The Naked and the Lens

Lou Benjamin

Second edition

The Naked and the Lens

A Guide for Nude Photography

Focal Press
Taylor & Francis Group
NEW YORK AND LONDON

Second edition published 2016
by Focal Press
711 Third Avenue, New York, NY 10017

and by Focal Press
2 Park Square, Milton Park, Abingdon, Oxon OX14 4RN

Focal Press is an imprint of the Taylor & Francis Group, an informa business

First edition published by Focal Press 2009

Library of Congress Cataloging in Publication Data
Benjamin, Louis.
The naked and the lens : a guide for nude photography /
Lou Benjamin. — Second edition.
pages cm
1. Photography of the nude. I. Title.
TR674.B36 2016
778.9'21—dc23
2015017358

ISBN: 978-1-138-82940-4 (pbk)
ISBN: 978-1-315-73781-2 (ebk)

Designed and typeset by Alex Lazarou

To Denise,

who never ceases to inspire, amaze, and love.

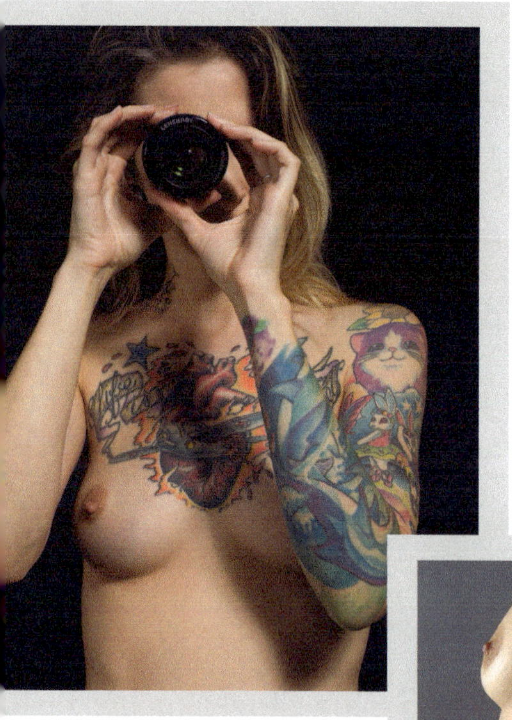
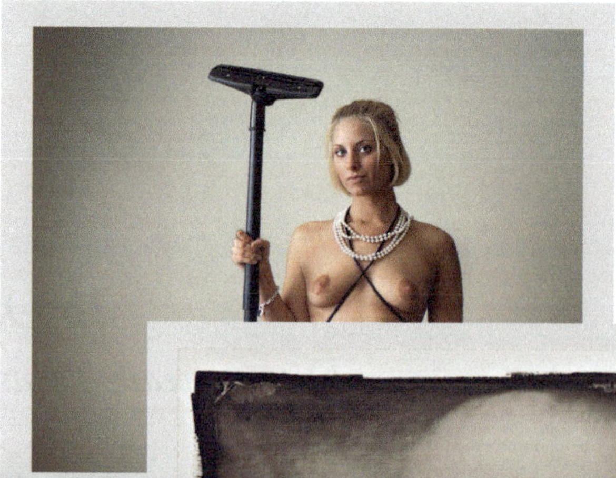
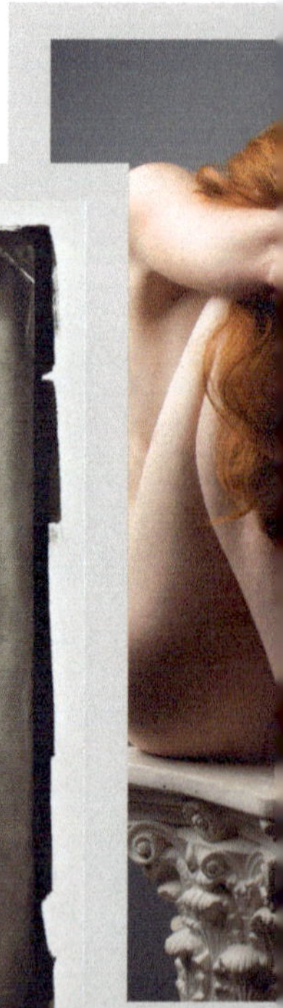
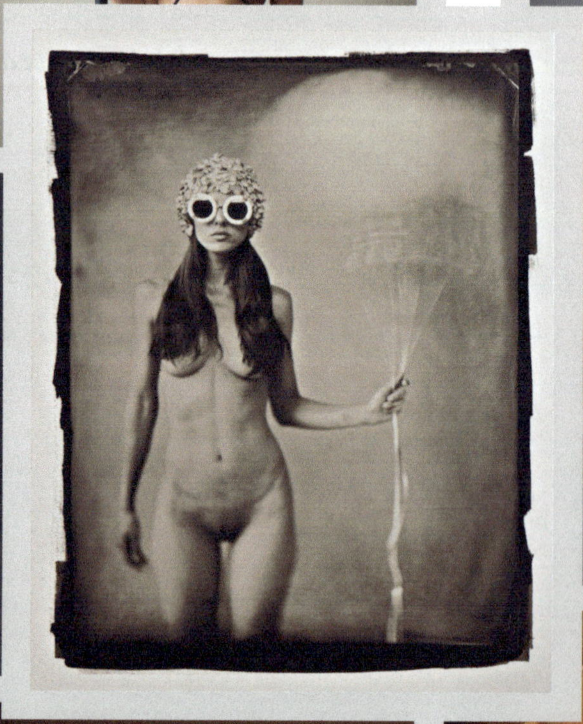
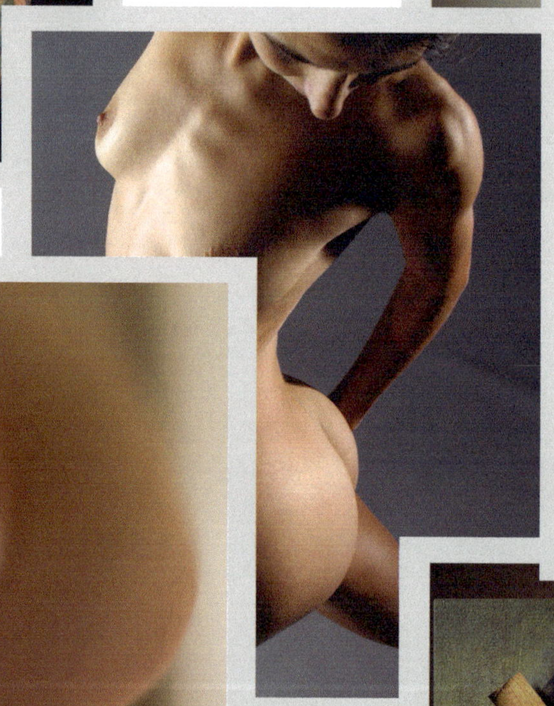
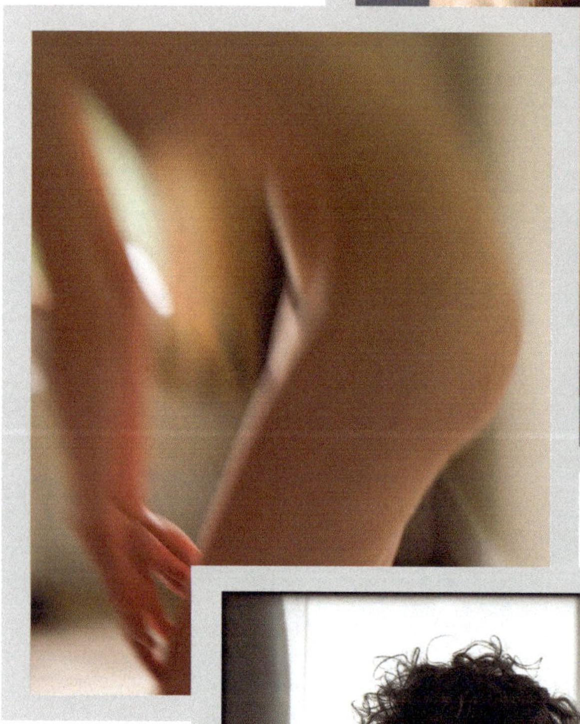
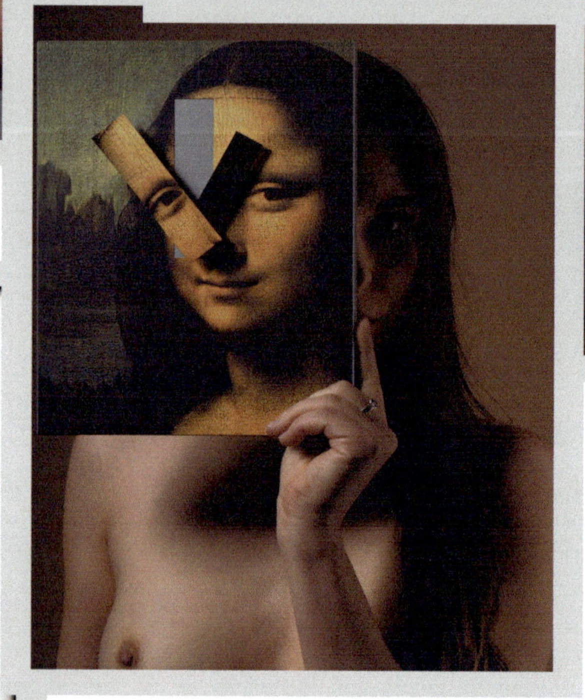
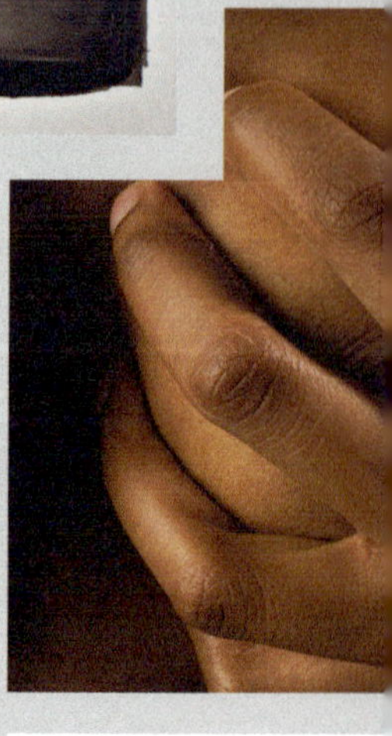
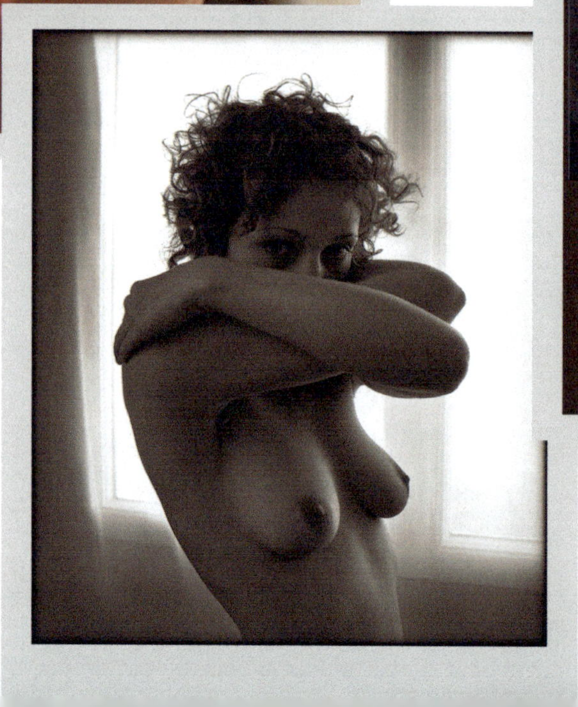

Contents

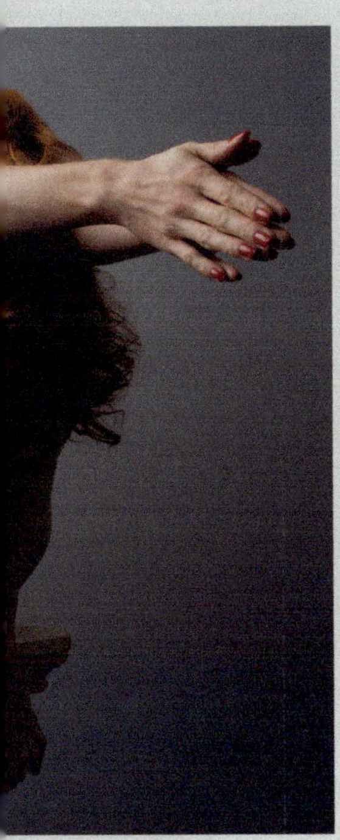

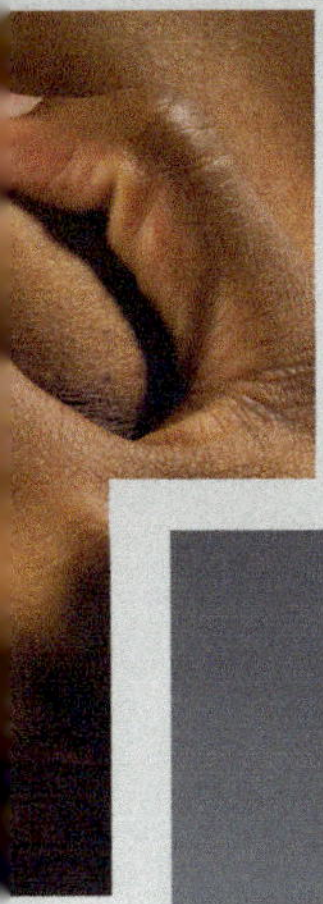

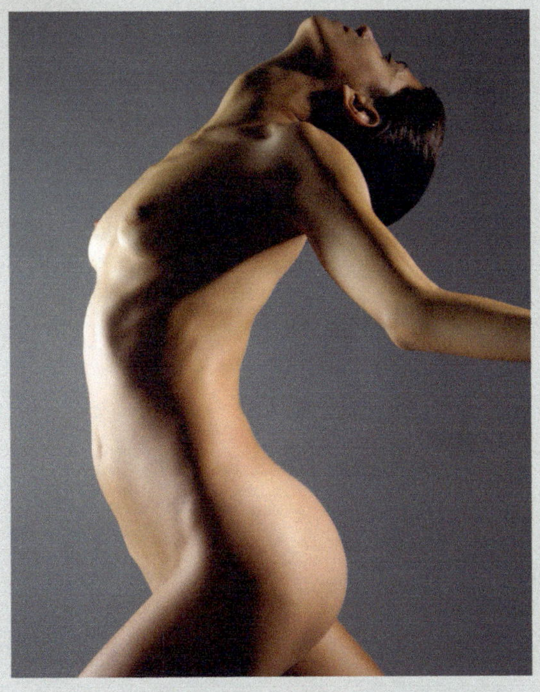

Acknowledgments

THE MODELS, artists, and curators who performed, contributed work, and participated in the interviews gave this book its real substance. I am standing on their shoulders. Eric Scott's insightful feedback helped me refine it. Frank Franca is both a gifted artist and an imaginative and innovative teacher. His lighting classes inspired my approach to the lighting material, particularly looking at Caravaggio and examples from cinematography. Their extreme generosity and talent inspires me:

Matt Barnes—ThatsTheSpot.com
Steven Billups—billupsphoto.com
Gary Breckheimer—GaryBreckheimer.com
Cheirodon
Steve Cherrier—stevecherrierphotography.com
Barney Cokeliss—barneycokeliss.com
Terry Donovan—midbrowart.com
Abigail Ekue—abigailekuephotography.com
John Evans—johnevansphotography.co.uk
Scott Foltz—scottfoltzphotography.com
Alan Fresco
Robert Gregory Griffeth—robertgregorygriffeth.com
Saddi Khali—saddikhali.com
Alfred Laij—alienlifephotographs.com
Donna Feldman Lasky—provoculos.com
M A N I F E S T/Jason Franz, Executive Director—manifestgallery.org
Gaspar Marquez—gasparmarquez.com
George McClintock—georgemcclintockphotography.com
Osmyn J. Oree—OsmynJOree.com
Nina Pak—dreamloka.com
Jafar M. Pierre—jmpphotos.com
Marcus J. Ranum—http://photography.ranum.com
Richard Rasner (Unique Nudes) of Nakayama Studios—uniquenudes.com
Saelon Renkes—saelon.com
Pascal Renoux—pascalrenoux.com
P.J. Reptilehouse—pjreptilehouse.com
Ned and Aya Rosen—nedandayaerotic.com
Ed Ross—edrossphotography.com
Daniel Sikorskyi—sikorskyi.ca
Pet Silvia—http://bit.ly/1HNN5Hy
Terry Slater—terryslater.co.uk
Tobias Slater-Hunt—tobiasslaterhunt.co.uk
J. D. Yezierski—jdyez.deviantart.com
Mayumi Yoshimaru—http://www.mayumism.com

Thanks also to Anna Valutkevich, Deirdre Byrne, and Sioned Jones, who patiently and professionally shepherded this project to publication. They are the ones who made sure that the book got into production, even as I missed more than a few deadlines on the way to finalizing the manuscript. I sincerely hope I didn't cause them any gray hairs! I remain grateful to Neil J. Salkind, Ph.D. When he connected me with Focal Press to write the first edition, he didn't just do a book deal, he catalyzed a new phase in my writing career.

Juanita and Louis Benjamin, Sr., my parents, have supported my artistic exploration and development throughout my life. Starting with 120 roll film and plastic cameras bought at a drug store in New Orleans, they have supplied me with a long stream of photography tools, including a Polaroid Swinger, my first two 35mm SLRs, and my first digital camera. During high school, they encouraged me to use one of the bathrooms as a darkroom, and they didn't seem to mind when this biology major enrolled in photography courses at college.

Introduction

There is nothing in Nature with more character than the human body. By its force or its grace it evokes the most varied images. At times, it resembles a flower – the flexion of the torso imitates the stem, the smile the breasts, the head and the sheen of the hair represent the blooming of the corolla … And at other times, the human body curved back is like a spring, a beautiful bow on which Eros adjusts his invisible arrows. And then there are times when it forms an urn. The human body, is above all the mirror of the soul and that is where its greatest beauty comes from.
Auguste Rodin

WELCOME TO the second edition of *The Naked and the Lens*. To create it, I essentially tore the old book apart and assembled a new one—adding new material, and subtracting or rearranging older material—with an eye toward refining the best elements and addressing some of the weaker points of the first. You will find ideas, photos, and even whole paragraphs carried over from the previous edition, but if I got it right, those ideas are presented here with more clarity and a better structure.

For the most part, the topics covered here are not unique to photographing the nude—a book about portrait photography or even general technique would cover many of the same topics—but as Rodin has noted, there is no other subject like the human body. The context of creating nudes, whether they be portraits, abstracts, formal, or transgressive, makes the technique of photography more compelling. It is my hope that you will enjoy this exploration of art, photography, and the nude, and that you will find new ideas, inspiration, and possibly even liberation among these pages.

Part I
Seeing Beneath the Skin

It's no accident that the words "image" and "imagine" come from the same root. Photographic images are the product of your imagination. Those photographs—whether they are carefully thought out and constructed tableaus, or chanced-upon scenes with a "snapshot aesthetic" guided purely by instinct—are the result of a process that you set into motion. Your intentions, where you choose to stand, and when you trip the shutter, make all the difference and uniquely shape your art. You can see this at play when photographers in a workshop all shoot the same models with the same setup and lighting—the results are often dramatically different.

It all starts with an idea, an impulse, a curiosity, a drive, or something you want to say. However you go about making photographs, the work you produce will always say a lot more about you than it says about the person or scene you're photographing. What is your work about? By examining your own interests, ideas, and influences, you can enhance the imprint that distinguishes your work. In this section, we'll look at the ideas behind the work of a number of photographers with the aim of raising your artistic self-awareness and sharpening your ways of seeing.

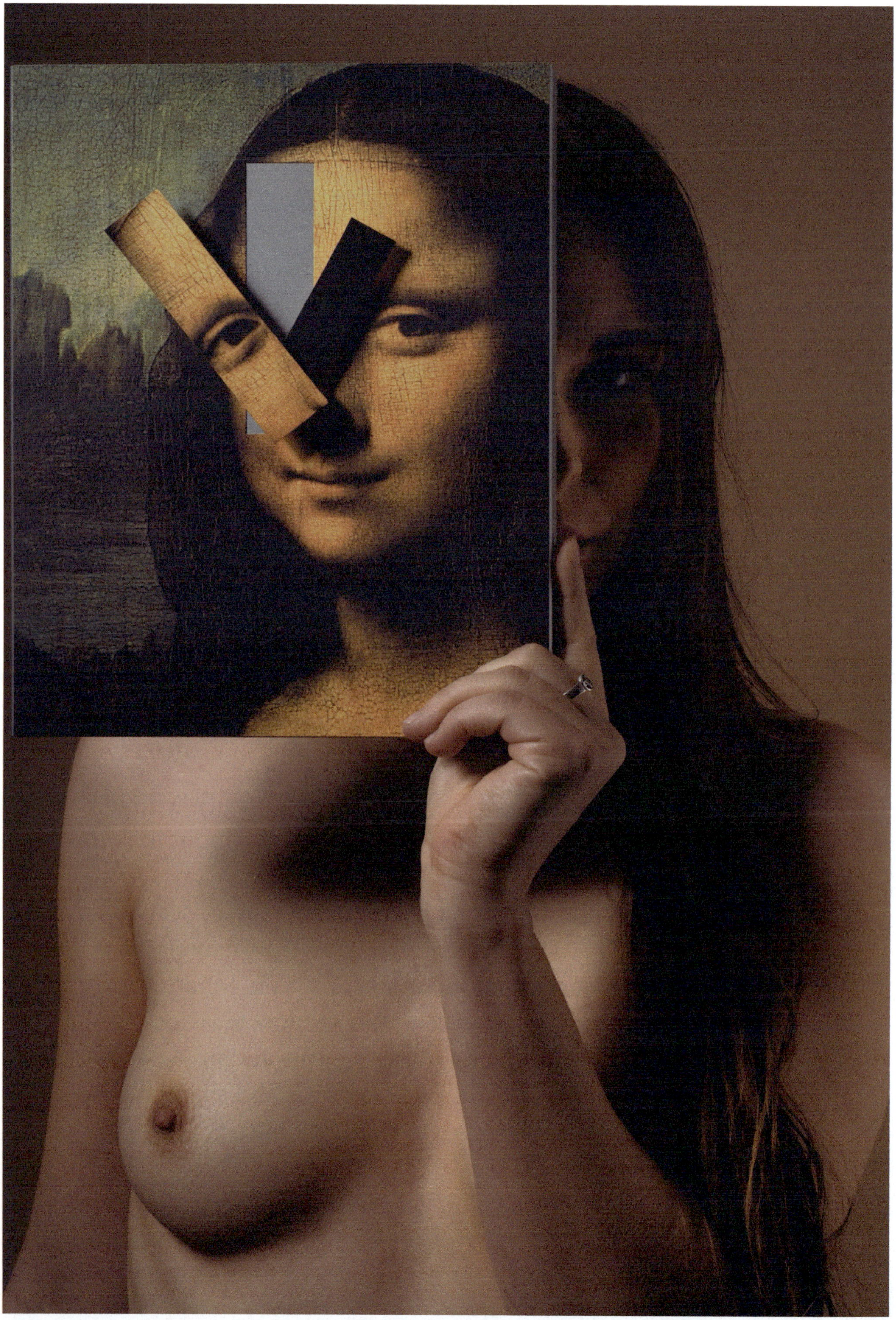

Chapter One | Focusing In

LET'S BEGIN by focusing on what we're talking about in this book—nudes in art photography. It is also about finding and strengthening your photographic voice. This is a wide-angle view that traces the complete arc from the initial concept or impulse through making and presenting the final image. We're talking about work that is determined solely by the photographer's vision and interests, rather than a client brief. This is the kind of work that appears in art salons, exhibitions, galleries, museums, and art publications. These are photographs produced for consideration or sale as art objects in their own right, rather than illustrations used to sell something else. While all of the topics covered may be relevant to producing commercial work as well, we will focus on photographers producing contemporary and fine art work.

This book takes an interdisciplinary approach to the field, drawing from art, science, and history. At its heart, it is concerned with four questions:

- What constitutes a strong artistic nude photograph?
- How are different artists approaching the field?
- How does photography work?
- What's involved in translating artistic vision into an image?

Facing: "Time Does Tell," © Lou Benjamin. Model: Aubrey. Shot in digital and referencing both art history and the passage of time, this photo touches on many of the facets of photography that this book will cover.

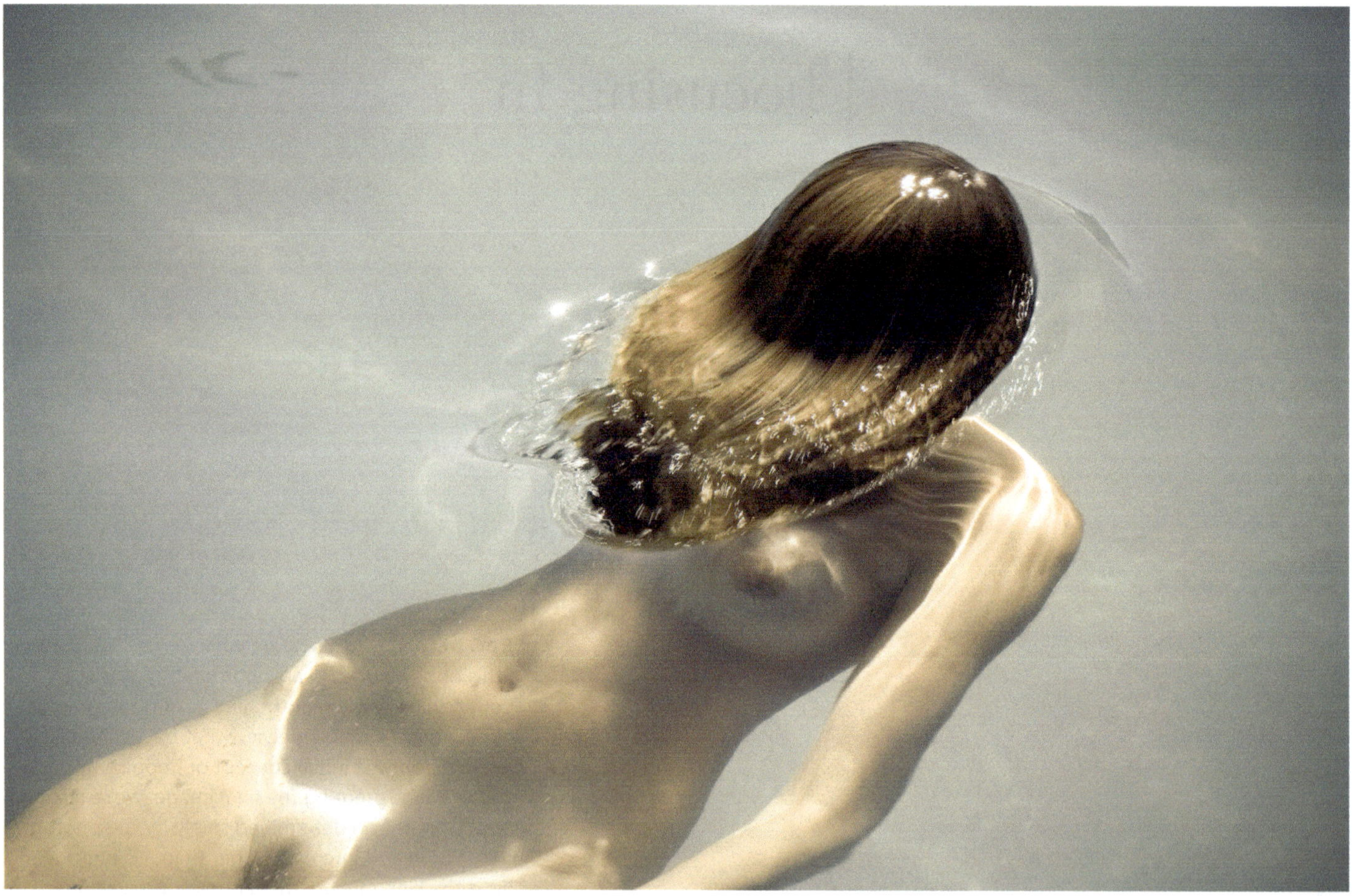

"Jordan Swimming" © Saelon Renkes.

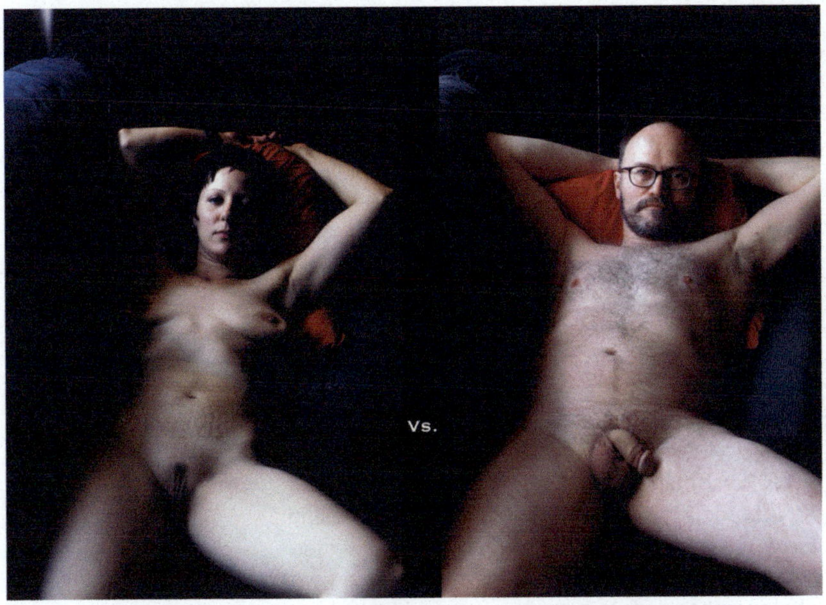

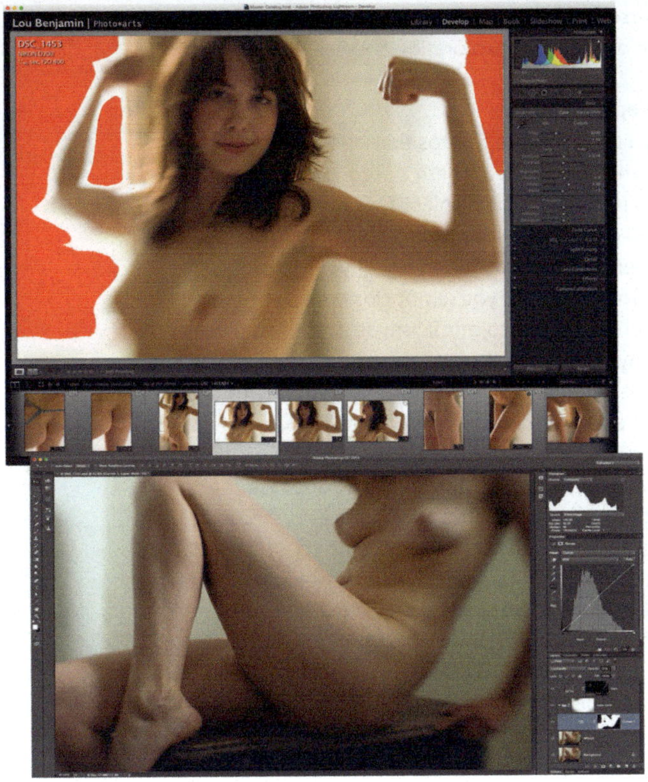

One caveat here: in photography, the term "fine art nudes" often refers to a very specific genre of nude photography, but fine art photography in general is much broader than that. We'll be looking at a broad range of artists' approaches to their personal work, including many that go beyond the very specific genres of "classic," "art," and "fine art" nudes.

Labels are tricky. If you search the Web for "art nudes," you're likely to find an almost overwhelming variety of imagery, including pinup and porn, as well as amateurish and "naughty" smartphone selfies. Among the types of images that are more germane to our discussion, you might find classics shot in the early 1900s, carefully crafted contemporary photos that reference the art of ancient Greece, and art images that have taken their cues from the commercial realm. You will also find that the terms "artistic photography," "art photography," and "fine art photography" all have different and sometimes contradictory meanings among various photographic circles.

The emphasis here is on photography that aims to convey a personal message—work that has more than just the look of art. We will be focusing on creating nudes as part of an artistic practice that goes beyond glamour, marketing, and exhibitionism.

Admittedly, there will be relatively few examples of male nudes. That has to do with the fact that the majority of nudes produced both by men and women artists feature female subjects—it seems that the default gender of art nudes is female. Part of the reason for this is an institutionalized bias ingrained in the culture among artists as well as patrons. A few of the artists presented in this book explicitly challenge that bias.

At the same time, you will find a significant amount of digital work in this book, even though the art world has not yet fully embraced digital, and a number of contemporary photographers shoot exclusively with film. The discussion of digital technique in this book will be limited to topics of relevance to photographing and maintaining an archive of nudes. We will look at digital technique with two types of photographers in mind: those who shoot digital, and those who work with scans from film.

Top: © Terry Donovan. For the series *The Model's Revenge*, Terry Donovan wanted to make himself as vulnerable as the models in his routine shoots. He turned over creative control to the model and allowed himself to be photographed in whatever way the model asked, with no limits.

Bottom: Photos © Lou Benjamin. Model: Sie Ist Idaho. Photoshop and Lightroom work together to create a comprehensive set of tools for managing, enhancing, and transforming digital images.

Not Quite a Manifesto

At the close of this chapter, we return to the ideas behind the work. Some of the ideas, assumptions, and intentions that shaped this book are set forth below. You won't find any hard and fast rules set forth for you to follow. The intent is to highlight and emphasize the choices you can make that will sharpen your vision and shape the way you approach your photography. The photos you make are an outgrowth of the attitude you bring to the process.

"Photographs Are Made, Not Taken" —Ansel Adams

Photographs arise from a process that is a marriage of art and technology. From the moment you decide to pick up the camera, you set in motion a process of making artwork. You decide where to stand, where to point the camera, what's included in the frame, what's excluded, and when to trip the shutter. Later, you decide what to print, post, or publish, and what to discard.

Photographs Don't Capture Anything

The phrase "nice capture" is inaccurate. It's like looking at a person and saying "nice DNA." Not all of a person's DNA is expressed, and neither are all of the sensor data and camera settings in a digital shot. That's before we even consider that photographs compress the four dimensions of space-time into two. They are reasonable facsimiles at best. Photos are analogous to rubbings. Light bounces off the surface of a body and casts shadows on a photo-sensitive surface, whether it's film or a digital sensor. From there, chemical or electrical processes "fix" those shadows so that an image can be produced.

Art and Culture Are Linked

Art happens inside the context of cultural norms and art influences those norms. Art can be political and art can be subversive. You can't separate the nude from its cultural context or its default connotations of shame, sexuality, etc.

Art is a Response

Artists process their experiences by making art. Artwork comes through you—events, experiences, and social structures can all affect and shape the work we make.

Seeing is Thinking

What we see in an image is the product of a cognitive process. Our brains search for shapes and identify them. We look for relationships between the elements inside the frame and we overlay references to experiences and knowledge gained during our lives. As a result, what we see in a photo varies greatly from person to person. And the photographic artist sees the world in a particular way—that shapes their choice of subject matter and determines which shots are their best work.

Art is Personal

Art is based in your reality. It is always subjective, and the work is an outgrowth of you. Your work says more about you than it does about the person or thing photographed. In fact, it has been argued that all photographs are really self-portraits. Embrace that and be yourself. Many artists make nude self-portraits as a vehicle of both self-exploration and self-expression.

Go Deeper

This is a call to create photos that offer something more when you look at them a second or third time, images that make you think or feel. Robert Capa inspired generations of photographers to fully engage with their subject matter, saying, "If your photographs aren't good enough, you're not close enough." That applies beyond photojournalism and refers to more than physical proximity.

We're living in a culture that is obsessed with surface, and inundated with disposable imagery that has artistic pretenses. Real art goes deeper than merely "artful" work. Aesthetics is just one facet of art—it goes deeper than pretty pictures or decoration. In fact, good art doesn't have to be pretty.

This is an encouragement to color outside the lines. The classics are not the only relevant style of artistic nude. Every new movement in art started with a willingness to discard the rules of previous movements. Art defies narrow definitions and it continues to change. Many works of contemporary art even confront the question of "what is art?" head-on.

Facing: "Sister's Got Habit" © Gary Breckheimer.

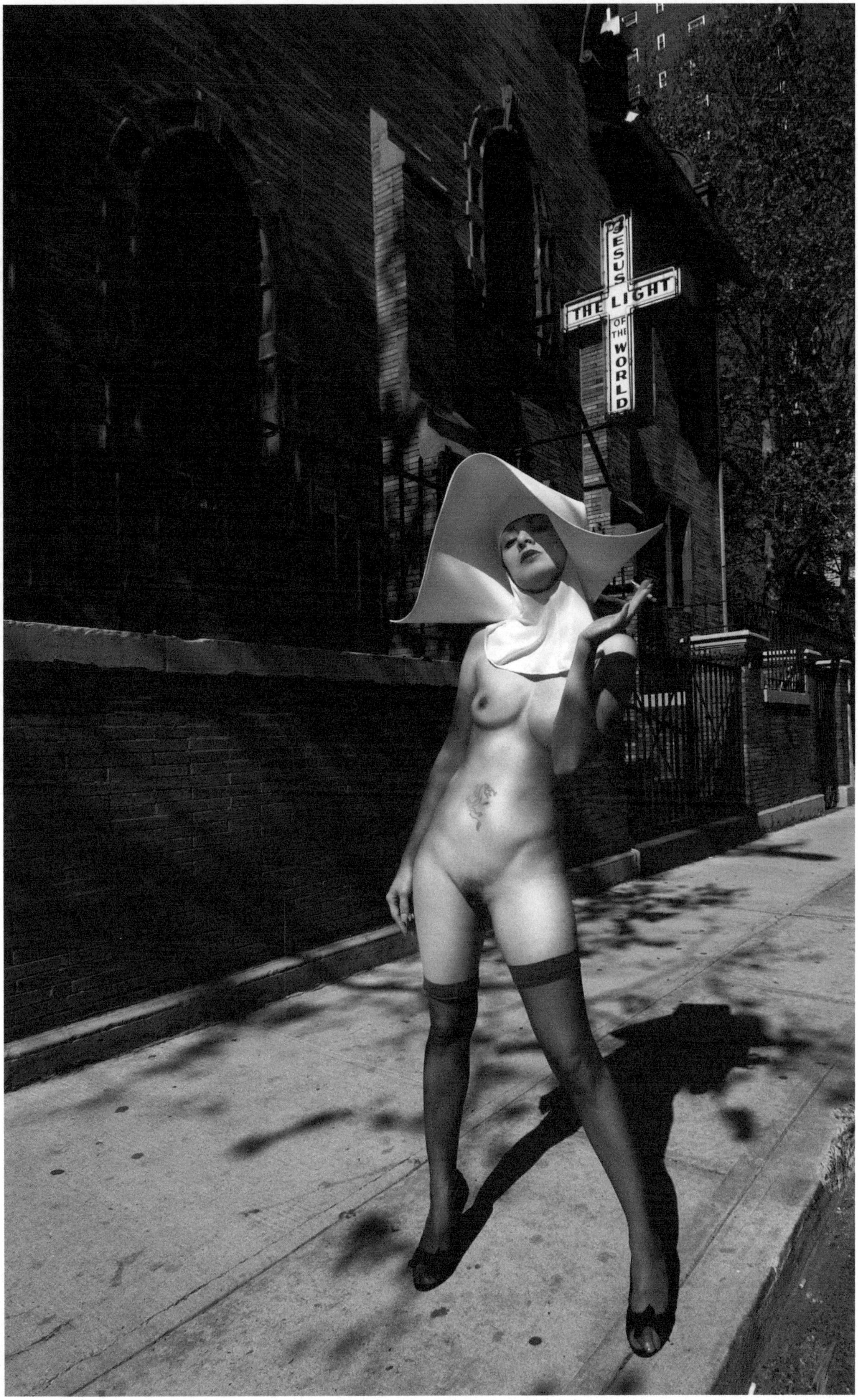
JESUS
THE LIGHT
OF THE WORLD

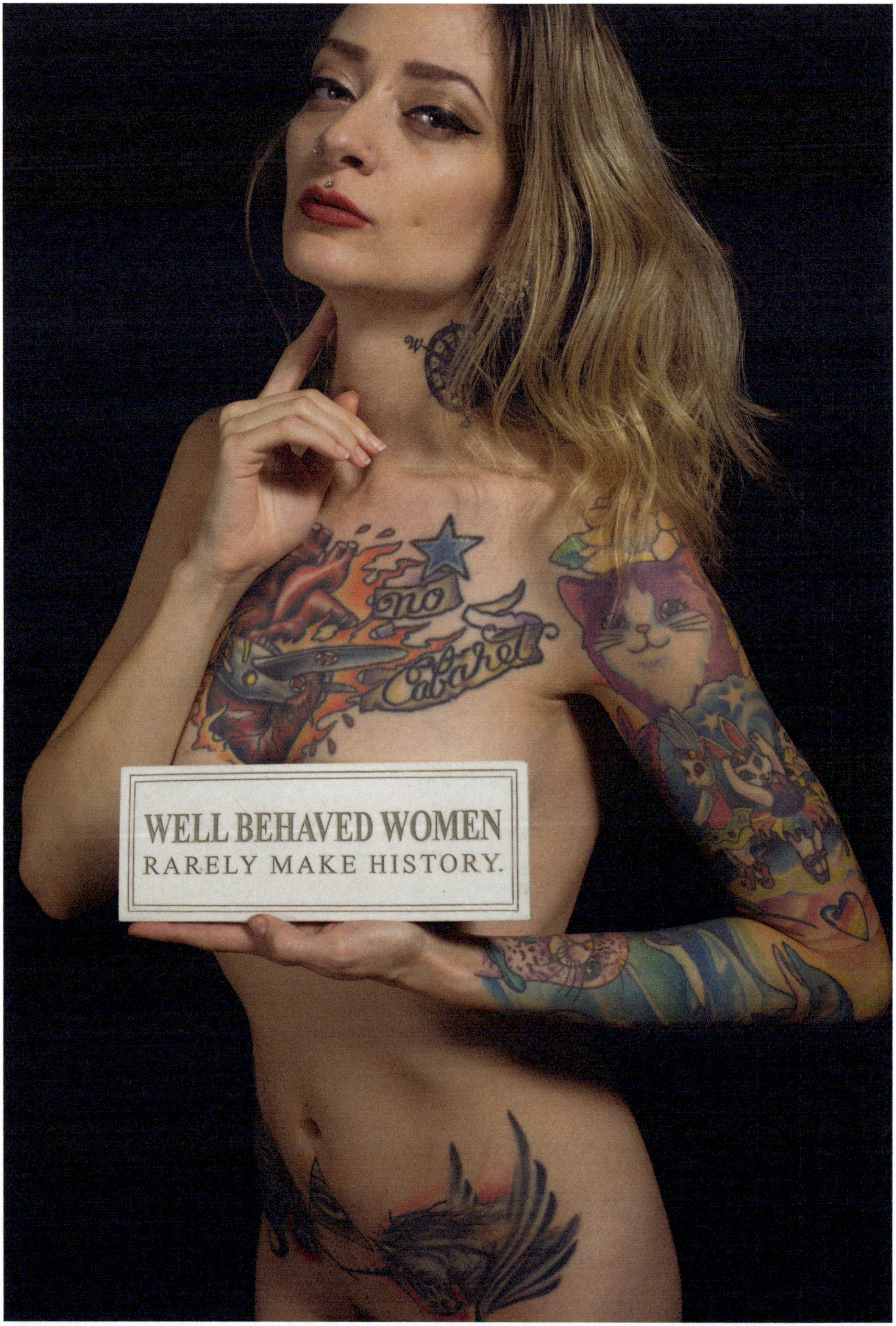

no
Cabaret
WELL BEHAVED WOMEN
RARELY MAKE HISTORY.

"It's so strange to me that anyone would ever think that a work of art shouldn't be disturbing or shouldn't be invasive. That's the property of work—that's the arena of a work of art. It is to disturb, it is to make you think, to make you feel. If my work didn't disturb from time to time, it would be a failure in my own eyes. It's meant to disturb—in a positive way."

Richard Avedon

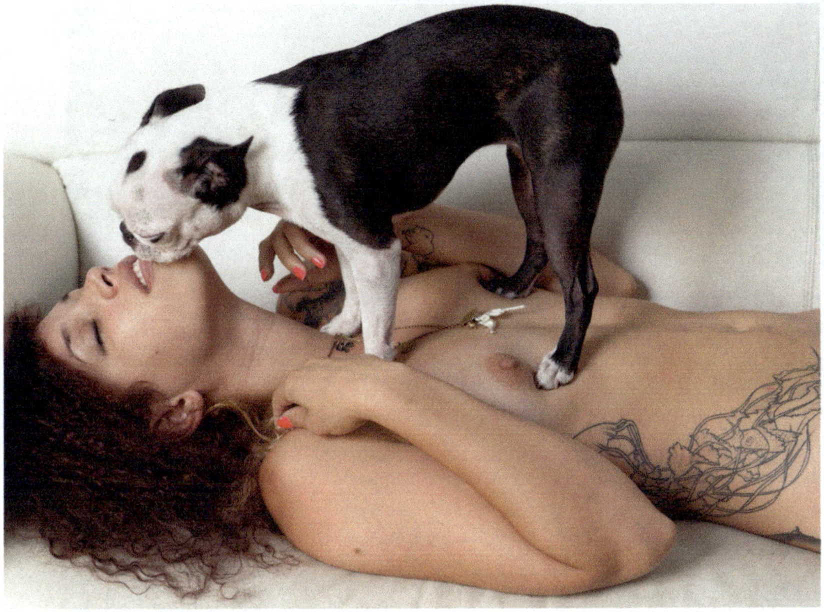

Photographs Are Rorschach Tests

Every person experiences a photograph differently. Photographs (works of art) are visual maps that viewers read, and reading is its own process of creation based upon that person's experience, culture, and biases. The viewer adds a lot that isn't there, and misses a lot that is. Once it's released to the world, the artist has no control over how their work will be (mis) interpreted.

Art Triggers Responses

Art can make you smile. Art can make you think. Art can be disturbing. Art can challenge beliefs. Artists can be provocateurs. For them, scandal is often free publicity. The more effective your work is at challenging beliefs, the more likely it is to trigger a negative response.

"Great Artists Steal"—Picasso

We're all influenced, and we all emulate. The pitfall is unconsciously aping work that touches us. Picasso was asserting that you should take elements of work that inspires you and express them in your own way, rather than simply "borrowing" those ideas. In other words, you can embrace your influences and still find your own voice. When you steal an idea and truly express it in your own way, it is no longer seen as someone else's.

The nude is compelling subject matter for contemporary photographers, many of whom draw inspiration from earlier works. That makes sense, because the nude has been a theme in photography since its very beginning, and nudes have featured prominently in the work of many of the pioneers who established photography as an art.

You can consciously cultivate your sources of inspiration and "prime the pump" with ideas that fuel your creativity. It is hoped that you will find inspiration and new ways of seeing your work in the coming chapters.

Facing: © Lou Benjamin. Model: Theresa Manchester. This quote by historian Laurel Thatcher Ulrich could well apply to all art photographers.

Above: Photo by Ned and Aya Rosen

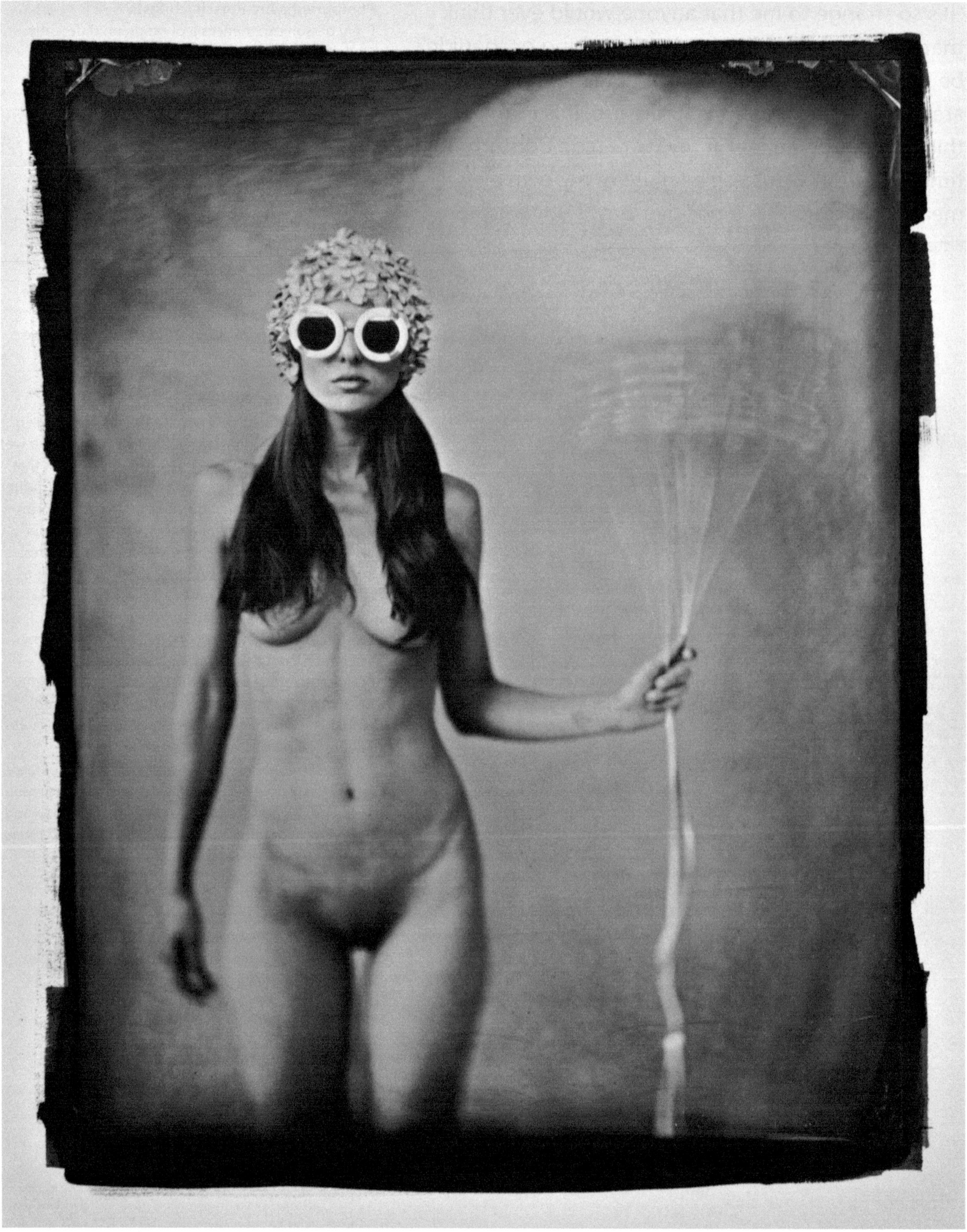

Chapter Two | Art Photography Laid Bare

"I have discovered photography.
Now I can kill myself.
I have nothing else to learn."
Picasso

THERE IS an inner game to fine art photography. The strongest works have to do with much more than the look or style of the surface. They have to do with a statement the artist wants to make or a question the artist wants to answer for themselves. Even in the case of visual artists who are terrible with words, you can sense a focus, an idea that drives their work. The ideas around the creation of artistic nudes literally trace back to prehistoric times, and the history of photographic art is closely entwined with that of the other fine arts. In this chapter, we'll look at how photos carry meaning and how the art of photography has developed over time.

Note: This chapter refers to a number of artists whose works could not be included. A list at the end of the chapter will point you to some web resources for those artists.

Reading Is Fundamental

In our highly visual culture, it's rare to stop and think specifically about how we take in photographs. There is a form of literacy involved, and we learn to read

Facing: © Ed Ross. Model: Shadia Ghantous. Palladium print from a 16 x 20 whole plate tintype, shot with a Voigtlander #8 lens from 1884. Ross scanned the tintype, then created a digital internegative to make the print. The internegative allows for some contract control in the print, which can be notoriously difficult with glass negatives.

images early in life. Visual literacy varies from person to person just as verbal literacy does, and developing an awareness of visual language and culture can give your work a powerful resonance.

Think of the times you've looked at a photograph and remarked that something about the image didn't work. We draw such conclusions by reading the image in complex ways, often in multiple passes, and unconscious of the thought process. Perhaps it was a technical issue: a hand was cut off by the edge of the frame in an unpleasant way, something in the background was distracting, or some detail was blocked up or blown out by poor exposure. Or, it could have something to do with the context or content of the image. The viewer often relies on things they know from their culture to assess what is being depicted and what that might symbolize. Certainly in US culture, a photo of a woman in green face paint wearing a pointy green crown and draped in a robe is likely to be read as the Statue of Liberty. The meaning of the photo changes immediately if Lady Liberty is depicted in the buff.

The 1916 and 1917 Type 1 "Standing Liberty" quarters are an interesting case in point. The two quarters featured Liberty standing on guard for peace, a shield protecting her left side, her right breast exposed. A revised design featuring Liberty clad in chainmail replaced the naked Liberty starting with the 1917 Type 2 quarter. There are competing theories on why the change was made, but certainly a naked Liberty can be read as being more vulnerable and less prepared than one fully armored.

The state of nudity has symbolic power and carries a charge that can be problematic. By default, images of the naked body are seen as sexual, dirty, and taboo. Much of that charge arises from the codified shame of being naked that so many of us learn at an early age (think of how young you were when you first heard the story of Adam and Eve and the fall from grace). Photographers working in some genres of the nude go to great lengths to make the body as abstract and asexual as possible. Another aspect of the power of nakedness can be seen in the way fashion operates: if the "clothes make the (wo)man," then stripping her clothes also strips away identity and a significant part of her social stature.

As we read a photograph, we also write ourselves into its narrative. Art critic John Berger observed that the protagonist of a nude photo is the viewer; a stranger standing in front of the picture, who is presumed to be male and fully clothed. We refer to this phenomenon as the male gaze. When viewers look at a photo involving nudity, they often project the shame and embarrassment they believe they would experience onto the artist and the model. From there, public discourse sometimes spins off into whether the work is art or pornography, or even further into whether the image should be on display at all. Two effects of this dynamic are an ingrained resistance to the portrayal of male nudes and the tendency to eroticize female nudes.

The visual language of photography has a very limited vocabulary and does not have the kind of syntactical structures of written or spoken language, but one thing that photography has in common with verbal language is metonymy—a photograph generalizes, so that an image of a man or woman is often read as representing all men or all women. That phenomenon directly relates to the resistance, for example, of showing men as being vulnerable or showing a phallus as anything other than mythic.

The language of photography is also context-sensitive. Much of the meaning in a photograph comes from the words and images you surround it with. The way you name photographs as well as number and sequence of photos surrounding it can change its meaning in profound ways. Context also comes from statements by the artist or curator. Photographs have been re-cast by curators who cherry-picked photographs from a number of artists to advance a particular idea. In 2004, the Museum of Modern Art presented a show called "Fashioning Fiction in Photography since 1990," in which photography that was shot for fashion was re-cast in an artistic context. Commercial pieces were converted into fine art, even though they were originally created according to a client brief. On networks like Tumblr, bloggers become de-facto curators to the consternation of many art photographers who found their work re-contextualized as pornography.

The male erotic gaze also creates a contextual challenge, particularly for heterosexual male

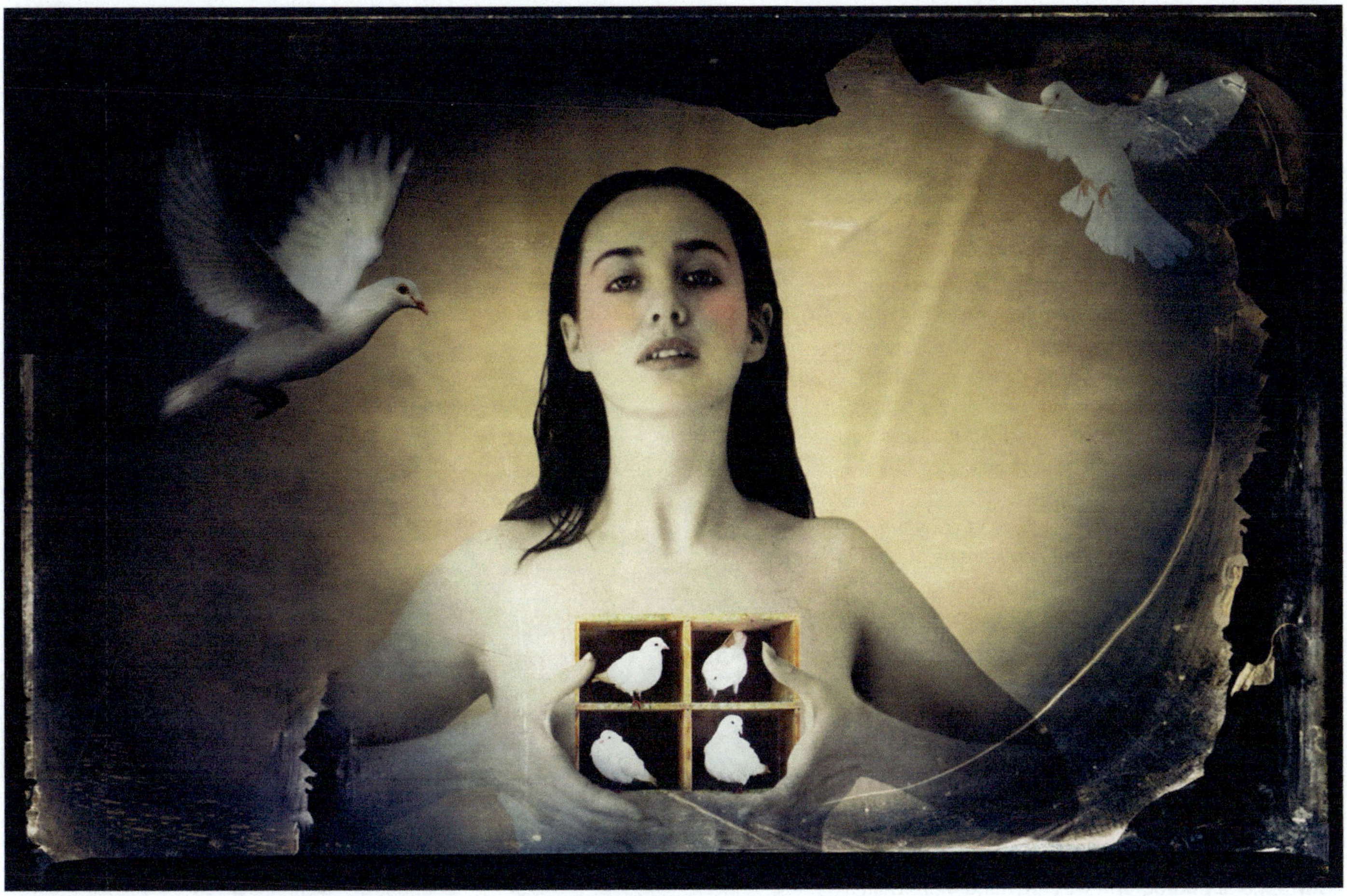

© Nina Pak.

photographers who shoot female nudes: how do you transcend the knee-jerk reaction to photograph women as objects or erotic spectacles for the viewer? One of the nagging critiques leveled against the Surrealists is the dominance of the heterosexual male gaze in the genre (we shouldn't forget that, much like the Algonquin Round Table, the Surrealists were a male-dominated clique). Surrealism's treatment of the nude is said to objectify and reduce the female body to a fetish object. The Surrealists argued that this objectification is simply a reflection of the true state of the (male) subconscious. The Surrealists were particularly interested in the subconscious and the irrational. André Breton, who wrote the 1924 Surrealist manifesto, and Salvador Dali, one of Surrealism's best-known figures, were both strongly influenced by the writings of Sigmund Freud.

The techniques of Surrealist photography are probably the most artful of all applications of photography. They were interested in using the photographic trace as a starting point for imagery rather than an end unto itself. The Surrealists are particularly interesting for their use of the nude and for the way they broke up notions about photography and the photographic object. Surrealist photography redefined the boundaries of lighting, pose, and what is now post-production. During the time of the Surrealists, the bulk of the debate about photography as an artistic medium centered around questions such as whether a photograph was anything more than a copy of the scene in front of the camera, and whether it was truthful or not.

At the center of the Surrealist movement was Man Ray, a photographic innovator who is credited with bringing a number of techniques to the forefront of art photography, including solarization (many of his nudes are solarized). The technique was brought to his attention by his muse, lover, and assistant Lee Miller, who went on to be a successful photographer in her own right. In addition to his art, Man Ray shot fashion. Two of Man Ray's assistants who also became well-known photographers are Bill Brandt and Berenice Abbott (who brought recognition to Atget after his death).

Another example of the role of context in validating a work of art is *L'Origine du Monde* (The Origin of the World) by Gustave Courbet. The painter was

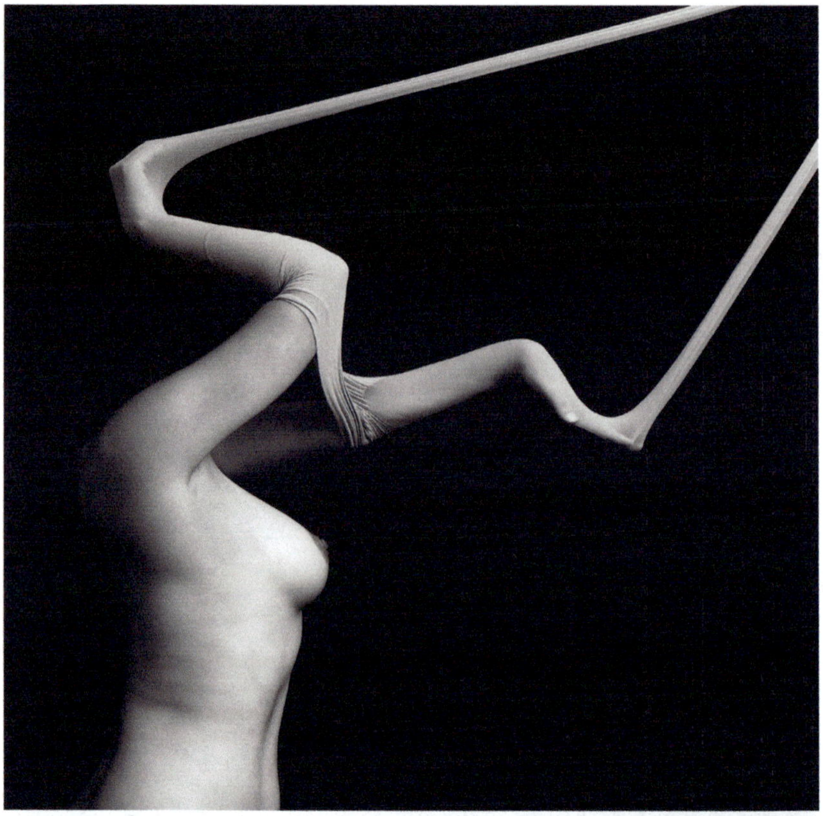

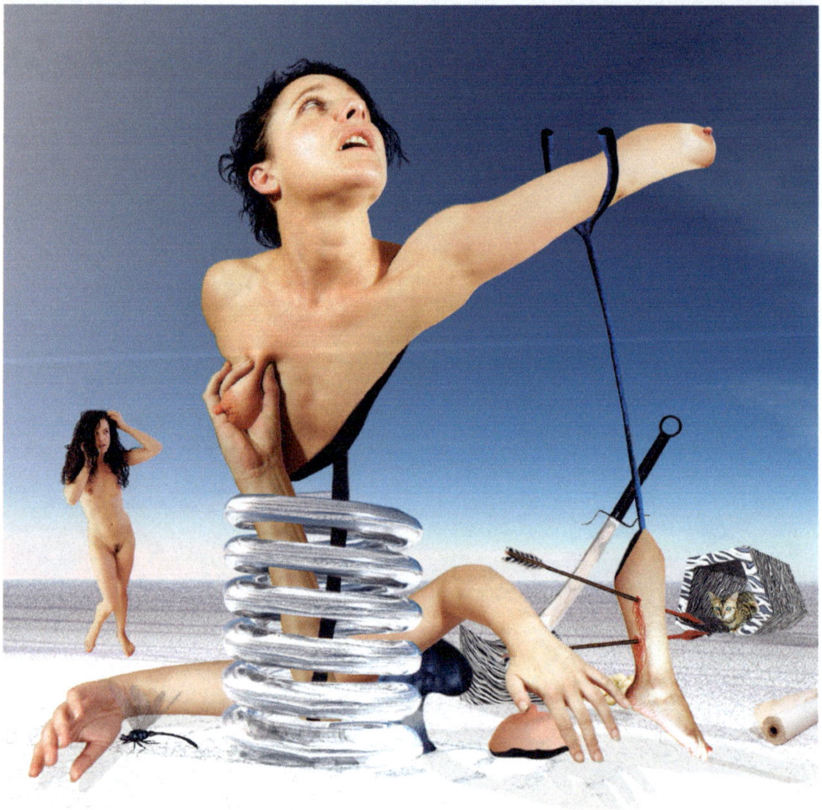

Top: "Pulling You Back" © Mayumi Yoshimaru.

Bottom: © Cheirodon. "LSD & The Mushroom (The Sequel)" uses the Surrealist visual language of Salvador Dali.

Facing: © Terry Slater. Solarization was one of Man Ray's signature techniques. This image was created by applying a blue toner to a solarized black-and-white silver gelatin print.

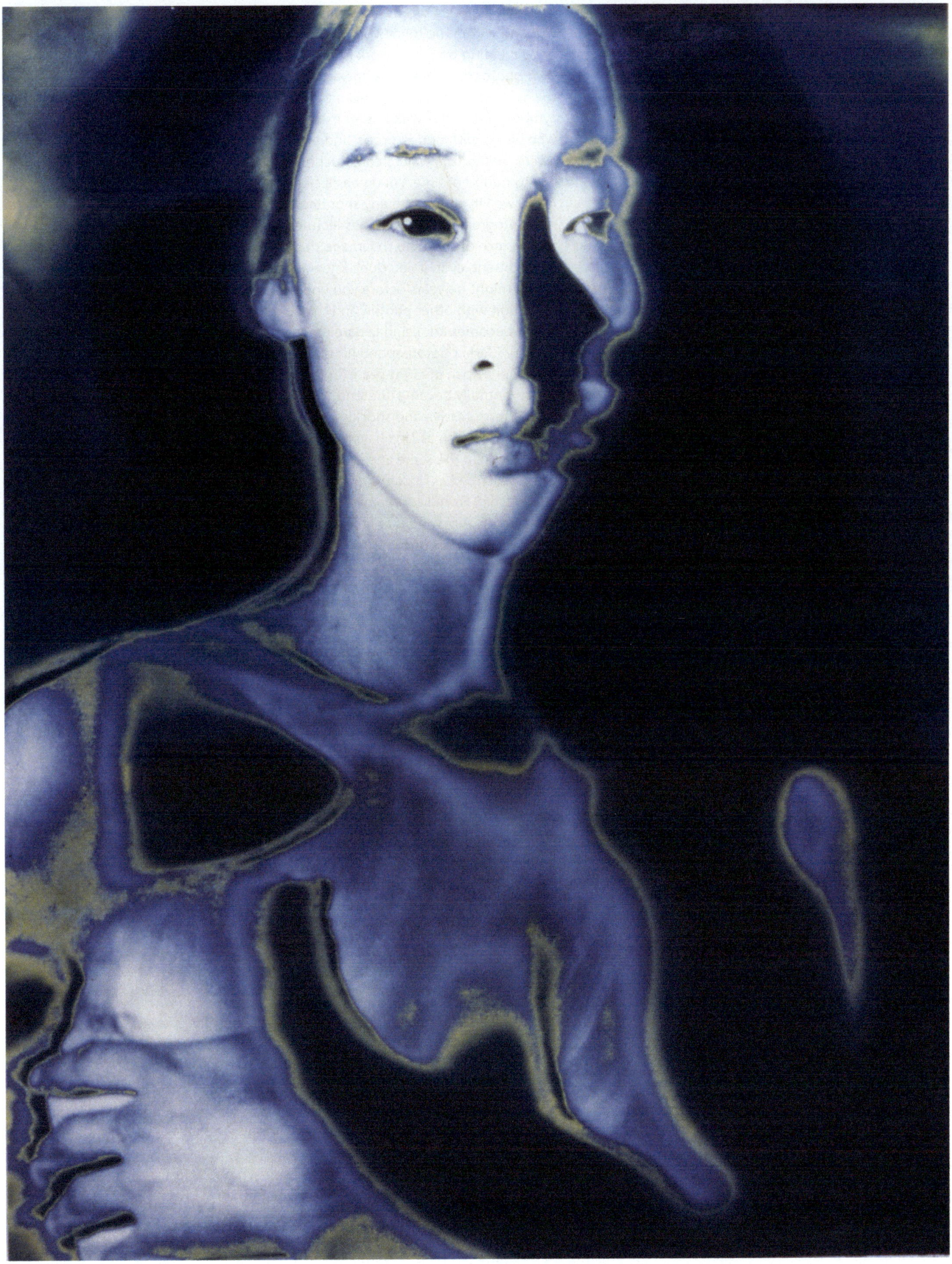

probably courting controversy when he created it in 1866, although it appears that he painted it for a collector rather than public exhibition. The highly realistic painting depicts a woman's bushy, spread-legged vulva from an up close and personal point of view, and it is likely that he referenced a photograph to create the painting. Her torso fills the canvas, with an undraped nipple kissing the top edge. Clever title or not, a photograph treating the same subject material in the same way is likely to have its artistic merit vigorously challenged; while contemporary painting has inherited a certain immunity owing to the legacy of works like Courbet's.

Today, *L'Origine du Monde* is on open display at the Musée d'Orsay in Paris, and without apology; it is not treated as something dirty on the museum's website. This suggests a difference in attitude about exhibitions of art in European culture, and yet the museum's curators seem a little defensive. This disclaimer appears on the site:

> The almost anatomical description of female sex organs is not attenuated by any historical or literary device. Yet thanks to Courbet's great virtuosity and the refinement of his amber colour scheme, the painting escapes pornographic status. This audacious, forthright new language had nonetheless not severed all links with tradition: the ample, sensual brushstrokes and the use of colour recall Venetian painting and Courbet himself claimed descent from Titian and Veronese, Correggio and the tradition of carnal, lyrical painting.
>
> *The Origin of the World*, now openly displayed, has taken its proper place in the history of modern painting. But it still raises the troubling question of voyeurism.

In short, the curators are saying, "folks, this is art, not smut—even if there is that troubling little issue of the male gaze—and here's why."

Photography that deals with sexuality is likely to be viewed as pornography by some. Terry Richardson has said that he enjoys the challenge of getting sexual images published in mainstream magazines, not porn magazines. His inner game is to push boundaries as far as he can, and still get his images run.

Photographers often create their own context by working within the framework of a long-term project or by creating bodies of work from an archive of their own photos. In some cases, the artist can take years to construct a single image from very specific visual symbols. Joel-Peter Witkin is an example of an artist who works with nudes, props, and even cadavers in a very methodical way to construct his images over a long period of time. Witkin has a clear-cut idea in mind, well in advance of any shooting.

Photographer Tim Davis has lectured about the importance of shooting the image that grabs you in the moment, even if you don't know why it calls to you. It might be years before you find that it fits into a collection with other photos, and that is the moment that it becomes art. Leigh Ledare (once an assistant to Larry Clark) photographed his exhibitionist mother Tina over a span of eight years for the body of work that eventually became "Pretend You Are Actually Alive." Transgressive and shocking in its frank depiction of situations such as Tina having sex with "Catch 22" (a young man the same age as Ledare), the work is often described as documenting a troubled, Oedipal relationship. From Ledare's perspective, "Pretend You Are Actually Alive" looks at archetypal relationships, fantasy life, social conventions and cultural taboos, with an effort to shine a light on some of our blind spots. He views it as a performance-based collaboration with his mother and insists that she doesn't get enough credit for her role in the work.

The specific meanings of visual symbols can also be lost with time as cultural norms shift. Consider the painting *Gabrielle d'Estrées et une de ses soeurs* (Gabrielle d'Estrées and one of her sisters) painted by an anonymous artist around 1594. The painting features two nude sisters in a tub, one holding a ring in her left hand while the other reaches over with her left hand to pinch her right nipple. The painting has been imitated many times in photography, including a 1999 Yves Saint Laurent ad shot by Mario Sorrenti and featuring a lace-clad Kate Moss as the "sister" with a nude man in the position of Gabrielle d'Estrées, though it is likely that the allusion to the earlier painting is lost on most consumers reading the ad. The photograph mimics the gesture of the sister pinching Gabrielle's right nipple, but the period-specific meaning of the

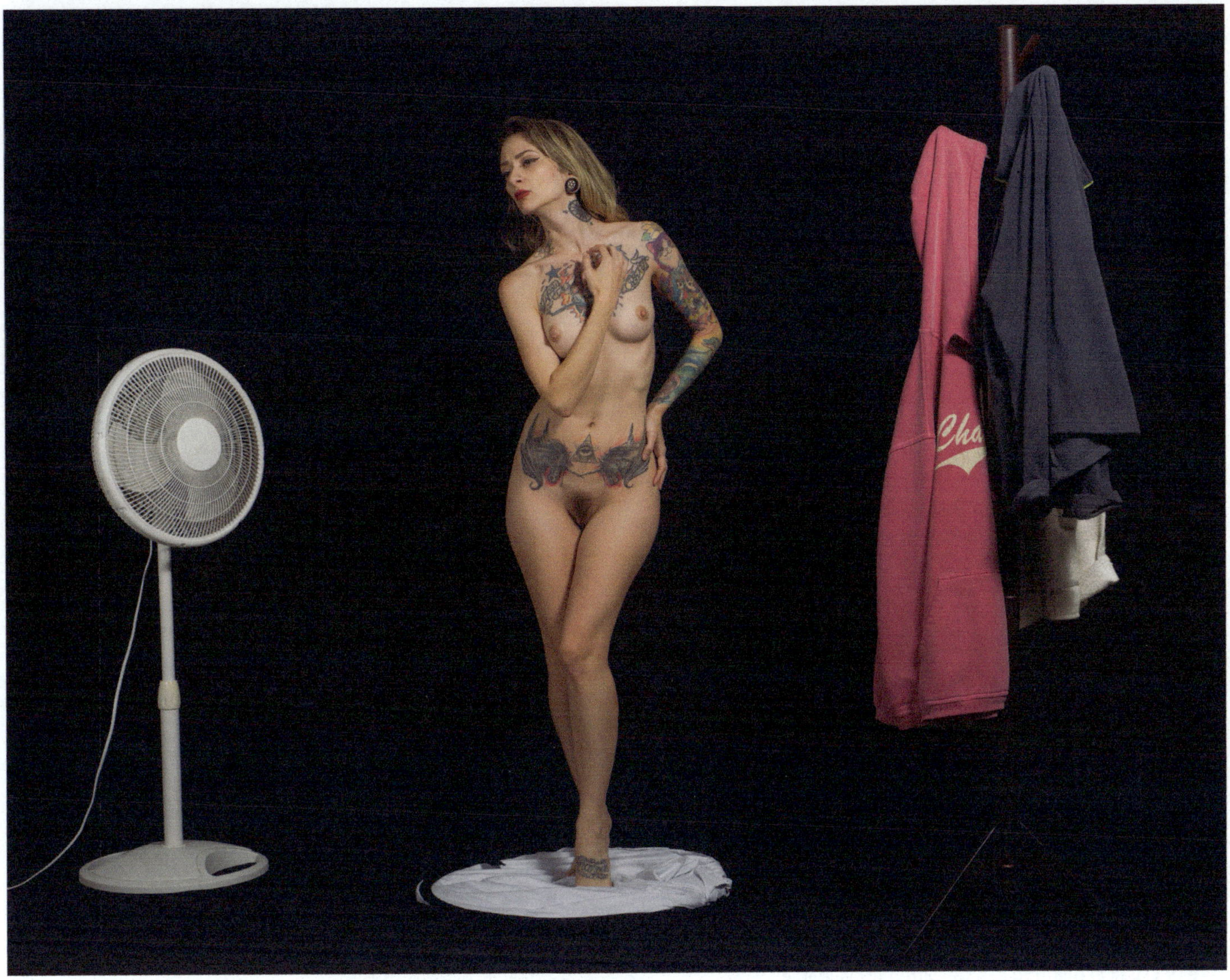

© Lou Benjamin. Model: Theresa Manchester. A modern riff on Botticelli's *Birth of Venus*, which in turn riffs on other works. The Botticelli painting is thought to be partially based on a Greek sculpture of Aphrodite known as Venus de' Medici and a Homeric hymn. In it, Venus is emerging full-grown from the womb of the sea, with the seashell symbolizing a woman's vulva.

gesture is lost. It is speculated to signify Gabrielle's pregnancy with the illegitimate child of Henry IV. Barring some marvel of technology or evolution, the gesture could not possibly have that meaning in the Saint Laurent ad. Instead, it simply reads as a quirky gesture. In the 1990s, the painting and its gesture also came to be understood as a homoerotic representation of lesbianism.

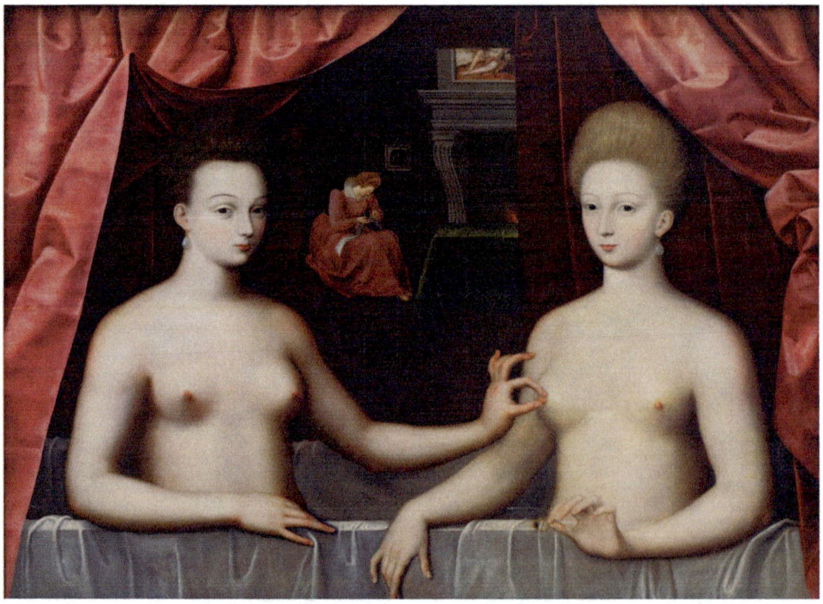

Learning from History

Today's artistic photography of the nude sits on a foundation woven from the historical threads of art, technology, culture, and law. If you only look at contemporary photography, you miss out on the opportunity to explore rich veins of ideas directly. As in the game of "telephone," artistic ideas developed earlier have been altered or even lost over time as works have been referenced and re-referenced by successive generations of artists.

A noteworthy artist who worked tirelessly to legitimize fine art photography by creating extraordinary work was Imogen Cunningham, who was still hard at work in 1975—at 91 years of age. Some of her most celebrated images are nudes. Bill Brandt, André Kertész, Wynn Bullock, and Harry Callahan all expanded the vocabulary of the photographic nude. Other important figures in the history of photography who created exemplary nudes include Paul Strand, Edward Weston, Erwin Blumenfeld (who declared himself "the erotic president of the Dada movement"), and Jan Saudek.

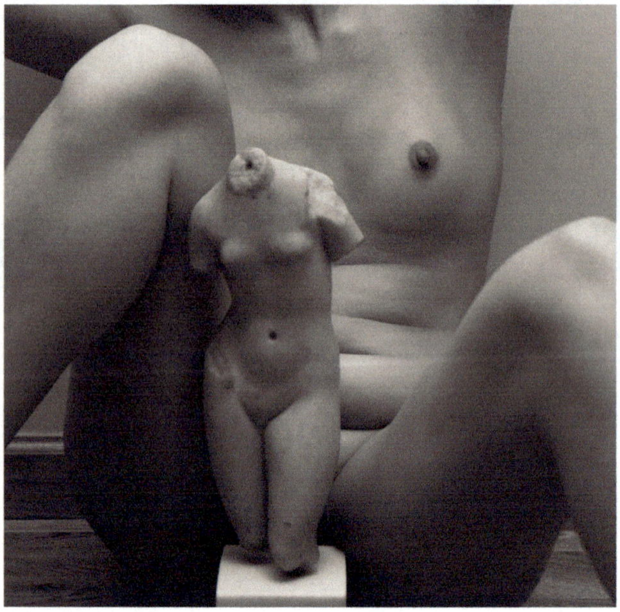

A visit to an art museum to study Greek sculpture or classical painting can be extremely valuable. Many contemporary models almost reflexively adopt a *contrapposto* stance, a pose developed during the Hellenistic period when the ancient Greeks deified the nude form by endowing it with idealized proportions.

Pictorialism and compositing are two mid-nineteenth-century approaches to photography that are worthy of reinterpreting today. Pictorial photography, as exemplified by Julia Margaret Cameron and John Edwin Mayall (who has been described as the earliest proponent of fine art photography), was concerned

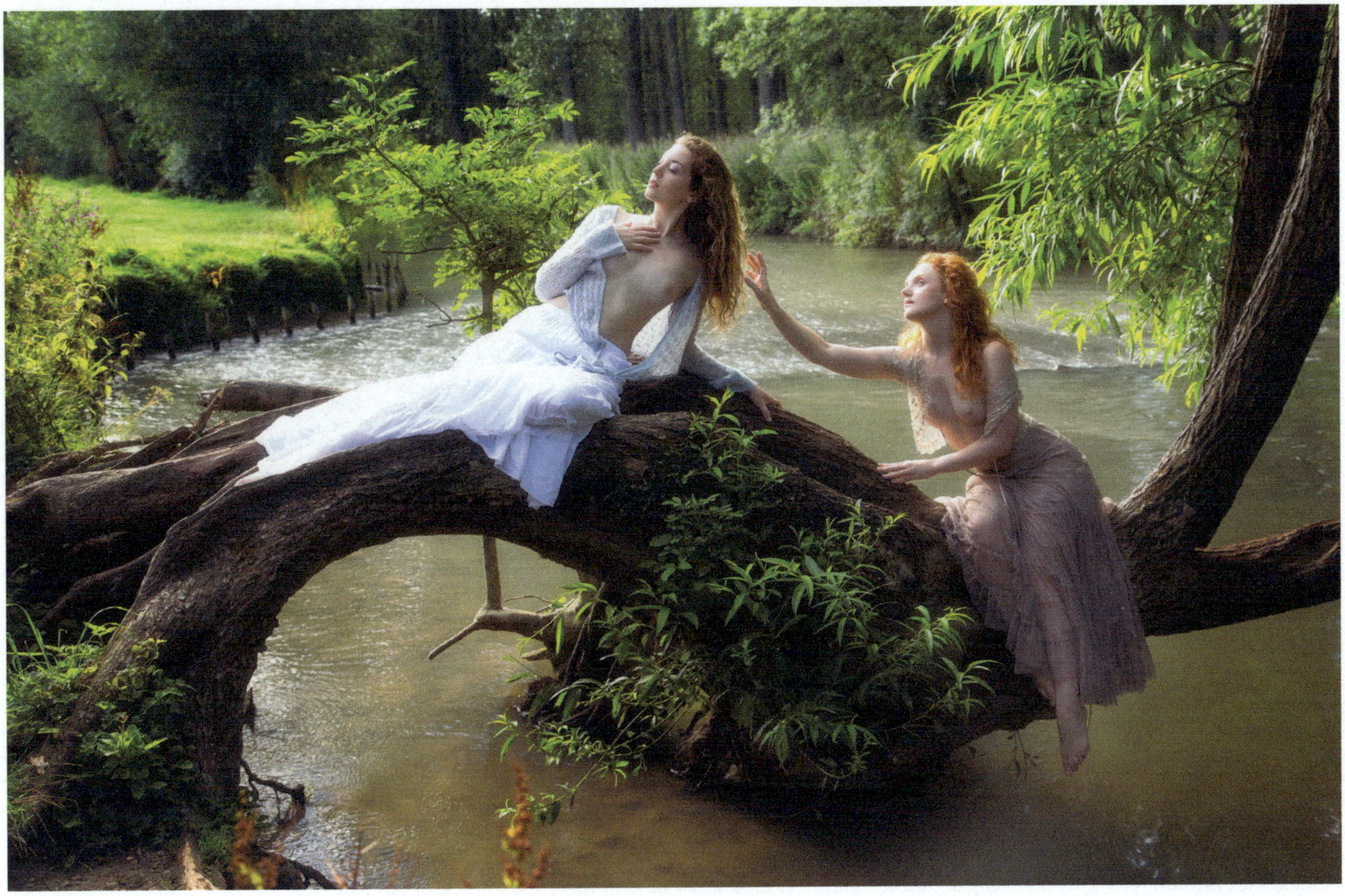

Facing (top): Anonymous, *Gabrielle d'Estrées et une de ses soeurs*, ca. 1594. The nipple-pinching gesture is often interpreted as a symbolic announcement that Gabrielle is pregnant with Henry IV's illegitimate child, César de Bourbon. The woman in the background may be sewing a layette for the child.

Facing (bottom): © Lou Benjamin. Photography of the nude today is often influenced by the idealized aesthetics of ancient Greece. The Venus replica here exhibits *contrapposto*.

Above: © Brian J. Connor. Models: Ella Rose and Ivory Flame. "Windrush" evokes the pastoral settings of painters like Fragonard.

with imitating what painting and drawing did by incorporating themes from the great works and using techniques such as soft focus. Alfred Stieglitz created fashion photographs in the style of the Pictorialists in 1911, making it some of the earliest published art photography.

Also in the mid-nineteenth century (more than a hundred years before the development of Photoshop) photographers were combining multiple negatives to create sophisticated tableaus and narratives. The technique, known as composition photography, was introduced by Hippolyte Bayard in the 1840s and expanded upon by Henry Peach Robinson and Oscar Gustave Rejlander in the 1860s and 1870s. Beginning in the 1970s, Jerry Uelsmann showed the extraordinary potential of combining images in the darkroom, though few have had the inclination to emulate his precise and demanding process. Since its introduction, Photoshop has brought compositing and photo manipulation within reach of far more photographers.

There is also much to be gained from exploring early fashion photography and Pop art. Pop artists made photography central to their work. Art photography reached a broader audience through fashion magazines, particularly *Vogue*, *Vanity Fair*, and *Harper's Bazaar*, all of which have featured nudes in their editorials over the years. Steichen even shot a nude that appeared in an ad for soap that ran in *Vogue*. Helmut Newton, especially famous for his groundbreaking nudes, shot fashion for *Vogue* and *Harper's Bazaar*. He also shot pictorials for *Playboy*, which, like the fashion magazines, aligned itself with the art world and gained legitimacy as a sophisticated promotor of art and artists. The *Playboy* aesthetic became a standard for many artists. Even today, *Playboy's* pictorials are offered as exemplars of "tasteful" nudity. Guy Bourdin was a contemporary of Newton who also shot for *Vogue* and frequently produced nudes for editorial and fashion. His fashion campaigns for Charles Jourdan inspire emulators today. A former protégé of Man Ray, Bourdin's fashion photography established the notion that the product was secondary to the image.

Fred Holland Day and Baron Wilhelm Von Gloeden were popular producers of male nudes in the early 1900s, but relatively few male nudes were created

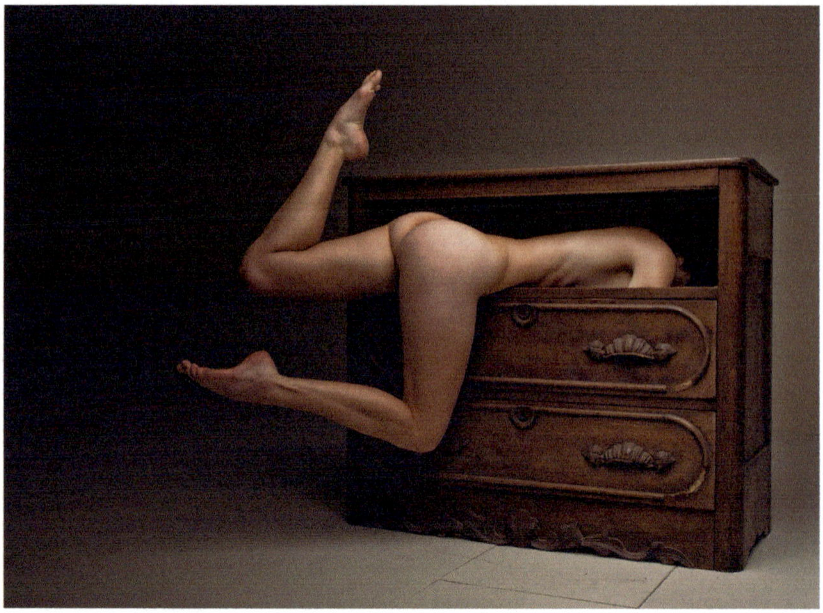

between 1910 and 1960 because of resistance, including institutionalized homophobia as well as religious and legal prohibitions. Still, George Platt Lynes (one of the leading fashion and portrait photographers in New York City), Edmund Teske, and Minor White were significant photographers of the male nude in the 1930s and 1940s. In the 1950s, Bruce of Los Angeles (Bruce Bellas) pioneered a distinctive style and created an influential body of work photographing male bodybuilders. The works of Lynes and Bellas were inspirations for Robert Mapplethorpe, Herb Ritts, and Bruce Weber (who shot the iconic first ad for Calvin Klein underwear in 1983 and the 2003 A&F Christmas Field Guide, which is legendary for its use of nudity).

Many cultures have tended to treat the male nude as being more immoral or obscene than the female nude. Two 1971 U.S. obscenity cases illustrate the discrepancy: in *Huffman v. United States*, the court ruled that depictions of female genitalia are not obscene, while in *Levin v. Maryland*, another court found that penile erections are obscene. The stigma of immorality and obscenity along with resistance to the presentation of male nudity have decreased, beginning with the

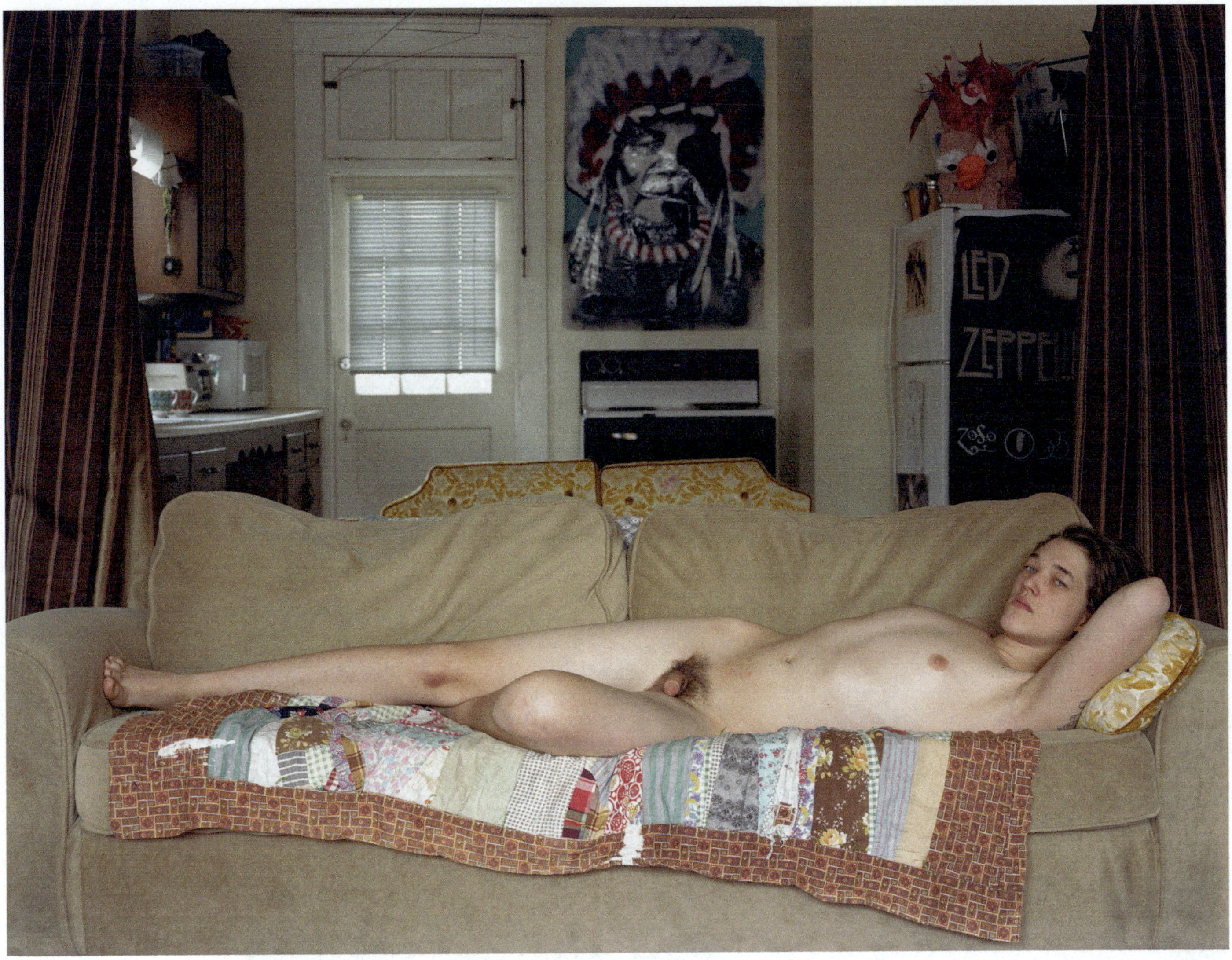

Facing: © Donna Feldman Lasky. Lasky's highly polished work resembles fashion photography and bears the pedigree of Surrealism.

Above: © Osmyn J. Oree. From the series *Exposed*, which aims to show portraits of men who are revealing, sensitive, and vulnerable.

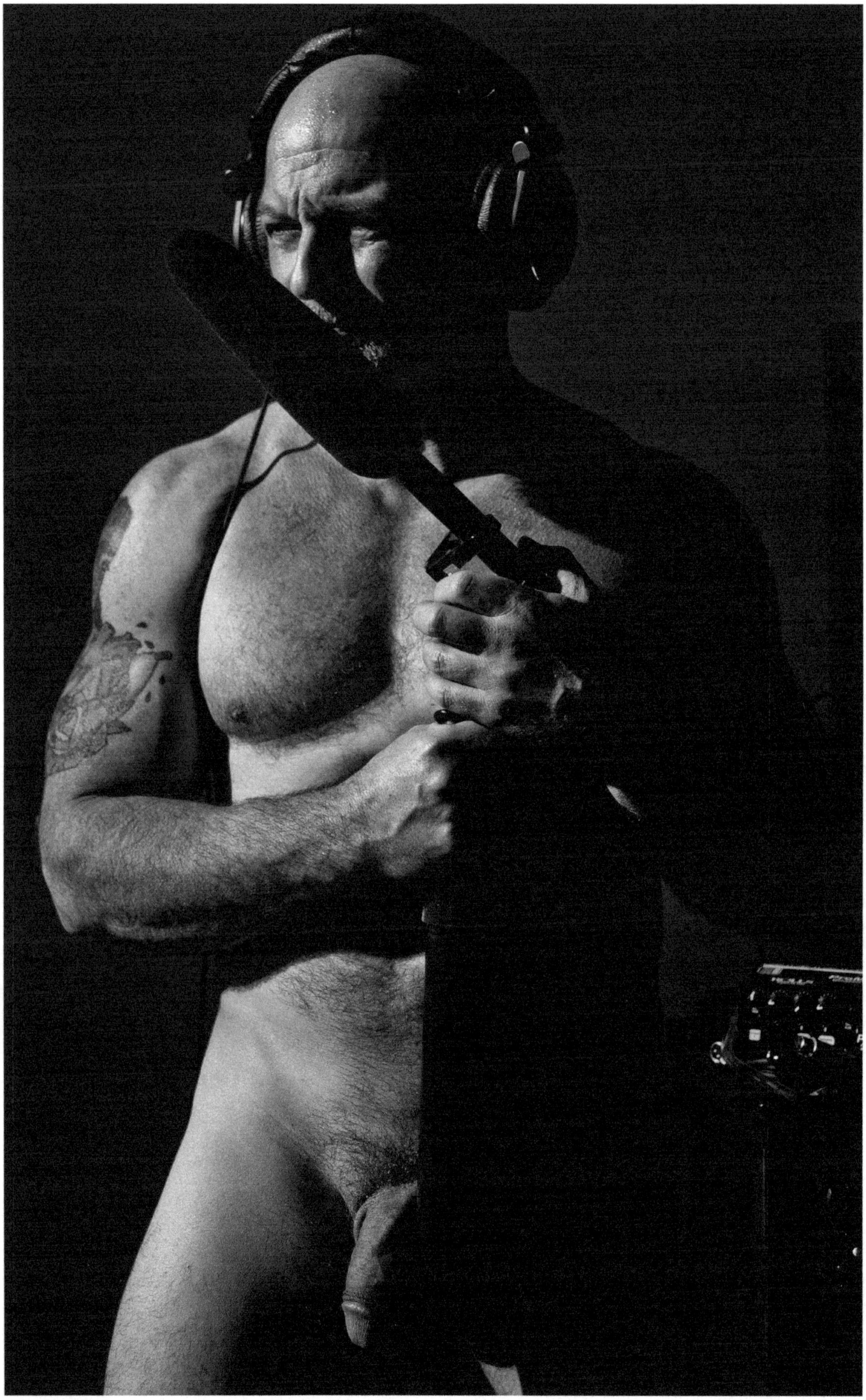

Sexual Revolution of the 1960s and accelerating with the rise of men's fashion in the 1980s (which made substantial use of male nudity in its advertising). However, there is a lingering cultural expectation that male nudes should signify virility and power and a persistent resistance to images that show men in any other way.

Web Resources

Berenice Abbott—www.iphf.org/hall-of-fame/berenice-abbott/
Diane Arbus—www.artnet.com/artists/diane-arbus/
Eugène Atget—http://ti.me/1BNIv5p
Richard Avedon—www.avedonfoundation.org
Hippolyte Bayard—http://bit.ly/1BNHOcu
Bruce of L.A. (Bruce Bellas)—www.bigkugels.com/content/Bruce.html
Erwin Blumenfeld—www.erwinblumenfeld.com
Guy Bourdin—www.louise-alexander.com/artist/guy-bourdin/
Bill Brandt—www.houkgallery.com/artists/bill-brandt/
Wynn Bullock—www.wynnbullockphotography.com
Harry Callahan—http://bit.ly/1CPpS5U
Julia Margaret Cameron—www.metmuseum.org/exhibitions/listings/2013/julia-margaret-cameron
Larry Clark—www.larryclark.com
Courbet, *L'Origine du Monde*—http://bit.ly/1akcFb0
Imogen Cunningham—http://lumieregallery.net/wp/247/imogen-cunningham
Tim Davis—www.davistim.com
Fred Holland Day—www.davistim.com
Baron Wilhelm Von Gloeden—http://bit.ly/1BRvGbe
Nan Goldin—www.matthewmarks.com/new-york/artists/nan-goldin/
André Kertész—www.brucesilverstein.com/artists/estate-of-andr-kertsz
Leigh Ledare—www.officebaroque.com/artists/11/leigh-ledare
George Platt Lynes—www.queer-arts.org/archive/show3/lynes/lynes.html
Robert Mapplethorpe—www.mapplethorpe.org/portfolios/
John Edwin Mayall—http://bit.ly/1Cy46SX
Steven Meisel—www.artandcommerce.com/artists/photographers/steven-meisel
Lee Miller—www.vam.ac.uk/content/articles/l/lee-miller/
Helmut Newton—www.artnet.com/artists/helmut-newton/
Nudity law—http://ncac.org/resource/art-law-library-nudity/
Obscenity law—http://ncac.org/resource/art-law-library-obscenity/
Irving Penn—www.artnet.com/artists/irving-penn/
Man Ray—www.manray.net
Oscar Gustave Rejlander—http://wp.me/p2gWss-Rz
Herb Ritts—www.herbritts.com/images/
Henry Peach Robinson—http://bit.ly/1P03rAb
Jan Saudek—www.famousphotographers.net/jan-saudek
Mario Sorrenti—www.artpartner.com/artists/film-print/mario-sorrenti/
Edward Steichen—http://bit.ly/1FjEi0u
Alfred Stieglitz—http://bit.ly/1CVad3K
Paul Strand—http://ti.me/1xZaEvk
Edmund Teske—www.craigkrullgallery.com/Teske/index.html
Jerry Uelsmann—www.uelsmann.net
Bruce Weber—www.bruceweber.com
Edward Weston—www.edward-weston.com
Minor White—www.getty.edu/art/exhibitions/minor_white/
Garry Winogrand—www.photogs.com/bwworld/winogrand.html
Joel-Peter Witkin—www.artnet.com/artists/joel-peter-witkin/

Facing: © Abigail Ekue.

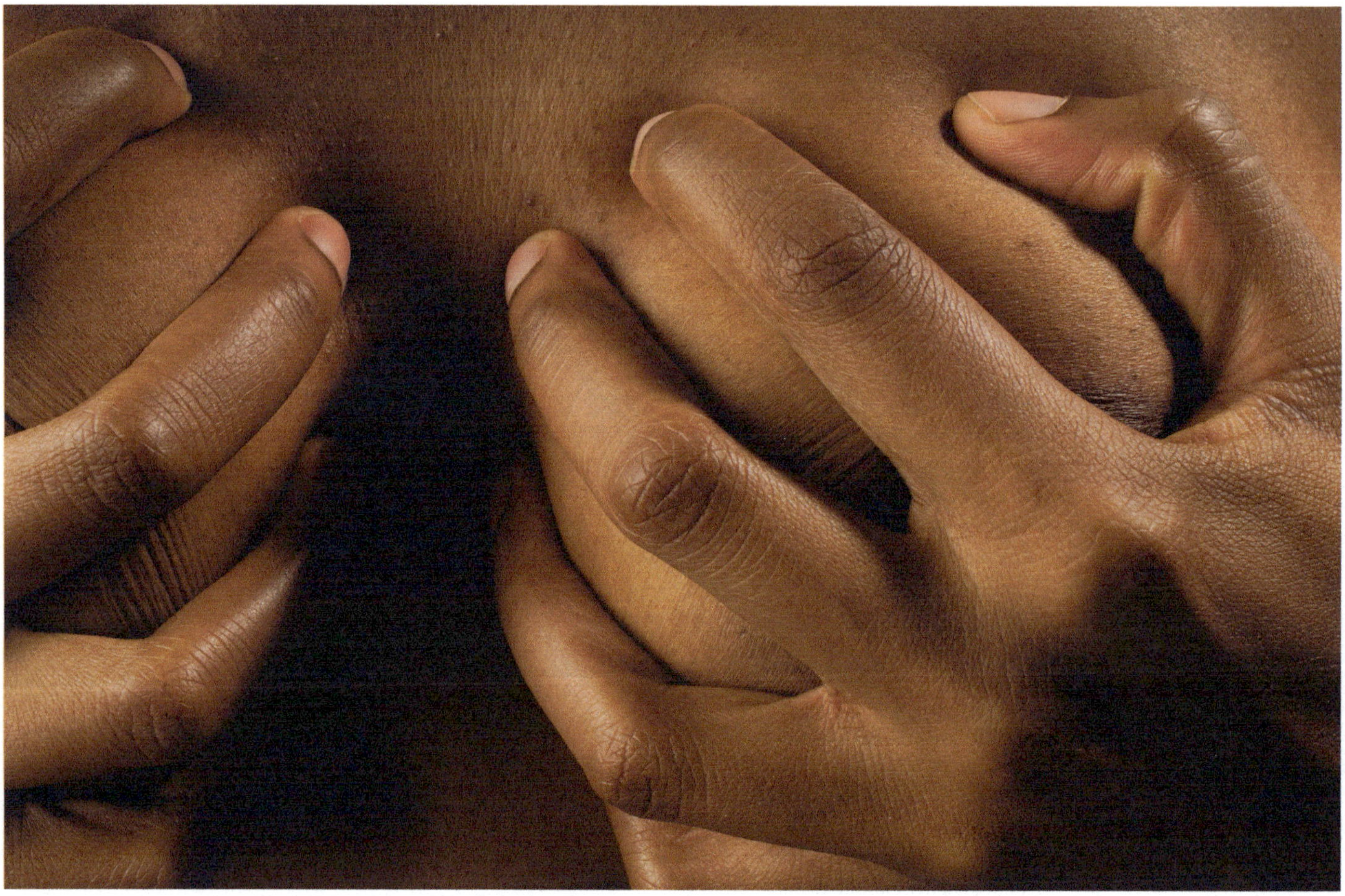

Chapter Three | Fleshing Out the Idea

"There is nothing worse than a sharp image of a fuzzy concept."
Ansel Adams

IT'S SIMPLE enough to find someone to sit in front of your camera, ask them to take off their clothes and improvise your way to artistic nude photos, but even when you're improvising, the most powerful artwork is propelled by a strong idea—a concept you're exploring, a question you're trying to answer, or a statement you want to make. In the most effective bodies of work, the clarity and integrity of the artist's vision is what drives everything else and gives the work resonance.

Some photographers explicitly set out to reshape the way people relate to photography. In the mid-1860s, Lady Mary Filmer pioneered the appropriation of images. Her transgressive photo collages questioned norms of respectability for the women of her time and showed that realistic-looking photographs don't necessarily present reality. Alfred Stieglitz was playing an even bigger game. Not only did he want photography to be accepted as an art form in its own right, he wanted to make it the dominant art form. In support of that aim, he founded the Photo Secession in 1902 to promote the idea that the photographer's unique vision is what makes a photograph significant.

Others took more personal, but no less impactful approaches. Cindy Sherman elevated conceptual

Facing: © Lou Benjamin.

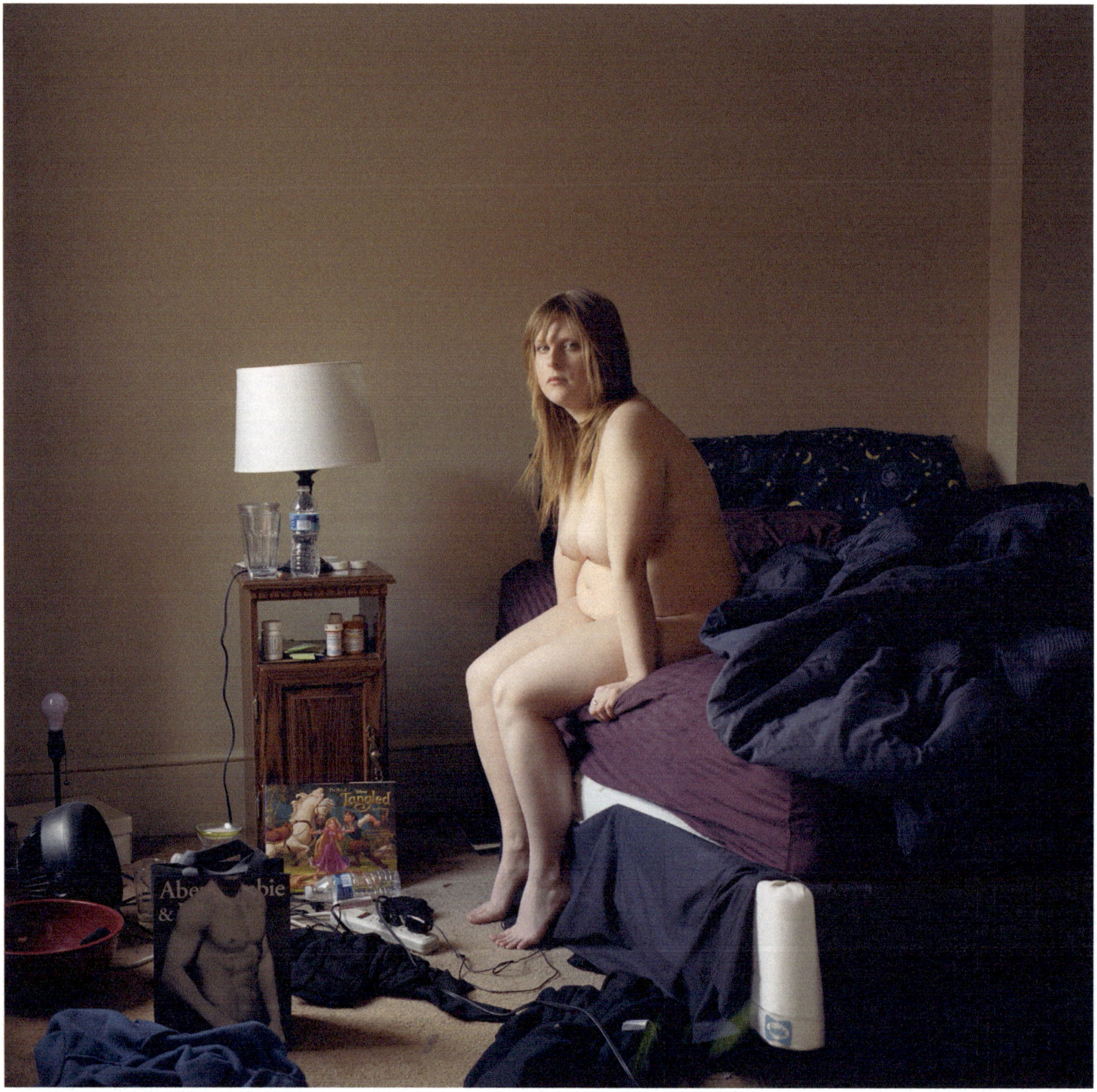
Tangled

photography by creating portraits of characters that she herself embodied. Ruth Bernhard wanted to portray women's bodies differently. "I felt that so many artists treated the female form badly, like it was an object that was tied up with their own sexual desires," she said. "I wanted to show the female form as filled with grace."

Environmental portraiture was pioneered by Arnold Newman, who said "I didn't just want to make a photograph with some things in the background. The surroundings had to add to the composition and the understanding of the person." When Lee Friedlander began his now famous series of nudes in the late 1970s, he incorporated some of those ideas and realized that he preferred to photograph the models in their homes, rather than the studio. His compositions included fabrics, potted plants, lamps, and other items found around the models' houses. Gravitating toward unconventional, even awkward poses, Friedlander also chose not to idealize or flatter—his photos show every mark and blemish.

David LaChapelle has shifted his focus from producing commercial work to fine art. About his work, he has said "The most important consideration is what is being communicated—what feelings or thoughts are being transferred to the viewer—through what has been created. My goal is clarity of intention." His idea is to have people leave the gallery feeling differently than they did when they came in. For his long-term project called *Paradise*, which is set in Maui, he combines religious motifs with references to the great masters.

Art making is often about turning convention on its ear. Such was the case when 21-year-old Irving Penn, already a successful fashion photographer for *Vogue*, shot the image known as "Nude No 1" in 1947. For the body of work that ensued two years later, he instinctively rejected the facilities of Condé Nast and the skinny idealized bodies of fashion models. Instead, he collaborated with fleshy art models who bore physical resemblance to a prehistoric fertility icon known as the Venus of Willendorf.

Jock Sturges is a highly respected fine art photographer who has also seen his fair share of controversy. His vision is informed by an "appetite for beauty." One distinguishing aspect of his work is that he creates "extended portraits," having photographed only a few people a great many times over the span of many years and generations. He had stopped shooting nudes for nearly a decade after attending a feminist workshop where he began to recognize the problem of objectification of women in nude photography. Then he had an epiphany—when you photograph someone over a prolonged period of time and present the portraits chronologically, the work comes to be about the relationship, instead of the body.

Three photographers of the nude who made their work truly personal are Harry Callahan, Nan Goldin, and Elinor Carucci. Callahan photographed his wife and muse Eleanor over a span of 50 years. Both Goldin and Carucci employ documentary-style photography to create intimate journals, photographing important people in their lives in an up-close and personal way. Their photographs represent slices of their own lives and the environments are pieces of their own worlds. Carucci appears nude in many of her own works.

Choosing Your Battles

As you develop ideas, one thing to get clear for yourself is the role of nudity in your images. Are your photos about pure form? Are you after shock value, or calling attention to some social norm by transgressing it? Is the naked body used to create some kind of visual dissonance? Or, perhaps you're using it as a narrative element. These are just some of the approaches worth considering.

František Drtikol, an influential pioneer of artistic photography of the nude, had a particular clarity about what he was after in a photograph: "I am inspired by three things: decorativeness, motion, and the stillness and expression of individual lines. I then use the background and props—simple objects such as circles, wavy lines and columns—accordingly. I let the beauty of the line itself make an impact, without embellishment, by suppressing everything that is secondary … or else I use the body as a decorative object, positioning it in various settings and lights."

Two broad categories of nudes are those where the image treats the body (which happens to be

Facing: © Osmyn J. Oree, from the series *Honesty*. Believing that fetishization—portraying the female body in a sexual, objectified way—detracts from photographs, Oree's series *Honesty* aims to reclaim the nude body and show it as something more important than simply an object of beauty or intrigue. "Each shoot I set out to make my photographs less about the nude and more about the meaningful portrayal of a person. I want to tell a story about the person through the photographs or give the viewer an insight into who the person is and make the nudity less about the eroticism or shock value and more about the universal sense of rawness and honesty."

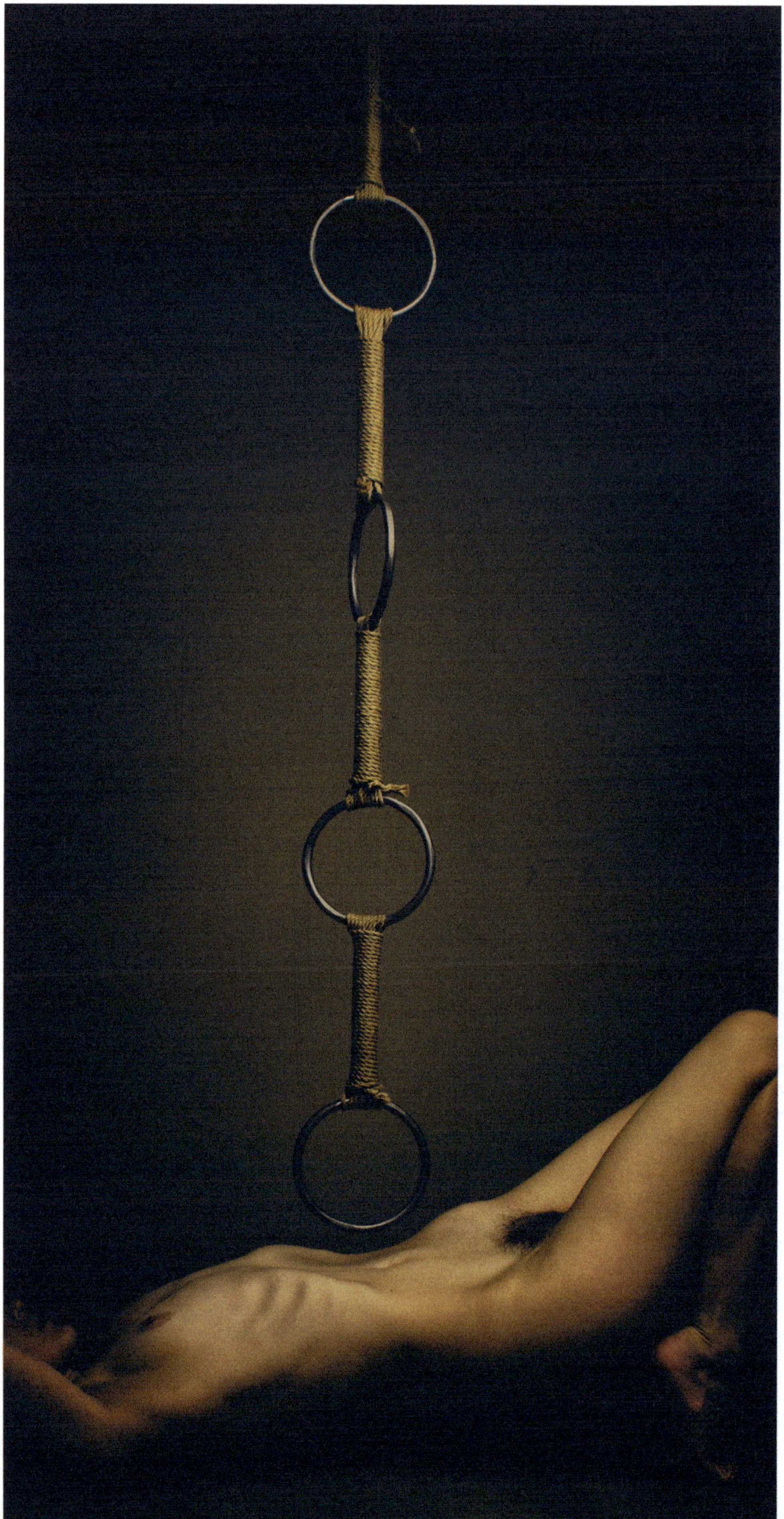

undressed) as a formal element and those where nakedness itself is at the heart of the image. Formalist images tend to be more restrained, leaning toward the abstract and downplaying the erotic. When the photo hinges on nakedness itself, the intended effect can often be to shock or to appeal to the libido, though other approaches include being humorous, camp, ironic, or dramatic. In more conceptual pieces, context is key in distinguishing artwork from pornography or other forms of photography.

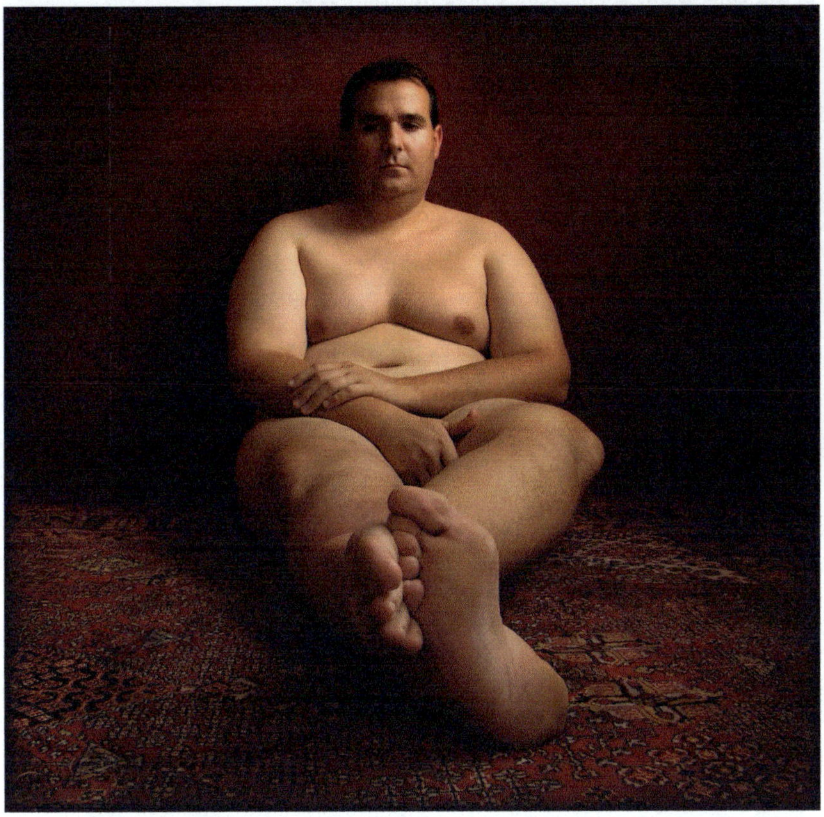

Naked/Nude, Nu and Nackt

In the book *The Nude: A Study in Ideal Form*, art historian Kenneth Clark famously wrote about a useful distinction between "nude" and "naked." Interestingly, the distinction came about in part because English has two words for being undressed, where languages such as French and German have only one word each ("nu" and "nackt" respectively). Clark posited that nudes represent idealized forms, while naked imagery does not idealize. According to Clark, nude is art, naked is not. To be naked is typically awkward or uncomfortable for both the viewer and the person seen. Consistent with that distinction, the painter Lucien Freud avoided the temptation to portray his sitters in a flattering way and referred to his works as naked portraits rather than nudes.

Clark wrote, "Every time we criticize a figure, saying that a neck is too long, hips are too wide or breasts too small, we are admitting, in quite concrete terms, the existence of ideal beauty." Art critic John Berger, who was writing about European painting at the time, expanded upon Clark's definition and suggested that by conforming to those ideals, the "nude" becomes a depersonalized form of dress. In Berger's view, the nude is idealized and abstracted to the point of being stripped of identity, while the naked retains its identity. As an extreme example, a contorted, faceless body is a nude, while a candid portrait of someone skinny-dipping is a naked portrait.

Extending this idea into composing a photograph, you can frame and light a shot in such a way as to obscure the face or isolate the torso to produce a piece that is anonymous. That anonymity emphasizes form and generalizes the body into something that signifies all bodies, the hallmark of the classic art nude. The absence of facial expression also removes the prime conduit for conveying emotion and makes it difficult, if not impossible, to ascribe personality. Photos that feature faces inherently signify a persona. Through cues such as eye contact, facial expression, and the direction of the sitter's gaze, we can read personality and emotional states. However, the presence of the face invariably de-emphasizes the figure.

It's worth noting that while Clark's distinction can be employed effectively to analyze art photography,

Facing: © Donna Feldman Lasky.

Above: "Le Salon Rouge" © Pascal Renoux. A portrait that runs contrary to the norms of "ideal beauty" and dispenses with taboos against male nudity.

it was his belief that photography was a tool of transcription that could not sufficiently transform the body to produce a nude. Thus, photography could not produce art in his estimation. For the purposes of this book, the term "nude" applies to all representations of the body in an undressed state. It's also worth noting that more current thinking on this distinction allows that at least some photography of the "naked" is still very much art. In fact, much contemporary work is more interested in the naked than the nude—pushing boundaries and re-examining assumptions. At least a segment of the current art market is interested in anti-beauty—unflattering imagery created in reaction to longstanding conventions of aesthetics.

Ideal beauty is a central element in the photographic genre known as "fine art nudes," which tend to have a very specific look and mood. Artists producing fine art nudes often describe their work in terms of "showing the beauty of the human body." However, the conventions of the genre seem to hold that only a limited range of body types are beautiful. When bodies that don't meet those aesthetic standards are offered as fine art nudes, they are typically presented in an anonymous form, such as bodyscapes—perhaps that was the influence of Penn and later, Friedlander.

Training for Your Eyes

A very powerful tool in developing your artistic vision is being able to distinguish what works or doesn't work about an image. Most of us are accustomed to saying whether we like a photo or not, but stop there. You want to learn to articulate in greater detail what catches your eye about a photo and what makes it successful or unsuccessful for you. Is it the subject matter? The tonality? Does the framing work? How is the color handled? Is there too much or too little contrast?

Learning to critique work functions much like ear training for a musician, where you listen and identify the notes being played so that you can recreate them at will. John Szarkowski (pron. Shar-COW-ski), who was Director of Photography at the Museum of Modern Art (also known as MoMA) in New York from 1962 to 1991, contributed a key set of tools for critiquing photography—his framework of five dimensions.

Locating the Nude within Szarkowski's Dimensions

In 1966, John Szarkowski published *The Photographer's Eye*, which set forth a framework of five dimensions specific to photography for assessing the artistic qualities of a photograph (i.e. the frame, the thing itself, vantage point, the detail, and time). In the introduction to the book he wrote that he hoped his framework "may contribute to the formulation of a vocabulary and a critical perspective more fully responsive to the unique phenomena of photography." Szarkowski was aware that the five dimensions he outlined in *The Photographer's Eye* were not the medium's only issues then, and art photography has continued to change and expand since he held sway. Still, Szarkowski's dimensions provide a useful critical framework for assessing art photography today. Each of the dimensions are presented here with particular consideration of photography of the nude.

The Frame

Szarkowski described framing as "the central act of photography, the act of choosing and eliminating, [which] forces a concentration on the picture edge—the line that separates in from out—and on the shapes that are created by it."

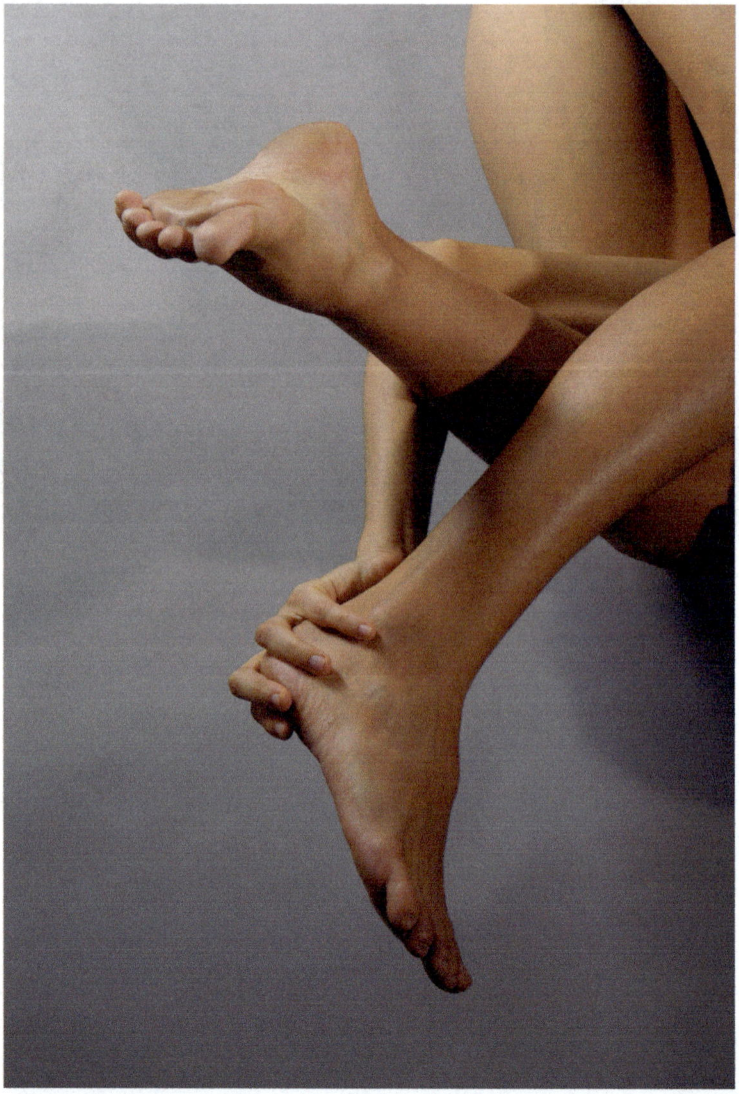

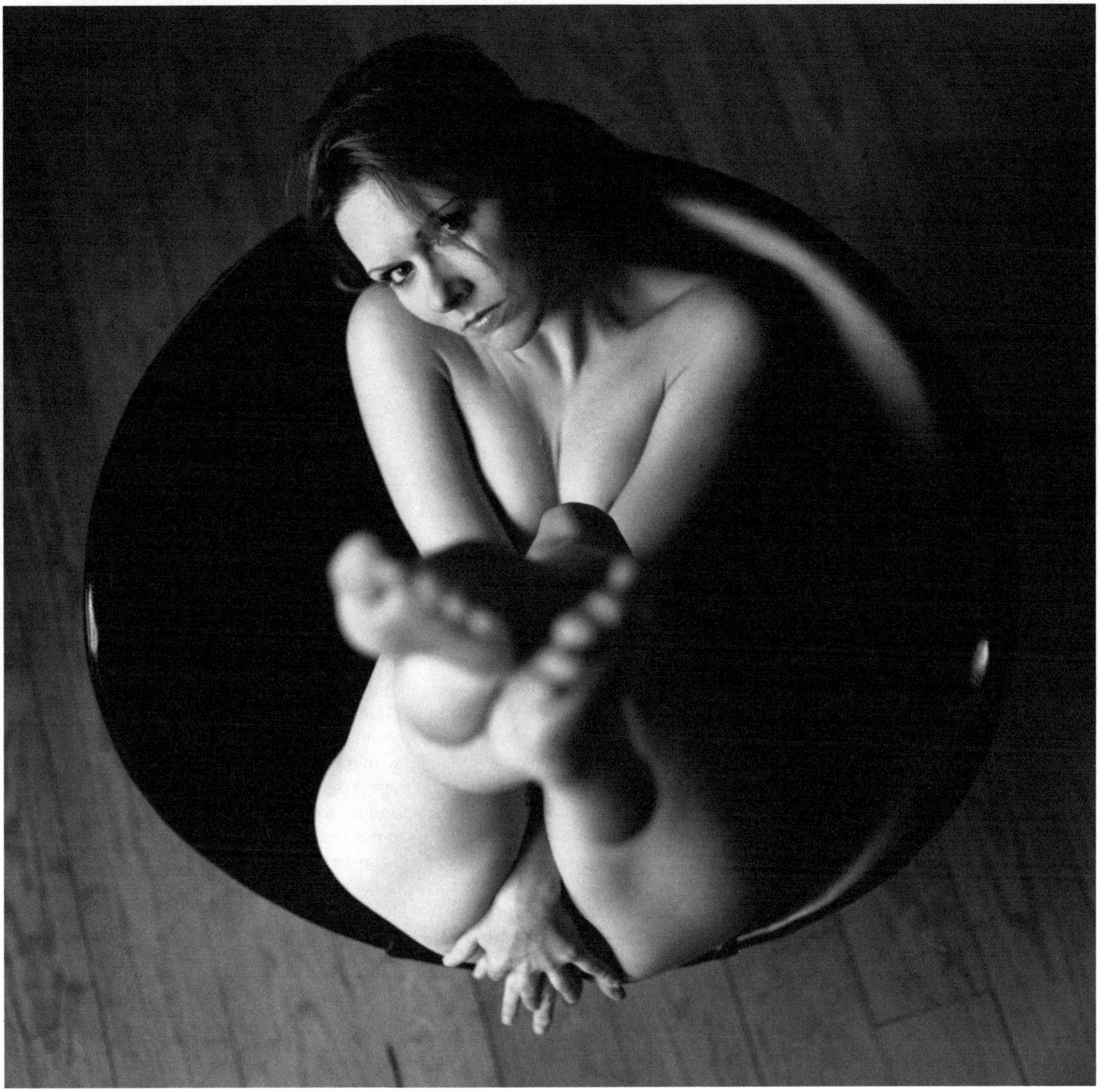

Facing: © Lou Benjamin. Model: Béu Tornaghi.

Above: © Steven Billups. The square framing and the circle interact with the figure in a powerful way, with the circle creating a frame-in-frame effect. The shallow depth of field presents a third dimension of framing which emphasizes how the feet are extended upward. The soft focus, however, de-emphasizes them.

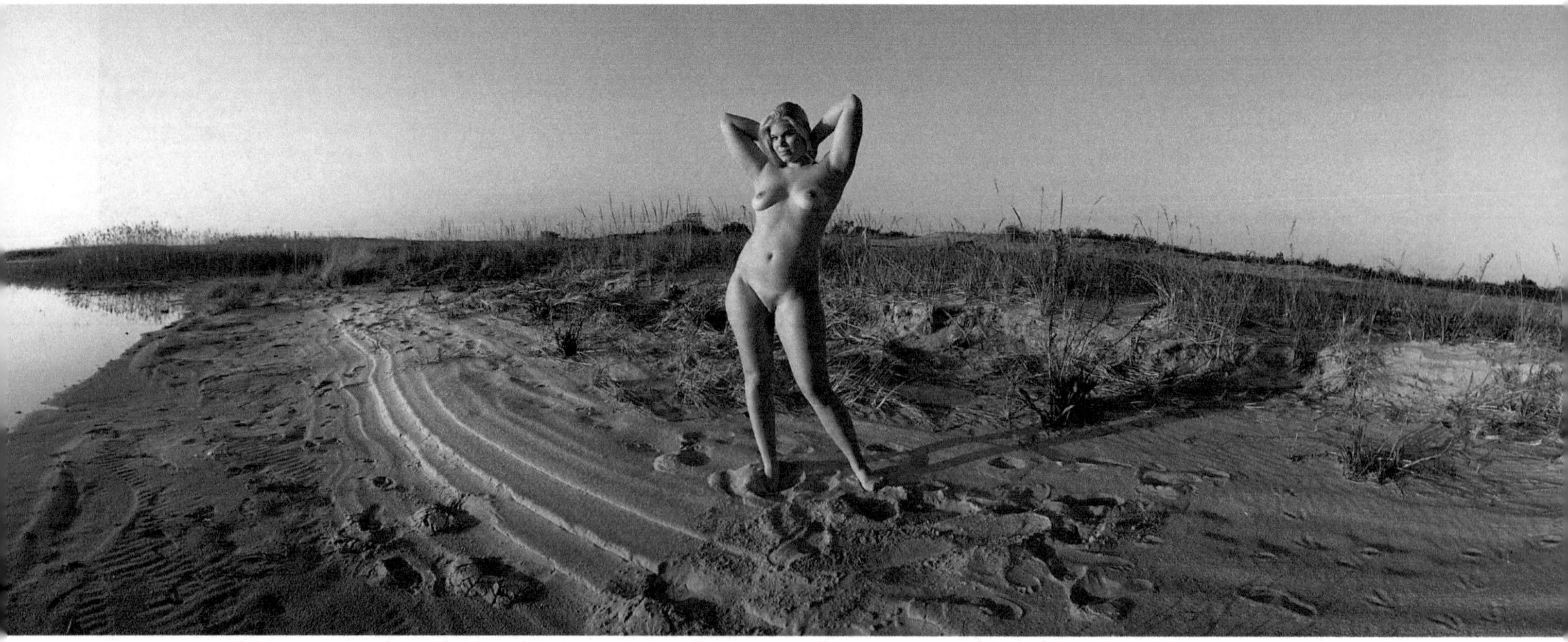

The body can be enclosed in the frame, constrained, or truncated by it, or included in an expanse of what graphic designers call negative space. A small figure near the bottom of the frame seems grounded. Placing the figure dead center in the frame can create a kind of ambiguity. Placing it near the top tends to give the impression of floating upward, or of an impending plunge.

Another graphic design concept is visual tension or imbalance, which is created by moving elements away from the center of the frame. A three-quarter portrait nude with the same pose and expression will have very different visual qualities depending on whether it is shot with the bridge of the nose on the center line, with the right eye (camera left) on the center line, or with the shoulder touching the center.

The proportions (aspect ratio) of the frame also matter. The aspect ratio of the 35mm frame is 2:3, and that's also what most 35mm-format DSLRs conform to. That aspect ratio is thought to mimic the field of view of normal human vision most closely. The square format poses very specific compositional challenges, while 4 x 5 is considered large format. Point and shoot cameras often use a 4:3 frame that matches the shape of conventional TV. Panoramic cameras create images in a range of proportions that are short and wide and have a cinematic feeling. HD movies are typically cut in 16:9, and 70mm theatrical films like *Alien* are in 2.20:1. Still other theatrical films are in 2.35:1. Each of these formats creates a distinctive compositional space and can have a subtle, yet important, impact upon the way an image is read.

Top: © Alan Fresco. The expanse of the landscape setting takes on significance because of the elongated aspect ratio of the frame.

Facing: © Alfred Laij. The ball, the ring, and the splayed fingers are salient details. Shallow depth of field (85mm lens at f/1.8 wide open) functions as a framing device to emphasize the gesture of extending the hand and render the face abstract. Warm tone gives the photo a vintage quality reminiscent of Pictorialism.

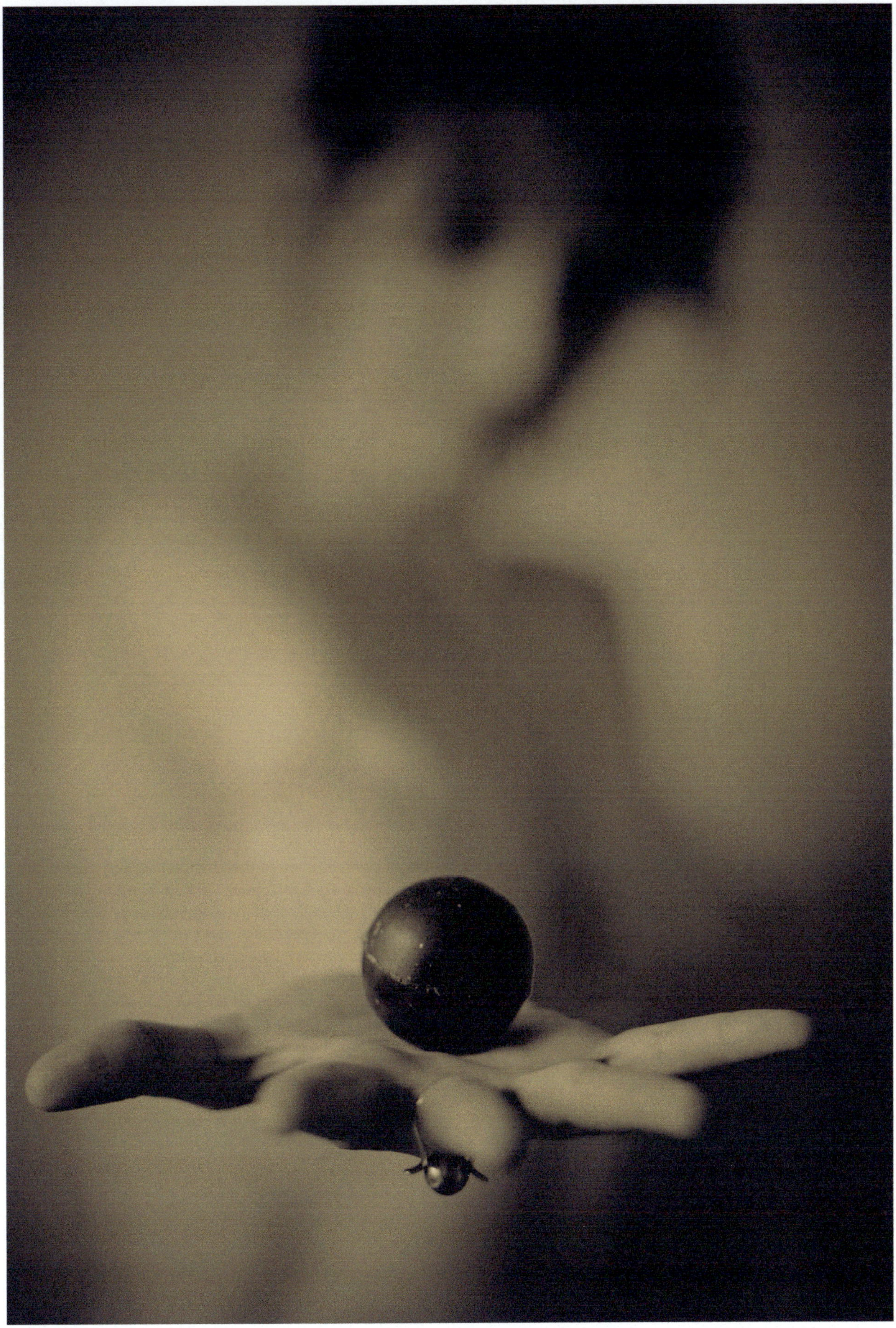

The Thing Itself

In a famous series of paintings called *The Treachery of Images*, the Surrealist René Magritte inscribed "Ceci n'est pas une pipe" (This is not a pipe) on the canvas beneath an illustration of a pipe, emphasizing that the illustration is not the thing itself. Szarkowski asserted that even though the viewer often fails to distinguish between the picture and the thing(s) depicted, the photographer has to be clear about this distinction and to think in terms of the photo.

The camera doesn't see the way we do, enlarging the distinction between the way we see the thing itself and the way its representation appears. Artists often make use of the transformation inherent in the photographic process. Bill Brandt's figures in *Perspective of Nudes* were transformed by the curvature and spatial distortion introduced by the vintage lens of his 100-year-old camera. André Kertész used a fun-house mirror to create even more dramatic distortions.

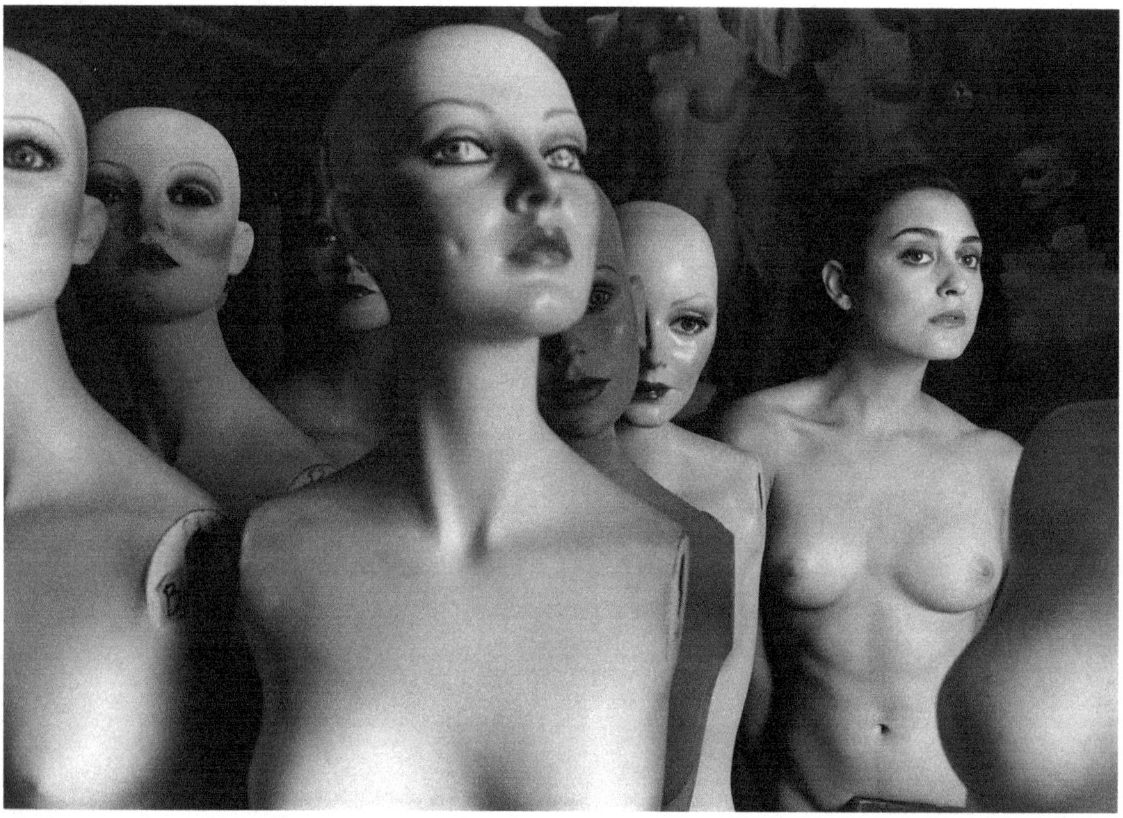

Simply by being attuned to the physicality of the subject and the play of light, the naked body can be rendered in many ways through photography. The same body in the same pose can produce results that range from a documentary-style portrait to melodrama, to abstraction; and all of these outcomes are the product of artistic choices that the photographer makes.

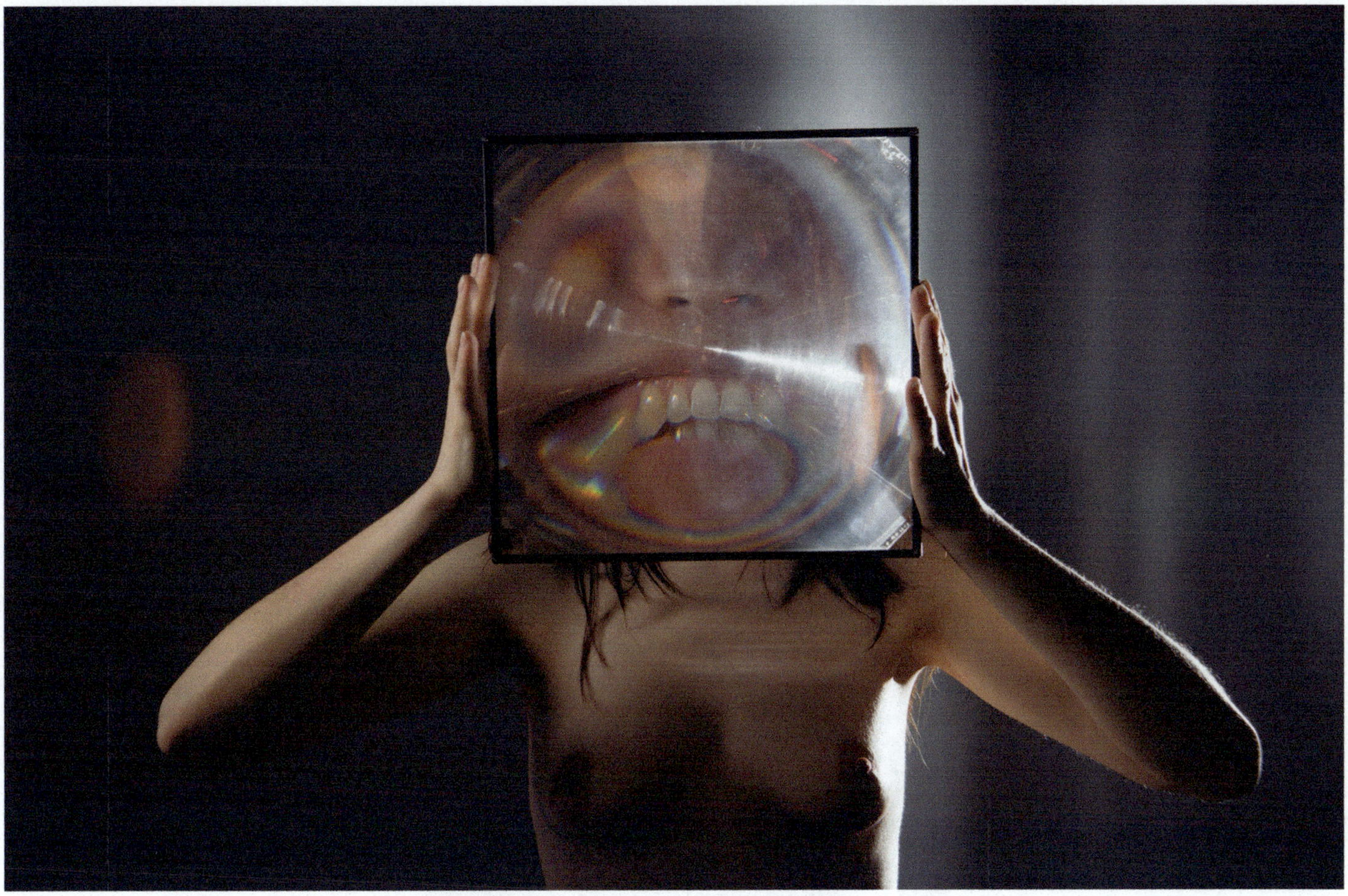

Facing: © 2009 Harvey Stein. A depiction of a person imitating representations of people.

Above: © Terry Slater.

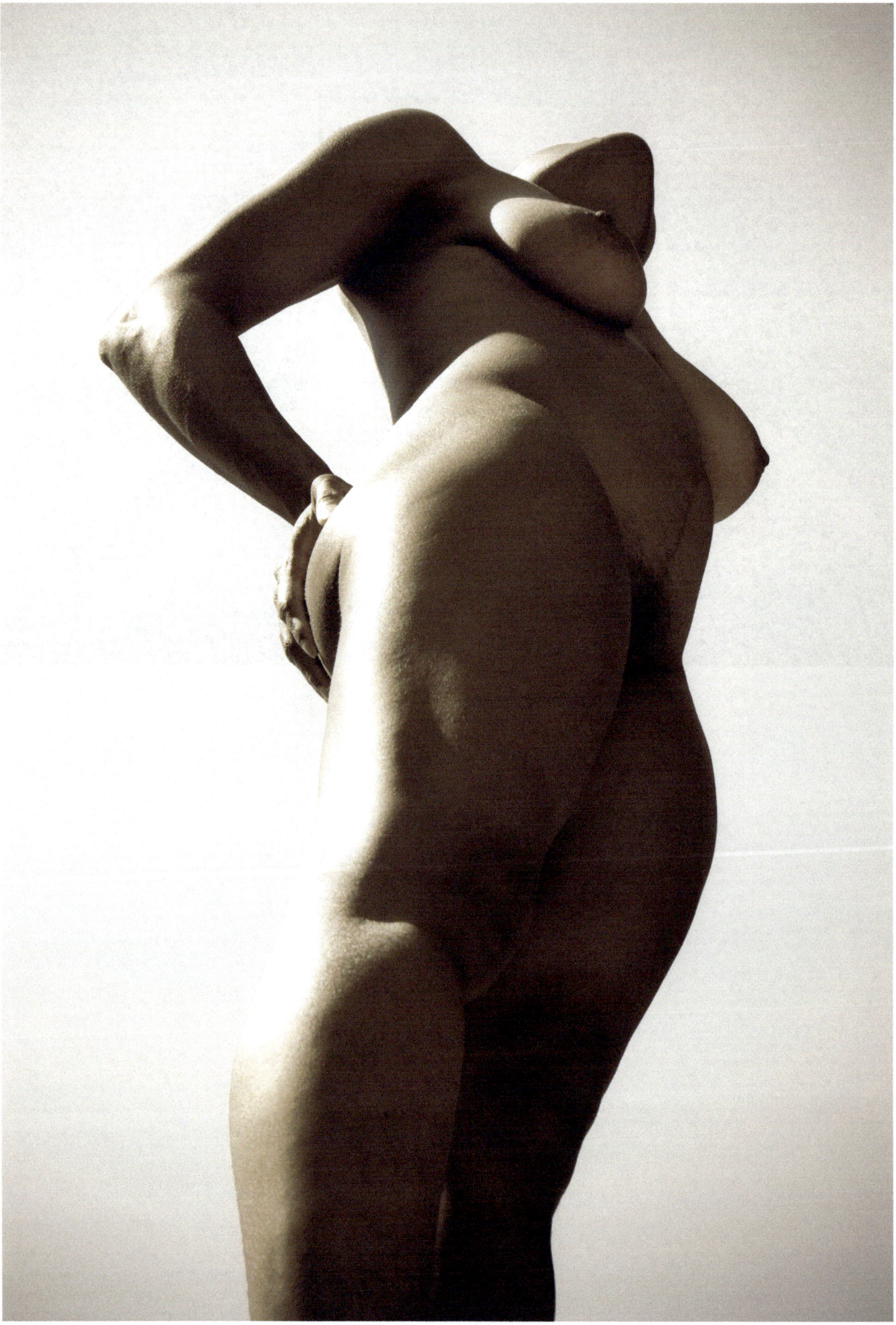

Vantage Point

Alberto Korda's famous 1960 portrait of Che Guevara demonstrates how powerful the low "heroic angle" can be in elevating the perception of the person portrayed. That shot is so iconic that a great number of images imitate it. The web is full of amateur cell-phone nudes shot "Hail Mary" style, with the camera positioned at arm's length, above the head, and tilted downward. Pornography has turned the "upskirt" into a pop cliché. Each of these approaches emphasizes seeing the subject from a point of view that we wouldn't normally see unless we were extraordinarily tall or short at the very least.

Szarkowski suggested that there is also a more expansive interpretation of vantage point: it can be seen as a particular attitude toward the subject. For example, the body can be depicted as an inert object, a symbol of sex, or even a non sequitur. It can be photographed in a way that suggests perfection, or emphasizes deficiency. Pictures can be about nudity itself, about morality, or simply a description of what someone looks like. The artistic nude can be about embracing ideals of beauty or subverting them.

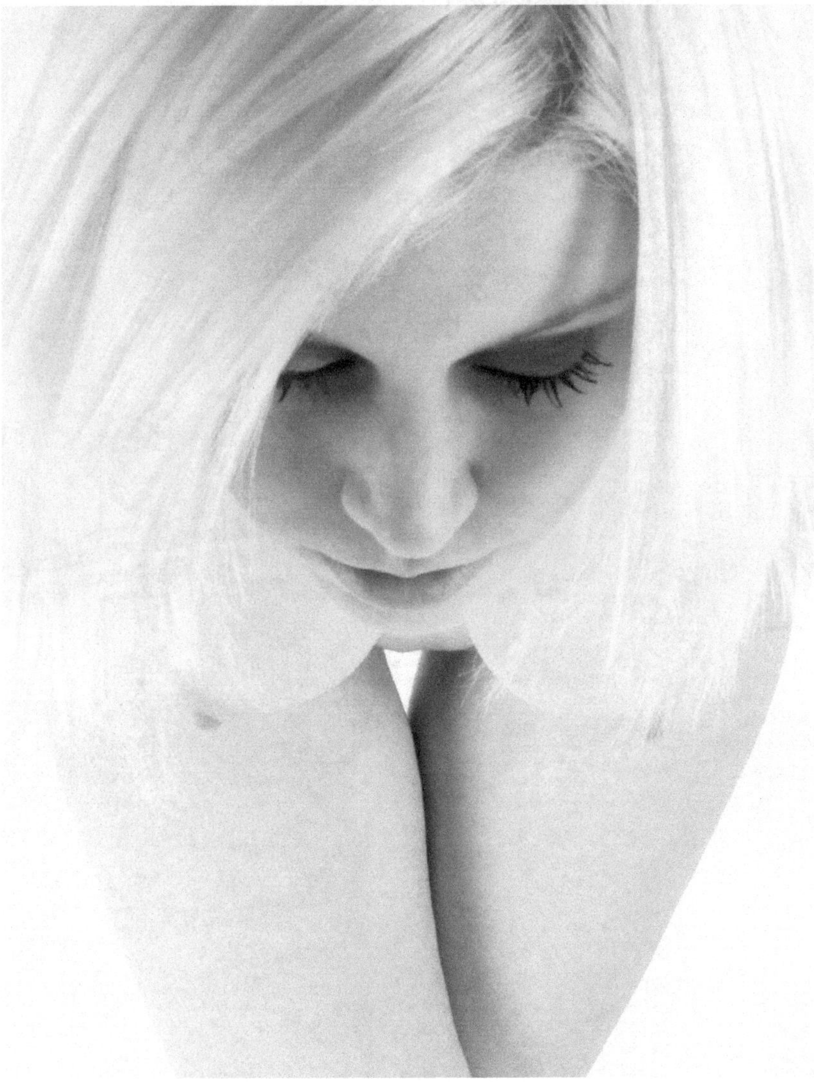

Facing: © Saelon Renkes.

Above: © John Evans. Vantage point, tight framing, and high key lighting combine to produce an image that borders on the abstract.

Nudity in a work of art carries a certain symbolic power, and one possible vantage point of the photographer making nudes can be that of exploring the very nature of such power. By formulating, articulating, and adopting a particular vantage point, the artistic photographer can build a cohesive and effective body of work.

Conceptualism and performance art have become much more important aspects of contemporary photography than they were in the time of Szarkowski, and while they are not unique to photography, they are also useful ways of thinking about the artistry of a photo. You could see them as aspects of vantage point, but you could also argue for them being something distinct from that. Vanessa Beecroft's conceptual works are live performances, often involving multiple nude models. She relies on photographs and video recordings to document the events.

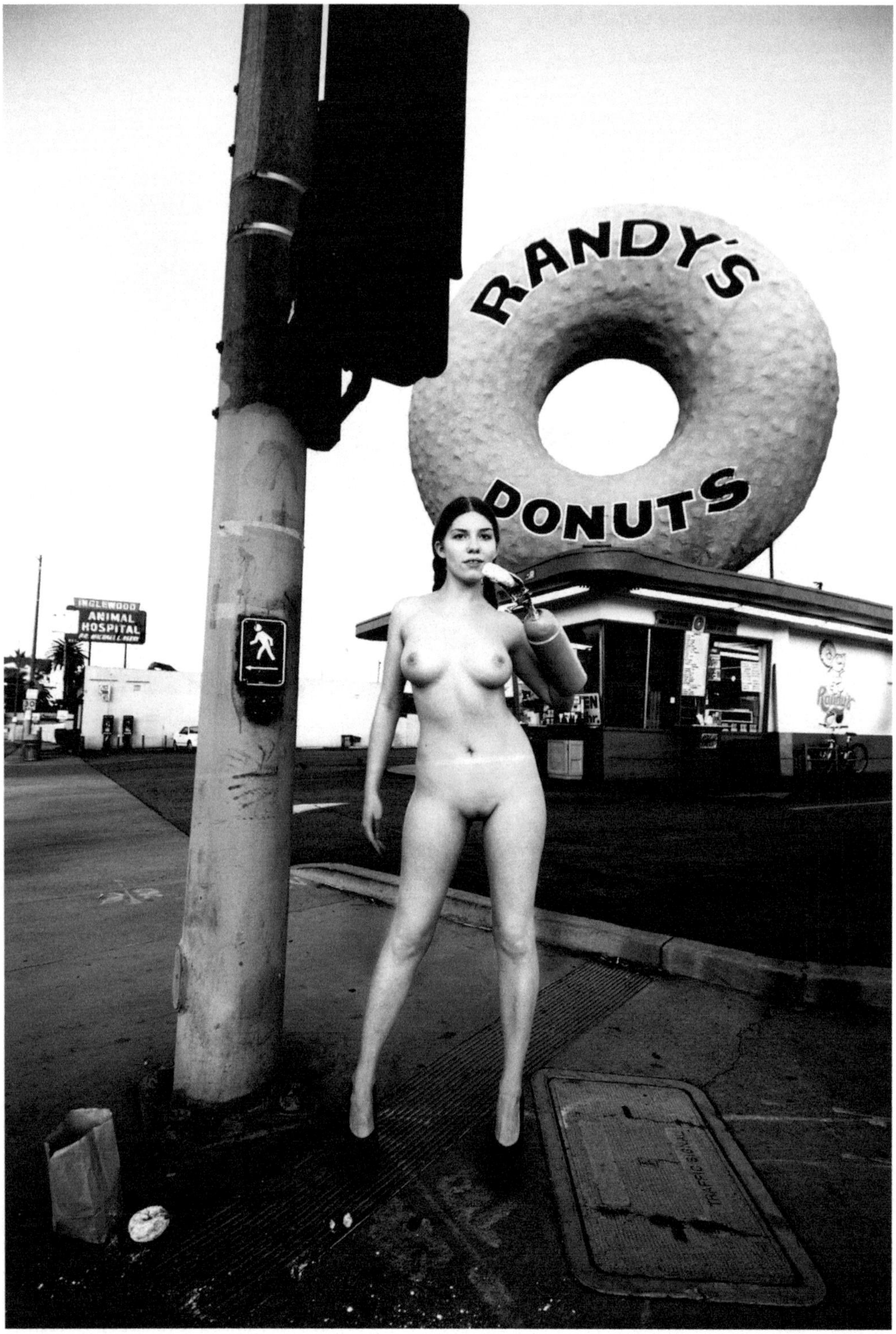

The Detail

Three issues of detail that photographers continuously confront are sharpness, shadow detail, and highlight detail. "Soft" lenses obscure detail, particularly texture. Over- or under-exposure can cause salient detail to be lost.

In isolating fragments of the thing itself (by means of placing the frame), a photographer can elevate what seems trivial and imbue it with symbolic meaning. John Coplans made nude self-portraits that famously isolated portions of his aging body in surprising ways.

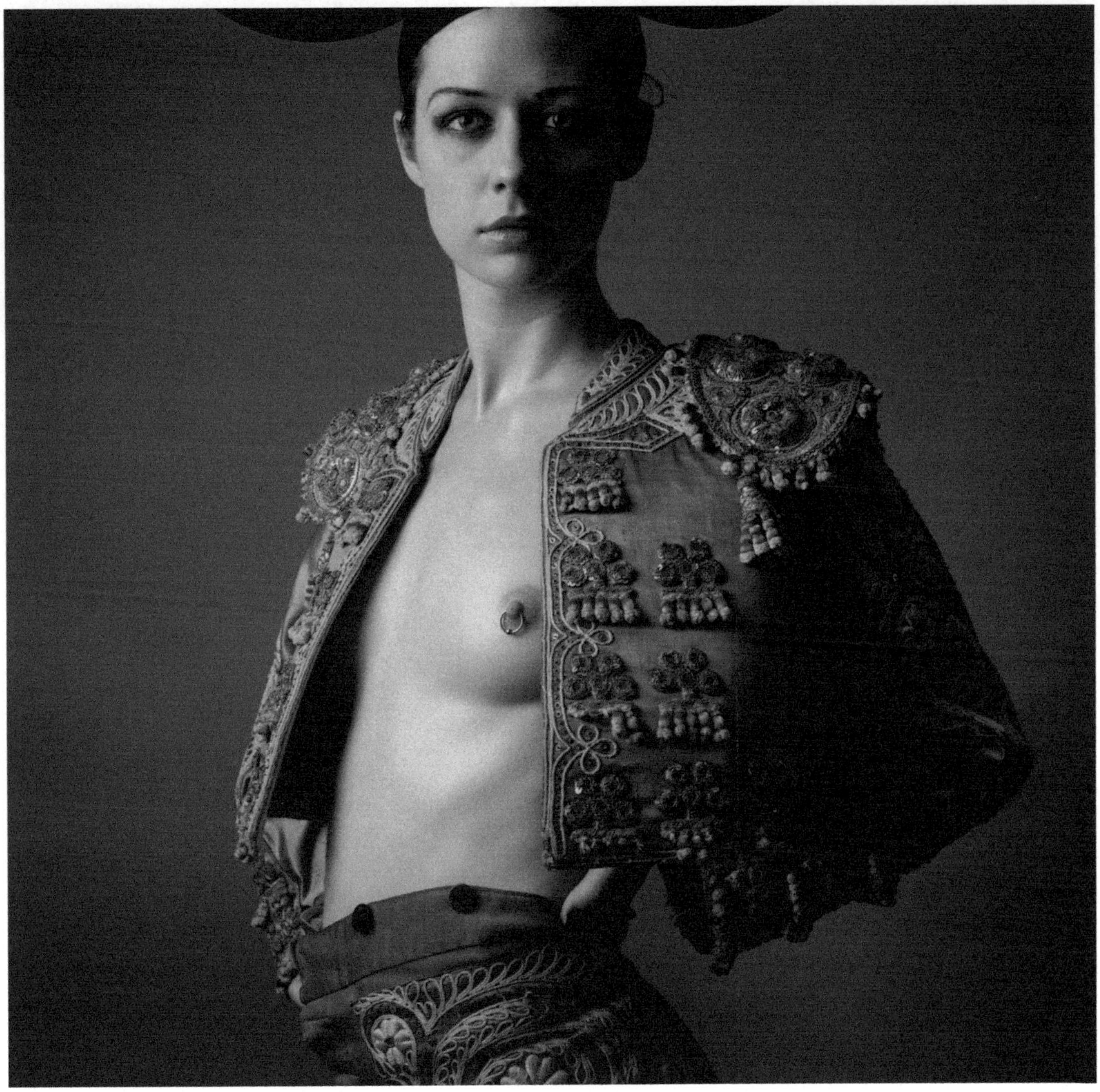

Facing: "Randy's Donut" © Gary Breckheimer. A detail that's easy to miss is that the model is holding the donut with a prosthetic hook. Choice of location and careful composition gives richness to this photo, which rewards a second look.

Above: "Of Mice and Matadors" © Tobias Slater-Hunt. From the series *Iconival.* Shot with a Twin Reflex Rollei in Gardena, Los Angeles, 2005.

Time

Just as the edge of the camera frame slices through space, the opening and closing of the shutter slices through time. Photos are never really instantaneous, even if they look that way. They can be made to emphasize the passage of time as an impressionistic smear of motion blur, or to isolate momentary events that we can only appreciate because they were recorded in less time than an eye blink.

In 1878, Eadweard Muybridge was commissioned to photograph a horse at full gallop for railroad baron Leland Stanford (the university is named for his son). Muybridge produced a succession of frames that froze the action and showed without a doubt that a horse actually lifts all four feet off the ground simultaneously when it gallops. The images are often referred to as being stroboscopic, but they are not. Harold "Doc" Edgerton would not develop the electronic flash for another 50 years. Using an array of twelve stereoscopic cameras with an elaborate tripwire system, he captured the frames at 1/1000 second. The R&D to create the high-sensitivity photographic materials he used had been bankrolled by Stanford.

Using this technique, Muybridge went on to document locomotion in animals and humans extensively, including sequences that feature men and women in stereotypical roles—men wrestling, women descending staircases, or one woman dumping a bucket of water onto another.

Doc Edgerton first began experimenting with flash tubes in 1926 after he noticed that the arc from some lab equipment that he was using to test motors seemed to freeze motion. The Edgerton flash tube design is still the basis of all flash tubes made today. In 1937, he began collaborating with photographer Gjon Mili. Using a stroboscopic "multiflash" device that could flash up to 120 times per second, the duo photographed Bobby Jones swinging a golf club in 1938. The result is reminiscent of Muybridge's galloping horse sequence, except that all of the phases of the arc of the swing appear in a single frame. Where Muybridge used multiple cameras with 1/1000-second shutter speeds, Edgerton and Mili used only one camera with a 1/2 second shutter speed. The 60 discrete flash exposures are separate slices of time rendered in composite on the film.

In the late 1970s, Francesca Woodman made groundbreaking images, using her own body as subject matter. In some of those images, she would move parts of her body during long exposures to produce nude self-portraits that suggested she was evanescent or blending into her surroundings.

Beyond the duration of the exposure, choosing the precise moment to trip the shutter is essential in the classic Cartier-Bresson "decisive moment" photograph. Szarkowski noted that Cartier-Bresson's idea has been misinterpreted. It's all about the photographer's awareness and exploitation of time in the context of the visual composition within the frame. The photographer waits to trip the shutter at the very moment when patterns and lines emerge from the flux of activity within the viewfinder and coalesce to produce a visual crescendo.

Facing (top): © Alan Fresco. Strobe light seems to stop time, while 1/60 second f/8 ISO 200 exposure allowed the environmental details to render. The camera is a Nikon D200 converted to full-spectrum sensitivity and fitted with an SB900 hot shoe flash. The photo is distinguished from the thing itself by the transformation produced by full-spectrum (IR + visible light + UV) sensitivity.

Facing (bottom): © Terry Slater.

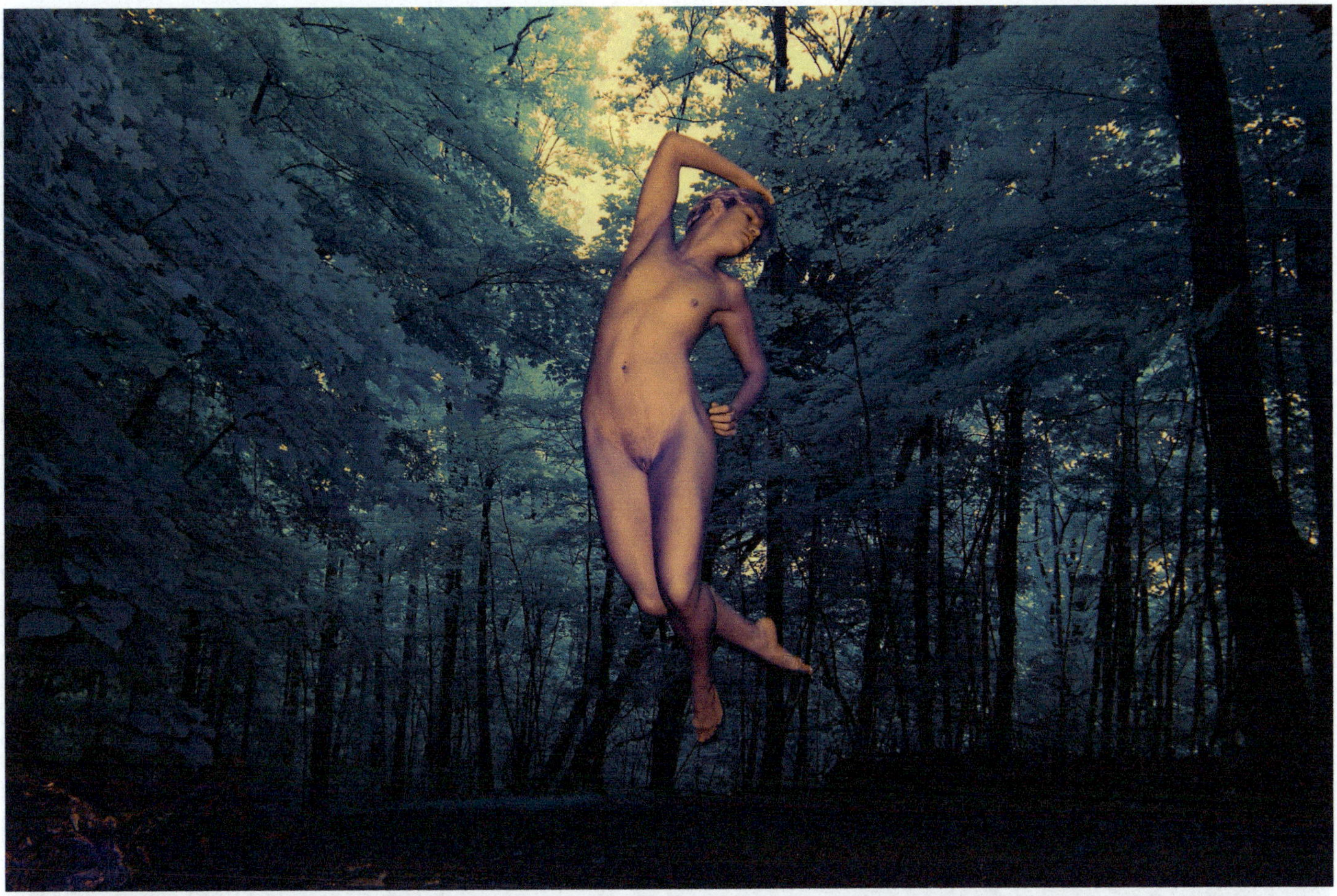

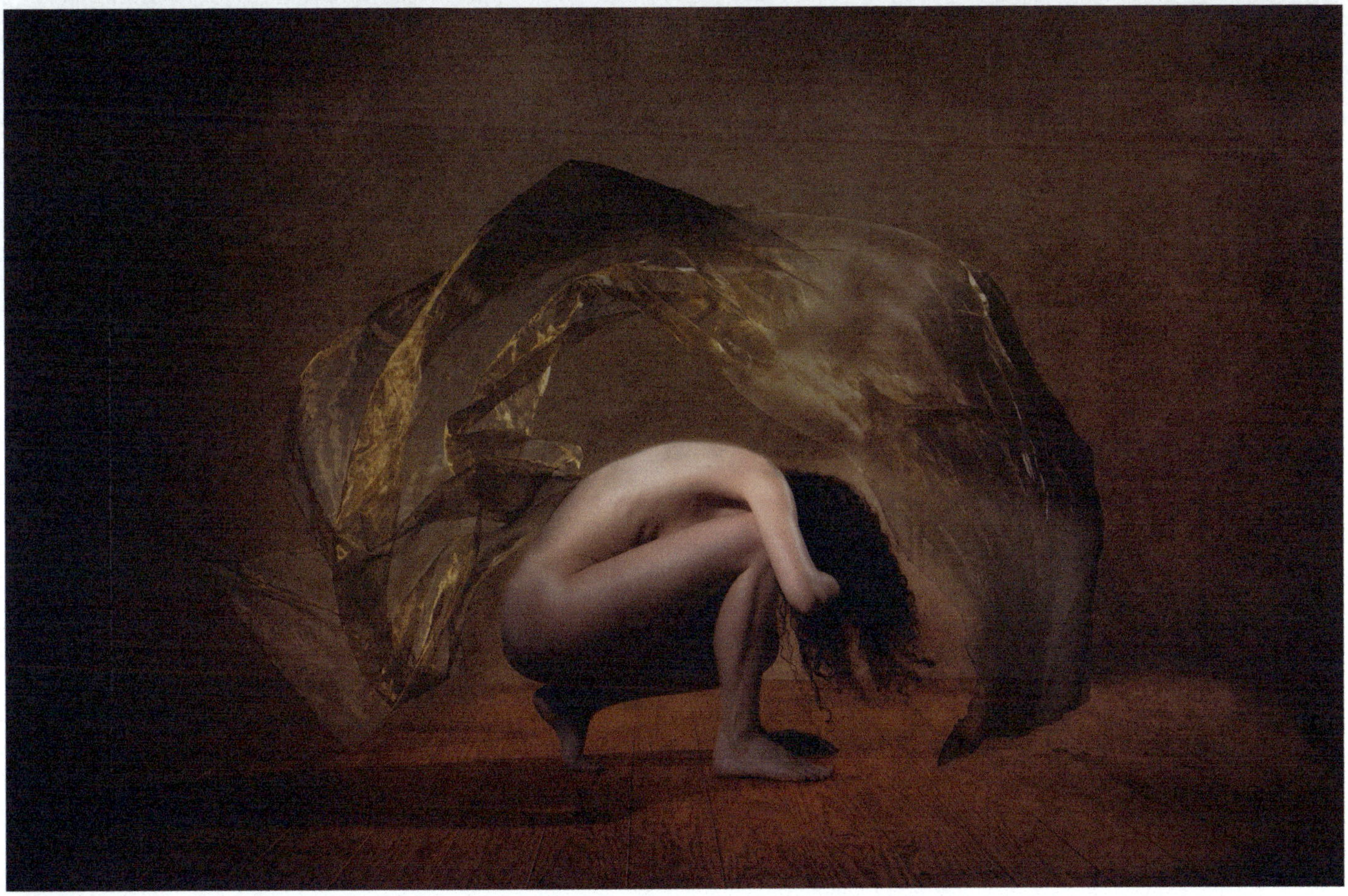

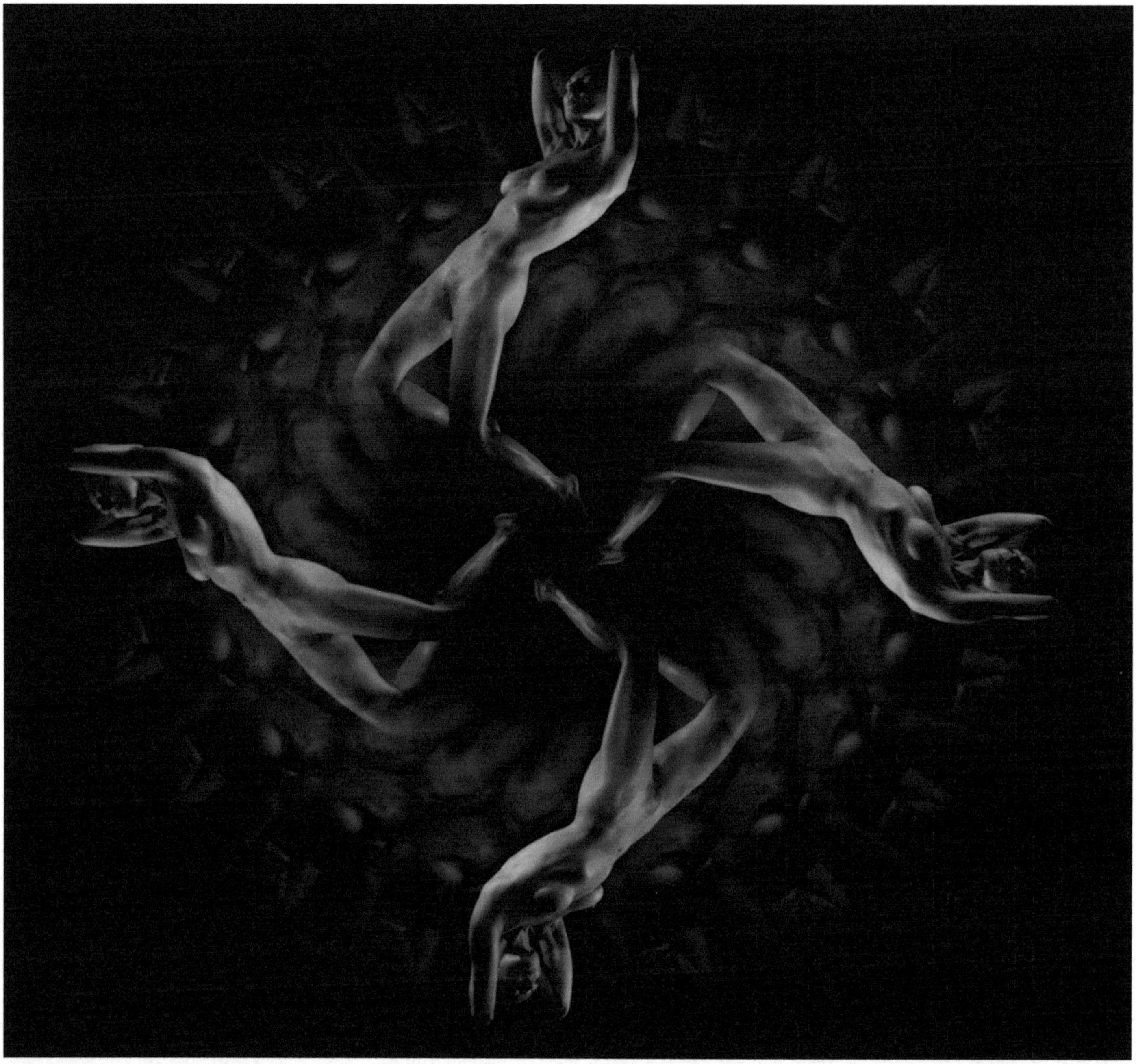

Above: © P. J. Reptilehouse. Where Edgerton's camera was always fixed, P. J. Reptilehouse uses a computer-controlled armature to move the camera. In this eleven-second exposure, the camera rotated on its axis while twenty variable-intensity pulses of light from LED strobes illuminated the figure. The model stood fairly still for this image, but often moves as well.

Facing: © Lou Benjamin. Model: Lauren Babree. Camera was affixed to a tripod. Exposure 0.8 sec. f/10, ISO 100.

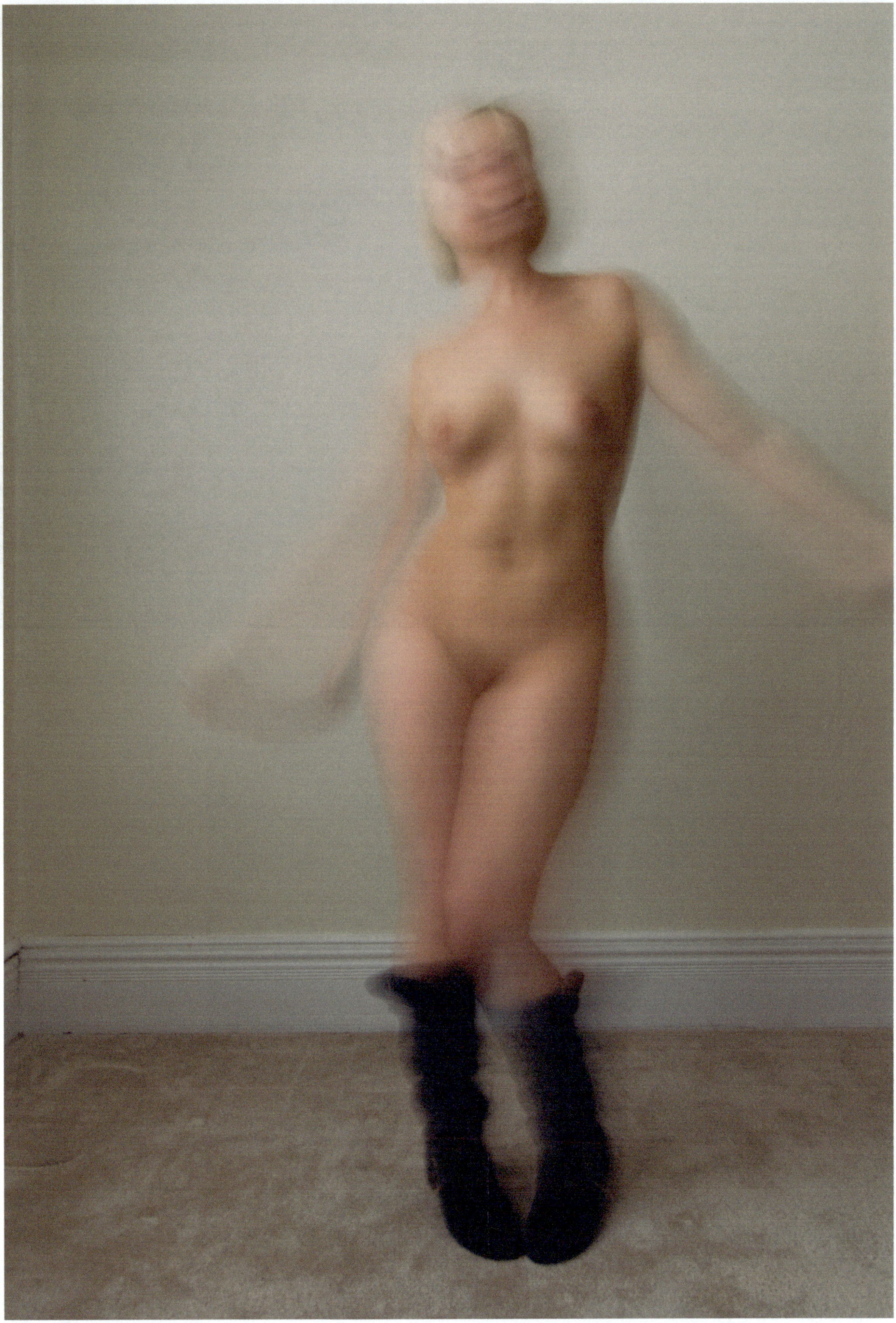

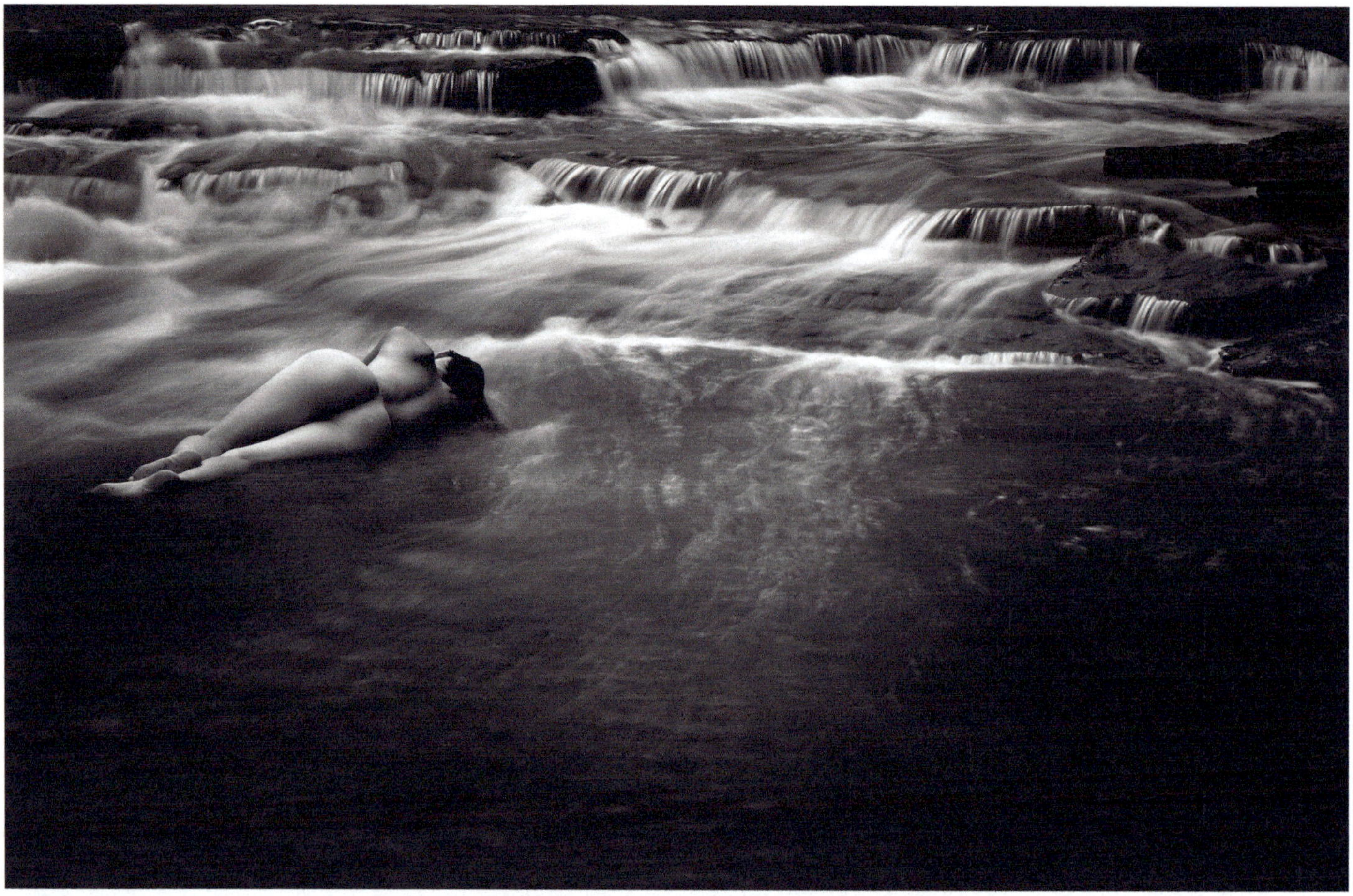

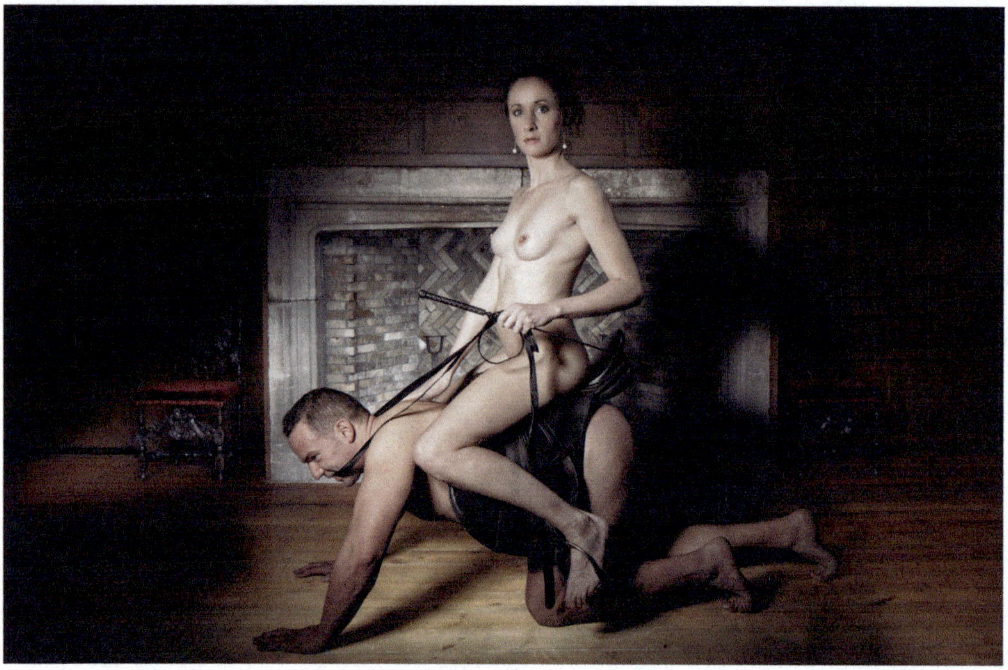

It's Not Just About the Body

Art photographs can be studies in pure form, but often they're more than that. For example, they can be portraits, explore narrative, or provide social commentary.

The idea of narrative in photography is easy to see in photographic sequences, where the viewer creates the action by deducing what has changed between each frame. Within the single frame, narrative can arise from the relationship between compositional elements, but it also often arises out of the way in which the viewer processes an image linguistically. This starts with mentally naming the objects perceived within the picture plane.

Environmental portraiture is largely about using the surroundings to tell a story about the person depicted, and environmental nudes can have a similar narrative quality. While a portrait tends to be a story about an actual person, environmental nudes are more often about a character in a setting or an idea. Environmental nudes often place the subject in a setting where nakedness is not acceptable or expected, emphasizing nakedness itself. In other instances, the environmental nude is more about the sculpture of the body in a space. A popular trope is

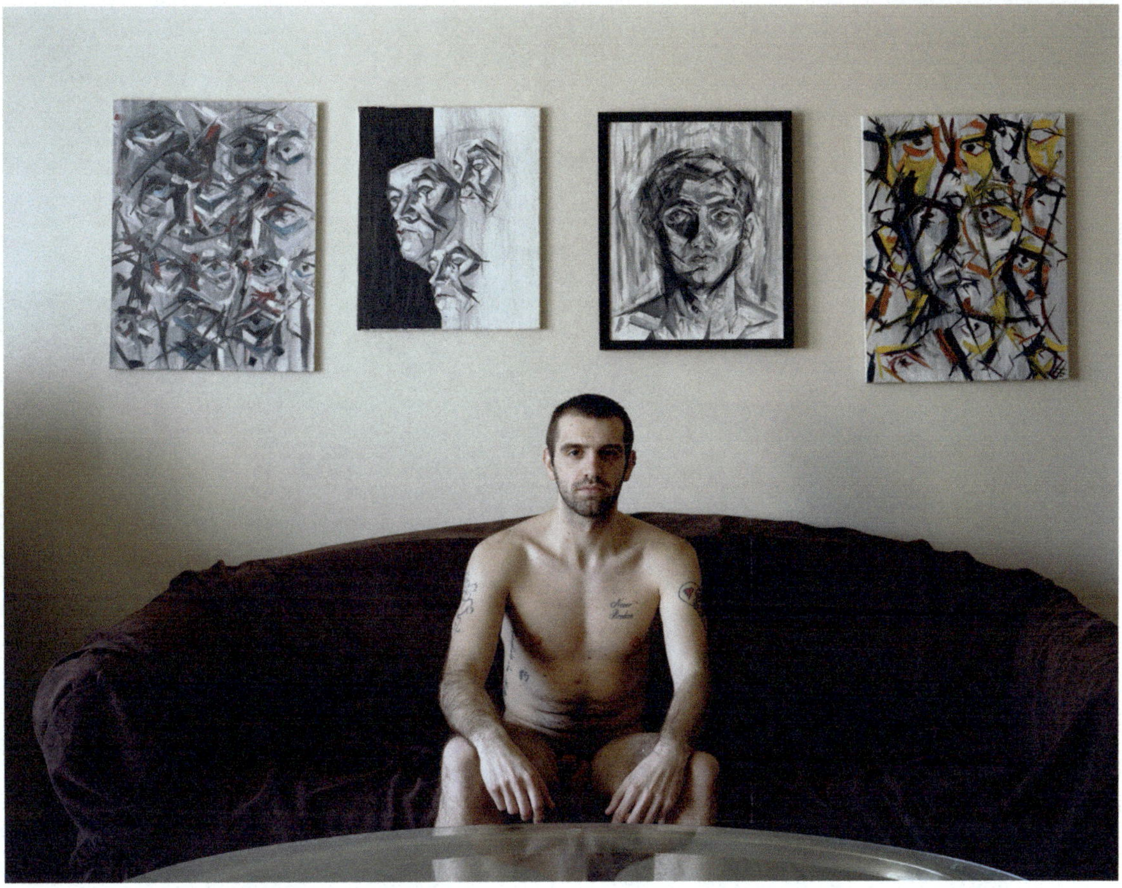

Facing (top): © Scott Foltz, from the series *Waterscape Nudes.* Dragging the shutter gives the flowing water a glassy quality while the perfectly still model is rendered tack-sharp.

Facing (bottom): © Terry Slater.

Above: © Osmyn J. Oree, from the series *Exposed.* "In our society, males are seen as pillars of strength that must not show any sign of weakness. The photographs in *Exposed* confront this stereotype and show portraits of men that are both revealing and sensitive … The men in the images are now vulnerable while the viewer has the power … I understand the reluctance to expose one's body and seek to explore that through my photographs."

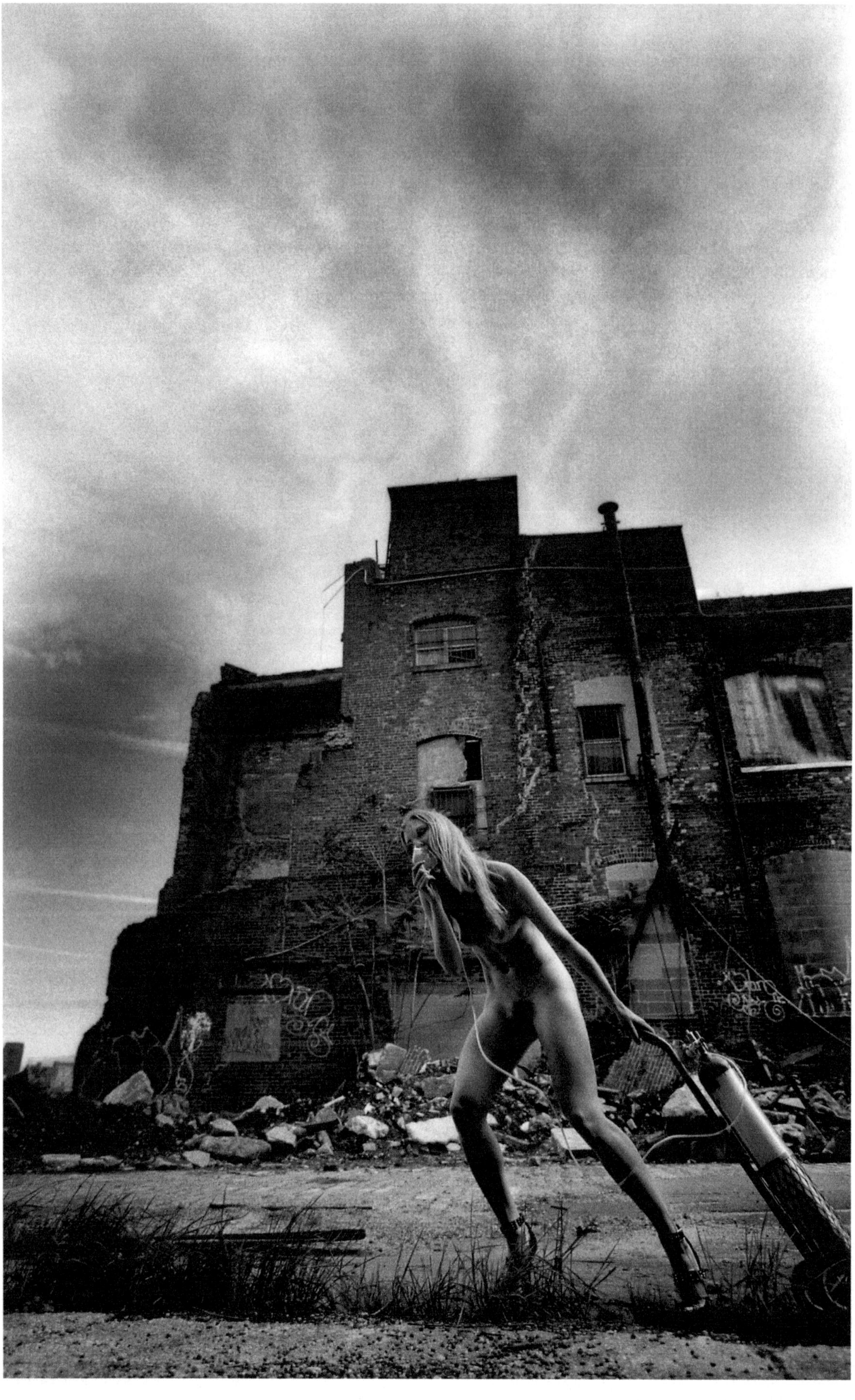

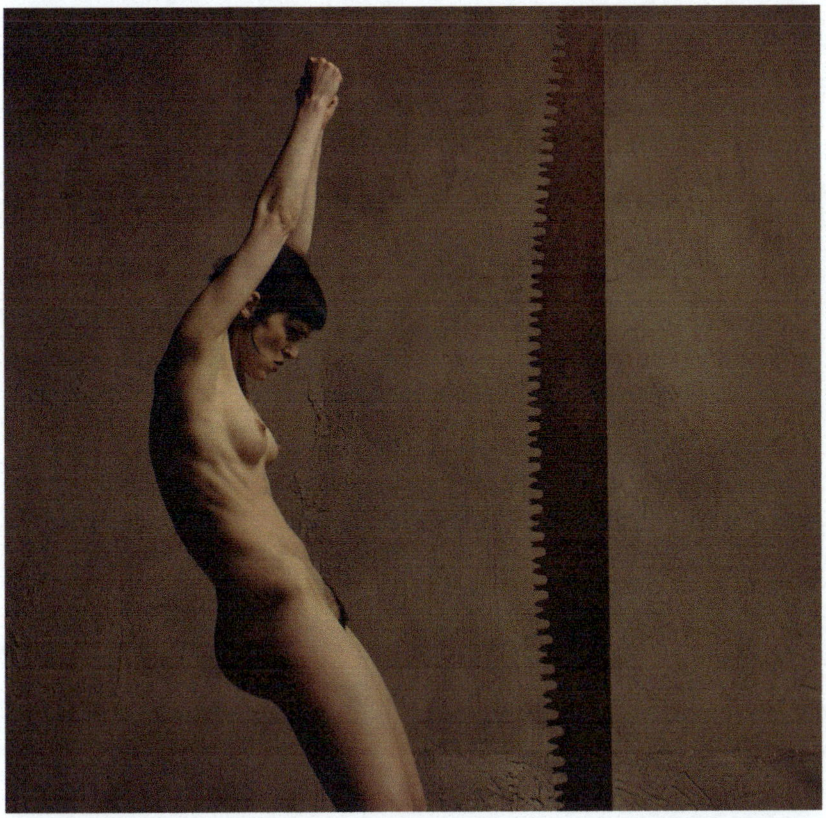

placing a naked woman in a dilapidated space. The opposition of decadence and the female form in images often dramatizes the quality of beauty itself.

Gary Breckheimer is a master of the environmental nude. He considers himself a rule-breaker, and he gets a rush from creating daring and beautifully crafted street nudes. In his work, he focuses upon the juxtaposition of the female form against the environment and adds erotic overtones. The clever works often bristle with subtext. Breckheimer has spent twenty years refining his art, and cites Robert Farber's "Moonscapes" as an early inspiration that still calls to him today.

Another form of environmental nude is an extension of environmental portraiture, where the subjects happen to be nude. Both Nan Goldin and Elinor Carucci use photography as a kind of personal journal, photographing important people in their lives in an up-close and personal way. Their photographs represent slices of their own lives and the environments are pieces of their own worlds.

Props provide another means of adding narrative to an image. The subject often focuses attention on the prop, or uses the prop to relate to other characters in the scene or to the viewer. A lot of props carry a symbolic charge; for example, boas and beads carry a heavy association with burlesque. Guns and knives are often cliché, and so are crosses, but such props can still be used in ways that transcend. Certain props are so loaded with meaning that the challenge in shooting with them can be a matter of keeping the prop from hijacking the image!

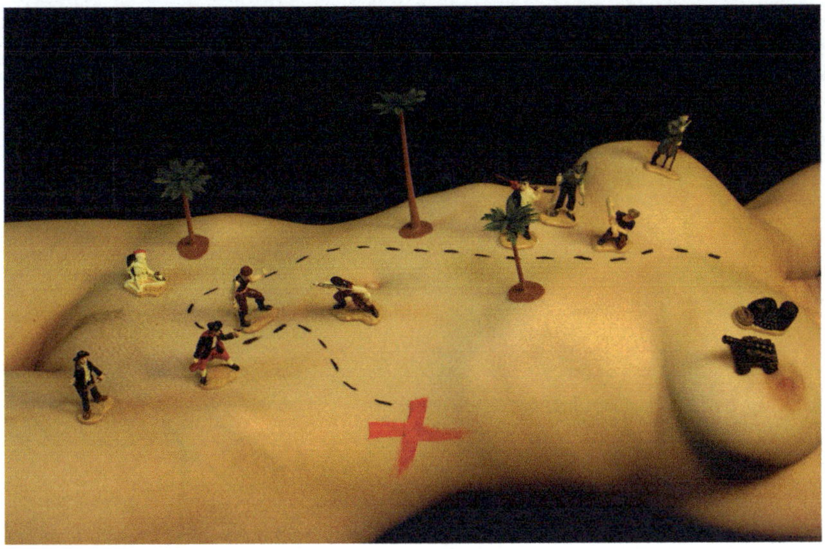

Facing: "Gass" © Gary Breckheimer.

Above (top): © Donna Feldman Lasky.

Above (bottom): "The Legacy of Pirates," © Richard Rasner (Unique Nudes) of Nakayama Studios.

Bodyscapes borrow heavily from landscape photography that dates back to the beginning of photographic art. In most cases, framing, lighting, and surprising points of view are often used to turn body parts into visual metaphors for mountains, dunes, and other geological phenomena.

There are also landscape photographs that strongly suggest the human figure, mirroring the effect of bodyscapes. An interesting twist is the hybrid that comes about by dominating the foreground of a landscape image with a bodyscape. The styles of landscape and bodyscape merge, and the bodyscape returns to its roots.

Reference, parody, and commentary are three ways in which images have employed the nude very effectively, and often controversially. Terry Donovan's *Model vs. Photographer* series creates a kind of parody rarely seen. In it, he has reprised shots he did with models with himself as the subject. The project was invented out of necessity: he had no one to shoot with, and he wanted to keep shooting. While many photographers of nudes recommend that we get in front of the camera ourselves to experience what it's like, a male photographer assuming the poses of a female model is a proposition that ups the ante. In an email exchange about the series, Donovan said this about his process: "The early shots were done months, even years after the original shot had been taken. Most of the recent ones are taken at the same time as I'm shooting the model ... The biggest challenge is trying to match the pose when I'm not using a mirror, and ... I have to rely on my memory of the model's pose as my only guide. As you can see, I miss more often than hit."

Donovan eventually took the idea a step further with *The Model's Revenge*, a project where he turned over creative control to the model and allowed himself to be photographed in whatever way the model asked, with no limits. The intention was to make himself as vulnerable as the models in his routine shoots.

Renee Cox did a body of work called *Flipping the Script*, which reinterpreted European religious masterpieces including the Pietà, Adam and Eve, and Michelangelo's David, using contemporary African-American figures. The lightning rod of the series is a piece called "Yo Mama's Last Supper," in which a nude Renee Cox stands in for Jesus in a rendition of the Leonardo da Vinci work that inspired it. Cox says her work is about breaking down stereotypes, and describes the image as a tongue-in-cheek piece dealing with issues of race, gender, and stereotypes. Provocative, yes, but she says she wanted to have fun with it. She also acknowledges that one of the inspirations for her work is that while Christianity is big in the African-American community, its iconography does not include images of black people. As a response, she took it upon herself to re-envision those classic images. That is a powerful, and controversial, context.

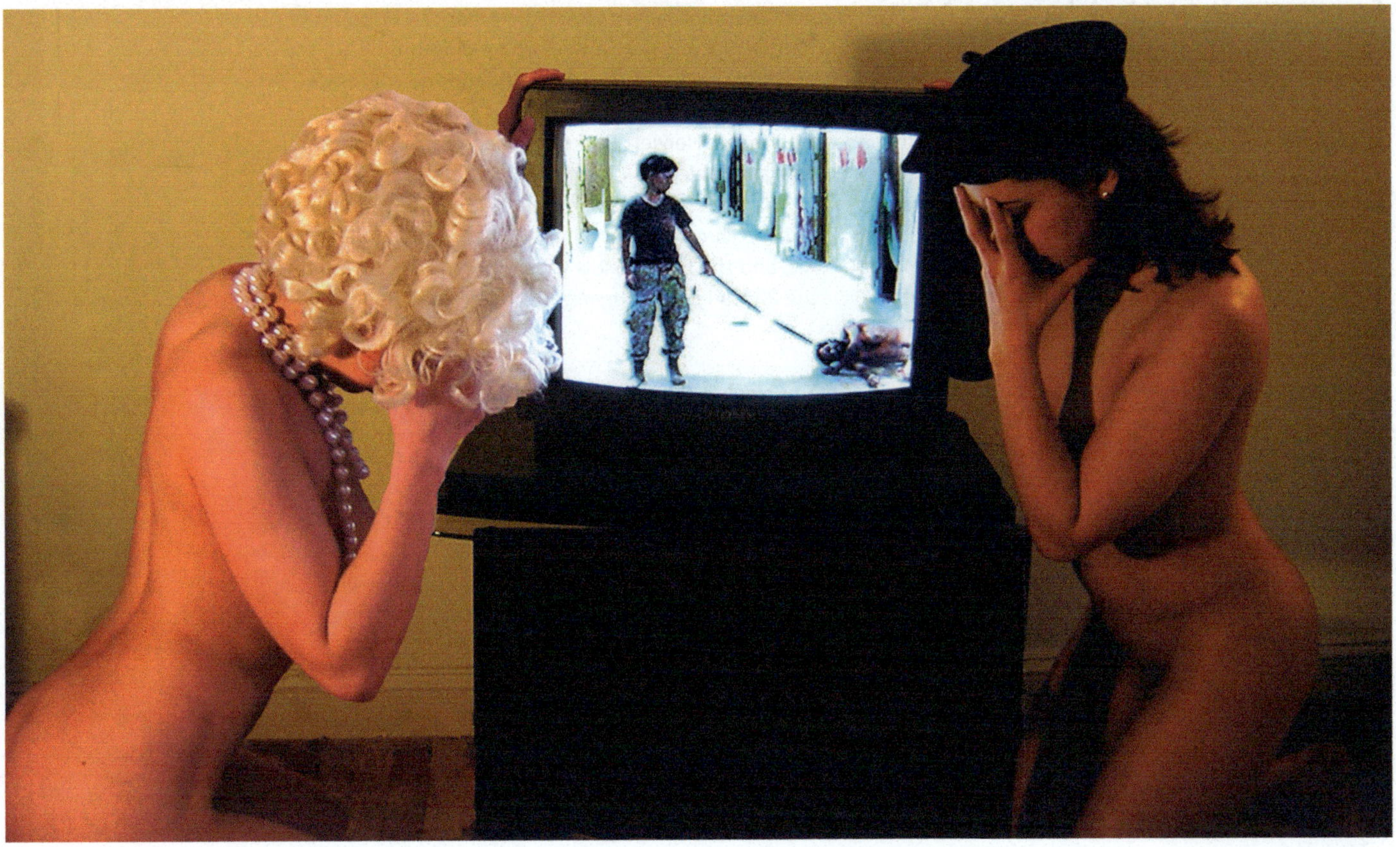

"American Pieta" © J. D. Yezierski. Model: Melissa Troutt. Referencing the Abu-Ghraib scandal and the Pietà of Michelangelo, this photo calls attention to ideals, politics, and shame. See Terry Slater's photo in Chapter Six for a more direct reference to the Michelangelo work.

Interview with Harvey Stein (HarveyStein.com)

Harvey Stein is a professional photographer, teacher, lecturer, curator, and author based in New York City. He currently teaches at the International Center of Photography, and in the Master of Professional Studies Program in Digital Photography at the School of Visual Arts. He has also been a member of the faculty at the Rochester Institute of Technology, Drew University, the New School University, and the University of Bridgeport. Stein is a frequent lecturer on photography both in the United States and abroad.

A recipient of a Creative Arts Public Service (CAPS) fellowship and numerous artist in residency grants, Stein had a book of photographs, *Parallels: A Look at Twins*, published by E. P. Dutton in 1978. Stein's second book, *Artists Observed*, was published by Harry Abras, Inc. in 1986. A color volume of photographs called *Coney Island*, was published by W. W. Norton in 1998. His book *Movimento: Glimpses of Italian Street Life* was published in December 2006.

Stein's photographs have been published in such periodicals as *The New Yorker, Time Life, Esquire, American Heritage, Smithsonian, The New York Times, Reader's Digest, Glamour, Forbes, Psychology Today, Playboy, Harpers, Connoisseur, Art News, American Artist, New York, People, Der Spiegel, Die Zeit*, and all the major photo magazines, including *Camera Arts, Black & White Magazine* (cover), *Popular Photography, American Photo, Camera, Afterimage, Zoom, Photo Metro, fotoMagazine*, and *View Camera*.

Stein's photographs have been widely exhibited in the United States and Europe—over 70 one-person and 135 group shows to date. He has also curated numerous exhibits. His photographs are in more than 50 permanent collections, including the Bibliothèque Nationale, the Art Institute of Chicago, the Museum of Fine Arts (Houston), the Brooklyn Museum of Art, the New Orleans Museum of Art, the International Center of Photography, the Denver Museum of Art, the Carnegie Museum of Art (Pittsburgh), the Portland (Oregon) Museum of Art, Museet for Fotokunst (Odense, Denmark), Musée de La Photographie (Charleroi, Belgium), the Portland (Maine) Museum of Art, the Corcoran Gallery of Art, the American Museum of Natural History, the Santa Barbara Museum of Art, the Addison Gallery of American Art, and the corporate art collections of Polaroid, Reader's Digest, Johnson & Johnson, Hewlett Packard, LaSalle Bank (Chicago), Barclays Bank, and Credit Suisse.

His work is represented by the Bruce Silverstein Gallery, Throckmorton Fine Art, June Bateman Fine Art, and the Forest Scott group, New York City; and by the Photo Researchers Agency, New York City.

You teach a course in photographic seeing at International Center of Photography. Many argue that ways of seeing cannot be taught. Do you feel you're teaching your students to see, or awakening them to their own unconscious ways of seeing?

▸ I think it's a blend of both. In the "Photographic Seeing" class that I teach at ICP, we look at the major individual elements that make up a photograph, such as light, color, line, focus/blur, perspective, shape and pattern, etc. Each week I give a shooting assignment that concentrates on one of these elements. So we atomize the photograph, and look intensely at each element individually and intensely. This heightens the student's awareness and appreciation of this photographic "property" and they practice featuring it in their work. Simultaneously, I am always talking about being intuitive, emotional, and accessing the submerged parts of our psyche.

How does teaching relate to your creative process, and how does it affect your photographic practice?

▸ Teaching means I have to pause every week to really consider many and various issues about photography, rather than just making work. In preparing classes, I must do research, think about issues, look at other photographers' work as well as books and exhibits, etc. So I learn in preparing to teach and I learn from my students. Occasionally, the students inspire me and I get ideas for my own work from the classroom.

Facing: Portrait of Annie Sprinkle © Harvey Stein.

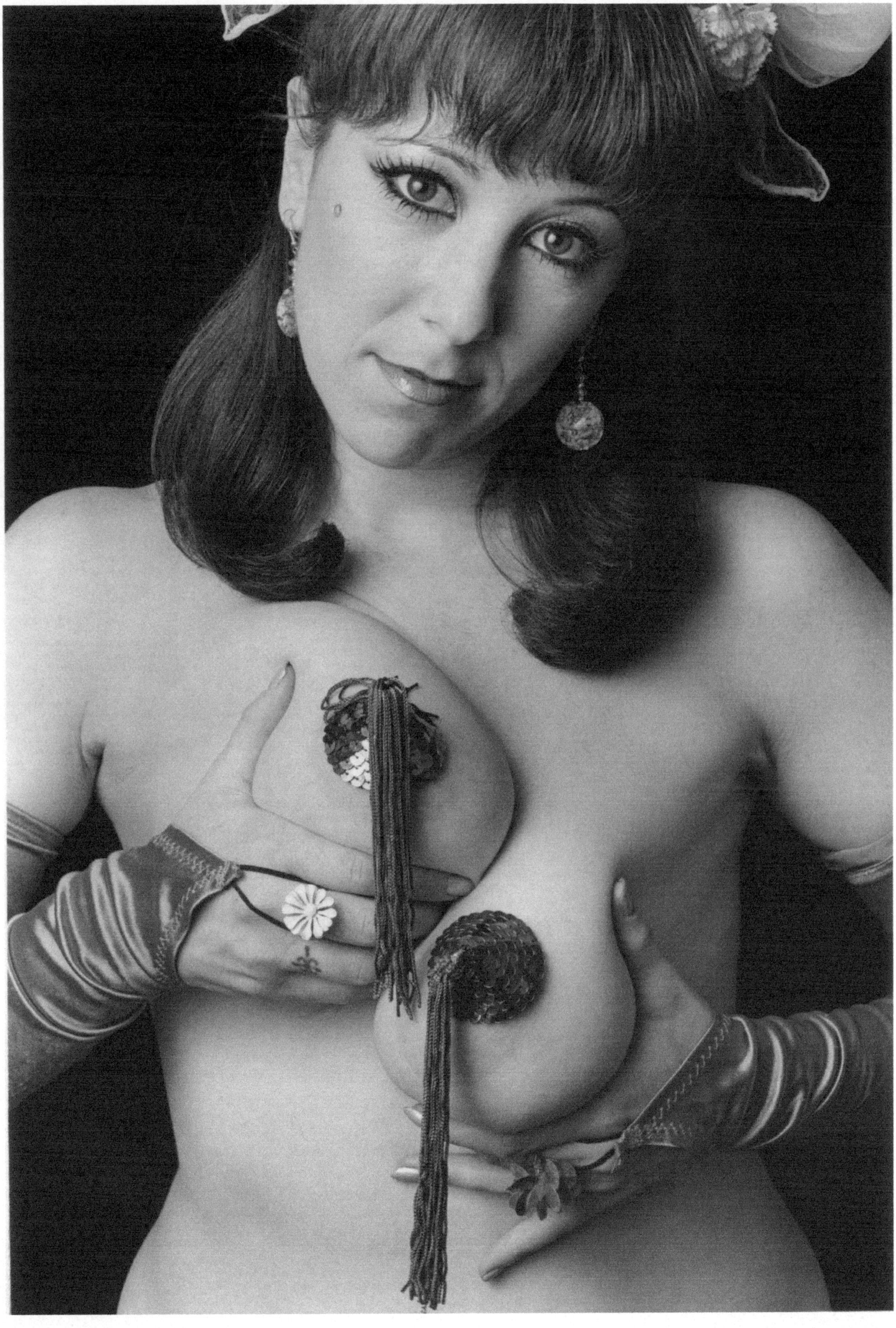

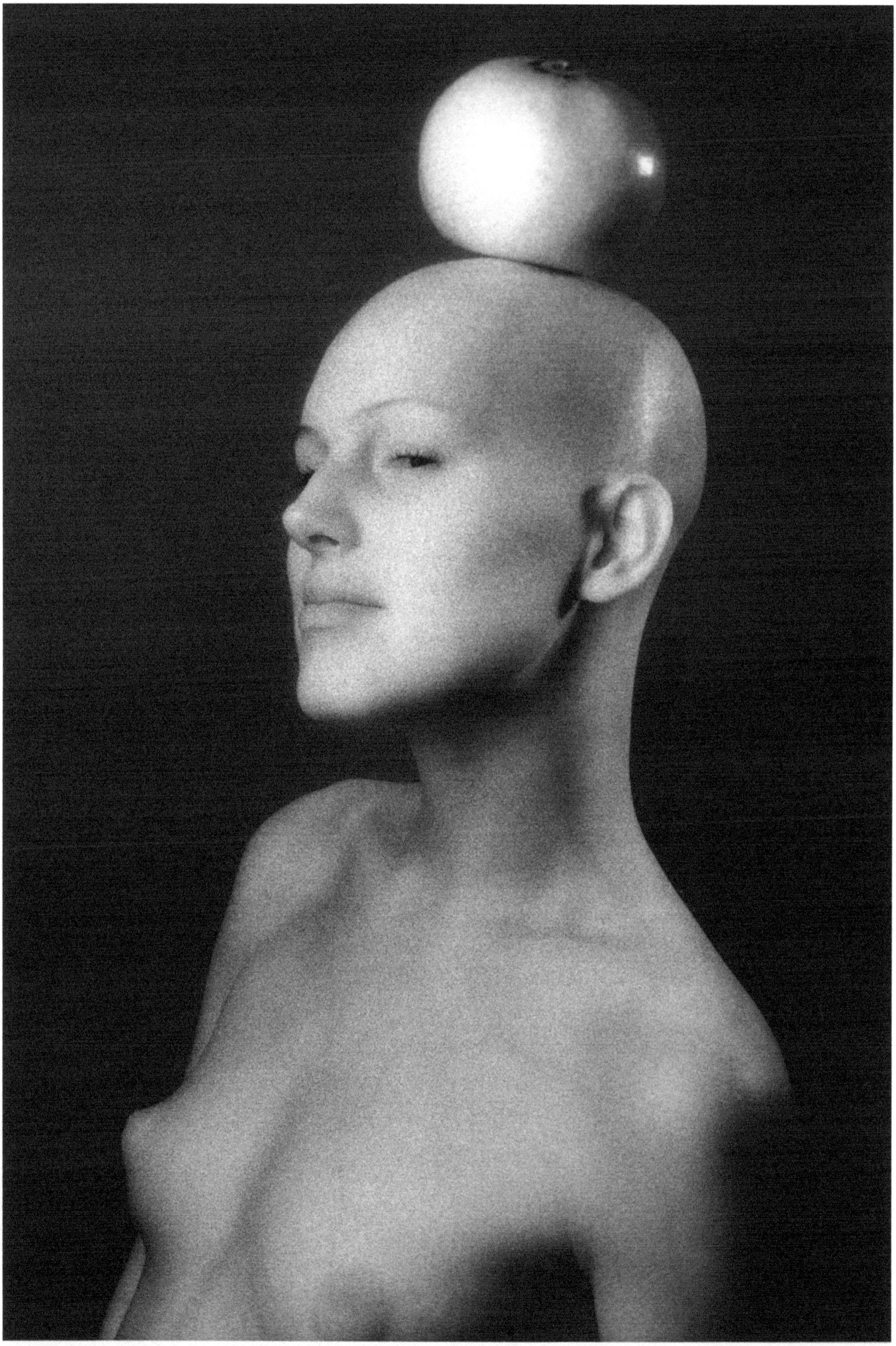

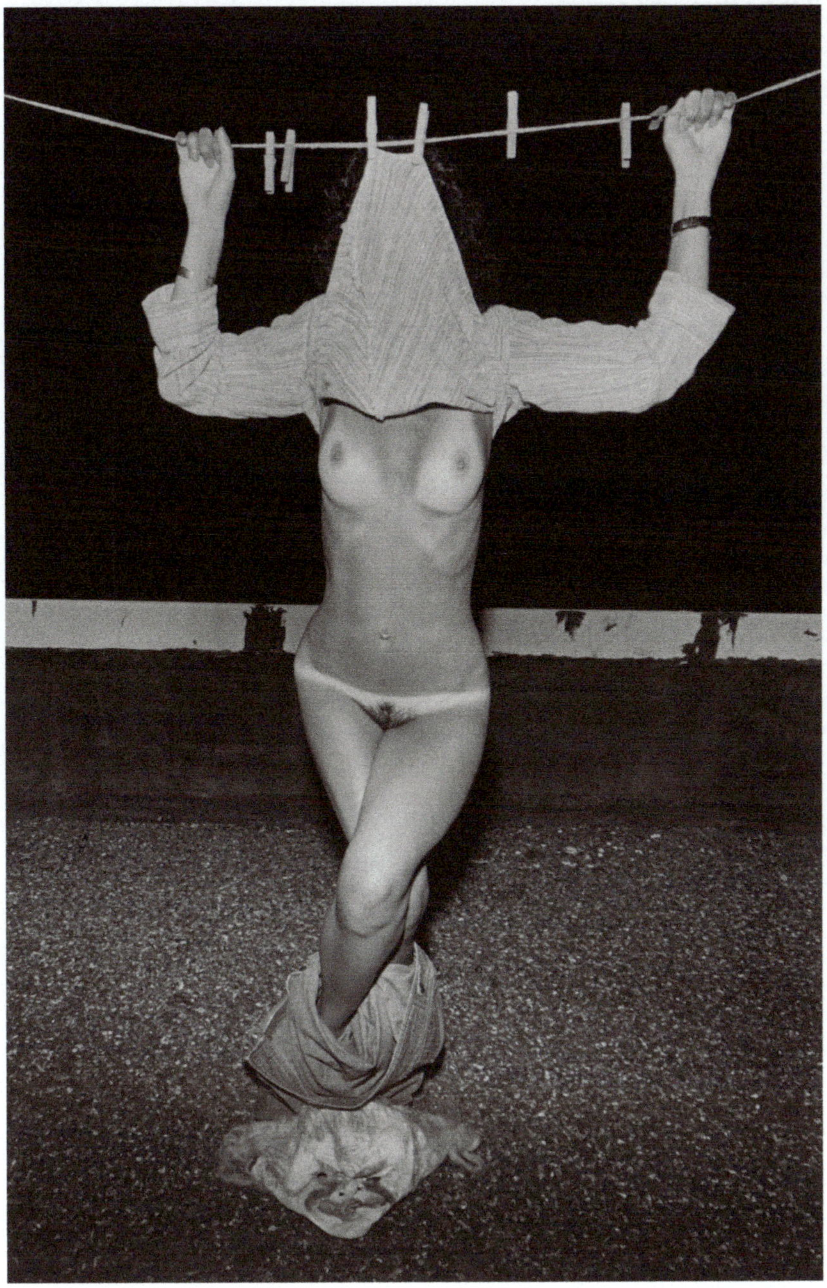

Do you think that it is important to look at other artists' work, and is a knowledge of art history or the history of photography valuable? For your own work, there seems to be a psychological dimension as well. Is that something you studied?

▶ I've always been interested in people and the human condition. I love people; they make life meaningful and rich. So all my life, I've studied them, formally in school and informally just being alive and around them. And most of my photographic practice revolves around photographing them. If there is some psychology that seeps into my images, that's great, it's one of my aims, in the spirit of learning and understanding more.

I think a knowledge of what others in your field have done in the past and are currently doing is always valuable. Not to copy or emulate them, but to build upon. Knowledge is always positive; it can build confidence and help further your practice. If it gets in your way, jettison it.

Is there a core idea or set of ideas that shapes your approach to shooting nudes?

▶ Usually my subject and I agree to do some nude photography so we think about location, props, and perhaps why and what I want to shoot and show. Each situation is different. My overriding idea is to enjoy it, be playful, somewhat different and even surreal, and to work collaboratively with the subject. And perhaps to learn more about myself and the subject. And always to make the best image I can.

Do you consider yourself a technical photographer, and how important is the technical aspect of the work that you make?

▶ I don't consider myself a technical photographer but I know technique, especially lighting. This comes from taking classes in the past, from reading and looking at photographs, from common sense and from learning while teaching. I think of myself as being intuitive yet thoughtful, and very open to taking chances photographically. Technique for its own sake is an empty exercise. Technique should always be in the service of the image and what you are trying to say.

Facing: © Harvey Stein.
Above: © Harvey Stein.

What recommendations do you have for someone who wants to begin shooting fine art nudes?

- My suggestions for someone beginning to shoot fine art nudes is to not be overly serious about it, to have fun with it, to practice, and to avoid clichés and what others have done. Also, do it tastefully with humanity and humility, and always treat your subject with respect and kindness.

Many contemporary photographers are very focused on getting that first solo gallery show, getting their work into a magazine, or putting together their first book. You've achieved those things many times over. Have those accomplishments affected the way you work? Were those milestones ever key motivations, or were they a product of something else? What motivates you now?

- These accomplishments do not at all affect the way I work. I don't think of any of that while doing my photography. That is the past. I'm interested in moving forward and always making new images and learning more about the world and myself through my art. I'd say trying to get shows or gallery exhibits or books published is always a motivation, but not the prime motivation. My main motivation is to make the best images I can, to stretch and grow through my work, and to impart some of the things I have learned back to my students and fellow workers. Doing photography makes me happy and a better person, it has sustained me for many, many years. There is nothing else I'd rather be doing.

Interview with Barney Cokeliss (BarneyCokeliss.com)

Barney Cokeliss grew up in London and was shooting record covers and book jackets as a photographer before he left school. He studied English Literature at Oxford and spent a year at Princeton in the Film and Creative Writing departments before winning a place on the prestigious BBC TV training scheme.

His directing career began with *Tea*, a short commissioned by MTV Europe, which went on to be the shortest film selected at Sundance. Barney then wrote and directed *Queen's Park Story* for BBC2's 10 x 10 strand. The *Observer* called it "the best British drama on television this year." It was in the official selection at the Venice Film Festival and won Best Director at Toronto.

Barney is represented by Ridley Scott Associates for commercials, and by United Agents for film and television. He has directed commercials for clients such as Volkswagen, Lexus, Typhoo, Toyota, and BMI Airlines. His films for the National Health Service have won advertising awards year after year and his safe-sex film *Spoiled* was voted Scotland's favourite ad.

In 2009, Taschen America published Barney's photographic nudes alongside the work of Jan Saudek and Terry Richardson. His portrait subjects have included Gil Scott-Heron, Ravi Shankar, John le Carré, Ray Liotta, and Jacques Derrida among many others. A monograph of his nudes is in preparation.

In 2010, Barney shot a new short film for Hill Holiday in New York, sponsored by Liberty Mutual, and had two feature films in development: one original and one based on a short story by the celebrated British author J. G. Ballard.

You have a lot of commercial work and portraiture in your CV. How does your experience of making that work affect the way that you approach shooting nudes, and what impact do your nudes have on your commercial work?

▸ I moved through portraiture to nudes—a lot of my early work was of famous people and making nudes was a way of getting around the focus on the individual that's inherent in portrait photographs of eminent people. At the same time, I like my nudes to feel in some way like portraits—I don't want the model to seem anonymous or just there to provide a body or an abstract form—but portraits of people whose identity isn't known. Portraits and nudes are on the same spectrum for me—essentially the fascination is in taking pictures of people and of human situations. I still love both.

As for my commercial work, that's mostly moving image so it doesn't relate directly to my photographs. I'd love a commercial brief that fit the style of my nudes, but often the commercials have another focus—comedy, storytelling, and so on. Maybe the closest I've come in my commercials to the look of my nudes is a safe sex ad I shot for the NHS (National Health Service) in Scotland: there's a contemplativeness in that one that has something in common with my pictures.

Your images seem to have a very strong sense of subtext. Is that a result of the discipline of filmmaking? Are there specific storylines driving your images?

▸ I love images that imply a narrative, even if it's not clear what exactly the story is. The tension between feeling there's a story there and not being able to say for sure what it is can be a real force in an image. This preference may be related to my film work, though in film the aim is usually to tell a story, not just hint at one! Painters like Kitaj and photographers like diCorcia are certainly an influence in the kind of suspended narratives they conjure. As for the parallel with film, I find it really exciting that, say, *The Piano* was apparently inspired by a photograph. But sometimes "cinematic" can be too obvious an effect for a photographer to aim for—unless you're Cindy Sherman and you're subverting the whole thing. I suppose my photography keeps my film-making image conscious, and my film-making keeps my photography aware of narrative. What I don't do is work out elaborate plots which I try to represent in the pictures—I'm more interested in leaving part of the story open to interpretation. Photo-stories can be wonderful—I've loved Duane Michals' work since I first saw it as a kid—but that's a whole other thing.

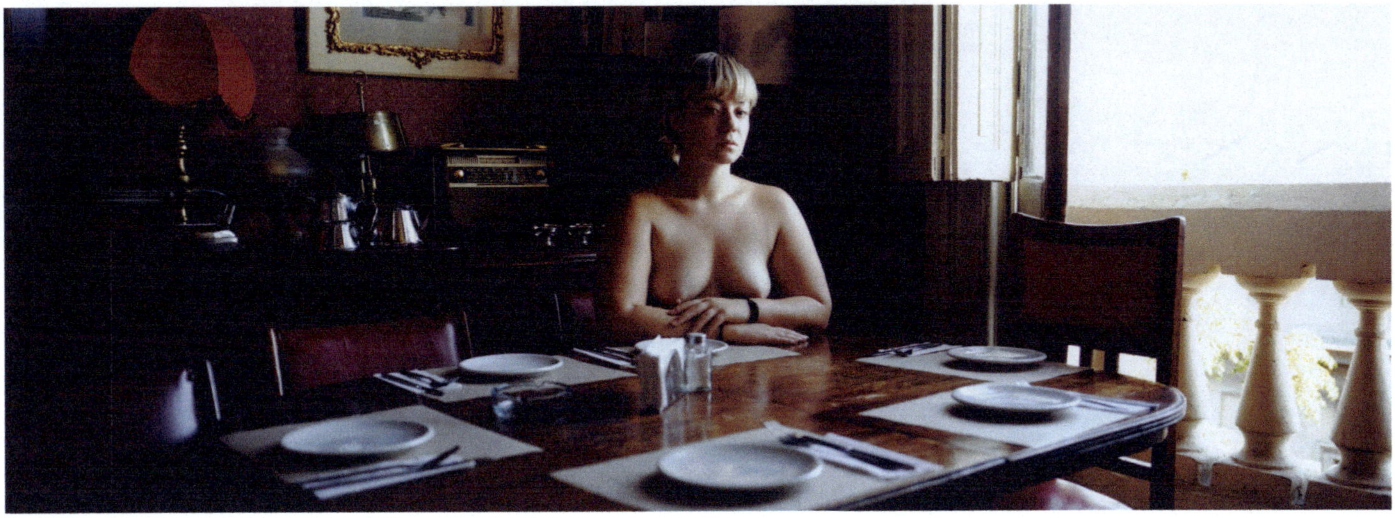

© Barney Cokeliss.

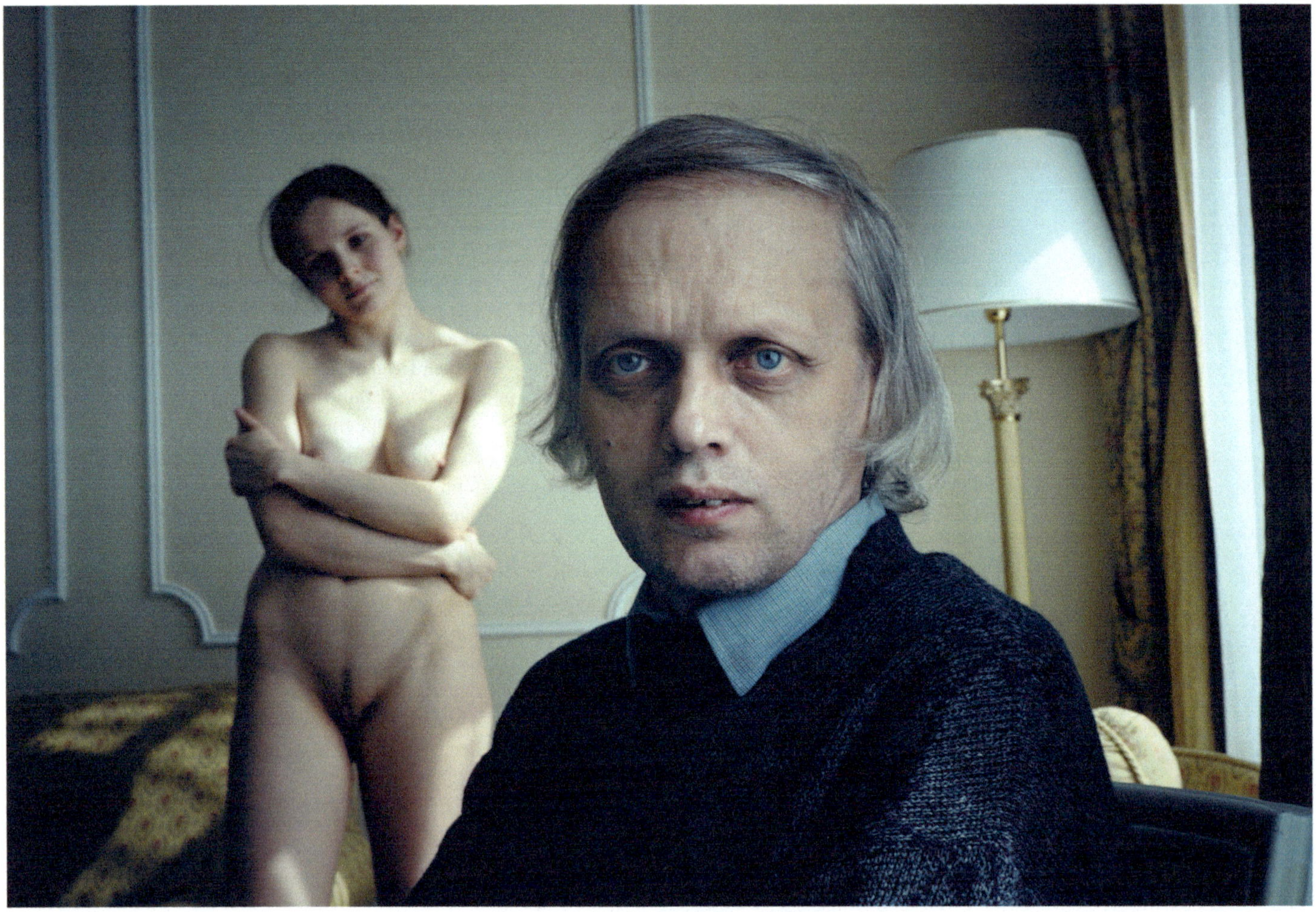

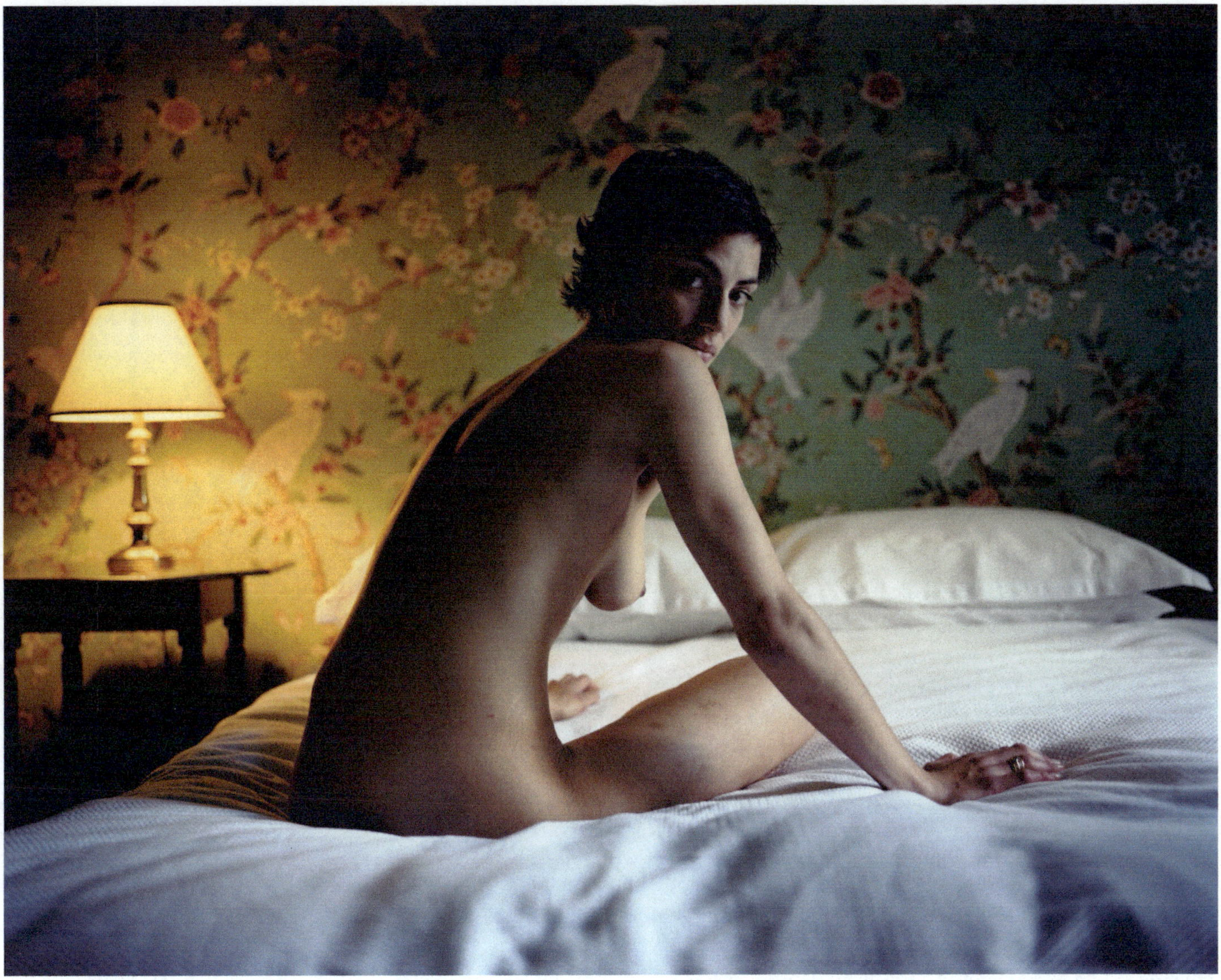

Facing: © Barney Cokeliss.
Above: © Barney Cokeliss.

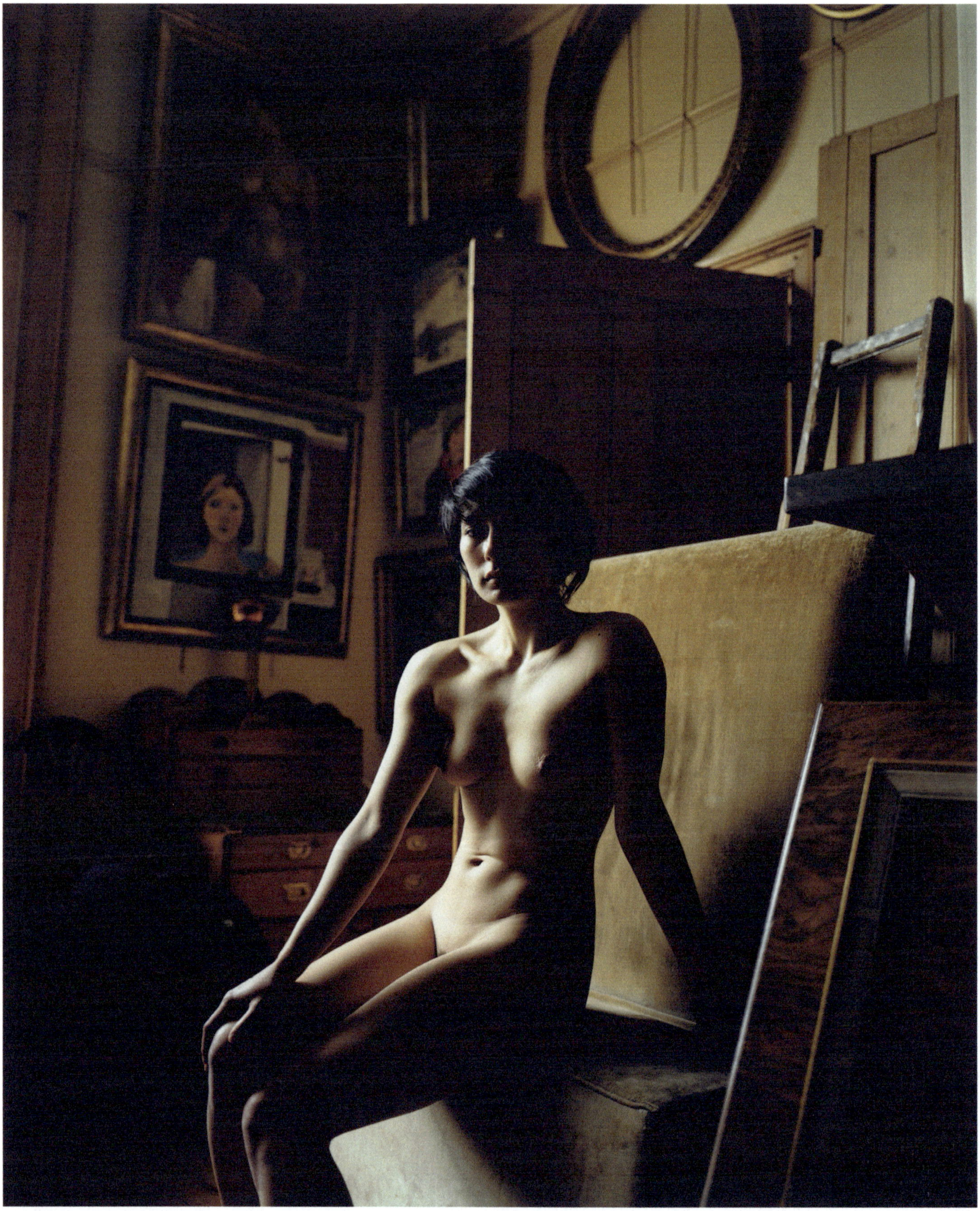

How would you say your photographic consciousness has changed over time?

- I think I started out, like a lot of beginner photographers, very focused on composition and form. Over time I've got more interested in atmosphere and implied story and let the compositional elements become more submerged. I think a good photograph has to be interestingly composed, but it doesn't have to make a big deal out of it.

Did Duane Michals or some other photographer inspire you to pick up the camera?

- Drtikol and Duane Michals were probably the two photographers that most impressed me when I was first picking up the camera—they don't have much in common! Cartier-Bresson is unavoidable too—I spent a few of my teenage years taking pseudo-Cartier-Bresson portraits of all my friends.

How much pre-visualization goes into your nudes? Do you go so far as to sketch or storyboard what you plan to shoot? How much do improvisation and "happy accidents" figure in your work?

- It varies. I always spend some time thinking about what I want to achieve from a shoot, and I have a bank of references for poses and situations that I'd like to explore. But I spend a lot of time trying to work against anything that looks posed. Often it's the position the model takes between rolls of film that I end up focusing on. So in that respect I try and find a little bit of documentary in what is essentially an artificial situation. One reason I don't tend to do sketches in advance is that my film work is very thoroughly prepared—it has to be given the number of people involved—and I like my photography to be opposite to that.

When and how do you decide that a story should be told as a still, or perhaps a series of stills, rather than as a film?

- Right at the beginning—I think the ideas come from different parts of my brain. But, now that you mention it, cross-pollinating them might be a good idea!

When you shoot stills, are you thinking in terms of capturing a single image? When do you know that you have something that works?

- I certainly feel that I only need one successful image for a shoot to be success—sometimes having too many from one shoot feels like a waste as it's harder to use them all without seeming repetitive. But I try to leave space to see what happens spontaneously, rather than just homing in on one key shot. I can know very early if I'm getting something that works—if the model and the location are right then the odds are very good. I rely a lot on casting and locations, so when one or both is disappointing then it can be a struggle. The location has to have a tonality that lets me create some contrast (so many rooms have pale walls, which make things much harder for me) and the model has to have something truthful about them—my biggest struggle is when the model is too professional-seeming: I'm not interested in pictures of models modeling.

Light seems to be an important part of your shots. Is everything lit, or do you rely on available light? How much does the lighting affect the amount of work you can produce in a session?

- I work with as little additional lighting as possible. I've been lucky enough to work with some of the great cinematographers (people like Eduardo Serra) and I've learned that it's often a case of what you don't add rather than what you do.

Has working with cinematographers strengthened your ways of thinking or communicating about visual ideas?

- Working with cinematographers can be a wonderful dialogue—it's a collaboration you don't really experience as a photographer. There's always a dual aspect to the dialogue—it's partly about storytelling and partly about aesthetics. Good cinematography is when the aesthetics are a key part of the storytelling, and not merely decorative.

Facing: © Barney Cokeliss.

Many of your photos have a look that evokes the painted portraits of the likes of van Dyck, and possibly Sargent. They also remind me somewhat of Tina Barney's photographs, and she has said outright that she was influenced by Dutch painting. Is this semblance in your work the result of a conscious intent? What would you say are your primary visual influences?

▸ My primary influences probably aren't directly comparable to my own pictures. I'm certainly not trying to restage the masters. Tina Barney's work has a different texture to mine but the way she presents people is very interesting and unforced so I'm flattered by the comparison. Aside from the people I've already mentioned, I'd say Kirchner, Hockney, and Modigliani are painters that I love. Photographers I'd mention are Drtikol, Goldin, Roversi, Penn, Brandt. More recent enthusiasms for me have been the photographs of Bill Henson, David Hilliard, and Elinor Carucci.

If your influences are not visible in the look of your work, then your connection to them is not about the surface. Can you say a little more about some of the ideas that come from these influences?

▸ I think the biggest influence I get from looking at other people's work is in expanding my idea of what can make a photograph. It's easy to get caught up in your own spiral of obsessions, and seeing another photographer create fascinating images from something totally different can free you up a bit.

What do you think is the value of being aware of your influences?

▸ Being aware of your influences can help you avoid merely aping them.

Your images seem to be set in pretty affluent surroundings. Are you trying to make a particular statement or portray a particular idea? Is there a central theme uniting your images?

▸ There's no statement in the location choice whatsoever. The affluence of the surroundings is coincidental and the result of upmarket hotel rooms of a certain sort being one of the surest sources of mid-tone (or darker) walls, deep colours, and a bit of window light. A lot of my shoots are quite opportunistic—I'll find myself in a strange city with maybe one day to spare and there won't be time to do a big location recce, so I often end up in a hotel. But my mental list of locations to explore next is hotel-free.

Can you describe the sort of direction that you give to your nude subjects? Do you direct your subjects for still shots in the same way that you direct film actors?

▸ I think the fundamental interaction is similar in that you're trying to relax people so that they can give of themselves unselfconsciously. But I don't put my nude subjects through the kind of exploratory, improvisational process that I find works well for actors. Maybe I should. Then again, I often find inexperienced models produce the best results and they've usually got enough on their mind doing their first photo shoot without me throwing drama games at them.

What do you think your sitters need from you to give a great portrayal in front of the camera, and how does one learn to be an effective director?

▸ I think actors need to feel simultaneously that you know what you want but that you are also open to what they want to try. With my photographs there's an element of trying to normalize an odd situation—the model is in a strange place with someone they don't necessarily know well, possibly taking their clothes off in front of the camera for the first time. So a large part of my direction is just maintaining a normal, relaxed interaction. I've had some first-time models move, in just a few minutes, from apprehension about being naked to actually forgetting that they're naked and wondering why passers-by look at them strangely if they stand by the window during a break. I think this has a lot to do with the atmosphere you create.

Web Resources

Ansel Adams—http://bit.ly/1aKDc1c
Diane Arbus—artnet.com/artists/diane-arbus/
Eugène Atget—http://ti.me/1BNIv5p
Tina Barney—http://bit.ly/1a5Z1qV
Vanessa Beecroft—vanessabeecroft.com
Henri Cartier-Bresson—http://bit.ly/1iV9w2h
Elinor Carucci—http://www.elinorcarucci.com
Renee Cox—reneecox.org
Philip-Lorca diCorcia—http://bit.ly/1GZ9Kk8
František Drtikol—http://www.artnet.com/artists/frantisek-drtikol/
Harold "Doc" Edgerton—http://edgerton-digital-collections.org/galleries/iconic
Walker Evans—http://ti.me/1PjWJFh
Robert Farber, Moonscape—farber.com/nudes/
Lady Mary Filmer—http://bit.ly/1DeEOY5
Lee Friedlander, nudes—fraenkelgallery.com/portfolios/nudes
David Hilliard—davidhilliard.com/info_pages/about.html
International Center of Photography—icp.org
André Kertész—brucesilverstein.com/artists/estate-of-andr-kertsz
R. B. Kitaj—http://www.tate.org.uk/art/artists/rb-kitaj-1416
Alberto Korda, Che portrait—rebekahjacobgallery.com/alberto-korda/
Magritte, treachery of images—http://collections.lacma.org/node/239578
Duane Michals—http://bit.ly/1GLhXbo
Gjon Mili—http://nyr.kr/1O9kX3C
Eadweard Muybridge—http://bit.ly/1a5N58v
Irving Penn—www.artnet.com/artists/irving-penn/
Cindy Sherman—http://bit.ly/1fwjdiY
Edward Steichen—http://bit.ly/1FjEi0u
Alfred Stieglitz—http://bit.ly/1CVad3K
Jock Sturges—http://bit.ly/1Nge2c0
Garry Winogrand—photogs.com/bwworld/winogrand.html
Francesca Woodman—artnet.com/artists/francesca-woodman/

Part II
Photo Anatomy

Photos work because of certain conventions of visual literacy that we all have internalized to a greater or lesser degree. One can learn things about how to make better photos by taking them apart and examining how they function. At the same time, one can never forget that a great photo is more than the sum of its parts.

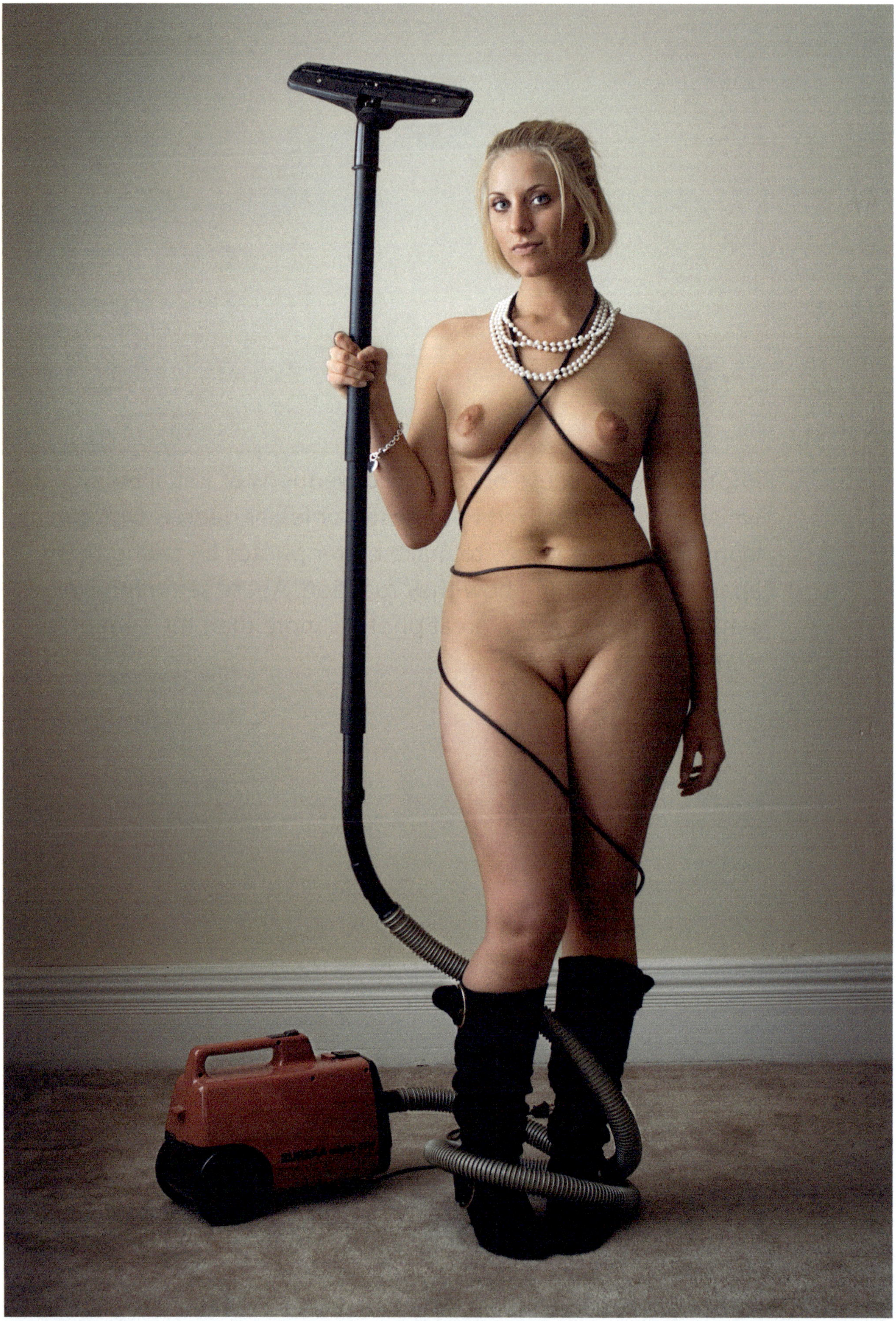

Chapter Four | Portraying the Body

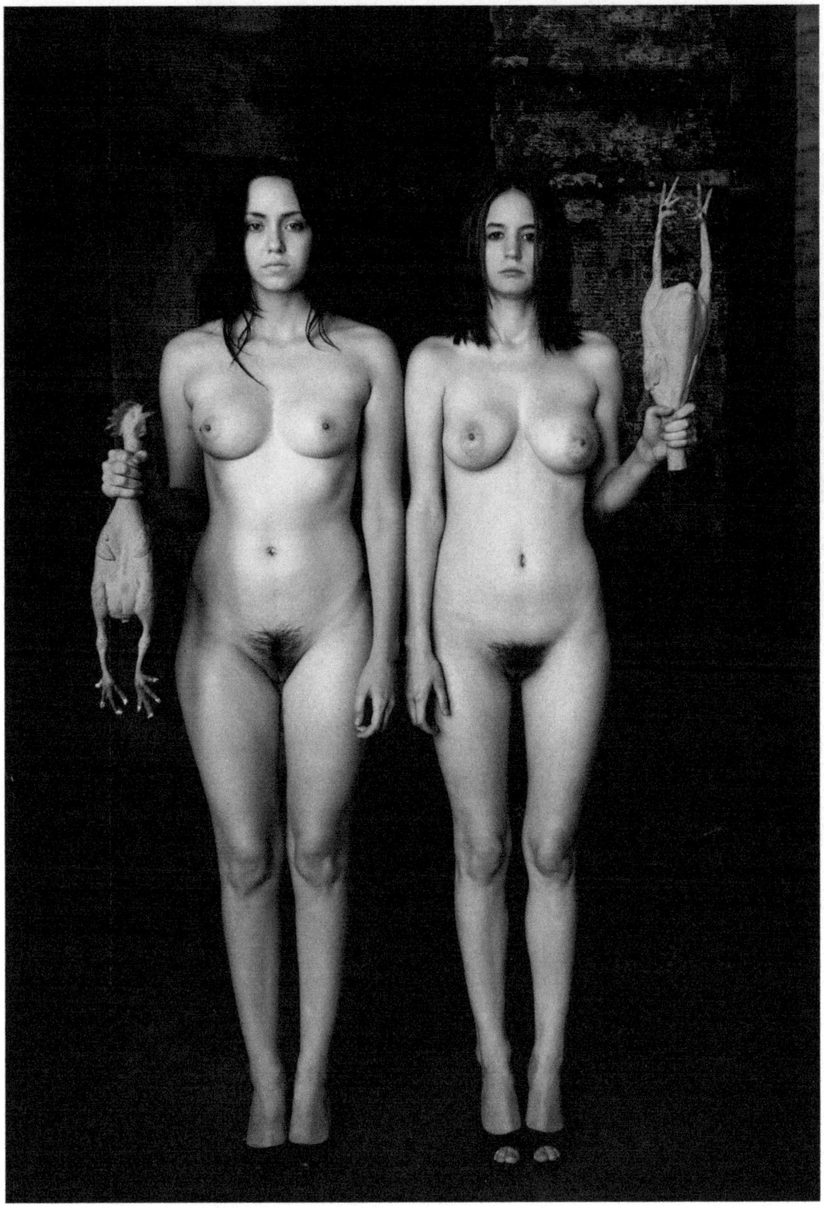

WHEN SOMEONE looks at a photo, one of the first things they're interested in is the meaning, story, or theme of the photo. Some of the perennial themes of the nude are form, beauty, life and love, sexuality, shame, and rebellion. In conveying stories, photos often reference or parody other artwork, or make social commentary. It is easy to see narrative in sequences of photos, where the viewer deduces the action by observing what has changed between each frame. Creating narrative within a single frame is more challenging, but it can be suggested by the relationship between compositional elements, such as people or props. Narrative can also arise linguistically, as the viewer perceives and mentally names the objects in the frame.

As we observed in Chapter Three, photographs involving nudity can be divided into formalist images that can be about the form or texture of the body in a more abstract sense, and more conceptual photos that focus on the state of nakedness to create contradiction, provoke, shock, or arouse. Various approaches to portraits of subjects in the buff can fall into either category.

We can also separate photographic nudes among several sub-genres or modes of portrayal, assessing

Facing: "June C's Newtonian Gothic Fantasy" © Lou Benjamin. A mash-up of tropes from Grant Woods, "Leave it to Beaver," and Helmut Newton.

Above: "Chicken Gothic" © Gary Breckheimer. A tongue-in-cheek reference to Grant Woods' *American Gothic.*

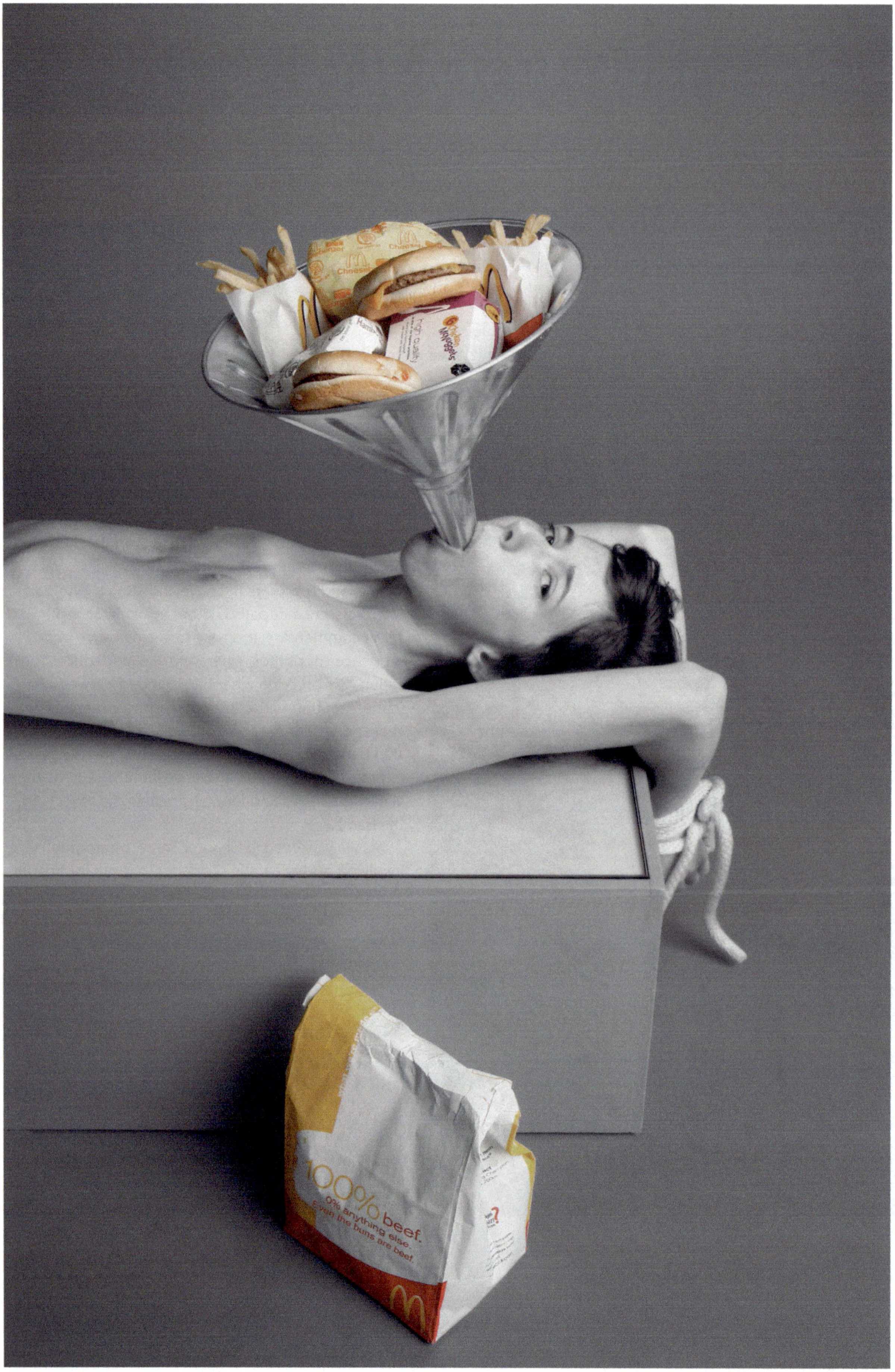
100% beef.
0% anything else.
Even the buns are beef.

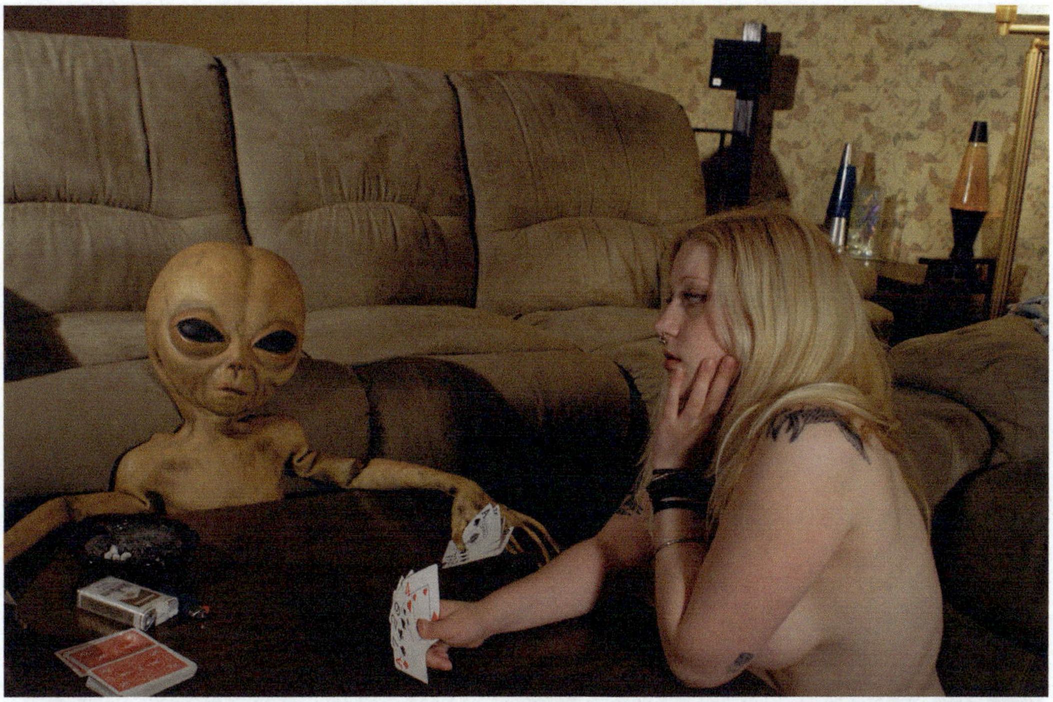

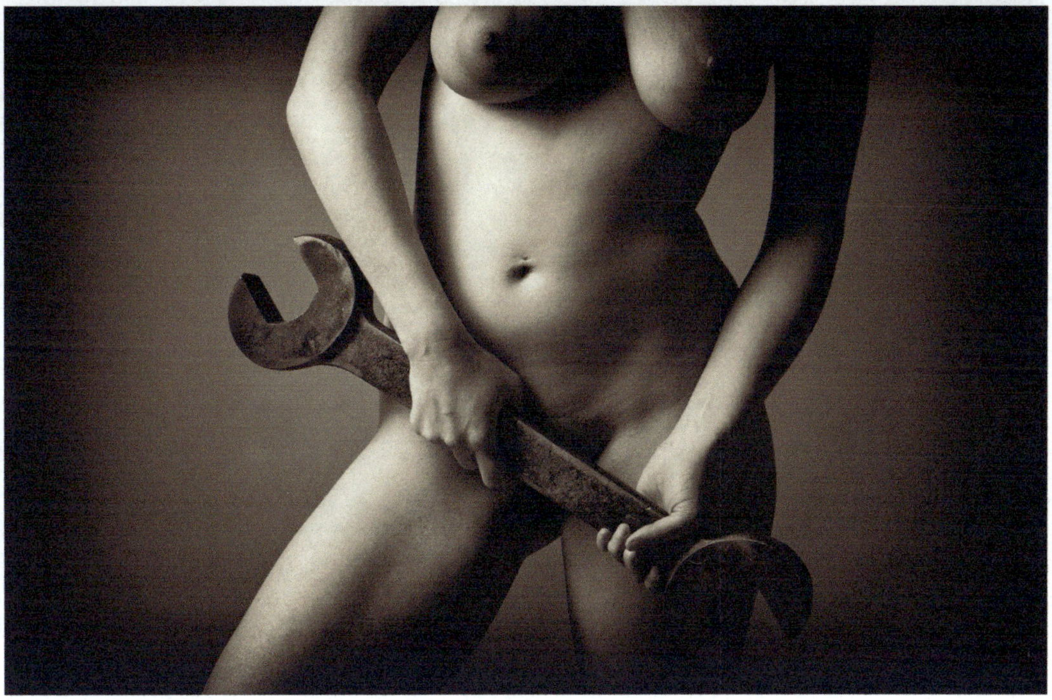

Facing: © Marcus J. Ranum (http://photography.ranum.com). Model: Kaitlin. A bitingly satirical photo that makes use of props and localized color. Artist's statement: "I find it amazing that people are so concerned whether a complete stranger is fat, or thin, or tattooed, or—whatever. As if it's their business somehow? Well, if it's my business, I make sure my models are well-fed."

Above (top): © Terry Donovan. An image rich in narrative.

Above (bottom): © Terry Slater. Even with the prop, the emphasis of this photo is on the figure.

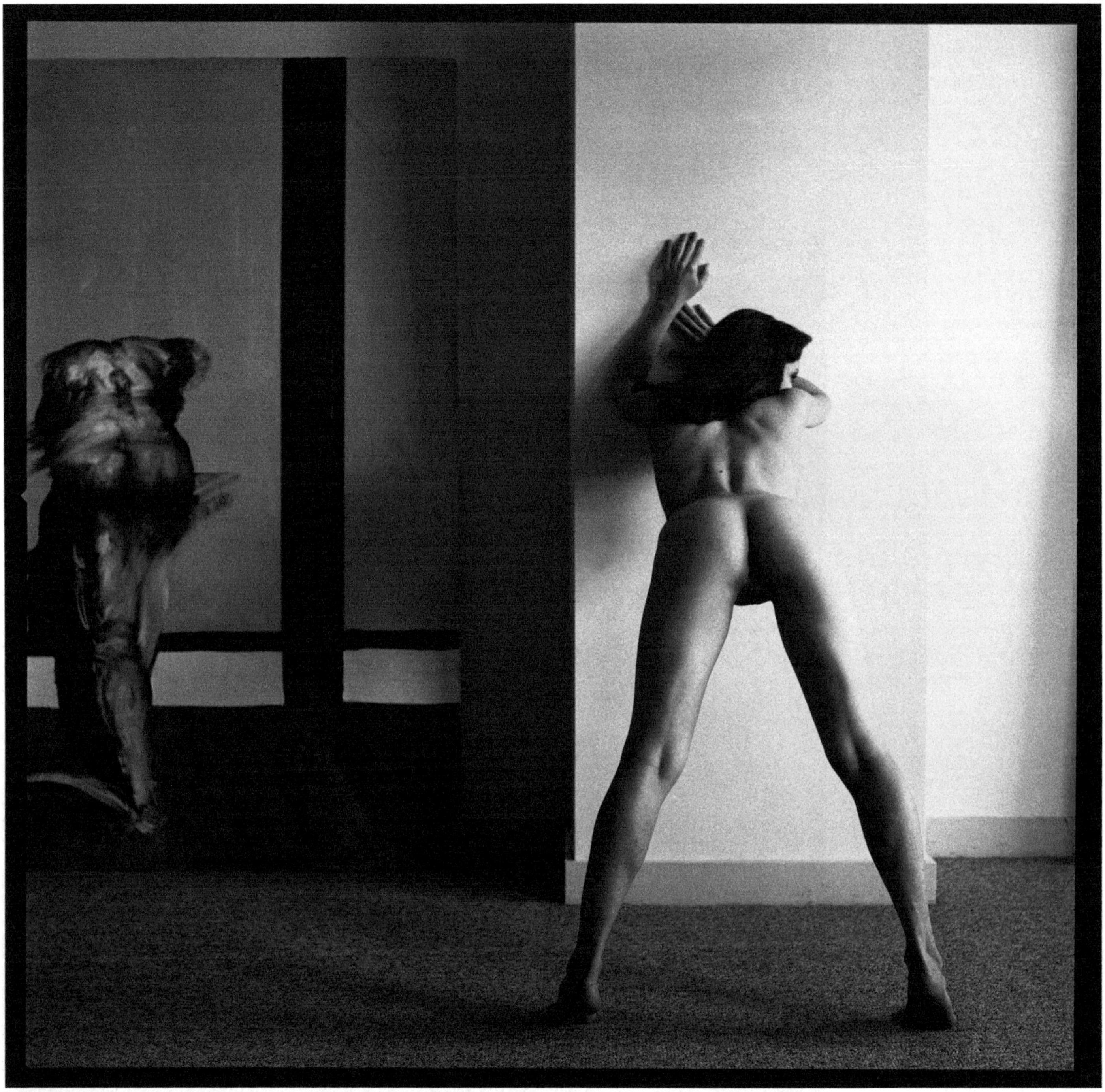

Top: © Sikorskyi, Chiaroscurist. The model's pose mimics, but does not exactly duplicate the pose in the painting, which in turn seems to reference the work of Francis Bacon.

Facing: © Alan Fresco. In this surrealistic photo, the model's legs look like outstretched arms on a headless torso. Distance, setting, the athleticism of the pose, and the false color of infrared photography combine to make this photo into something that is intriguing rather than transgressive.

the images in terms of how much of the body is shown, how clearly it is revealed, and even whether or not the head is shown. We'll look at some modes of portrayal shortly. As you explore nude photography, you will probably encounter many images that don't clearly fit any of the modes mentioned here, as well as some that combine modes (e.g. environmental abstracts).

The various modes discussed in this chapter are not hard and fast and it is doubtful that a comprehensive listing of modes can ever be compiled, but they can still be a useful way of surveying the wide range of approaches.

Note: This chapter refers to a number of artists whose works could not be included. A list at the end of the chapter will point you to some web resources for those artists.

The Edges of Acceptability

Though the Greeks idealized the nude form and third-century Hindus even carved erotic statues into their temples, there is a long history of societal suppression of imagery that represents nudity, especially when it can be read sexually. Painters such as Egon Schiele and Amedeo Modigliani are celebrated artists today, but in their time some of their works were removed or banned from shows. Schiele was jailed for obscenity in 1912. Others had entire shows shut down, and some had works destroyed.

Photographer Paul Outerbridge is respected for his artistic genius today, and was a pioneer of color photography, nudes, and fetish photography. In 1935, he sent a roll of film to Kodak for processing. When it came back to him, the "offending" areas in his images had been scratched out. His frustration with what he considered to be "infantile and ridiculous" attempts to legislate morality caused him to retire from photography sometime around 1945, saying that he felt he was being forced into making clandestine a matter that should be public.

Charis Weston, the model in some of Edward Weston's most famous nudes, recalls that about a year after Outerbridge had his Kodak moment, Edward Weston was using a magnifying glass to carefully inspect his print of "Nude, 1936" to decide whether it could be sent through the mail—if you look very closely, you can see a few pubic hairs.

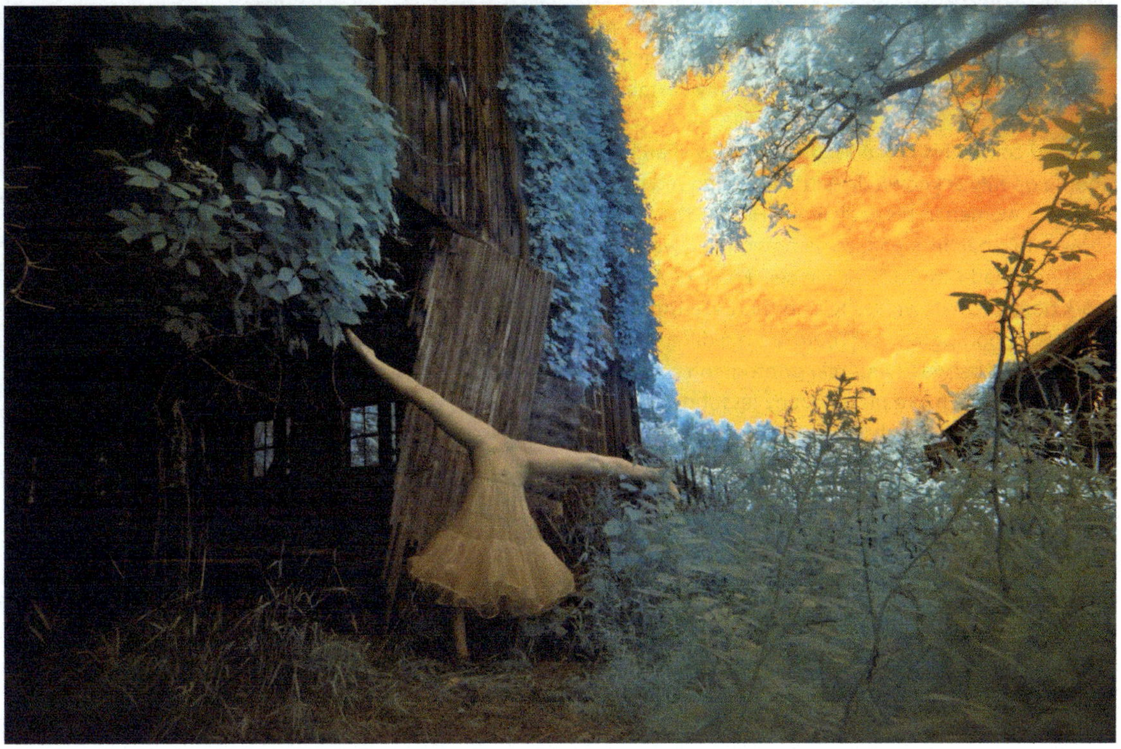

The ambiguous phrase "tasteful nudes" is commonly used on networking websites frequented by models and photographers as if everyone has the same standards of taste. In actuality, tastes vary widely. Often, the implication is that "tasteful" imagery is not very sexual, aggressive, or confrontational in style. In those same communities, people often use the phrase "artistic nude" as a shorthand for nudes devoid of eroticism—full frontal nudity is discouraged and open-leg poses are out of the question. However, a great many artistic nudes are challenging. Anyone familiar with the work of Nobuyoshi Araki or Robert Mapplethorpe will be aware that their nudes are exemplars of fine art and yet they are highly eroticized; clearly, artistic nudes are not constrained to being chaste, formalistic images.

Mapplethorpe famously blurred the line between art and erotica. While even his photos of flowers could be read sexually, his more explicit depictions of sexuality could be read aesthetically. The artist was gay and some of his work depicted gay life, sexuality, and kink in a very frank and unflinching way. He was a master technician, and his lighting was outstanding. Despite the obvious artistic and technical merit of his work, some people took offense with some of his subject matter, and because an exhibition that included some of his works had received funding from the National Endowment for the Arts (the NEA), he and photographer Andres Serrano became lightning rods in the political movement to limit public financing of works that are controversial or portray certain content.

Araki coined his name as an allusion to anarchy, and he openly acknowledges that he intended to objectify women in his early work. He was the first to show pubic hair in Japan, challenging the laws and creating a bad-boy buzz for himself. Much of Araki's work doesn't go down easily, and there are those who consider it pornographic. (There are big differences aesthetically between an Araki photograph and porn, but that doesn't make his work any less shocking.) His work catalogs his obsession with women, and especially their vulvas, but it also shows a fascination with and love for life in Tokyo. His photographs of flowers are very different from Mapplethorpe's work,

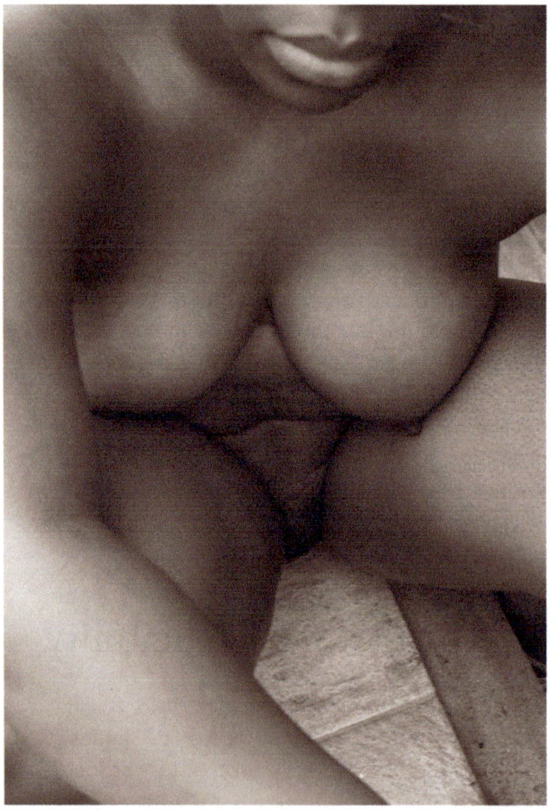

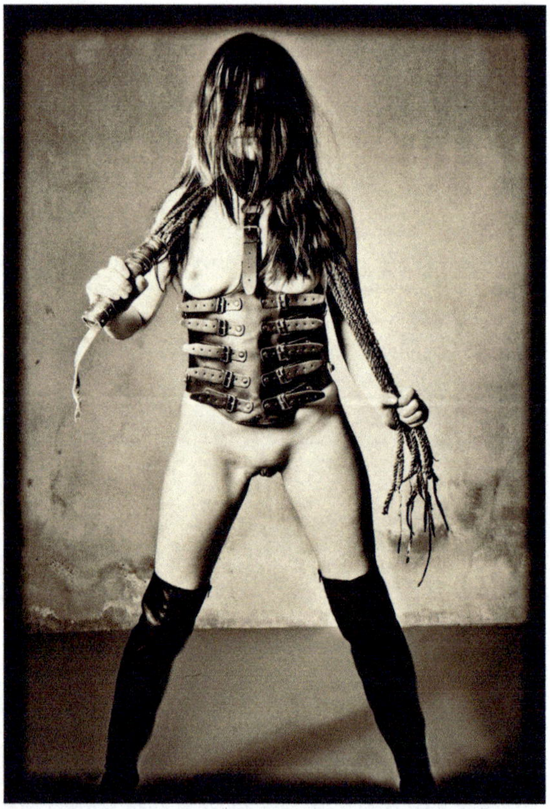

Top: © Lou Benjamin.

Bottom: © Terry Slater.

and demonstrate how much the artist's vision can transform the presentation of a subject.

Helmut Newton's aesthetics were very different from those of Araki and Mapplethorpe, but his work is certainly erotic, as well. His family called him "Dirty Helmy," and in interviews, his wife June has said that he sometimes went too far with his ideas. His pursuit of ideas near the edges of acceptability, coupled with his obvious love of women and the female form, produced work that still has strength decades after it was produced.

Portraits

Faces are our primary way of identifying people, and we tend to relate to the image in terms of a specific character or person. When the face is not shown, the person immediately becomes more anonymous, and we tend to relate to the image in terms of figure or form. Critics of the nude in photography also see the faceless figure as the height of objectification. Many contemporary models sport tattoos. These markings are often distinctive enough to identify the person even when their face does not appear in the shot. Following Kenneth Clark's distinction that the nude is anonymous (often representing all bodies) and idealized, the tattooed body is anathema.

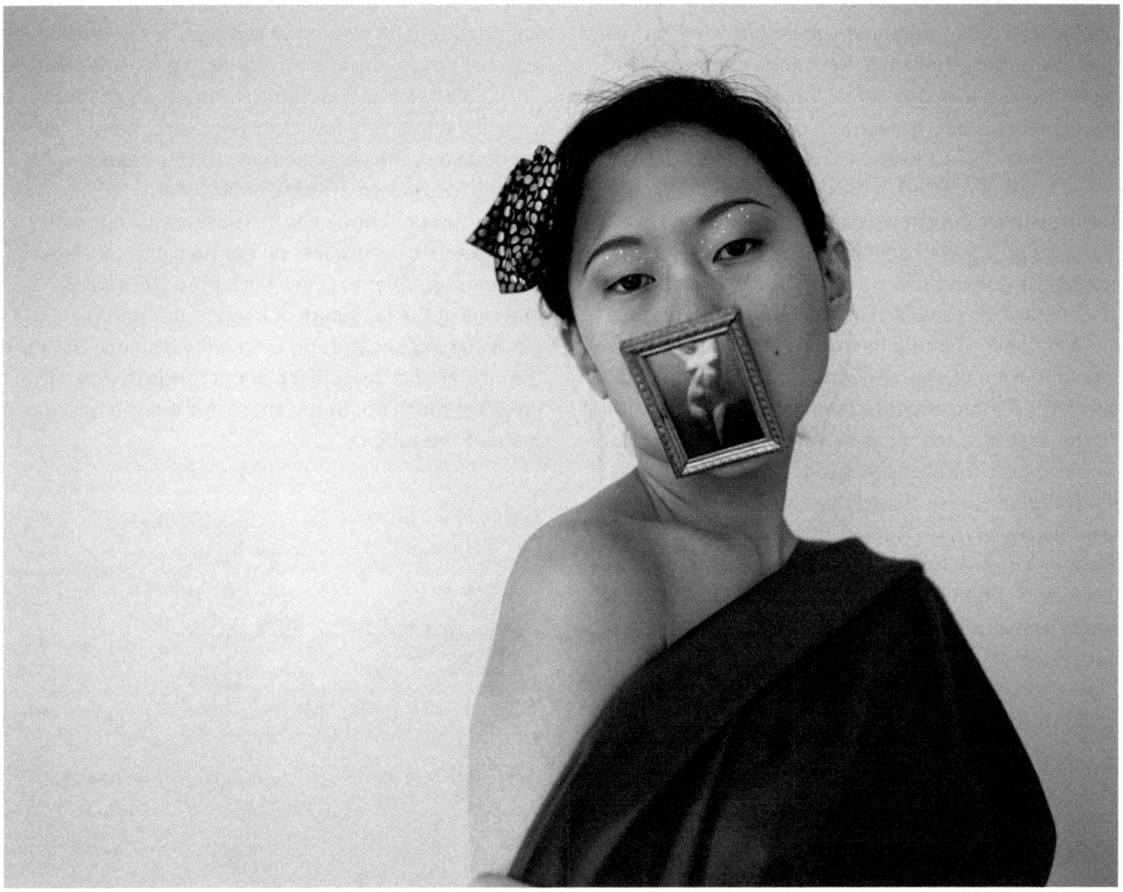

Untitled, 2013 with PAPA, © George McClintock. A compelling variation on the notion of portraiture.

In some ways, tattoos function like clothing—people make value judgments based on their appearance. Removing clothing removes cues about social stature that are closely associated with identity. Absent the distinctive markings of tattoos, the body can be abstracted and idealized to the point of being beautiful, anonymous (and often asexual), forms and contours to be lit and framed; although it ceases to be a portrait. For those reasons, and likely others, some photographers decline to shoot tattooed subjects and others go to great lengths to remove tattoos in post-production. However, some models object and even decline to shoot with photographers who do.

It's worth noting here that people really do look better from some angles than others. The distinctions can be amplified by your choice of lens and lighting. It's a good idea to be aware of that, and maybe even do a few test shots to evaluate first. Once you've found those stronger points of view, use them, unless you're out to do something subversive, in which case you might only shoot the "bad" angles. Word to the wise: Your sitter might object if they don't understand that you're turning convention on its ear.

Neither Richard Avedon nor the painter Lucien Freud were interested in making flattering portraits. It is possible to portray naked people in ways that are more about the person inhabiting the skin and less about conforming to a stylistic norm such as boudoir, cheesecake, or some other idealized representation.

A number of artists have found that putting themselves in front of the lens, rather than working with a model, is a more effective (and more economical) way to get access to the ideas they are trying to express. There are technical challenges to shooting self-portraits, but for these artists, the benefits are worth the trouble. If you read critiques of photography, you're likely to come across the notion that the photograph itself, and certainly any given photographer's body of work, acts as a kind of self-portrait. The stronger the artist's voice in their work, the more this holds true.

As you move in closer and the subject fills more of the frame, the viewer often experiences a stronger sense of intimacy with the subject. Directing the subject's gaze into the lens can intensify this effect, which is usually read as an acknowledgment of the viewer's presence. At the same time, it is quite possible to create a sense of intimacy without even showing the face.

Slightly parting the lips is also read as a kind of openness. Eye contact and glossy lips are played out in the extreme in cheesecake photography, where the model often appears to be seducing the viewer with a "come hither" expression. In the early days of photography, such an attitude signified that the sitter was a prostitute and the photographer risked jail.

At the other end of the spectrum are fashion nudes, where the model sometimes breaks eye contact and doesn't acknowledge the viewer, often seeming to look above, beyond, or through the camera. John Berger observed that the effect of the detached gaze is to trigger a kind of envy in the viewer that in turn makes them want whatever fashion is being depicted. Romantic longing with a touch of envy is a central theme in the work of Bruce Weber, who routinely uses nudes and pushes boundaries in his fashion photography. Advertising, especially in America, is increasingly concerned with selling lifestyles and attitudes, rather than product benefits. When very few clothes or no clothes at all are depicted, the message that comes across can be sharply focused on attitude or lifestyle.

Shooting full-body has its specific challenges. It places certain constraints on lighting, and requires the photographer to move back from the subject. In terms of the language of images, it also has a particular impact, putting emotional distance between the viewer and the subject, and it tends to make the image as much about the space around the figure as it is about the subject.

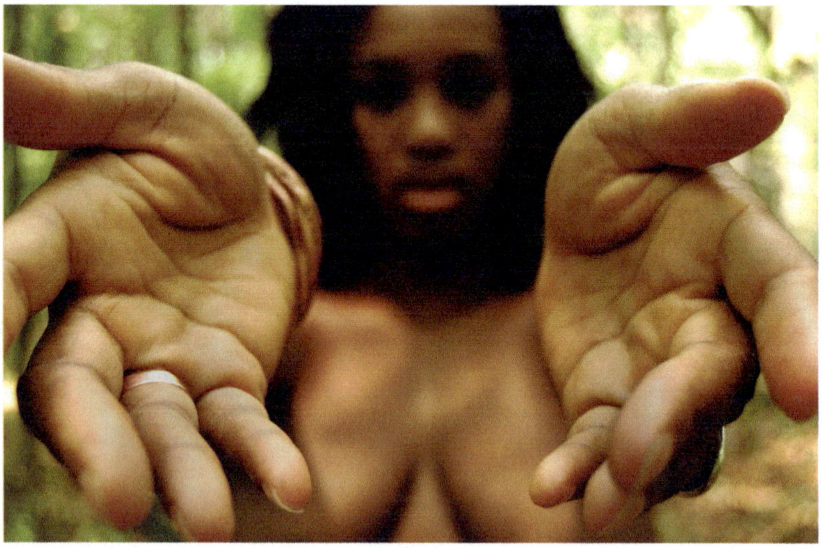

Top: © Saddi Khali. Even without actually seeing the subject's eyes, the gesture of her outstretched arms conveys an impending embrace. Shallow depth of field places the focus on her hands and emphasizes the sense of space.

Facing: © Alan Fresco. Props and an odd color palette resulting from infrared photography create a sci-fi narrative. Portrait orientation allows the bodies to fill more of the frame.

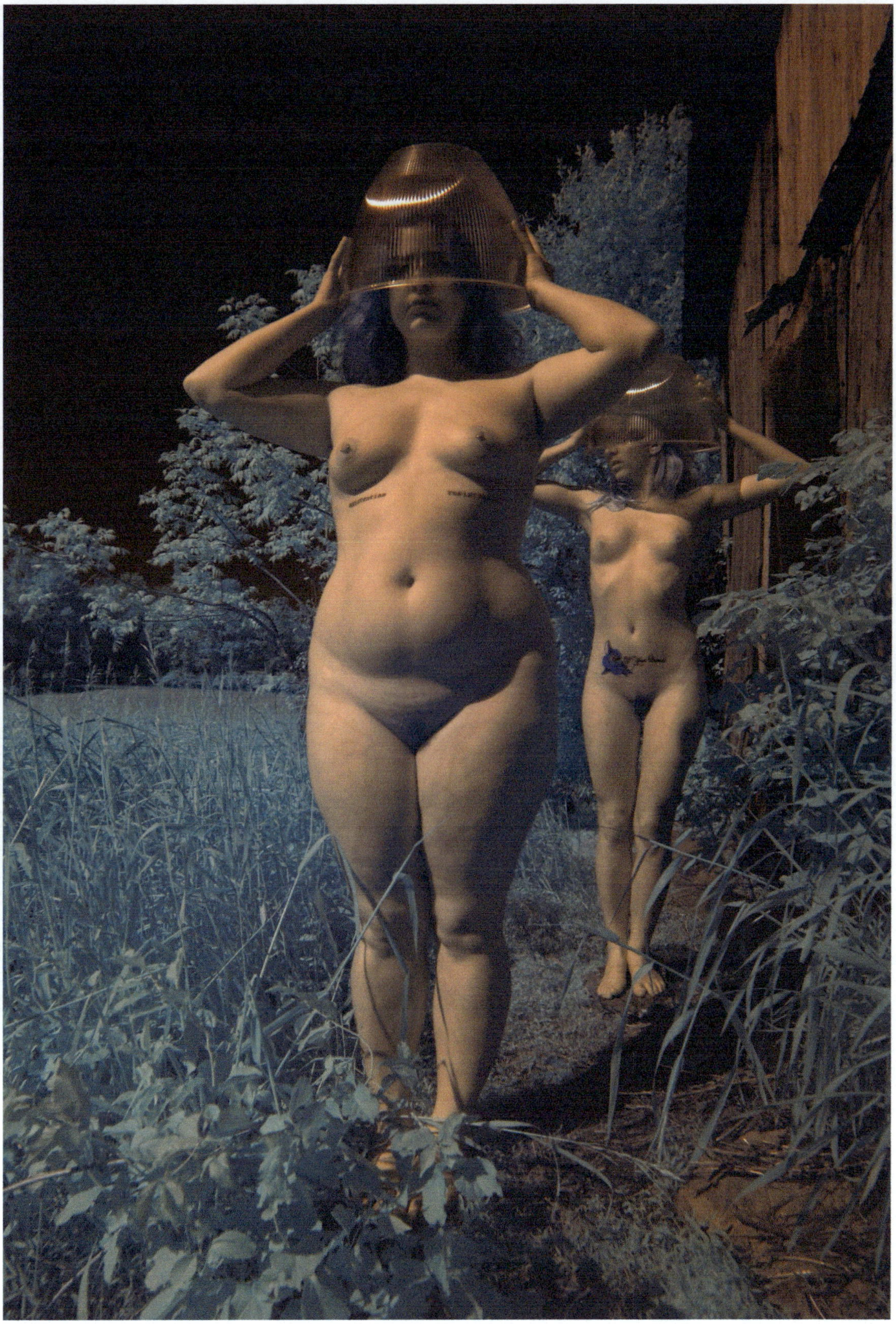

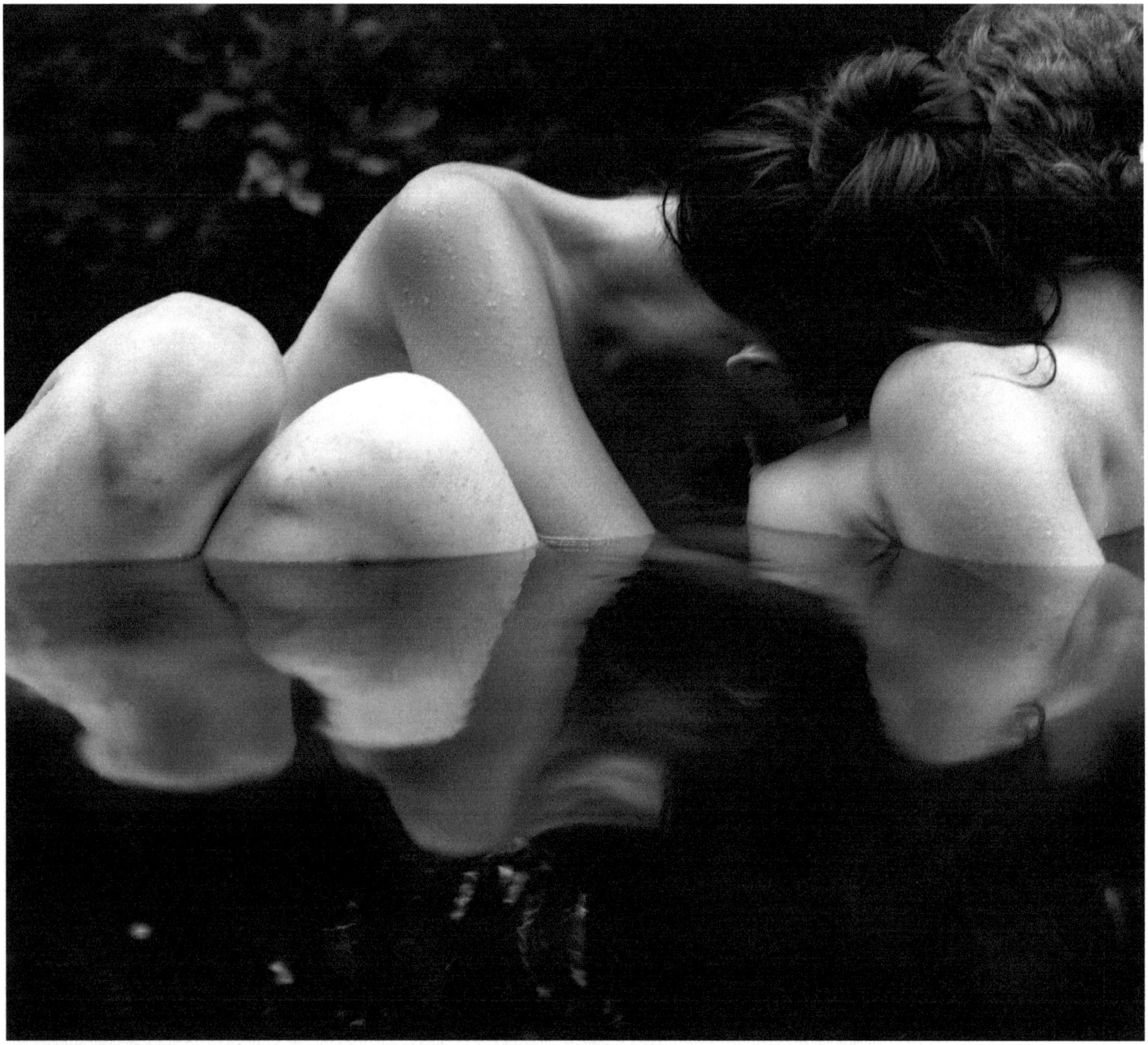

Top: "Water Study 5" © Stephen Billups.

Facing: "Silent" © Mayumi Yoshimaru.

Scapes

For some, the term "fine art nudes" is almost synonymous with bodyscapes. The bodyscape emphasizes the body as abstraction, and the form almost requires that the figure not have a face; after all, with the exception of Mount Rushmore, Georgia's Stone Mountain, and perhaps a few other sites around the world, landscapes don't usually have faces. Lighting (discussed in depth in Chapter Six) is often an essential ingredient in bodyscapes. It can be used to strategically place shadows and highlights that emphasize form and obscure detail.

When a bodyscape is set within a landscape, the framing is looser, and the portion of the image taken up by the body varies greatly. The portion of the frame taken up by the body helps to define the significance or insignificance of the body relative to the rest of nature. Landscape nudes offer an excellent form to explore questions of whether humans are outside of nature or part of it. Urban landscape nudes tend to emphasize the footprint of humankind on nature.

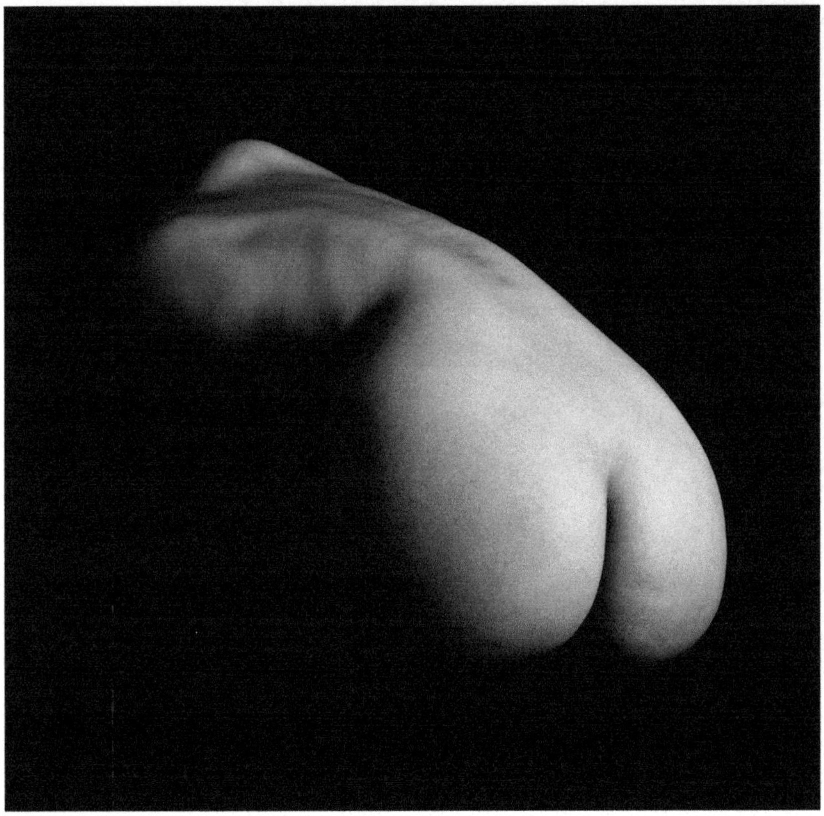

Abstract and Sculptural

Moving in close to isolate parts of the body tends to make it more abstract. When the face is not visible, the contents of the frame have more to do with lines, shapes, forms, or textures. Additional degrees of abstraction can come from throwing the figure out of focus or using high-contrast lighting, such as that produced by grid spots (see Chapter Six), to obscure.

Often, the abstraction results at least in part from making the body less identifiable as a body and relating it to something else, but this is not always the case. Henry Horenstein's series, *Humans*, features isolated parts of models' bodies that are clearly recognizable for what they are, yet they transcend simple recognition. An image of an eye becomes a meditation on form. It is rare that we get that close and simply stop and stare. A photograph gives us permission to stare and to see something anew.

Sculptural nudes derive many of their qualities from lighting, the physicality of the poses, and the point of view of the camera. They can be abstract, but that abstraction is more the result of factors like foreshortening and shadow than the imposition of the frame.

Some of the earliest works of Kishin Shinoyama were concerned with the body as pure form, where he posed curled naked bodies on boulders to emphasize the similarities. Austrian Andreas Bitesnich has taken a very different approach to the figure, but his works also trade on the sculptural qualities of the body.

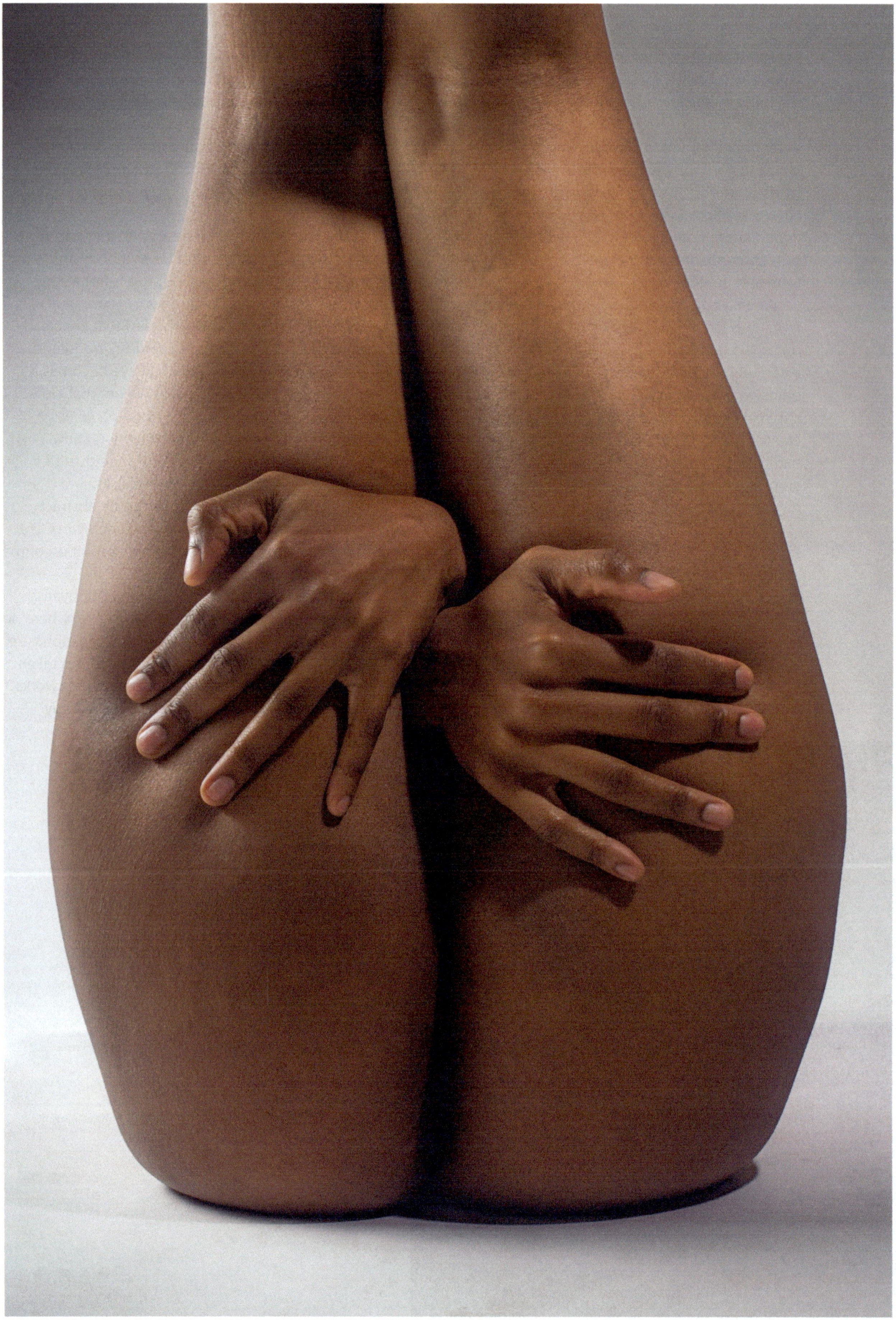

Covering the Body

Covered-up nudes are often referred to as "implied" nudes. The body can be draped in cloth, lit in a way that throws shadows over it, or turned in a way that obscures the genitals. The hands can be used to cover the breasts—the "hand bra." In some photos, the sitter is actually wearing clothes, but the use of props, angles, or framing obscures the view such that we see only skin and imagine the sitter is naked. On networking sites, some models will list that they shoot nudes, but insist on shooting only implied nudes. This relatively safe approach to portraying nudes can be beautiful, but it can also be read as timidity on the part of the photographer, the model, or both.

Covering the genitals with a sweeping gesture of the hand dates back to the fourth century BCE, when Praxiteles of Athens sculpted the Aphrodite of Knidos. That pose is often referred to as *Venus pudica*, or "modest Venus." The genitals can also be covered with a prop, referred to as a *cache-sexe*. Ironically, these tactics often focus attention on the genitals, rather than downplaying them.

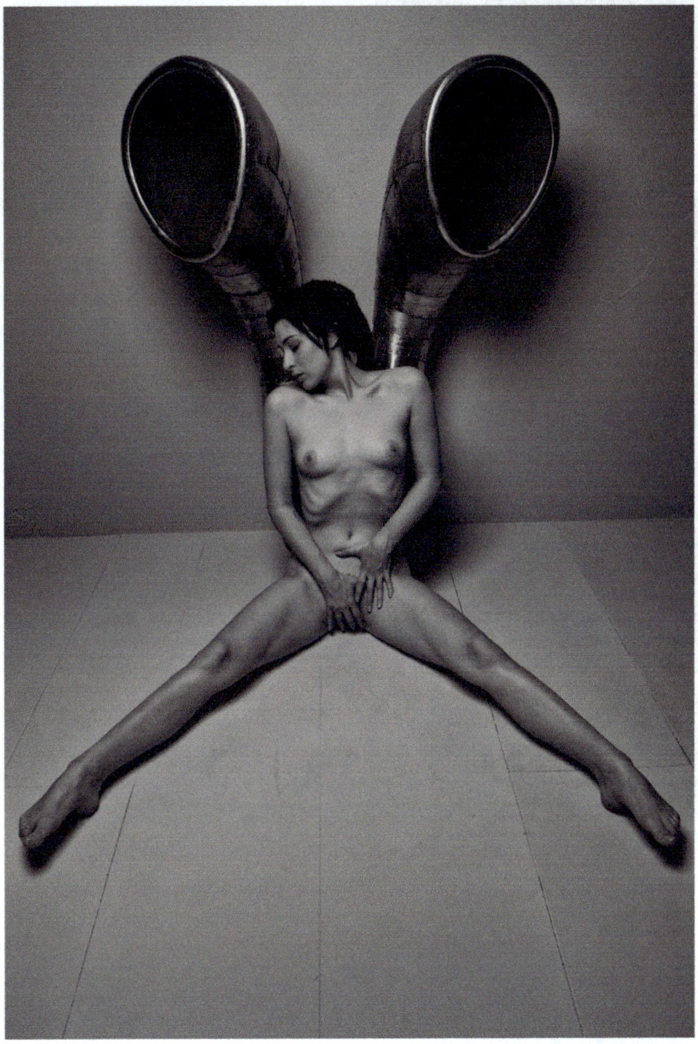

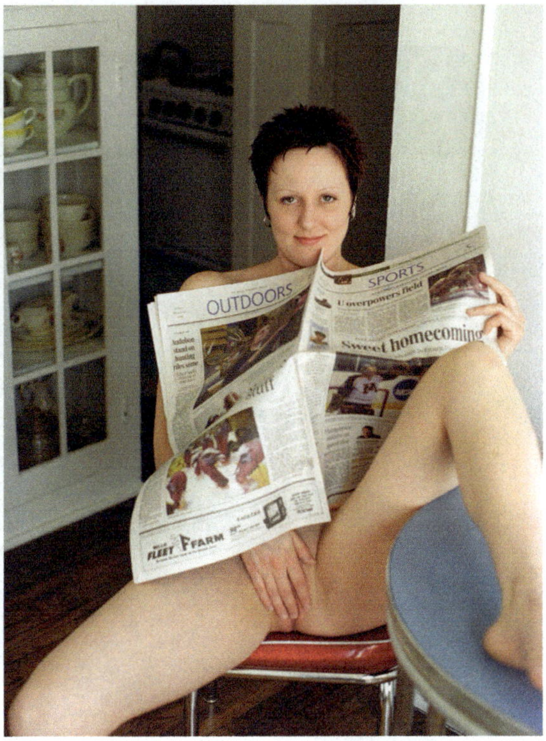

Facing: © Lou Benjamin. Lighting and framing are key factors in making this sculptural nude allude to a vase.

Above left: © Donna Feldman Lasky.

Above right: © Terry Donovan.

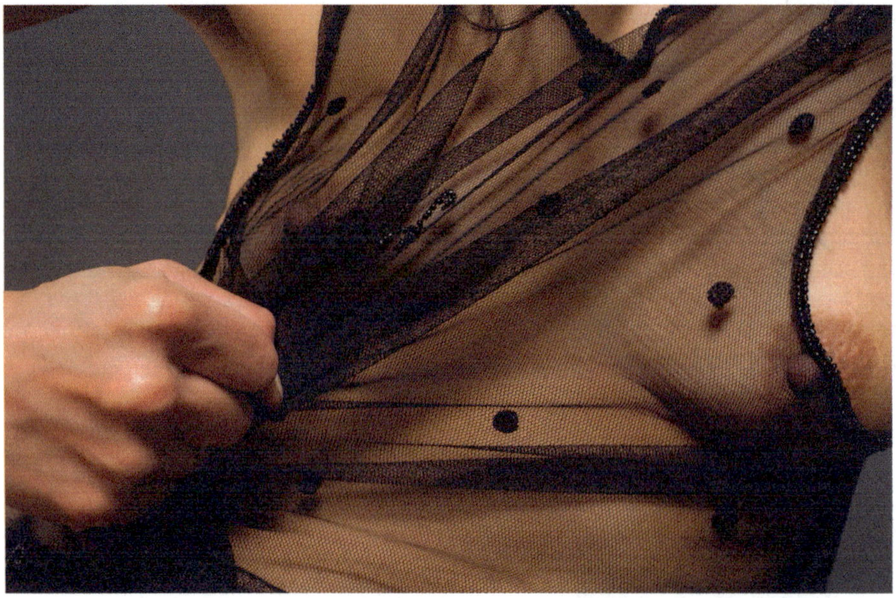

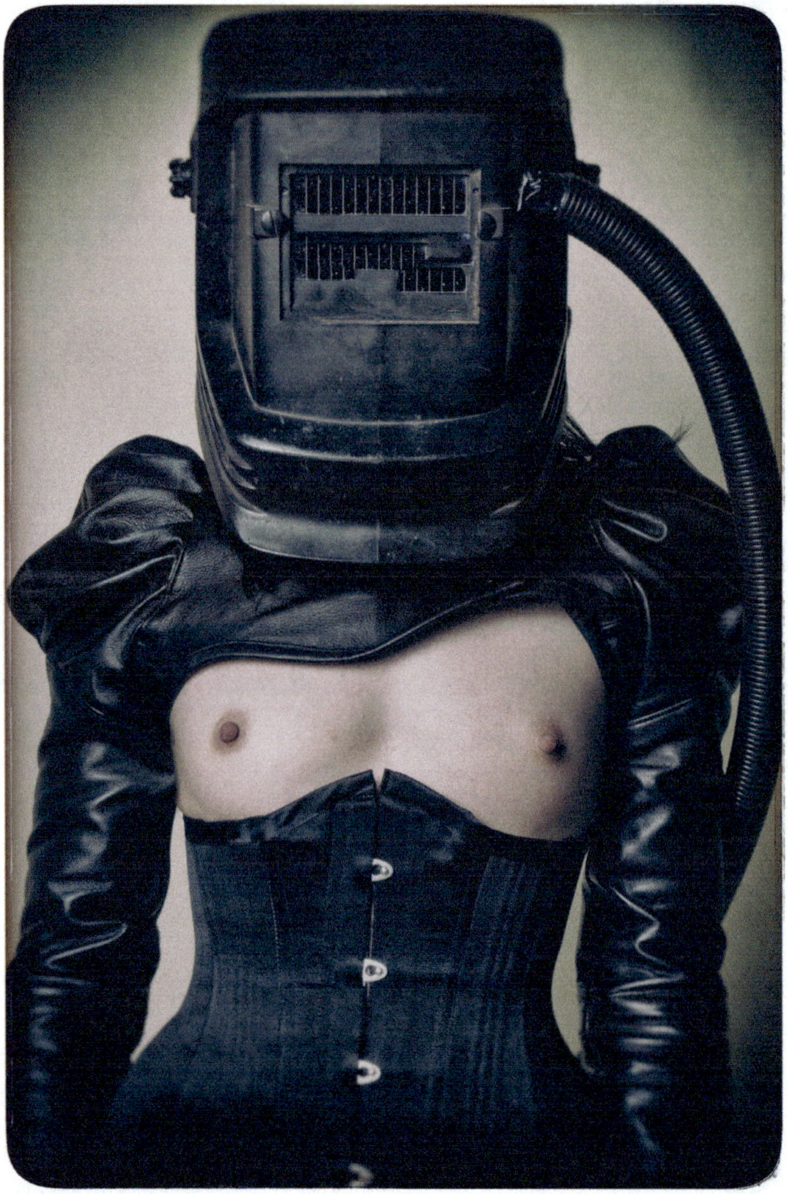

The fashion industry has understood that body coverings can also be used to emphasize awareness of the naked body from its inception. That understanding has been the source of the slitted cocktail dress as well as many fetish wear designs such as corsets and ropes that transform the shape of the body, clothing with cut-outs or holes, and sheer fabrics.

Shibari (kinbaku) is artistic rope tying meant to embellish the body. The texture of the rope and geometric patterns of the knots are contrasted against the curves and smoothness of the skin. Developed in Japan during the late Edo period (1603–1868), it lends itself to figurative erotic photography and has many Western practitioners. Nobuyoshi Araki is a famous Japanese contemporary artist who makes use of the form.

Female pubic hair can function as a body covering by concealing the labia, making certain shots a little less explicit. Some models who once shaved their pubic areas have chosen to grow out their hair for that reason. Hair covering the sex also signals sexual maturity, while a shaven vulva can suggest pre-pubescence. The bare pudendum can carry connotations of either classical painting or porn. As you develop project ideas, it is worth consciously considering how the presence or absence of pubic hair (and body hair in general) will affect your image.

Some models who shave will sometimes choose to wear a pubic wig called a merkin. Filmmakers have employed merkins for nude scenes to avoid more restrictive ratings. Photographer Rhiannon Schneiderman created a series of eight self-portraits called *Lady Mane*, in which she sports over-the-top styled merkins and adopts fashion posing and staging to satirize societal norms related to femininity and objectification.

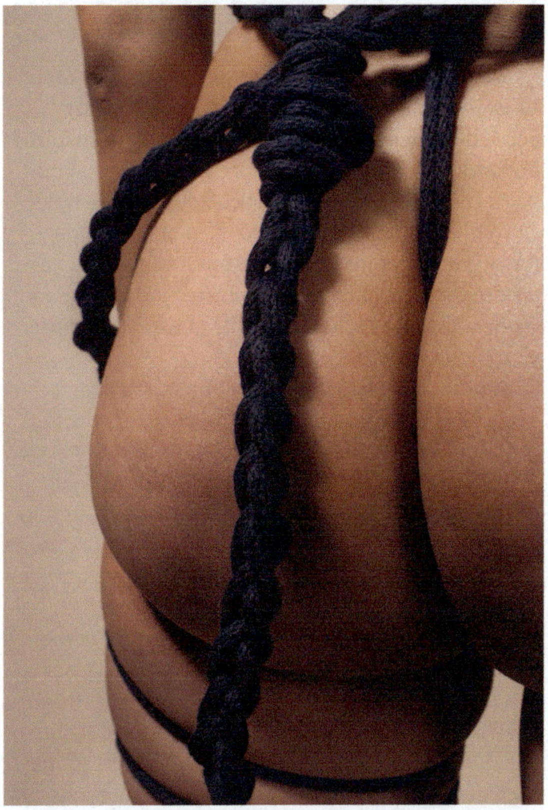

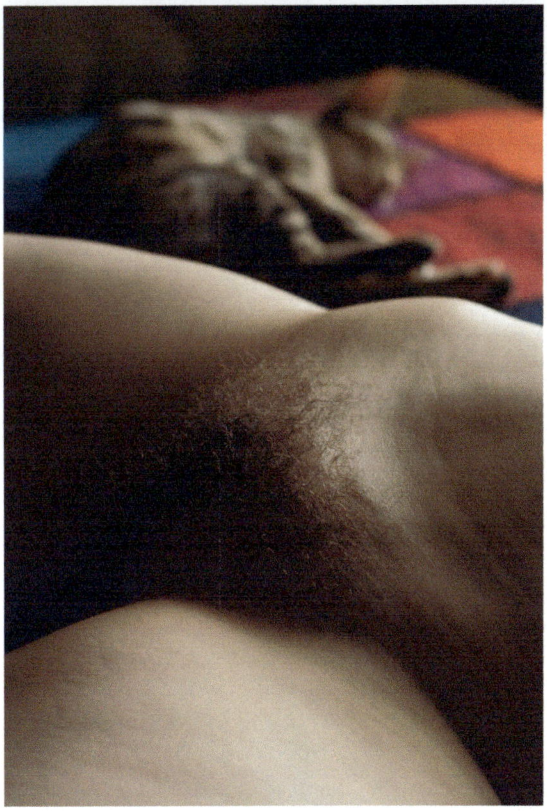

Facing (top): © Lou Benjamin.

Facing (bottom): © Terry Slater.

Above (top): © Lou Benjamin.

Above (bottom): © Lou Benjamin. This photo combines a visual pun while making the body nearly abstract. For some, pubic hair (and body hair in general) is erotic and aesthetic, while others consider it pornographic and prefer a bare pubis. Back lighting creates a bright edge and casts shadows that emphasize contours and conceal the genitals.

Skin and Second Skin

Fishnets, liquid latex, mud, flowers, honey, and other substances with strong textures or colors can be applied to the skin to call attention to the form of the body by altering the appearance of its surface. Body paint can do that as well, particularly if it is a single color (think of Mystique from *X-Men* or the Jill Masterson character in *Goldfinger*), but it can also act as a kind of camouflage that dominates the picture and renders the body unrecognizable in ways that most clothing cannot.

A potential pitfall is that the photograph can become about the painting or the painter, reducing the body to just another canvas. Writing on the body or affixing signs presents a similar challenge. Text tends to dominate an image, and the effect is usually more potent than attaching a caption. If the text is not legible but is recognizable as text, it creates a particular type of visual intrigue.

As you move in closer, the characteristics of the skin become increasingly prominent. Macro lenses can be used to bring the viewer so close that the skin itself is transformed into something abstract. Lighting the skin from the side with a directional light source such as a grid spot will emphasize its texture. This can be a very powerful effect on the faces and bodies of older men, but it might bring protests from anyone who sees lines and bumps in the skin as flaws. You can see examples of directional lighting with grid spots in Chapter Six.

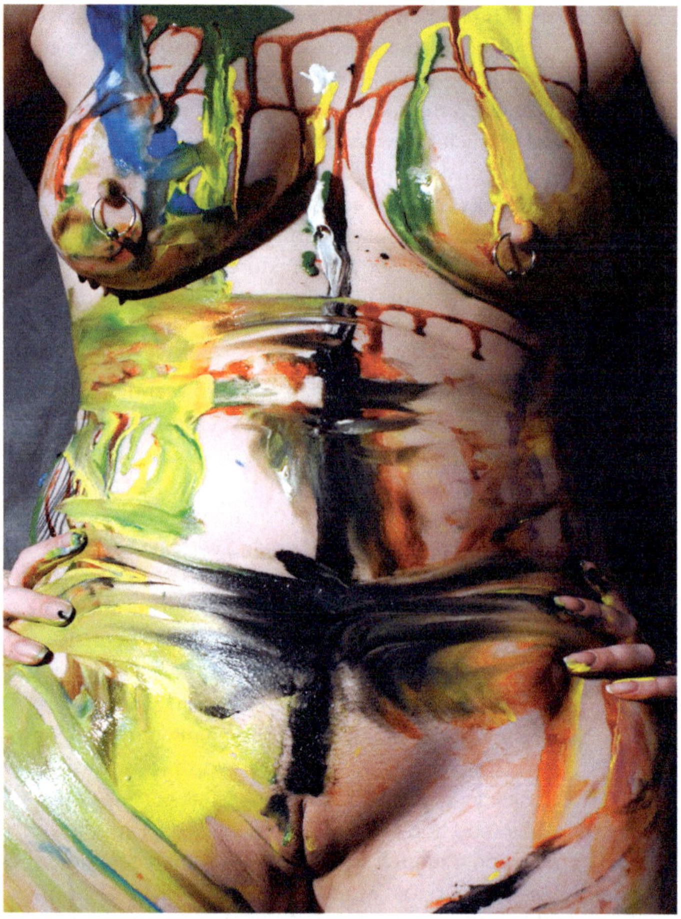

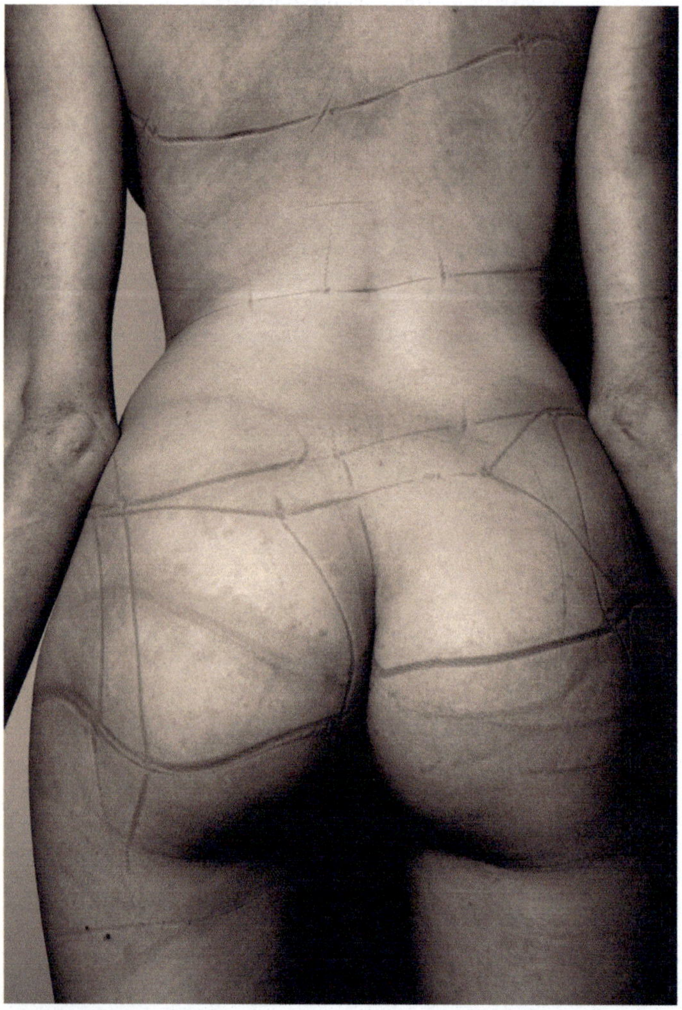

Top: © Terry Donovan.

Bottom: © Terry Slater.

Facing: © Ned and Aya Rosen.

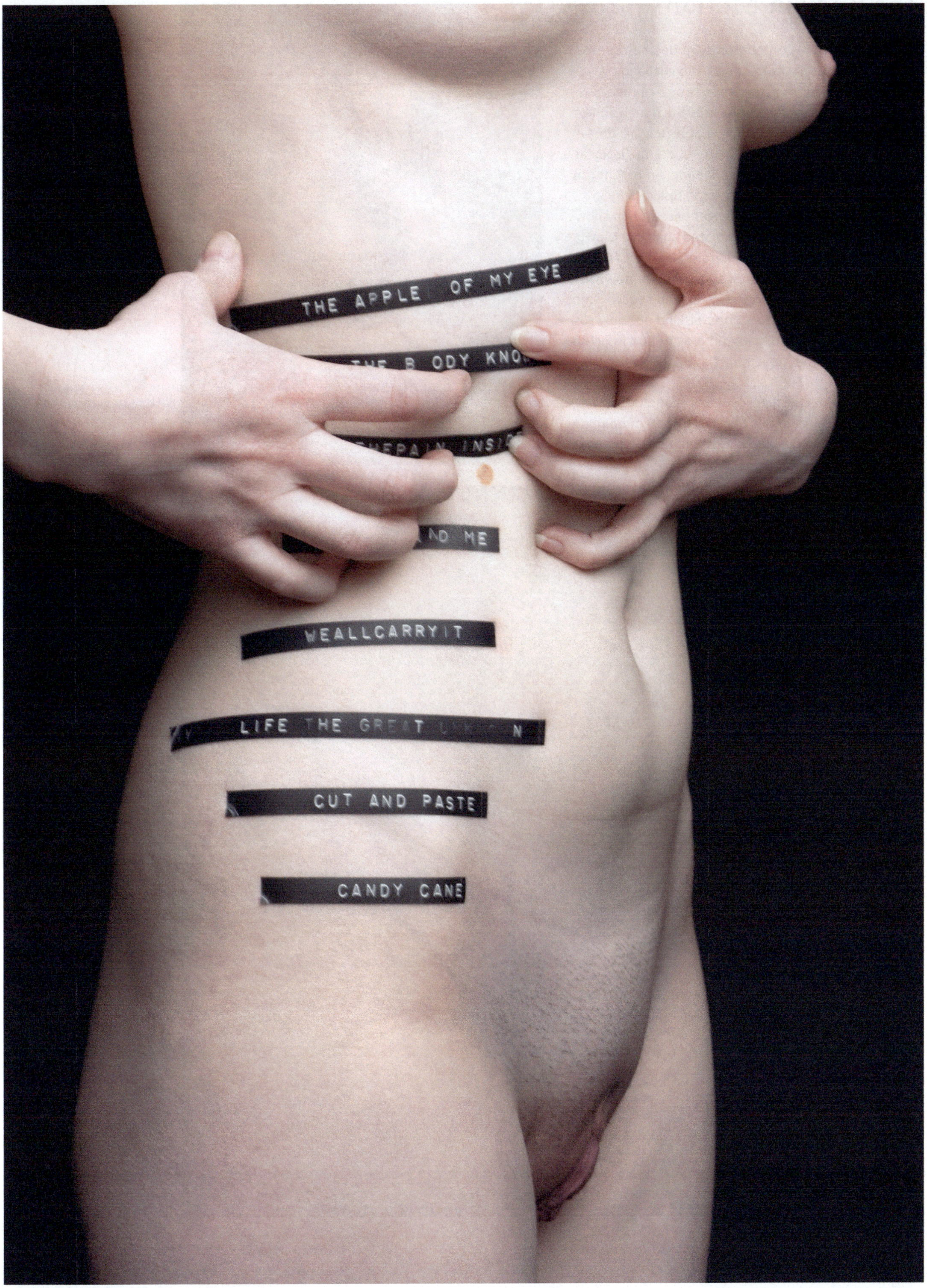
THE APPLE OF MY EYE
WEALLCARRYIT
CUT AND PASTE
CANDY CANE

The Body in Motion

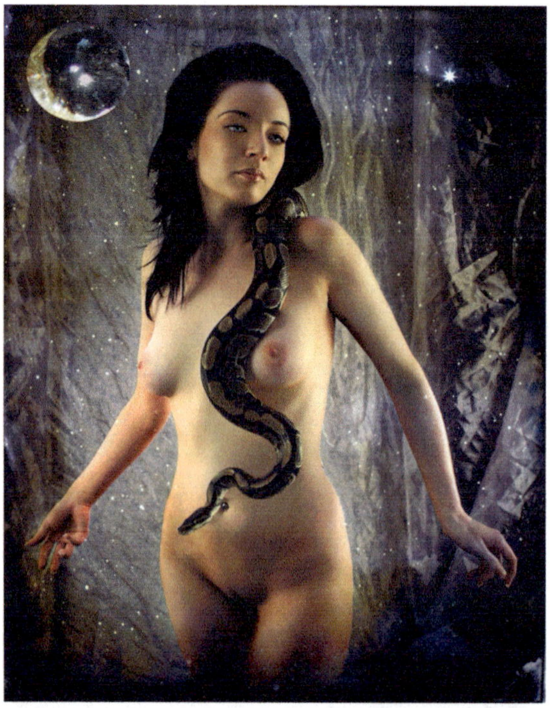

Body movement in contemporary nude photography borrows heavily from dance. The challenge is to find other kinds of activities to source our ideas from. Moving the body emphasizes the dimension of time, and the reaction of photography toward time is either to arrest movement or to render the body as evanescent, emphasizing how fleeting a moment can be and how temporal we are. Aaron Siskind's 1956 series entitled *Pleasures and Terrors of Levitation* shows swimming-trunk-clad divers isolated against a blown-out white sky, freezing them in mid-fall. There is no blur. Because there is no indication of up or down, the divers seem oddly suspended in time and space, limbs projecting in different directions. Siskind not only suspended time, he also disavowed gravity, and in doing so, emphasized the movements and the form of the body as it falls through space.

Gestures are a particular type of motion. They have much richer application across the history of painting than in photography. In religious paintings, gestures

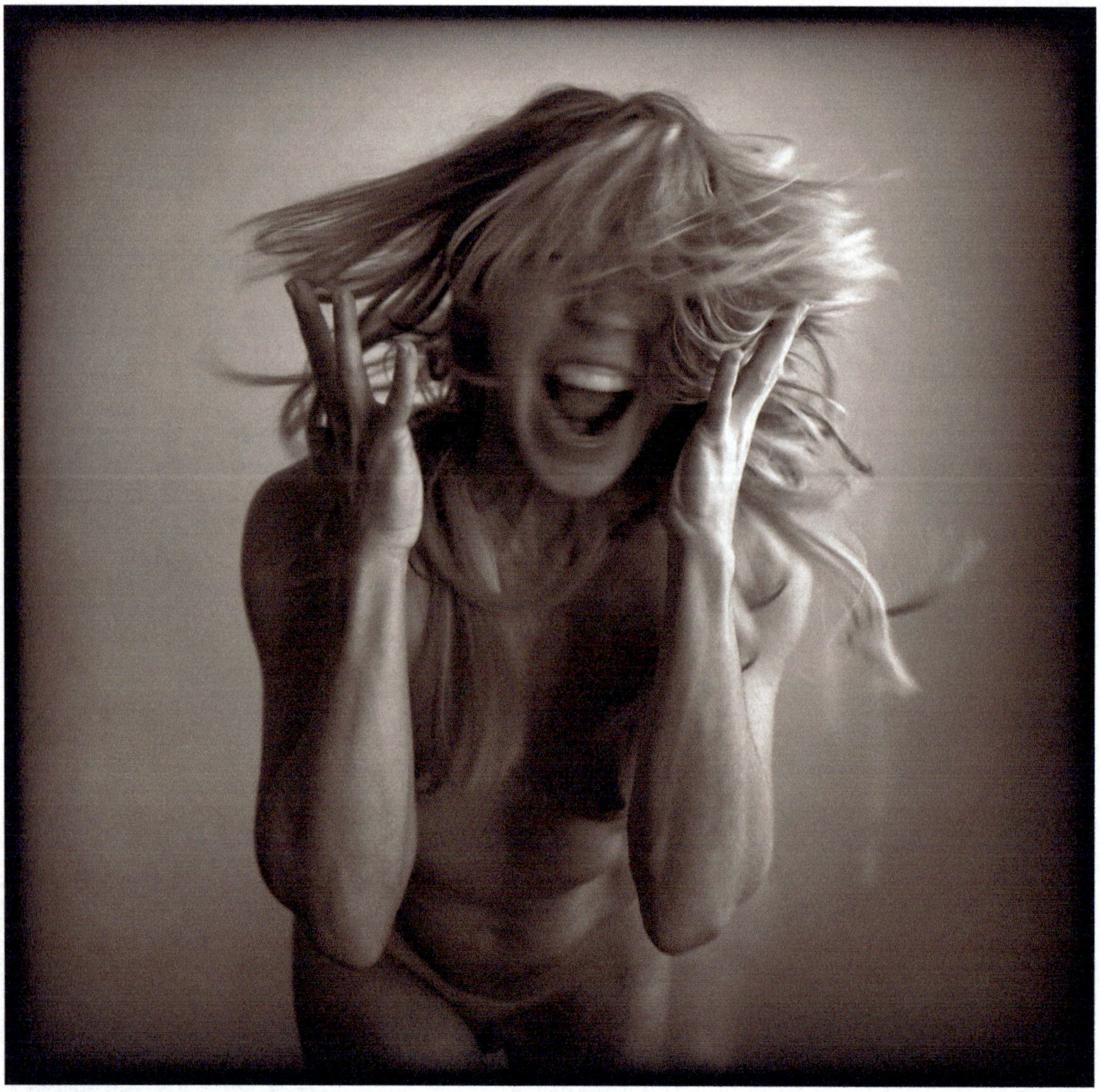

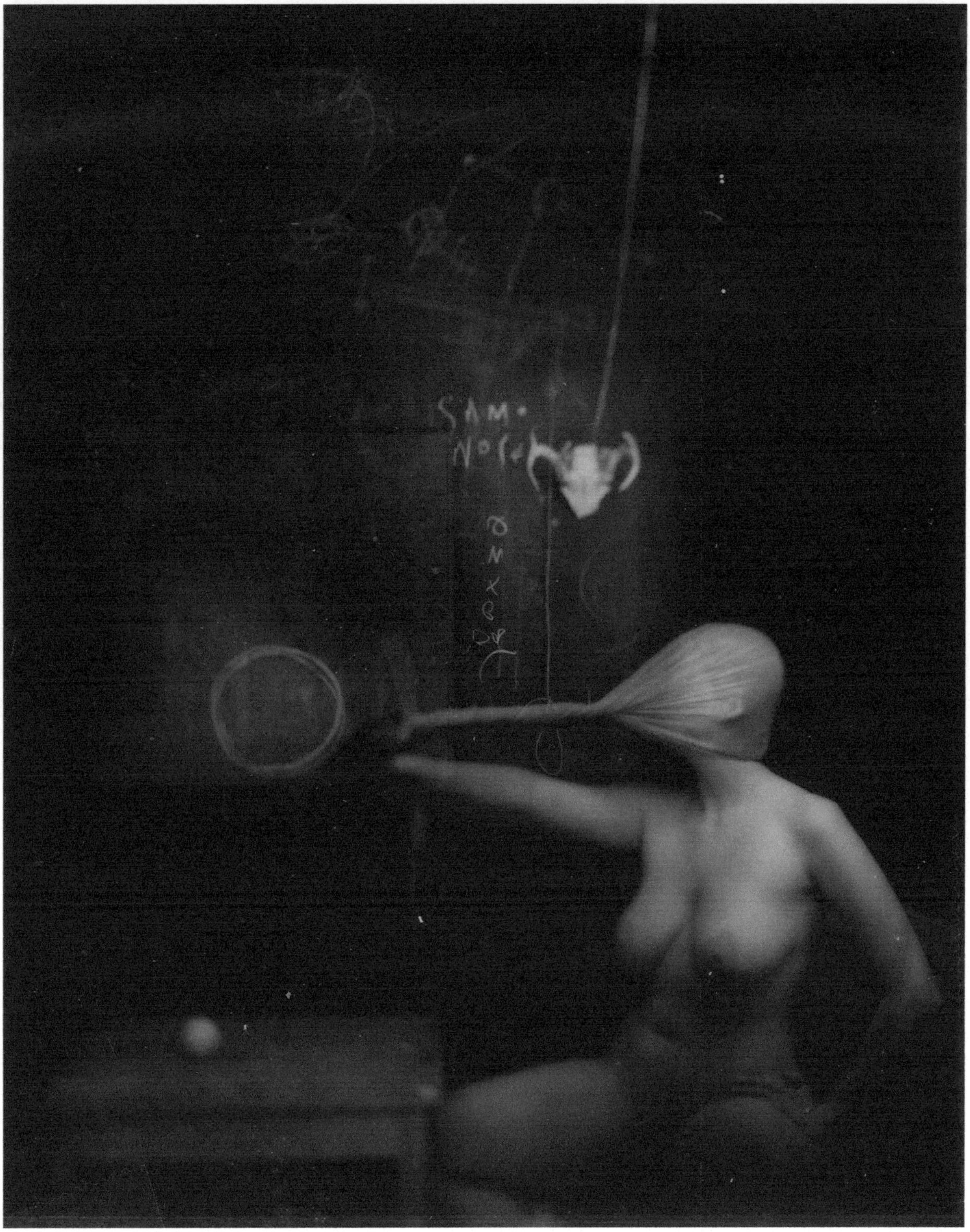

Facing (top): © Nina Pak. The expressive hands add a lot to this image, which references the Bible, mysticism, and classical painting.

Facing (bottom): © Pascal Renoux.

Above: © Robert Gregory Griffeth. Gesture is a prominent element of this constructed image. Griffeth cuts up, collages, and draws on negatives to create his images. He has been described as a photography outsider who developed his eye from looking at books and magazines, rather than from formal classes. He likens his process to dreaming, constructing the images freeform—"I layer the visual, just like a musician would layer the sound."

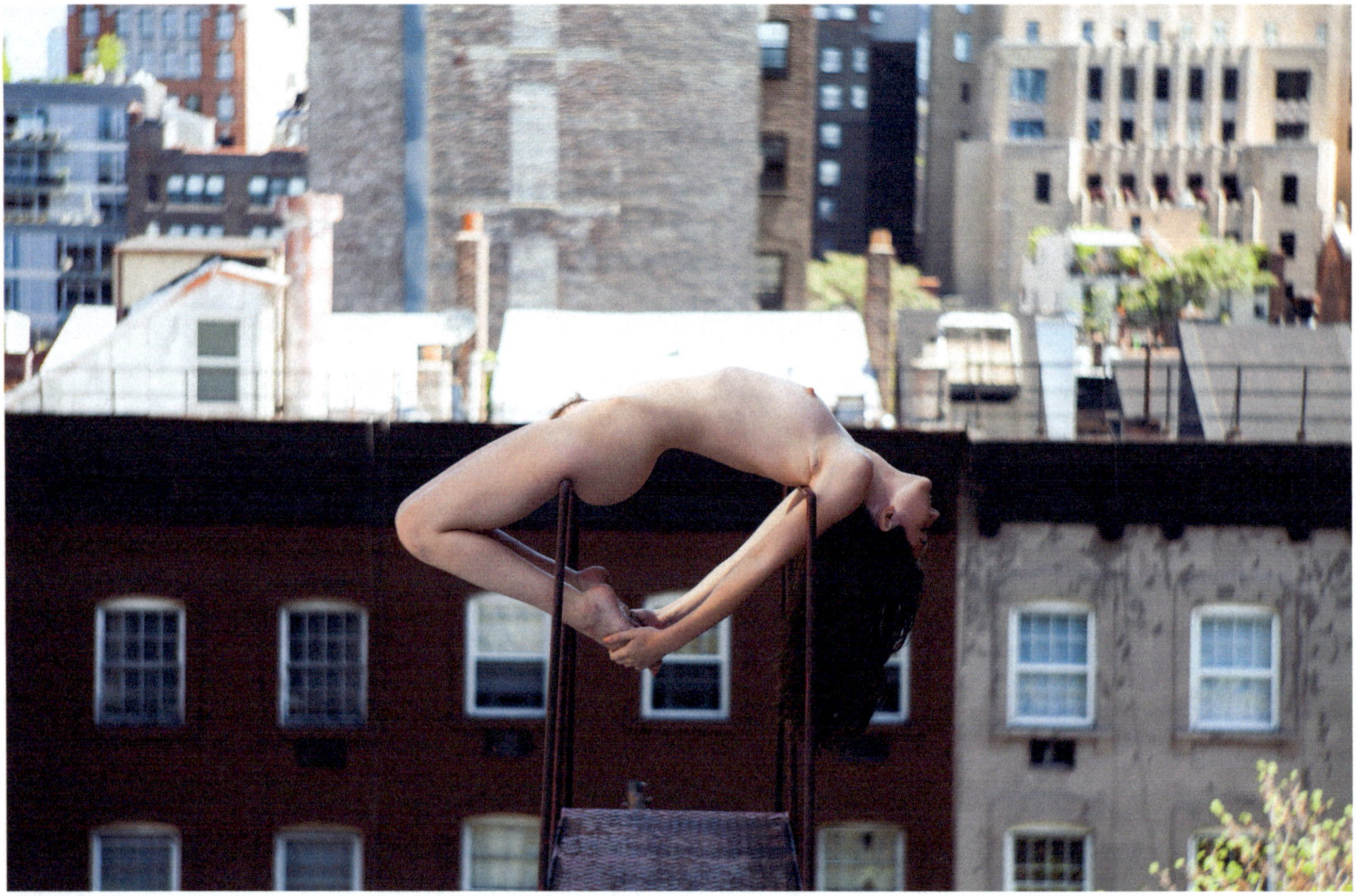

Top: "Fearless over 14th Street," 2014 © George McClintock.
Model: Erica Jay.

Bottom: © Scott Foltz.

often have specific meanings, such as the Holy Trinity, sovereignty, or protection. Austrian Expressionist painter Egon Schiele often used hand gestures to convey emotion in powerful ways. In glamour shots, the hands are often placed to bring attention to the face, making use of the principle of leading lines, but many photographers overlook the hands in favor of directing facial expression and posing the body.

Body vs. Setting

Environmental portraiture uses the setting to create context for the figure. With nudes, cues from the environment replace the cues that might be provided by clothing. In images that are not portraits, but more conceptual, the setting can give cues about the role of the figure in the image. Photos can compare the human form to nature or to human-made things, suggesting how humans are an extension of nature, or act in opposition to it. Placing bodies against architectural elements often exhibits how the entire scale and proportion of architecture is based on the human form. Two masters of this type of nude are Kishin Shinoyama and Spencer Tunick.

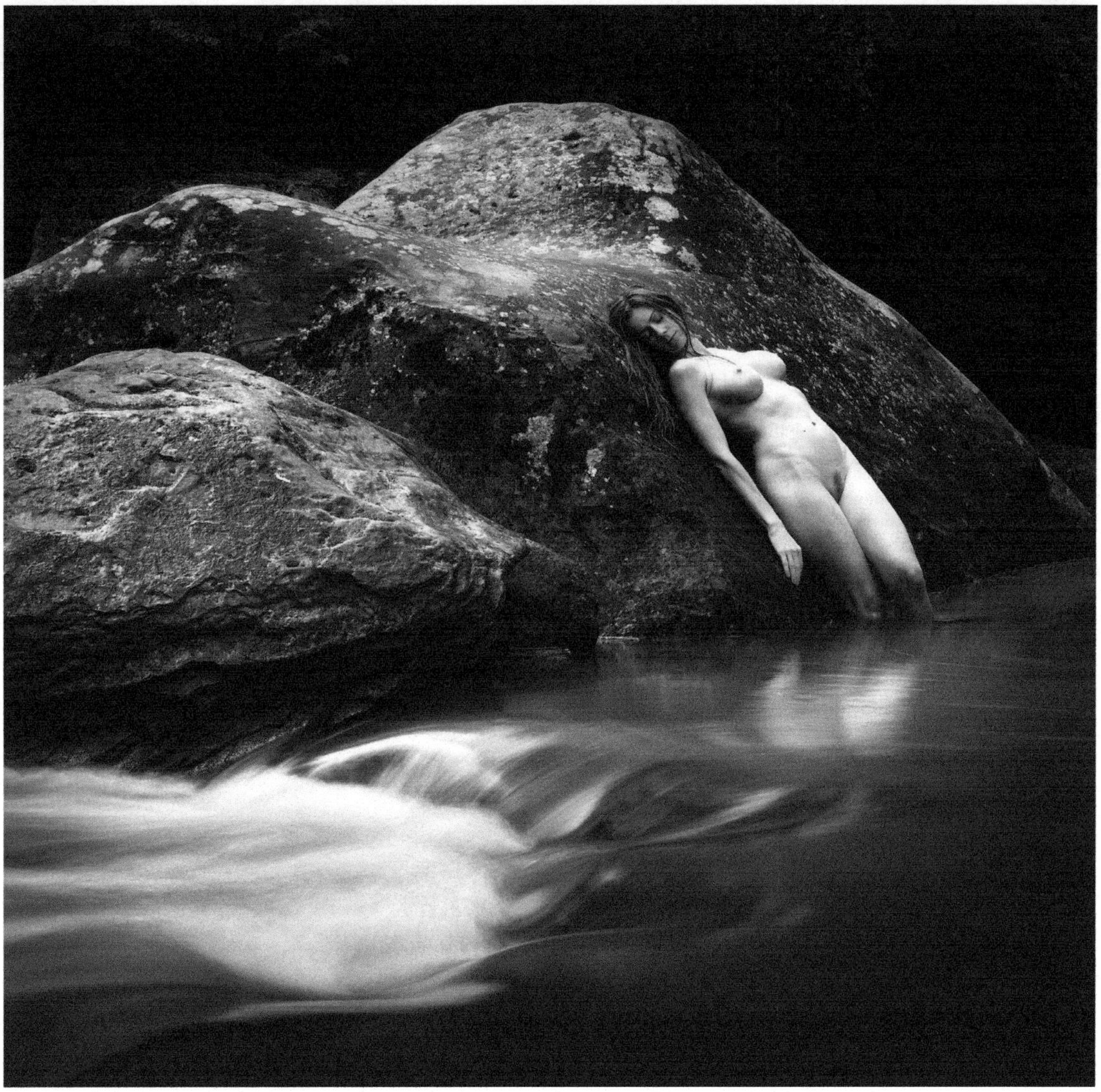

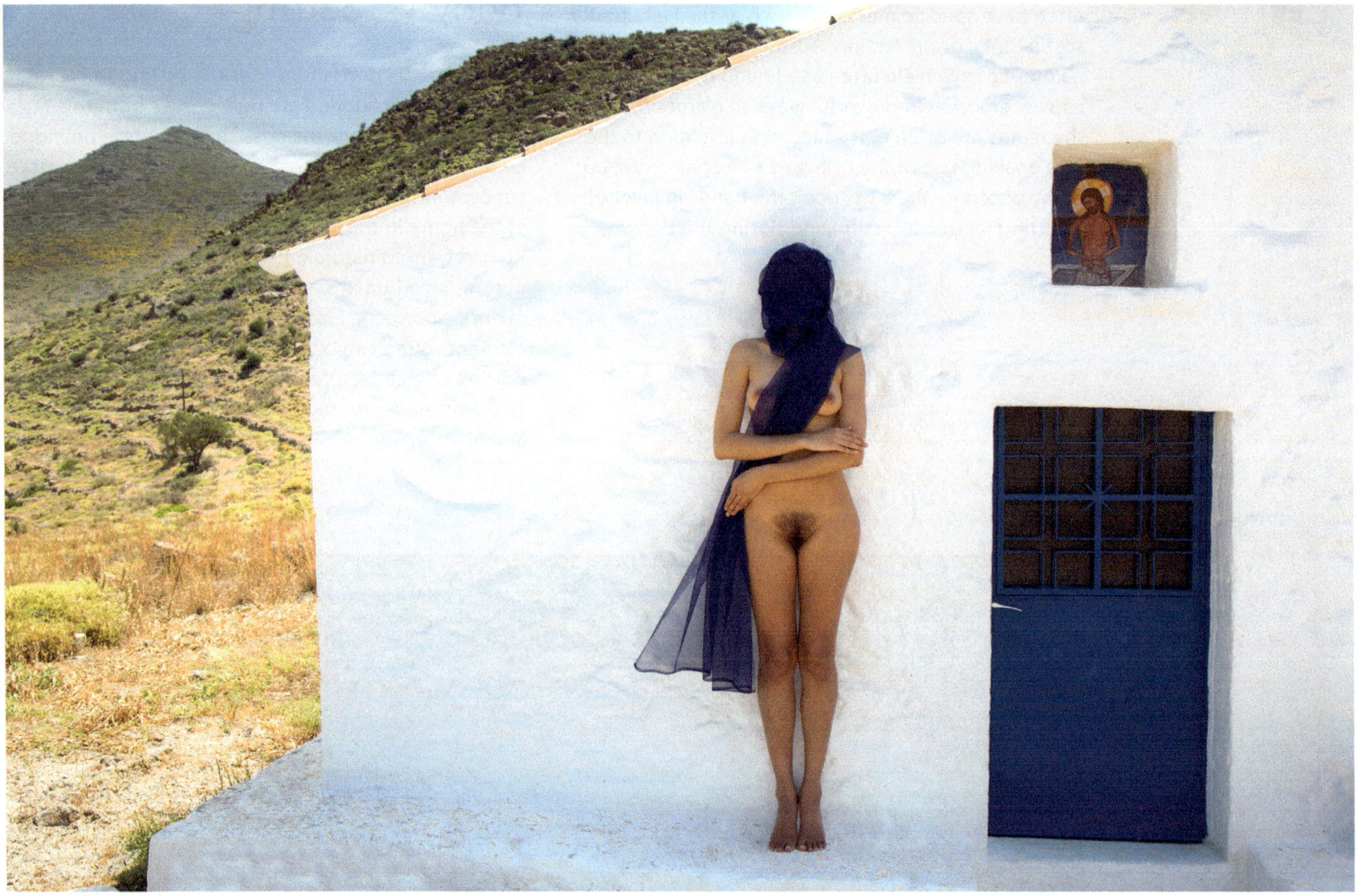

In "Modern Cycladic Idol", the setting, color scheme, and figure create a powerful synergy that compare and contrast civilizations, religions, and eras. The model has adopted the pose of an ancient Cycladic idol, the earliest female nude in Greek art, thought to be a goddess or symbol of fertility, nature, and sexuality. The popular figures were produced during the period between 3300 and 2000 BCE, and are the only known depiction of the nude female in Greek art until the fourth century BCE.

The modern idol stands in front of a present-day Orthodox chapel with Christ, the modern god figure, gazing at her. White Orthodox chapels with dark blue doors can be found everywhere in the modern Cyclades, the ring of Greek islands that surround the isle of Delos in the Aegean Sea. White and royal blue represent the ocean, dark blue sky, and bright white clouds that dominate the landscape.

Top: "Modern Cycladic Idol," 2014 © Brian Connor (Aspiring Imagery). Model: Kat Love.

Facing: © Terry Slater. Light from the left plays an important role in isolating and abstracting the couple.

Some environmental nudes place the subject in a setting where nakedness is unexpected or unacceptable, emphasizing nakedness itself. In other instances, the environmental nude is more about the sculpture of the body in a space. The body can blend in, or it can be made to stand out starkly. In some of her best-known work, Francesca Woodman juxtaposed her body against old interiors and used motion blur to seemingly dissolve into the walls amidst peeling wallpaper. The nude can symbolize life while a crumbling building represents death and decay. The opposition of decadence and the female form in images often dramatizes the quality of beauty itself.

Erotic

It has been said that, particularly in the United States, images depicting nudity are typically viewed in one of only two ways: either as abstract, artistic and asexual, or as erotic/pornographic. Exceptions to those two views, aside from academic medical imagery, are hard to find.

If you ask ten people what makes a photograph erotic, you're likely to get a dozen answers. If you want to make things more interesting, ask about the difference between erotica and porn. It's easy to find examples where the words erotica and pornography are used interchangeably, and the porn industry uses the word "erotica" to lend sophistication to some of its offerings. In 1964, Justice Potter Stewart famously declined to give a specific definition for "hardcore" pornography, but declared "I know it when I see it." This is an important distinction, since works deemed obscene are not protected as free speech in the United States, and communities can have dramatically different standards.

Whether you choose to enter into the art vs. pornography vs. obscenity fray or not, we can consider what might make an erotic image more artful. To the extent that it helps inform your artistic vision, it may be useful to come up with a personal distinction, but beyond that, the old adage applies: "One man's meat is another man's poison." If you choose to explore that kind of subject matter, be prepared to meet resistance.

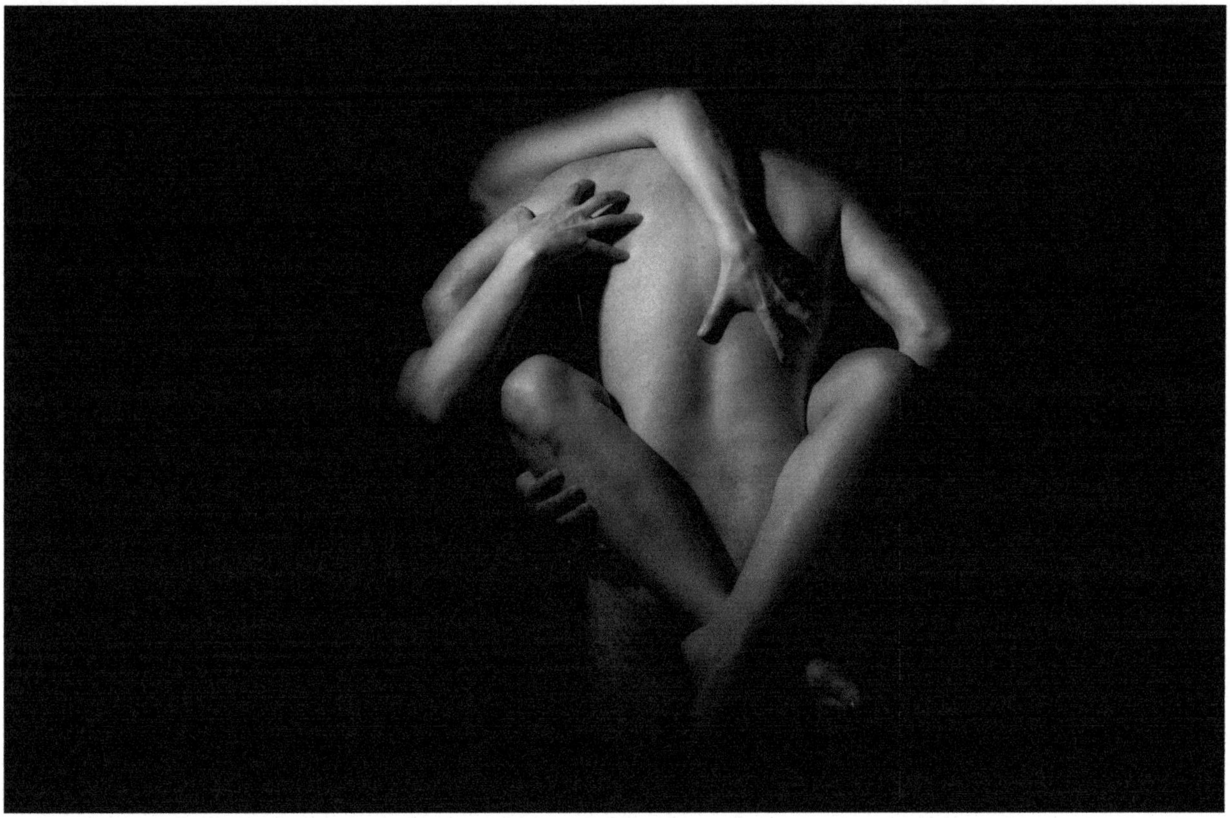

Nakedness, Sex, and Biology

Nakedness, sex, and biology are closely tied. The act of removing clothes is often a ritual precursor to sexual intercourse, a fundamental function of human biology. The naked body, (especially the female body) is often viewed as a signifier of sex or the site of sex. Theorists observe that in advertising, even clothed females symbolize sex. If you doubt that, visit the New York City subway and take note of the graffiti applied to advertising posters featuring women: Breasts or pubic hair are added, penises are drawn in proximity to their mouths or crotches, and lewd captions are often added. These are not rare occurrences, and the scrawl may simply be a restatement of the subtext that can be read in the images.

Pregnancy and motherhood are potential outcomes of sex, but it is noteworthy that representations of sex and sexuality are strongly segregated from imagery of pregnancy, motherhood, and family. Nudes of pregnant stars such as Demi Moore, Cindy Crawford, and Heidi Klum have all graced the covers of major magazines. The depiction of pregnant nudes in these settings tends to be very stylized and conventional. One of the more controversial examples of a pregnant nude is Daniel Edwards' life-size sculpture of a crowning Britney Spears on all fours caressing the head of a bearskin rug while giving birth as a monument to the pro-life movement.

As problematic as art involving pregnant (and especially birthing) women can be, depicting naked children is even more treacherous. Jock Sturges' work with nudist families is widely known, as are the stories of the FBI raid of his studio, and the celebrated legal case in which a San Francisco grand jury refused to indict. Some of the photographs in Sally Mann's "Immediate Family" show her own pre-adolescent children in scenes that have been described by some as sexualizing them. Mann consulted with a lawyer and waited until her children were older before ever exhibiting some of her work.

Artists who explore these areas have to become adept at defending themselves. Ironically, the controversy surrounding such cases can increase the cachet of the artist. Sturges has pointed out that artists in such situations also run the risk of being defined by the scandal instead of the art that they produce. Robert Mapplethorpe said that he hadn't intended to be a poster boy for free speech, he just wanted to be written about on the merits of his art.

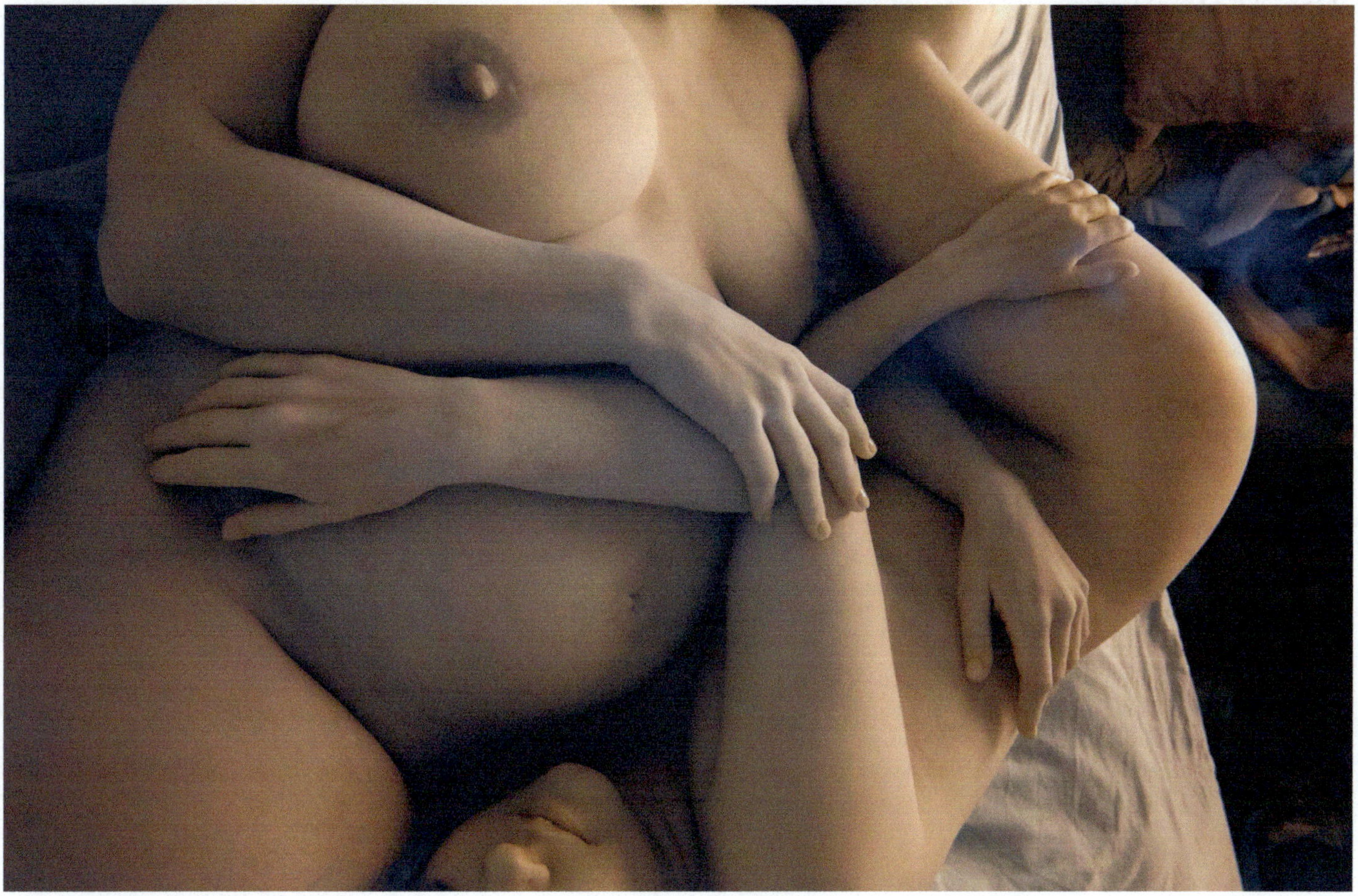

© Alan Fresco.

The Male Nude

It is obvious that male nudes in fine art are far rarer than female nudes. This may be due in part to the dominance of the heterosexual male gaze as a point of reference in art culture, which in turn may have had as much of a shaping influence on art production as the emergence of single-point perspective in Florence during the early fifteenth century.

Regardless of the tendencies of the mainstream, photographers such as Bruce Bellas, better known as Bruce of Los Angeles, blazed the trail of photographing the male nude. Beginning in the 1940s, he shot for "physique" magazines, such as those published by Joe Weider, at a time when gay pornography was illegal. His campy style and the slightly amateurish look of his early work helped define the look of male homoerotic photography, influencing fashion photographers such as Herb Ritts and Bruce Weber. Mr. Weber went on to change the face of advertising and launched a designer underwear business in 1982, when he portrayed a man as a sex object. Olympic pole vaulter Tom Hintnaus was the object of desire in that iconic campaign for Calvin Klein underwear. Weber's sometimes controversial advertising work has continued to push the envelope, and includes the catalog he did for Abercrombie and Fitch, which featured athletic male nudes.

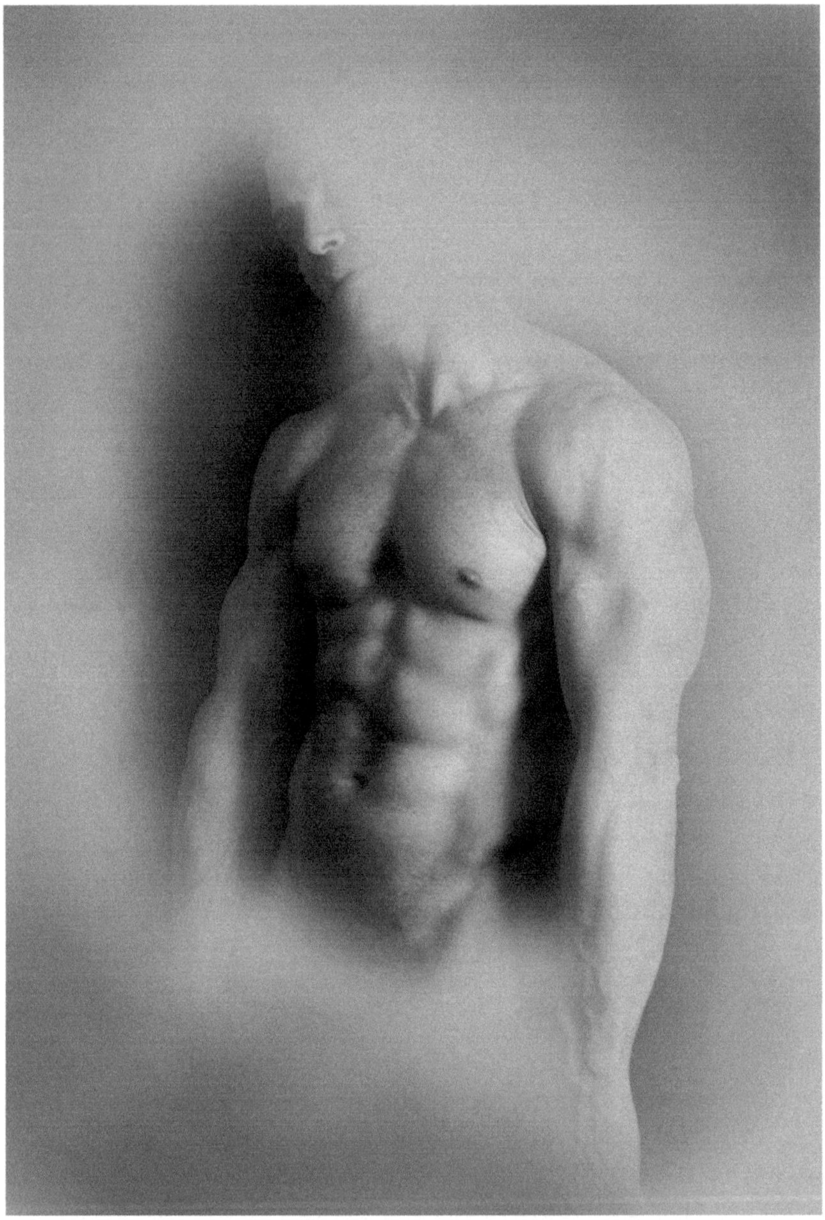

Top: "Myth" © Mayumi Yoshimaru.

Facing: © Terry Donovan.

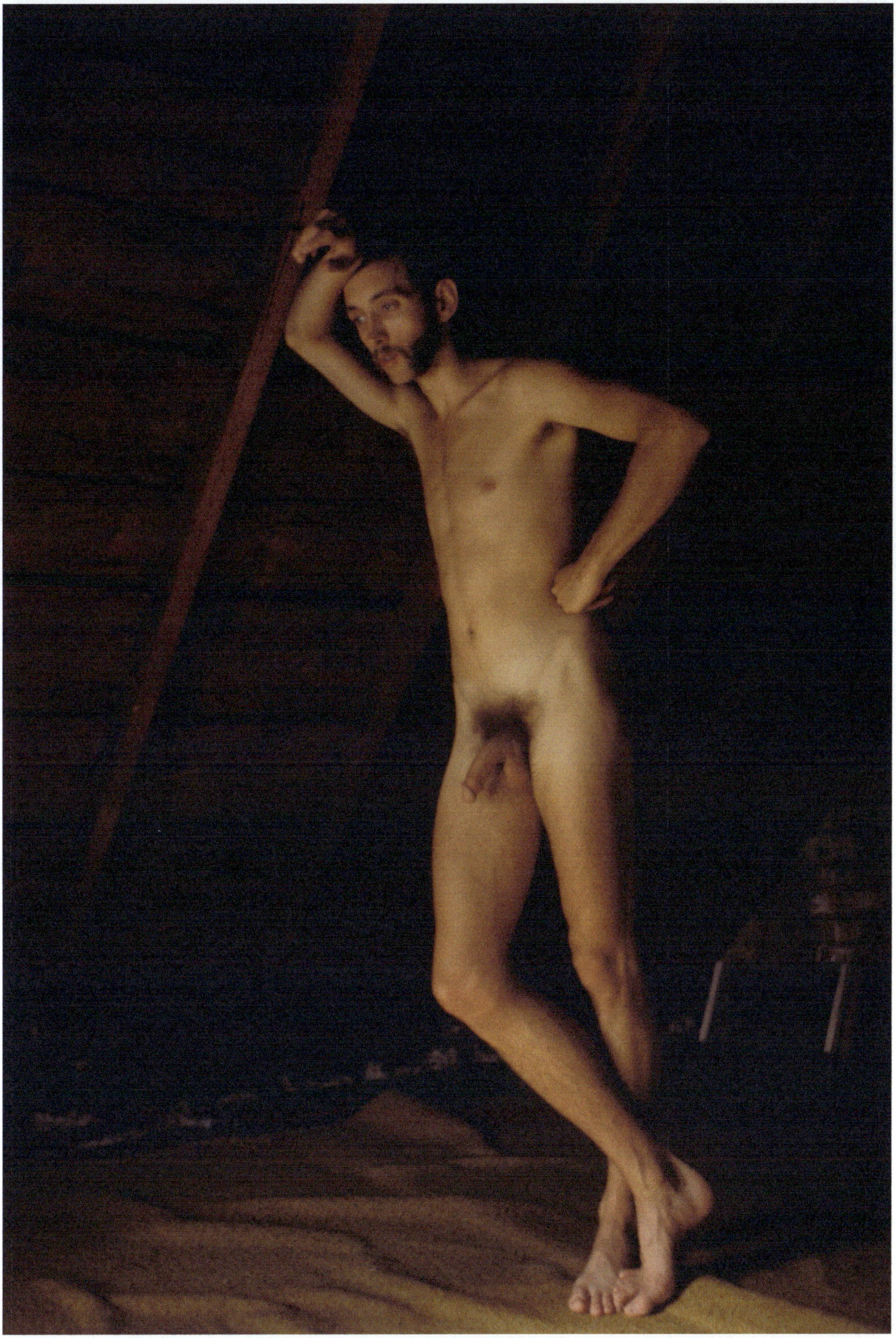

Interview with Osmyn J. Oree (osmynjoree.com)

Osmyn J. Oree photographs both men and women and is particularly interested in portraying people in ways that transcend the usual conventions of photographic nudes. His experience photographing men suggests that even potential models have a degree of resistance to portraying male nudity.

The biography on your website states that it is important to you to "represent the human body (male or female), in a tasteful, yet thought-provoking way." What do you want to provoke people to think about?

- With my work, I want people to look past the naked body and see the people in my photographs as just that, people. The body is often depicted as a sexual object or something directly related to sex and I don't want that in my photographs. My goal is to make work that is geared towards making the nudity or nakedness of my subjects seem commonplace and challenge why nudity might inspire aversion or fear.

What would you say are the differences between clothed and nude portraits?

- Nudity is vulnerability, but not the same kind of vulnerability as nakedness. Nudity implies that the subject is an active participant in the project, while nakedness implies a sort of breach of privacy. You're putting yourself out there for all to see. When you are clothed you are wearing a sort of protection and are more comfortable being that way. I think that clothed portraits can be just as interesting as nude portraits. I don't think there is a difference other than the feeling an image may give the viewer. People are more accepting of clothed portraits of course, but nude portraits seem to catch the eye more quickly.

When shooting nudes, are there differences between working with male and female subjects, either in terms of the interaction, or in terms of technical issues such as lighting?

- Males are more difficult hands down. The *Exposed* project is a good example of that. I was dealing with my own personal issues when I started that project, and I still deal with them now. At first, looking at the male body for a long period of time was difficult. That made it difficult to shoot and edit that project, and just spend time with these images. It was something different for me and a challenge. I have gotten a lot better at dealing with the nudity nowadays. The men are sometimes not as comfortable to start off with, and seem stiff. Sometimes it take a little while for things to get going and get the poses I want out of the males. On top of that, it's just harder to find males that are comfortable being naked in general. I sometimes run into those difficulties with females, but not as much. First-time models need time to get into the shoot, but after a while they are really comfortable and end up enjoying themselves.

What standard of taste are you referencing?

- My standards for photography have always been high, but even more so when it comes to nude photography. When I first started shooting nude photographs, I would always base my shots off of photographers I saw on the internet or local photographers in my hometown. As I grew and developed my style, I started to differentiate and think about what I thought was good or bad nude photography. A lot of what I saw when I first started was all about the body being sexy and attractive. The photographs that I was admiring were portraying the body in a highly sexual, objectified manner. I only found them to be good because the women in the photographs looked good. I began to realize that definitely wasn't what I wanted in my work. That's what I mean by taste: differentiating between objectification and intimacy. I think that as the photographer, I have a responsibility to be respectful and show my sitters as people and not just naked body-like objects in an environment. It is also worth mentioning that a lot of the people I photograph are friends, so I don't ever want them to be seen as sexual objects for a stranger's consumption.

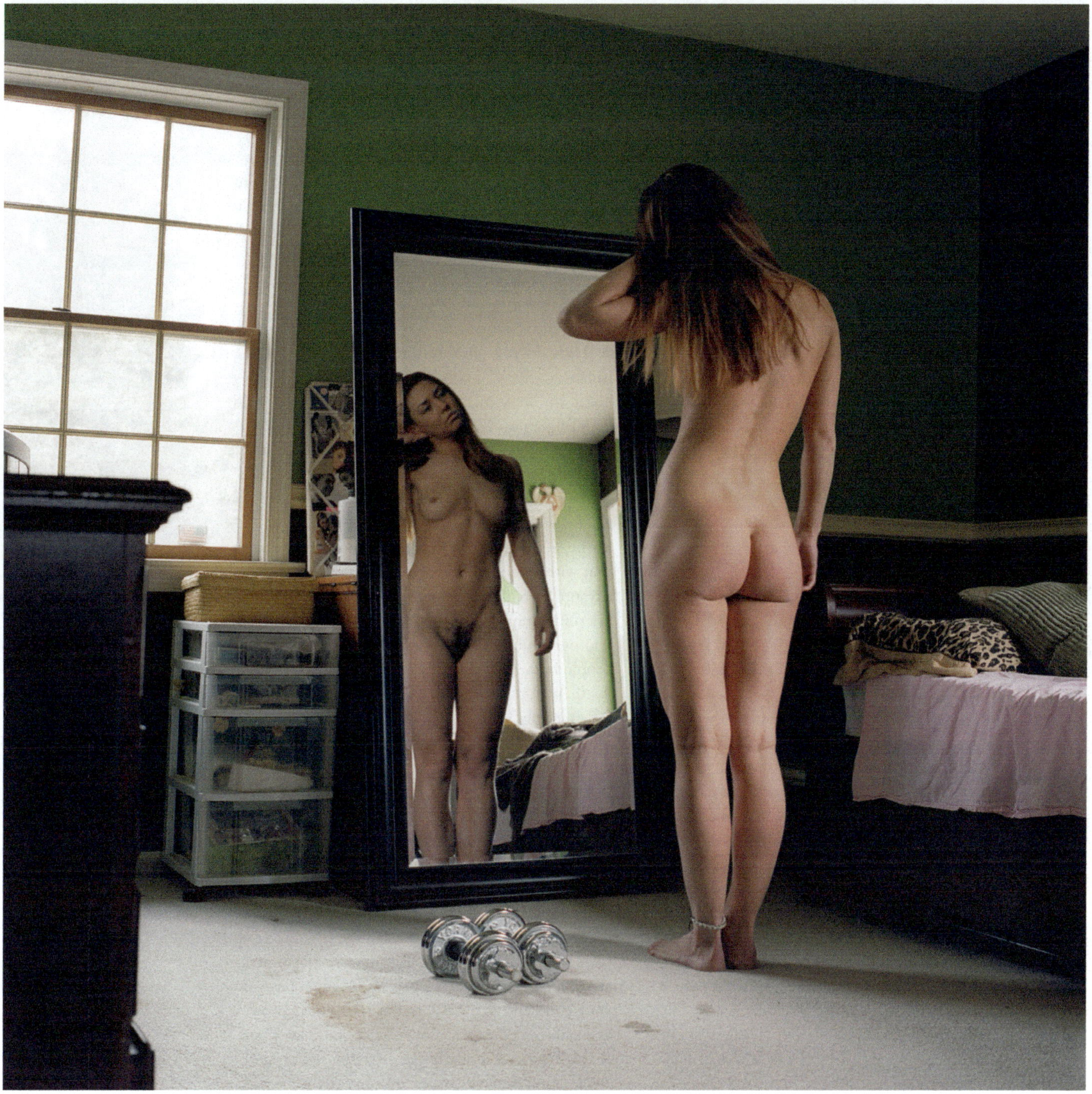

© Osmyn J. Oree.

The phrase "tasteful, yet thought-provoking" seems to suggest that tastefulness makes it harder to be thought-provoking.

▸ I don't think that tastefulness makes it harder for images to be thought-provoking at all. Sometimes I think the nude body is used in imagery just to draw people into the photo itself and that's it. I think tasteful images can be done without the shock value of women or men selling their naked bodies. You can present someone with an image of the naked body that can make them think critically and create a story around what they're seeing. There's this idea that just because clothes are absent, the image is intended solely to gratify the viewer, and I think that's why so much of nude photography is distasteful imagery of people as objects. That just makes it much harder to grab the attention of an audience that's used to seeing highly sexualized imagery and has those kinds of expectations in viewing nudes in general.

Does the conservative community in which you live and work further constrain what is meant by "tasteful"?

▸ I don't think that it constrains what I mean by tasteful, but I do feel that the community of photographers that I am surrounded by don't exactly present Lancaster's art community with the best examples of tasteful nude photography. Nudes in general are sort of looked down upon unless they are paintings, and even then they are difficult to show in town. Add to that the fact that most of the nude photography is ironically super-sexual and outdated. It's as if everyone around town takes something from everyone else and they all end up creating the same imagery. It's sometimes hard to tell whose work is whose. Another thing worth mentioning is that some of the main galleries in town, where most of the art is hung, don't really make an effort to put nude images on their walls. It's a conservative town, and they stick to their guns when it comes to what they want and don't want in galleries. It's hard enough getting photography in most galleries. Needless to say it's harder to get my work into galleries where people can see it.

You made five 32 x 40-inch prints for shows in Los Angeles. How important is scale in your work?

▸ I like to print things big. Ever since my senior show in 2011, I always wanted to print things as big as possible. I live in a town where people usually shy away from the nude body. I had to figure out how to present my images to people who wouldn't want to look, so I made them big. In particular, I wanted to make male images as large as possible, due to the fact that people aren't used to seeing the male form in that way, if at all.

Environment is central to much of your work. How do you go about selecting locations?

▸ Locations are something I always have an issue with. Shooting around Lancaster is always possible, but I've had my fair share of close calls shooting outside. The location usually depends on weather and the seasons. In the winter, I shoot indoors a lot, but have to deal with bad lighting due to the gloomy days. In the summer, I shoot more outdoors, but have to deal with the blistering heat. They both have their advantages and disadvantages. The locations I use for my photographs are ideally where the people I am photographing live. I try and photograph in a space people know to make the shoot enjoyable and easy for them. I don't have a studio or designated space for shooting, so it's really all I have. It also becomes more of a portrait of objects in the frame that are intimate and relevant to the subject.

Do you have any advice for photographers who are interested in shooting nudes?

▸ Use your friends first! It's the easiest and most comfortable place for someone to start, and it's always fun. When I first started, I had no idea what I was doing, but I pushed and just kept getting better and better. Don't doubt yourself if photographs don't always come out the way you want. You'll have your good and bad days, but at least you're growing as a photographer and doing what you love. Look at artists that you like to get a starting point, and always look at what others are currently doing. Also, read and engage other artists and critics. It's important to know your history, be it the nude, or gender, or still lives. Reading about and listening to different perspectives only helps your work. Shoot, shoot, and shoot some more. You can never shoot enough if you are passionate about something and you want to get better.

How do you go about finding subjects to work with?

▶ Friends are the best models. I would say almost 100 percent of the people I work with are friends, or friends of friends. I don't have money to pay people, so I use those around me that are comfortable and willing. Money can also influence how a shoot will go and I don't like that. I don't like the pressure of knowing I'm paying for someone to do a job like this if I'm trying to honestly portray this person in a vulnerable state. People contact me as well to be photographed because they like my work, and I am always open to meeting new people and making more photographs. Social media plays a huge role in finding people as well, but it's not as effective as using people you know to start with. Two problems I do encounter, though, are finding people of color and finding men who are willing. It's understandable why certain people don't come forward, but I do find it somewhat surprising that more females are willing to step forward than males.

Both your *Honesty* and *Exposed* series seem to be about going against type to a certain degree. Are there specific things you do (or ask your sitters to do) to avoid fetishizing female bodies or in portraying men as vulnerable and sensitive? What sort of responses have you encountered to your portrayals of men?

▶ A lot of times with the female nudes, the poses are just things that my friends do when they are sitting and waiting for me to get ready. I usually have a starting point and an idea I want to go with, but most of the time the photographs come from natural movement and coincidence. I try not to have much posing or any kind of planned gestures in my photographs because I think it gives the images a more natural and calm feel. With the male images, it is sort of the opposite. I want the men to be completely open and exposed and almost always looking at the camera. That project is about confrontation, and that's what I want in the poses of the men. I also try and pose the men in ways that you wouldn't normally see men in, to switch things up and create a better image.

What sort of interaction do you have with your sitters during a shoot? Do you give a lot of direction?

▶ Most of the posing and interaction happens by chance. I do compose the space, and am always thinking of composition when I'm with my subjects. I tend to wait for something interesting to happen that activates the space or frame and go from there. I'll make very small changes to hand or legs in photographs but most of it just comes from the person. I only really give direction when I want something very specific, but that usually ends with me scrapping the idea and going in a completely different direction. Also, I want to keep the shoot as comfortable as possible, so I try to give a small amount of direction to start and then let the person just do what they feel is comfortable.

Your photography was featured prominently in two juried exhibitions at the 1650 Gallery in Los Angeles, including the cover of the catalog for their 2011 show *Exposed*. How did that come about and what was your experience of working with the gallery?

▶ It might have been a friend who mentioned the call for entries to me. I just went for it and ended up getting in. It was a shock to get that cover, and it is still a surprise that my photo was on the front of the catalog. It was a huge accomplishment for me. Working with the gallery had its hiccups. Getting my work there was the hardest part, because the pieces were so big. There was also an issue with the people that dropped off my work. It was a big deal, but in the end the problem was fixed and everything worked out.

You've had several exhibitions since 2009, many of them in other states. How do you go about getting your work shown?

▶ It's a combination of meeting people and just submitting work to contests and galleries. I am a very sociable person and love meeting new people. I use that to surround myself with people that want to show my work. My first solo exhibition actually came from a photo-shoot I did with a fellow artist. When this person happened to come upon a gallery space and wanted another artist to show their work, I was her first choice. A lot of the exposure I've gotten has been a snowball effect from people seeing my work online and emailing me, along with doing small local shows where I can.

Interview with Ned and Aya Rosen (nedandayaerotic.com)

Honesty is a central concern in the work of husband-and-wife team Ned and Aya Rosen. They live together, work together, and spend almost all of their time together. Their work and life is an ongoing conversation about who they are as a couple, as a team, and as individuals. They feel they balance out very well. Aya's paintings are incredibly complex and rich with many levels, while Ned's photography has always been very minimalist.

"I think that because we each have such respect for each other's process, we maintain a trust that I have never felt towards another artist," says Ned. "We can hear each other without feeling criticized, and we both make room for each other in the work." Aya tends to take the lead in prep, and Ned holds the camera which is tethered to their computer, so that the two can be in communication about what is being shot. Ned adds that, "Aya is an amazing editor, and I am an amazing retoucher."

How would you describe the work that you do, and how much of that work is personal?

▶ For the past three years we have been focusing most of our energy on building our client base in fashion. But we do find it so important for us to shoot personal work to keep exploring ourselves.

Do you separate your commercial and art projects (do you even distinguish between the two), or do they all happen together?

▶ When we shoot commercial projects, we are hired usually by a fashion brand. The process of producing and determining the style of the shoot comes from our dialog with the client. We do maintain a cohesive "Ned and Aya" style, but our main goal is to supply our client with an effective tool for showing and selling their collection. Our personal work is about exploring something within ourselves and having a dialogue with each other and our model. The goal is to express our own feelings and thoughts. Fashion

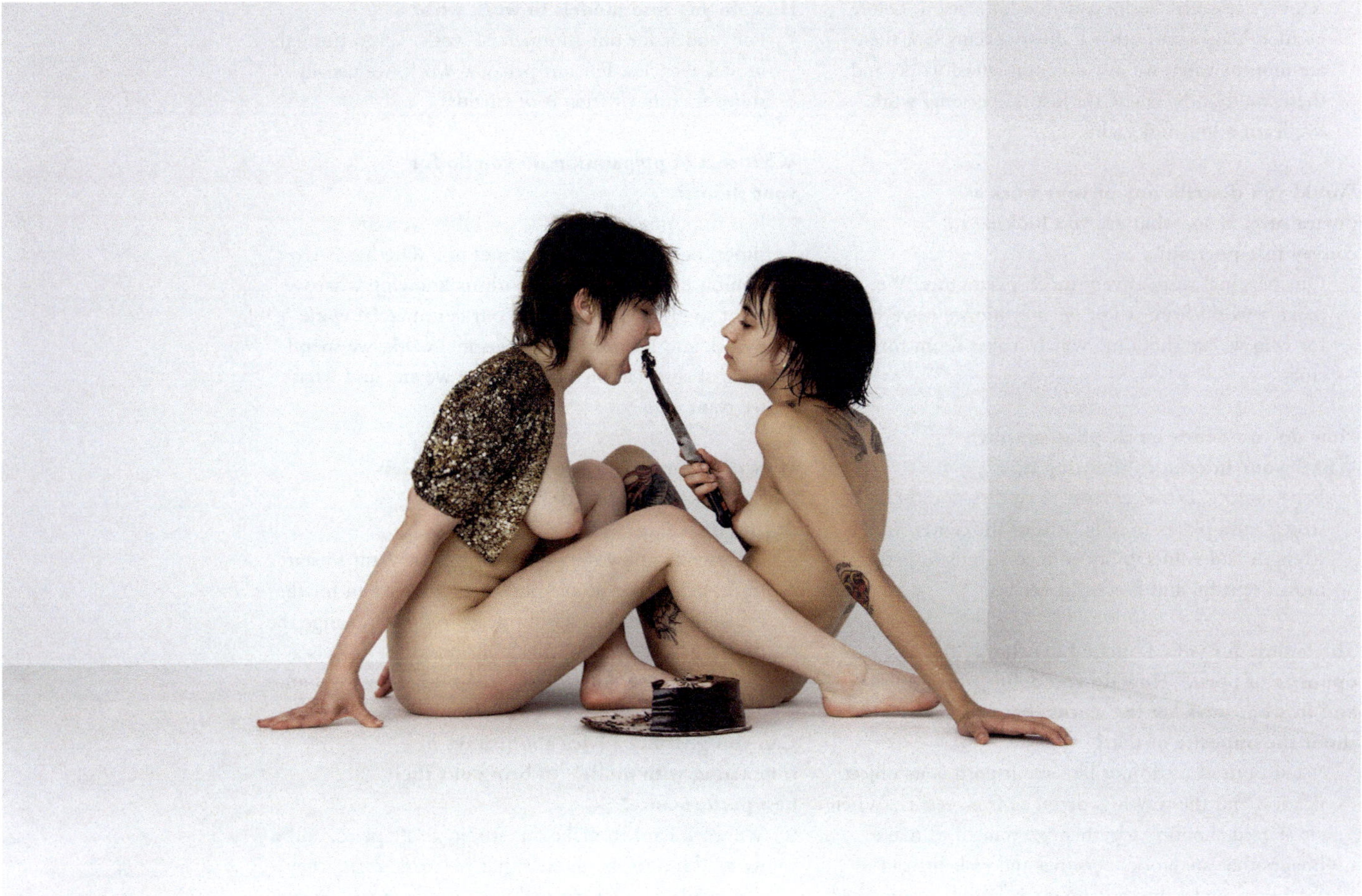

"Death by Chocolate" © Ned and Aya Rosen.

is a very seasonal business with a lot of work before Fashion Weeks and other industry events. So, there are months when we just do commercial work, and there are months where we just do personal work. We learn a lot from each.

Would you describe any of your work as portraiture? If so, what are you looking to convey in a portrait?

- Our personal work is very much portraiture. We make a world from where we are, and we leave space for who we are shooting, which makes room for their story.

How do you define erotic photography? What's your interest in shooting it?

- For us, erotic is the removal of clothes, social constructs, and places to hide. It is of the center, where strength and vulnerability connect. To us, it is the most beautiful and honest place.

The tagline for your Louche Lust site is "the opposite of porn." How do you define porn, and in what ways are the works that you shoot the opposite of that?

- What both of us do not like about porn is its objectification and the way it is divorced from reality. When we started shooting together, we wanted to make images that are erotic, personal and real. Instead of forcing a model into a defined sexual role, we wanted to create an emotional landscape for honest feelings and actions.

Sexuality and shame seem to be central to your work. Can you say more about that?

- When we met, we were each working on dealing with shame, in our work and in our personal lives. Both of us, at our core, are very lonely people who just want to feel connected and loved. Before we met, we each were exploring the idea of shame and fear, behind what keeps us all feeling separate. We each came to the decision to live our lives as honestly and openly as we can. We find it empowering to explore shame and sexuality openly and honestly in our work.

How do you find models to work with?

- For models for our commercial work, we go through model agencies. For our personal work, we usually shoot friends, or friends of friends.

What sort of preparation do you do for your shoots?

- It is important for us to know what we want to shoot, before the camera comes up. Whether it is fashion or erotic, it starts with us knowing what we want to say or to show. For our commercial work, we ask and listen. For our personal work, we spend a lot of time talking about where we are, and what we want.

How collaborative are you with the models and what kind of direction do you give during the shoot?

- We usually know the direction that we want to start from, before the shoot. But as we leave room for the model in the shoot, we also leave room to change the direction as we're shooting. Our personal work is a process and we don't always know where it will end.

Can you give any advice about ways of interacting with models to bring out their best performance?

- We work hard to make our studio a safe place, and we are kind to the models that we work with. They are people who we are making a project with. Everyone wants to do the best that they can. The more clear direction that we can give, the easier it is for the model to know what we want.

You seem to have a broad presence on the Web, with Tumblr and Pinterest bogs, a Twitter feed, two Facebook accounts, profiles on Model Mayhem and LinkedIn, Ned&Aya Erotic, Louche Lab, and Louche Lust to name a few. And you seem to keep them all up to date. Can you say a little about your strategy in creating and maintaining those presences?

- We met a little over nine years ago, and we each had a strong web presence. When we started shooting together, we wanted to have a website or a blog for the work that we did together. At the time, there weren't many options so we decided to learn html so we could design our own site. We got carried away and made a few. We used to have a few other sites, but after a while, they just seemed irrelevant to what we are working on now, so we just let them go. We try to keep everything up to date, though we are a few weeks/months behind. There isn't a lot of overlap, personal work goes on our erotic site, motion goes on Louche Lust, and commercial work goes on the Ned and Aya site.

Some of your nudes have been featured on television. How did that come about?

▶ It was really cool! The director needed a picture for a billboard in the background for the opening scene. It needed to be fashion, but looking a little nude, and it had to be able to pass the network's Standards and Practices. He saw our erotic site and got in touch with us. It went very well. We went on to work with him and a few other TV directors in the past few years.

Web Resources

1650 Gallery, Los Angeles—1650gallery.com
1650 Gallery, *Exposed* 2011—http://bit.ly/1CzY8xs
Nobuyoshi Araki—www.artuner.com/artists/nobuyoshi-araki/
Bruce of Los Angeles (Bruce Bellas)—www.bigkugels.com/content/Bruce.html
Andreas Bitesnich—www.bitesnich.com/gallery/
Cycladic idol—www.ancient.eu/article/457/
Daniel Edwards—http://nyti.ms/1y4YwZC
Calvin Klein Underwear—http://bit.ly/1Inn8jJ
Sally Mann—sallymann.com
Robert Mapplethorpe—www.mapplethorpe.org/portfolios/
Jill Masterson, *Goldfinger*—http://bit.ly/1Of7DuB
Amedeo Modigliani—http://bit.ly/19PnWza
Mystique, *X-Men*—http://bit.ly/SDjfjz
Helmut Newton—www.artnet.com/artists/helmut-newton/
Paul Outerbridge—http://visualmelt.com/Paul-Outerbridge
Terry Richardson—http://nyti.ms/1GNeFEg
Herb Ritts—ww.artnet.com/artists/herb-ritts/
Egon Schiele—http://bit.ly/1GlLwQl
Andres Serrano—www.artnet.com/artists/andres-serrano/
Kishin Shinoyama—http://gadaboutmag.com/interview-kishin-shinoyama/
Aaron Siskind—www.artnet.com/artists/aaron-siskind/
Jock Sturges—http://bit.ly/1Nge2c0
Spencer Tunick—spencertunick.com
Bruce Weber—bruceweber.com
Edward Weston—http://bit.ly/1bSPF3e
Francesca Woodman—www.artnet.com/artists/francesca-woodman/

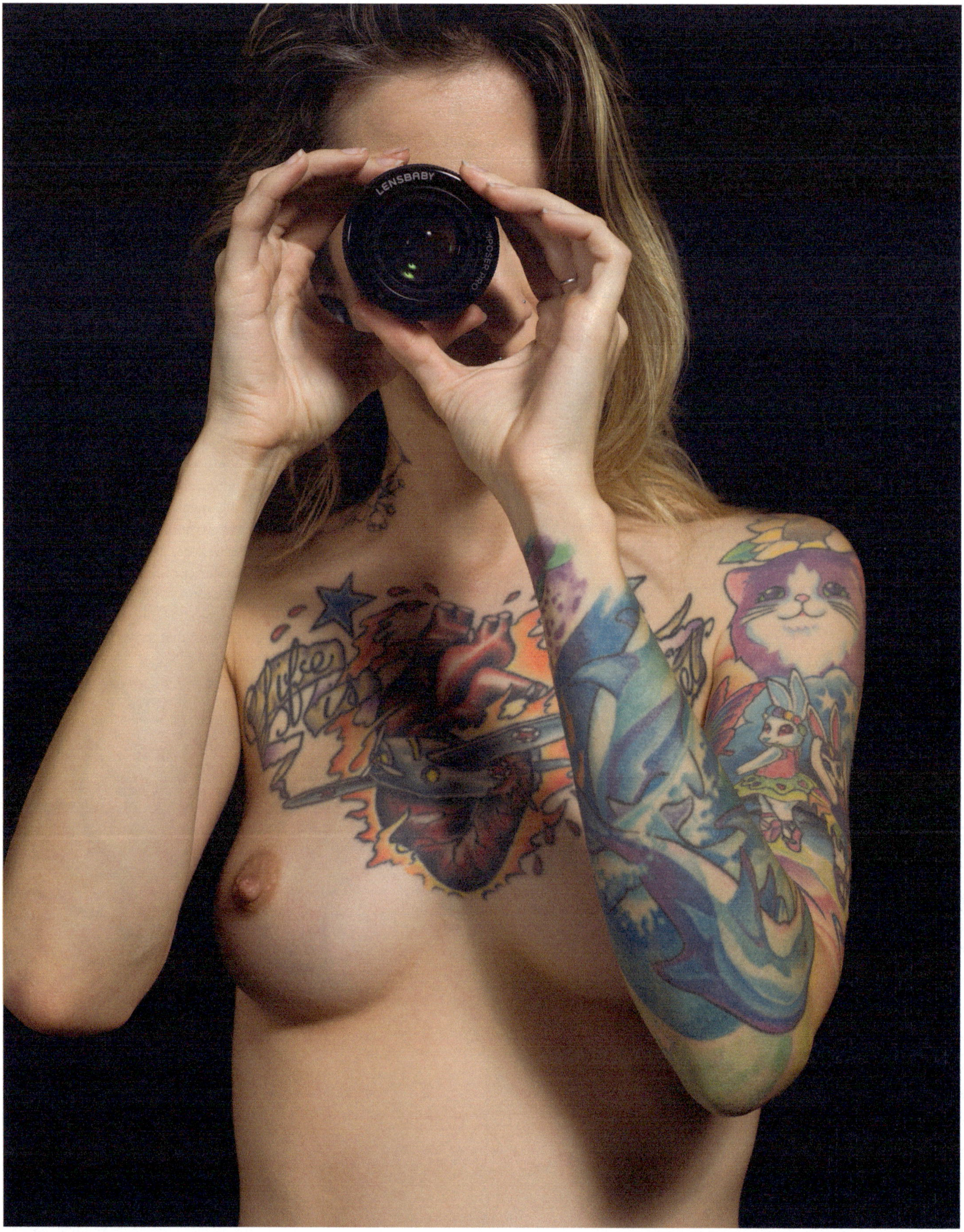
LENSBABY

Chapter Five | The Camera vs. the Eye

"The camera is something of a nuisance in a way. It's recalcitrant. It's determined to do one thing, and you may want to do something else. You have to fuse what you want and what the camera wants."
Diane Arbus

JUST AS the invention of resealable oil paint tubes made "plein air" and impressionist painting possible, choices such as camera, lens, film vs. digital vs. alternative process, color, or black and white fundamentally shape the type of images you can make. Artists often choose between digital, film, and alternative processes specifically because of differences in aesthetic qualities as well as the manner of working with the materials. For certain applications and ways of working, a specific type of camera can make a huge difference, but for the rest of us the way you use the camera matters far more than which camera you use.

The Camera Is Not an Eye

The camera has often been viewed as a stand-in for the human eye and as a validation of single-point perspective. Neither view is really accurate. Two initial differences between the camera and the eye are that the camera's dynamic range is more limited than that of the eye, and unlike the eye, most lenses are sharp across the entire image plane. Still, thinking about these factoids opens the door to a more artistic

Facing: © Lou Benjamin. Theresa Manchester with a Lensbaby.

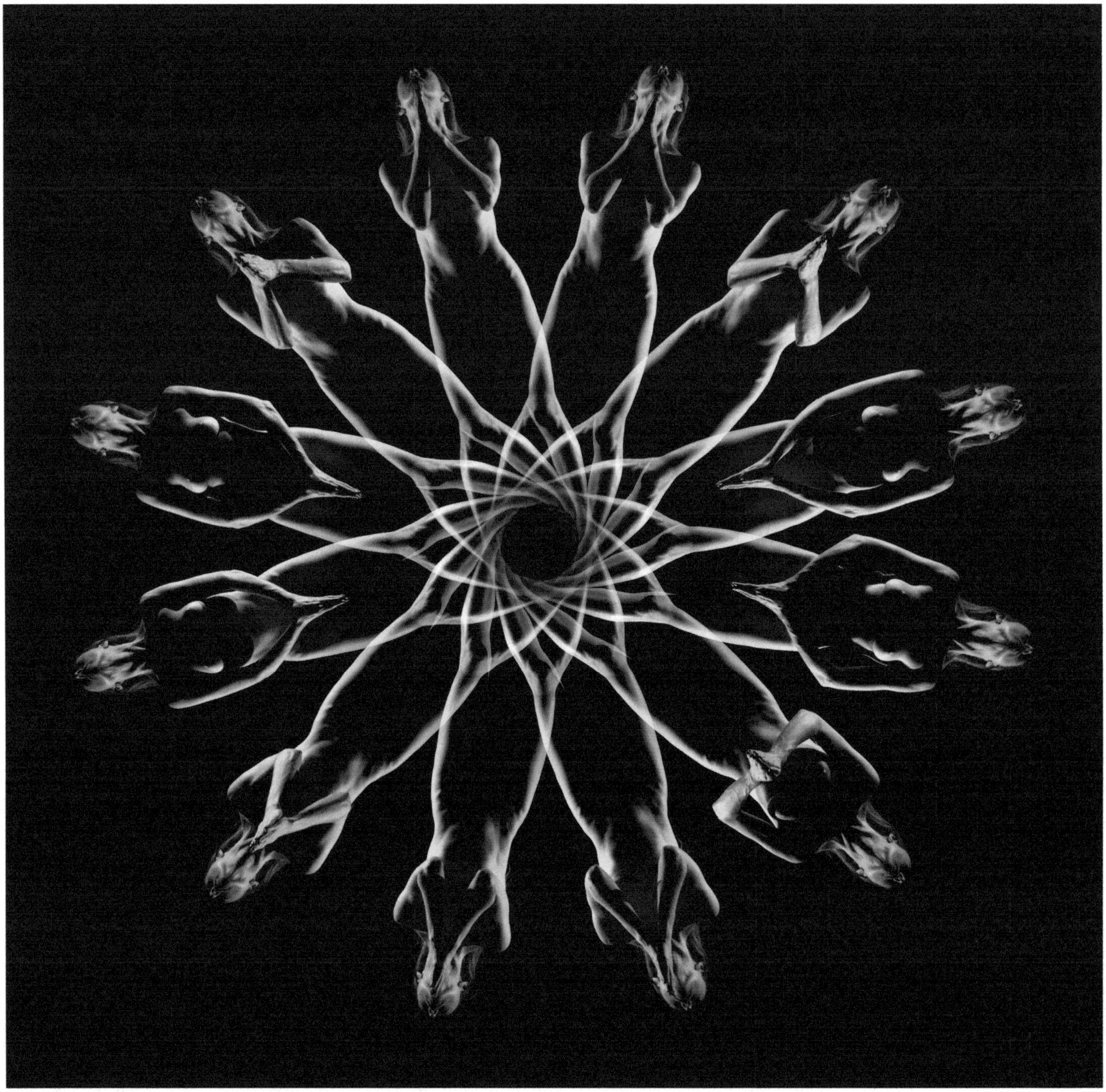

Above: © P. J. Reptilehouse. Look closely, and you'll notice that the model is not simply rotated around the frame, but that her hands change position. To produce often kaleidoscopic imagery in-camera (this is not a post-production effect), the artist takes advantage of long exposures coupled with computer-controlled LED strobes and computer-controlled camera movement. He often choreographs the model's movement to interact with the motion of the camera. The result is an uncommon image and a unique experience for the model.

Facing: © Harvey Stein. Black and white infrared film.

"When I began to photograph nudes, I let myself be guided by this camera, and instead of photographing what I saw, I photographed what the camera was seeing. I interfered very little and the lens produced anatomical images and shapes which my eyes had never observed."

Bill Brandt

relationship with the camera by consciously manipulating and exploiting the differences between the ways the camera and the eye sees. Despite all of the discussion of creative image creation that involves Photoshop and post-production, there is much that can be done better in-camera.

The ease of use and responsiveness of the camera can impact the flow of the shoot. Regardless of the camera you have, one key to making better photos is to learn the essential controls so that it effectively vanishes as much as possible. That way, you can focus on your subject and the image you want to make, rather than the process of making it. If you are looking to upgrade your camera skills, it's a good idea to prioritize the features of interest and learn how they work one at a time. If you've always used program mode, learn to use manual mode. Play with over- and under-exposing images to understand how the camera sees and how exposure relates to expression.

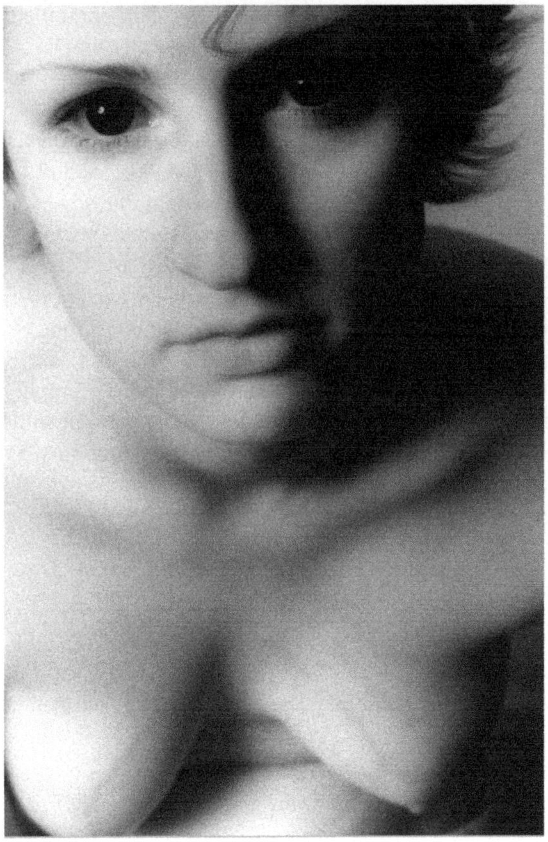

Black and White vs. Color

The decision to render a photo in black and white rather than color profoundly affects how the photo will be perceived. Certain compositions will be made substantially stronger by being rendered in black and white, without the confusion of color. On the other hand, there are photos that only work in color.

We literally see black and white photos differently from color photos because we process them with different parts of our brains. Carrie Leigh, former *Playboy* playmate and publisher of *NUDE* magazine, has gone so far as to say that fine art is in black and white, while porn is in color.

Neurologically, the visual system that we use to sense texture, form, and location functions in black and white, while the system that we use to identify things works in color. Consider how similar apricots, plums, and peaches are in appearance, and then think about how much harder it would be to tell them apart in black and white, with no scale of reference. Because black and white photography reinterprets colors as shades of gray, a fundamental transformation occurs, opening the door for a wide variety of expressive interpretations. Typically, none of those interpretations would be considered incorrect, where color that is "wrong" is quickly spotted.

Strong contrast with deep, black shadows can convey a sense of drama in black and white imagery, but absent facial cues or body language, black and white cannot convey emotional content the way that color can. We relate to black and white imagery in a more abstract way and respond to it in much the same way as pencil drawings, while we relate to color photos in a manner similar to paintings. Toned monochrome images are often thought of as black and white, but they are actually color images. Simply adding a warm toning effect (e.g. sepia) to black and white images can add an emotional overtone, such as nostalgia, to a photo.

Film vs. Digital

There is a quantitative difference between digital and film because the costs of shooting are no longer directly linked to the number of frames you shoot. The capacity and reusability of memory cards allow for prolific shooting. That can be a blessing and a curse. There is no longer anything at stake when you squeeze the shutter, so it's easy to be careless and waste frames. However, the immediate feedback of digital also takes at least some of the mystery out of whether you're anywhere close to the image you might have pre-visualized.

There is also a qualitative difference. Film and digital sensors respond to light, particularly in the highlights—those tones that are extremely bright, but not yet pure white—very differently. As the intensity of exposure gets closer and closer to the point of saturation (pure white), film becomes progressively less responsive—it becomes non-linear. A digital sensor responds to light in a completely linear fashion, matching the intensity of the exposure 1:1 right up to the point where it blows out. As a result, the highlights in film imagery are often described as being more "creamy" than the highlights in digital and the natural tonal compression of the highlights in film tends to retain more details than digital.

Another difference is that digital can typically produce more highly saturated color than film, and the color can be far more accurate than the result with film. However, digital color can be almost clinical and those saturation levels are often viewed as hyper-real when compared to film and print—the standard that we're used to. Film's color response has also been tweaked to look its best in the areas of "memory colors" such as skin tones. Even if the colors are not an accurate match to what was shot, it looks right. The majority of photographers working with film shoot positive transparencies. Negative film has wider latitude than slide film, but it's also much harder to get the color right if you're relying on a lab.

Facing: © Alan Fresco. Shot with a digital camera modified to respond to IR and visible light, 14mm F3.5 lens. 1/100 sec at f/9; ISO 1250.

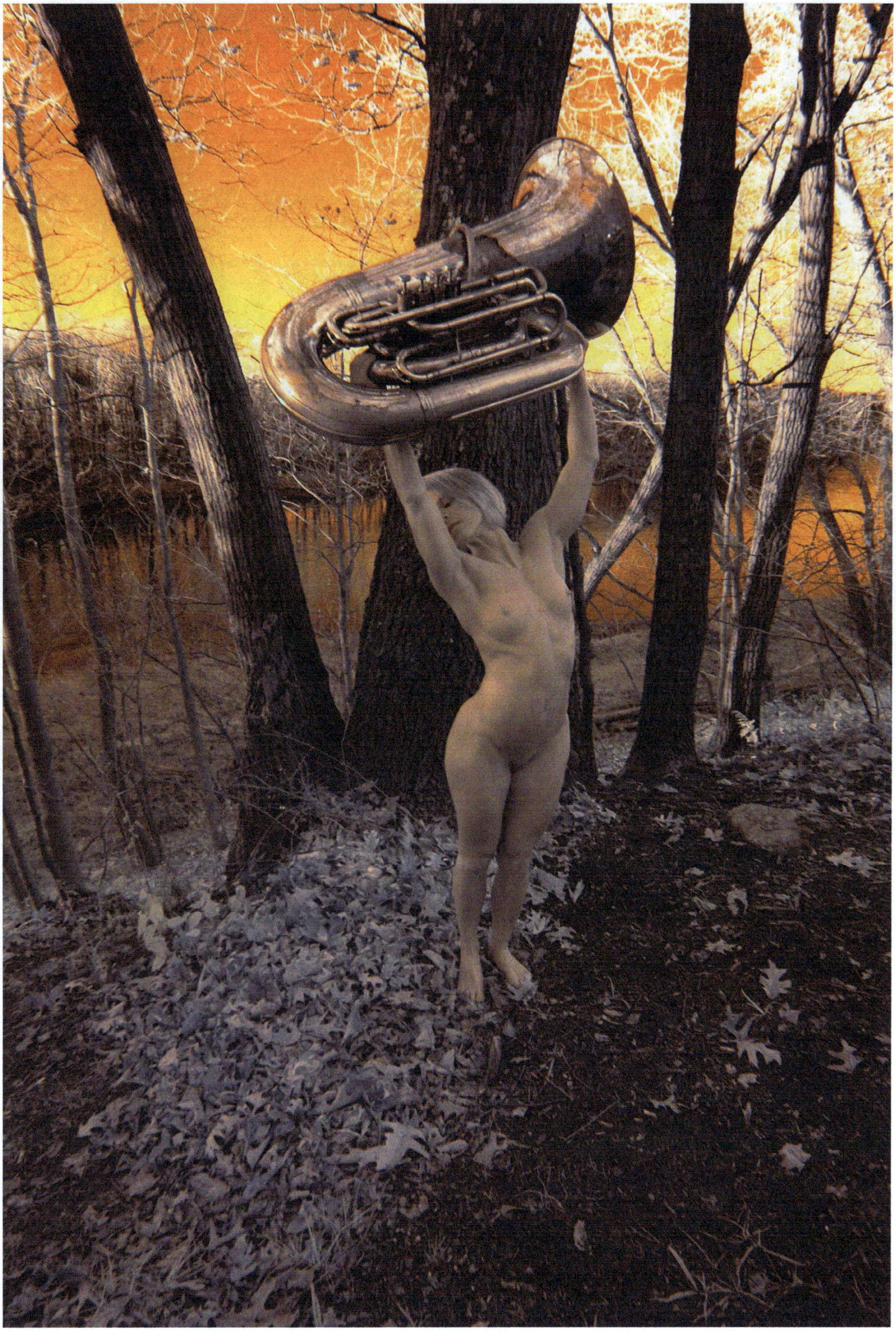

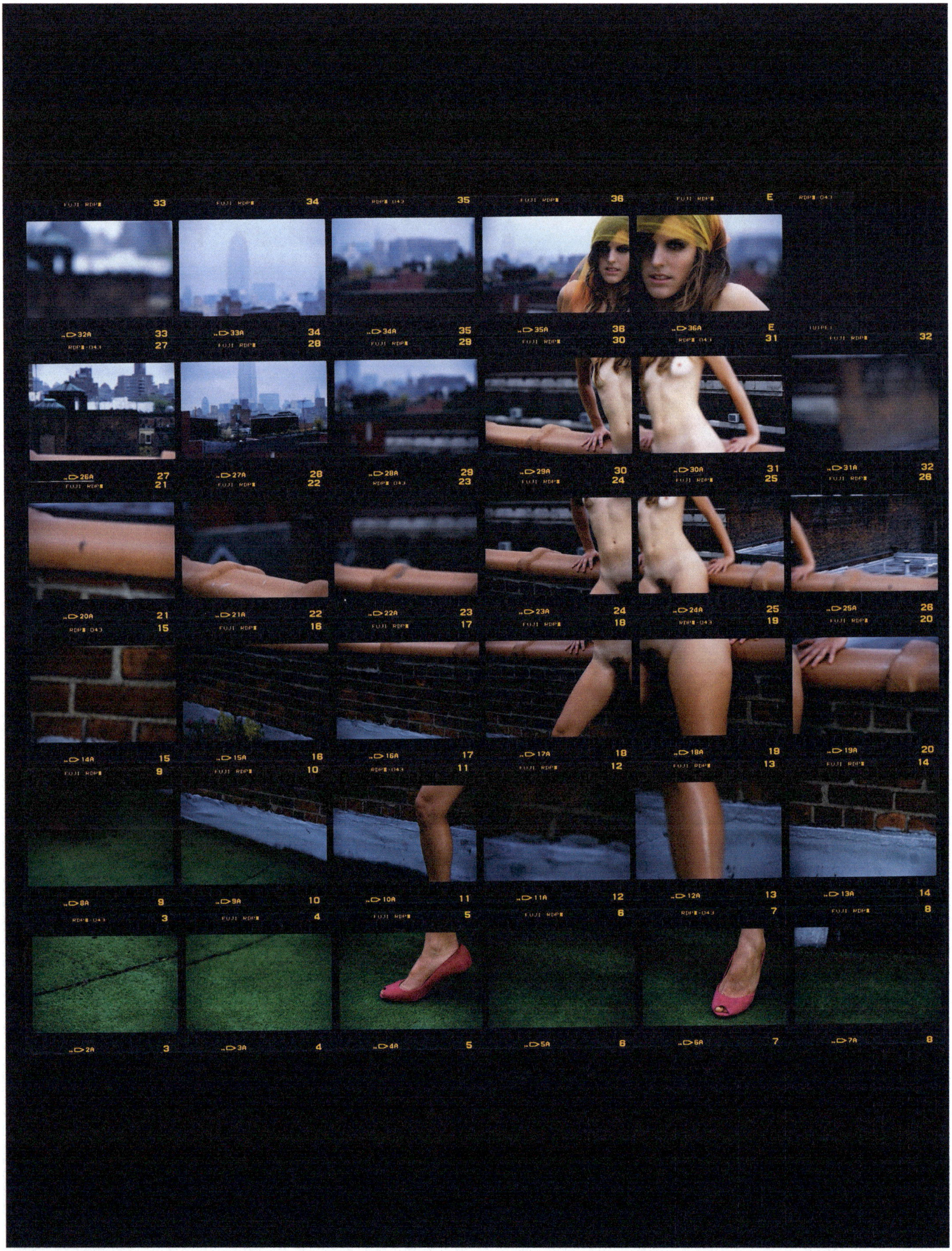

While film shooters often select film with a sensitivity between ISO 50 and 400, many dSLR shooters have a minimum ISO of 100 to 200 and can easily work with ISOs of 800 or faster. That means you don't need the fastest lens on the market and can shoot with a smaller aperture, a faster shutter speed, or a combination of both. High ISO sensitivity also offers new opportunities for working in low light.

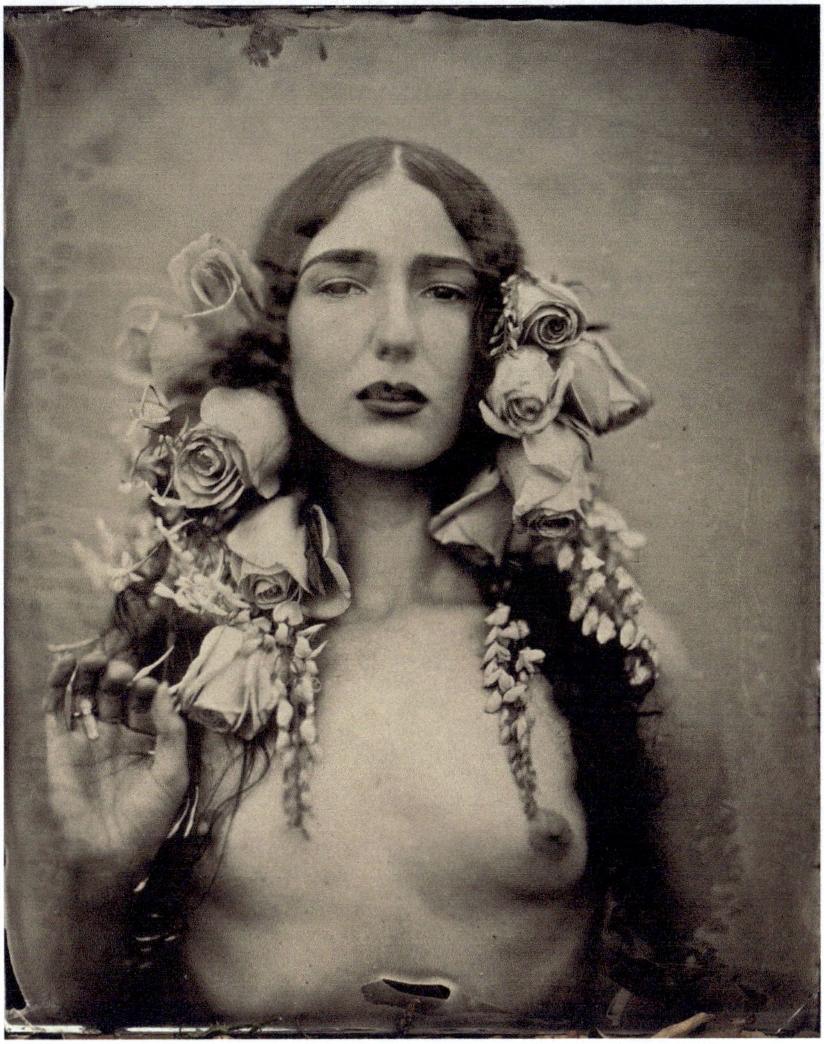

Historical processes

Many art photographers say they choose to shoot with vintage large-format cameras or reproductions because the format forces them to slow down their process. A number of them shoot tintypes or Ambrotypes (also known as collodion or wet plate, a process dating back to the late nineteenth century) and also use vintage lenses dating from the same time period. The nature and expense of operation of those cameras demands a careful, thoughtful approach.

With the Collodion process, each image is a unique positive, which makes it more valuable as an art object. To reproduce these images, you need to scan them and make a digital print. Collodion is only sensitive to blue light, which means that certain colors do not register at all, giving it a distinctive aesthetic quality. The long exposures needed for the early photographic processes also affected the behavior of the sitters: photographers would tell the sitters not to smile, because it made them look like corpses, and of course they had to remain very still.

When your sitter is aware that you're using a special camera, they're likely to relate to you in a different way, and that will come across in your photos. Timothy Greenfield-Sanders, who did the book *XXX: 30 Porn Star Portraits*, uses a vintage 8 × 10 Deardorf view camera. The antique-looking plain wooden box, with a lens in the front and a bulb shutter release, is a very different animal from the present-day dSLR that most sitters are used to.

Now working with a digital camera, Stephen Shore continues to apply the lessons he learned over his years of shooting with an 8 x 10 camera: "I never bracket, and never take more than one picture of the same thing," he says (*Image Makers/Image Takers*, Anne-Celine Jaeger, Thames and Hudson, 2010, p. 51).

Facing: "Woman with Hairband" © Gaspar Marquez. Marquez creates these images in-camera, intuitively shooting frames of 35mm film. He then makes a contact print from the negatives and scans the print to apply post-production and create large-scale prints.

Above: © Ed Ross. Model: Neptunian Haze. Scanned 16 x 20 tintype. Ross shoots with a camera made by Chamonix, in China. The camera's designer is a professor of photography who also shoots wet plate in China. Ross also has an 8 x 10 camera by Black Art Cameras, Rochester, NY. His lenses include a massive Voigtlander #8 from 1884 and two brass barrel lenses—a Dallmeyer 3b and Ross Cabinet Lens #3, from the late nineteenth century.

Infrared

Infrared photography, both film and digital, radically changes the way the camera sees, and offers rich aesthetic opportunities. Rather than responding to visible light, infrared (IR) photography responds to wavelengths of radiant energy that are shorter than those of red light, which includes heat. In digital cameras, this is done by removing the filter that normally blocks IR from reaching the sensor. There are techniques in Photoshop, mainly centered around emphasizing the red channel content over others, that attempt to emulate the look of infrared, but they are not the same thing since they are still based on the visible spectrum at the end of the day.

The Sigma SD1 Merrill features a removable IR filter, making it extremely easy to use for IR photography. Fuji makes a hard-to-get IR camera with a license agreement that specifically prohibits "unethical photographic conduct" (e.g. photographing through people's clothes without their knowledge). Two companies offering to convert digital cameras for IR photography are kolarivision.com and lifepixel.com. See www.wrotniak.net/photo/infrared for an overview of the process and more links.

Gazing at Glass

A key element of many artistic photographs is a sense of atmosphere. Light, color, contrast, and sharpness or softness can all convey that sense, and those factors are all products of the lens. Imperfections in the lens can transform the image in ways that can be used to your artistic advantage. The lens also affects the rendering of space, essentially bending the lines that represent space onto the picture plane in different ways. The focal length of the lens is one measure of the degree to which lenses bend light.

Wide-angle images emphasize foreshortening, meaning that objects in the foreground appear large relative to objects in the background. If you shoot a picture of someone's face with a wide-angle lens, their nose is likely to dominate the frame while their ears look minuscule. Tilting a camera fitted with a wide-angle lens also exaggerates the proportions of people and things.

Telephoto lenses in the range of 85mm to 150mm are particularly useful for intimate portraiture, because they can bring you in close to the face without distorting it. Some have macro focusing capabilities that allow you to focus at an even closer distance. Telephoto lenses compress space, and minimize the effect of foreshortening—objects in the background can appear as large as objects in the foreground. This effect makes objects appear closer together and emphasizes patterns.

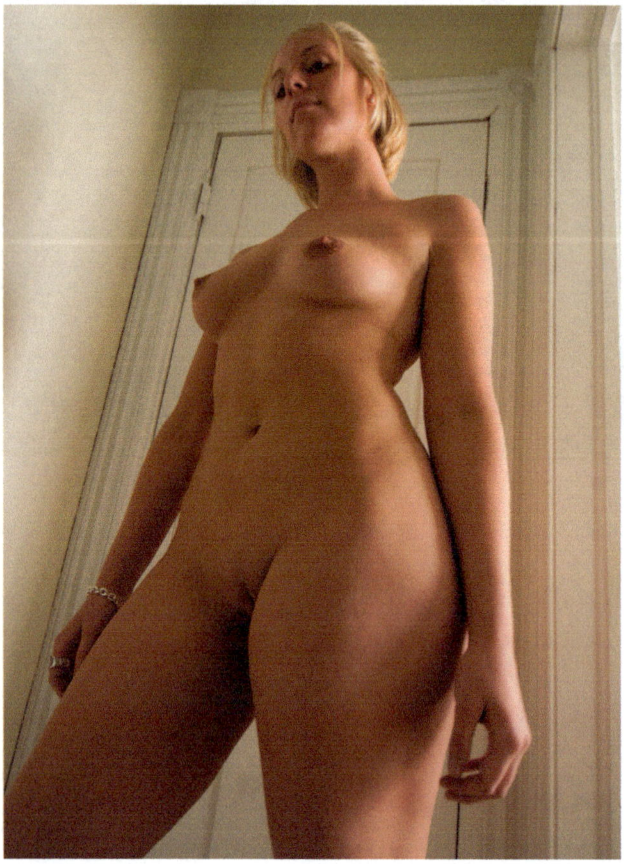

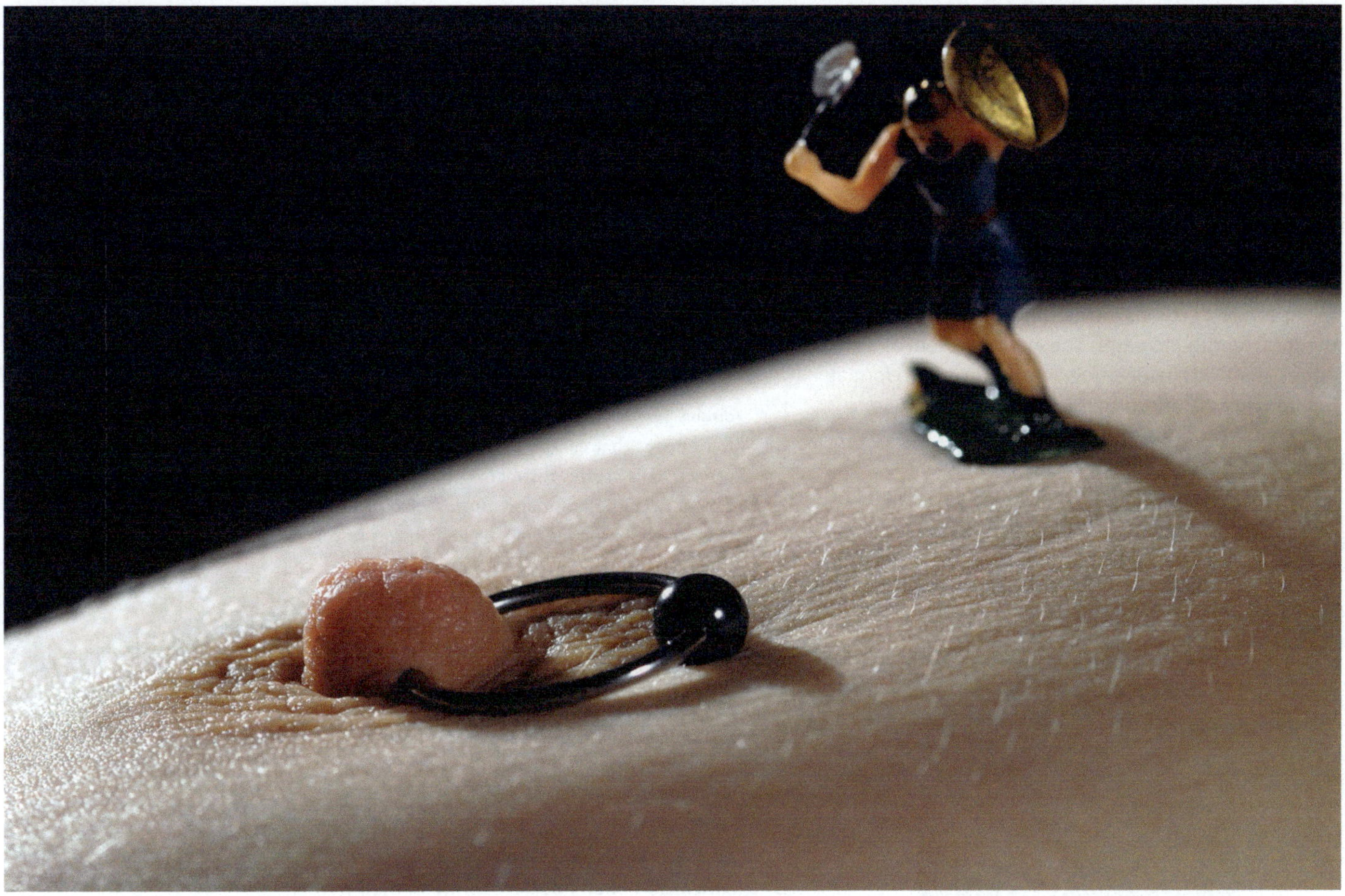

Facing: © Lou Benjamin. Model: Lauren Babree. The wide-angle lens exaggerates the keystone effect produced by the low angle, while the hips are emphasized by proximity to the lens. Shot with a Nikon D200 and Nikkor 12-24mm f/4 DX zoom lens at 16mm (equivalent to 24mm).

Above: © Terry Donovan. Shot with a 105mm macro lens. Even at an aperture of f/10, depth of field is noticeably shallow.

Lenses with a low-numbered maximum aperture, such as f/1.4 or f/1.8 are called "fast" lenses because they allow you to use a higher shutter speed to make an exposure. They also allow you to shoot in low light without having to bump up the ISO setting. Stanley Kubrick had a 50mm f/0.7 lens fitted to a movie camera for the making of *Barry Lyndon*. The fast (also extremely large and expensive) lens allowed Kubrick to shoot scenes that were literally candle-lit.

The depth of field effect produced by opening the aperture becomes increasingly pronounced as the focal length increases. The effect is essentially nonexistent with wide-angle lenses. On 35mm format full-frame cameras, portrait lenses such as an 85mm at f/1.4 can produce inches-deep depth of field, with the sitter's eyes tack-sharp while his or her ears are "soft." The most popular portrait lenses are designed to produce a very smooth, aesthetically pleasing bokeh effect. You pay a premium for this—an 85mm f/1.4 lens sells for roughly triple the price of an f/1.8 lens.

BOKEH

We refer to the quality of the out-of-focus parts of an image as the bokeh, or boke (pronounced "boke-uh"), an obscure term that apparently originated in Japan. This characteristic is actually designed into lenses, and certain lenses have reputations for good or bad bokeh. Lenses render images by creating thousands of tiny circles that become more apparent in the parts of the image that are out of focus. Good bokeh has soft-edged circles. With bad bokeh, these circles have hard edges that can be brighter than the center. This creates distracting highlights that can undermine an image. In post-production, over-sharpening out-of-focus areas of an image can turn good bokeh into bad.

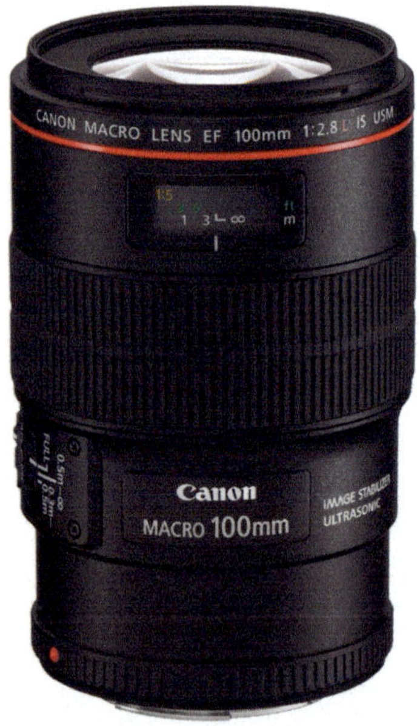

This Canon lens is a fast macro telephoto lens with image stabilization, making it an excellent choice for hand-held, close-up, and low-light situations. Its focal length is also good for portraits because it will not exaggerate facial features.

It can be a good idea to have a zoom lens in your arsenal, particularly if you're shooting in locations that don't allow you to move around to get the framing you need. Variable aperture zooms cut down on size, weight, and expense compared to constant aperture designs. You will recognize variable aperture zooms by the inclusion of an aperture range in their name, e.g. 100–400mm *f/4.5–5.6*. One caveat is that the maximum aperture of such lenses can decrease by as much as two stops over the range of the zoom, and the shutter speed has to decrease to compensate. In the case of a two-stop decrease, that could mean going from 1/250 sec. to 1/60 sec.

Weight and maximum aperture are important considerations in handheld low-light photography. While zoom lenses are convenient, single focal length "prime" lenses are lighter, faster, and cheaper by comparison. Some of the best zoom lenses come close to the sharpness of prime lenses, but for any specific focal length, a quality prime lens will typically be substantially sharper and less expensive. For some ideas on lens selection, see the "How Much Gear?" section in Chapter Eight.

Facing: © Alfred Laij. A warm monochrome composition with qualities of Pictorialism emphasizes form and sensuality. Laij created soft focus using shallow depth of field. He placed the focus point on the water droplets and used their distortion to add to the atmosphere. 17–35 mm f/2.8 zoom at 28mm, f/2.8; 1/100 sec; ISO 800.

Undoing Sharpness

A big reason for the success of the 35mm format, which ultimately gave rise to dSLRs, was the development of extremely sharp lenses. For example, the sharpness of Leica lenses is legendary. However, for some artistic approaches, sharpness is anathema. Around the beginning of the twentieth century, the Photo-Secessionists took up the cause of Pictorialism, which aimed to make photography emulate painting and etching, two dominant forms of art that had legitimacy at the time.

Many in-camera techniques of Pictorialism involve soft focus, effects filters, and lens coatings. You can approximate some of those effects by placing an inexpensive UV or skylight filter over your lens and applying materials to it. One possibility is stretching translucent fabric such as pantyhose or tulle over the filter. You can apply clear nail polish and then scratch it to modify the effect. To reuse the filter, take it off your lens, and then clean it with nail polish remover or acetone. Another technique is to spray a fine mist of hairspray up into the air, and wave the filter under the mist until you've built up the right thickness.

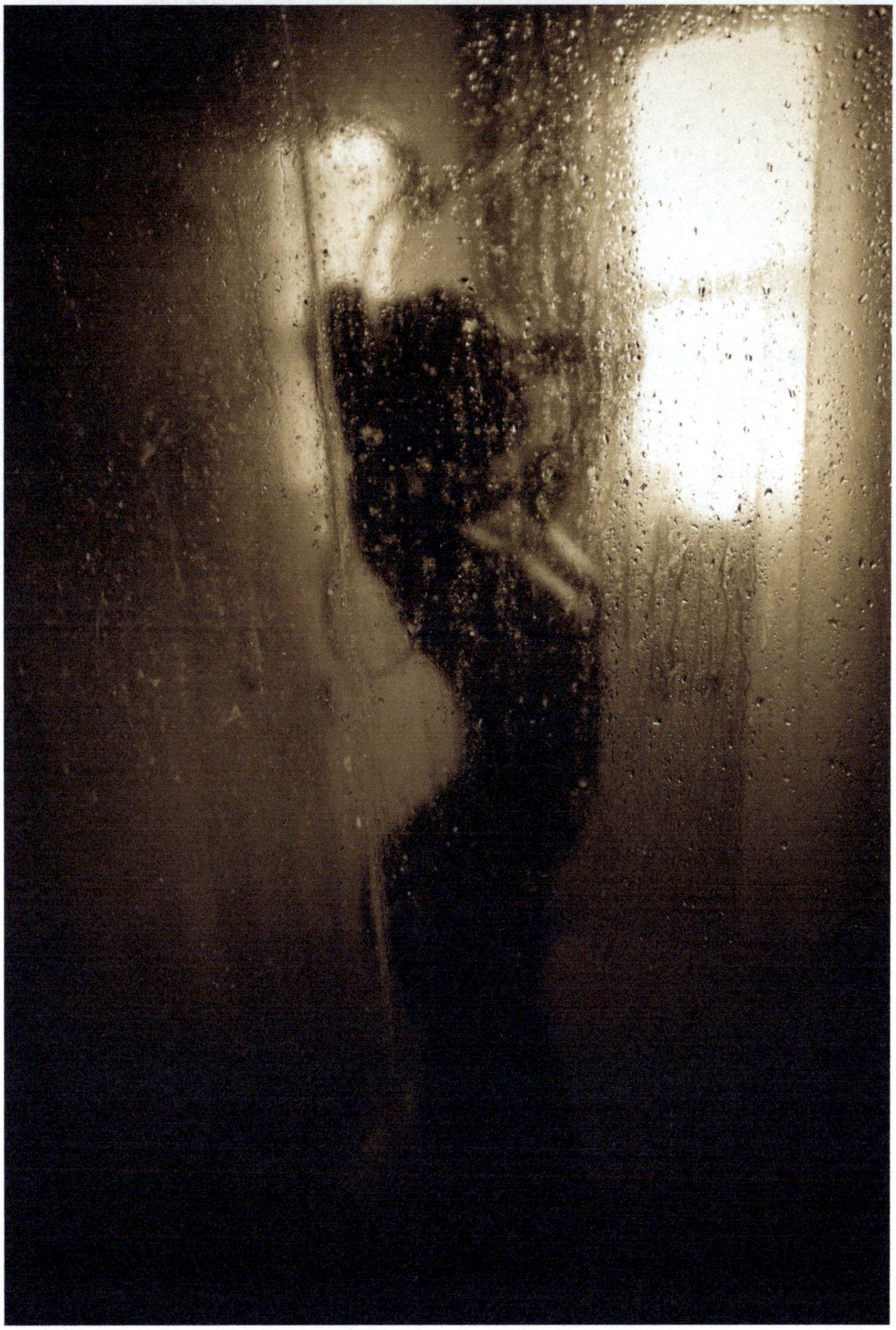

The hairspray washes off with warm water. Cinematographers have been known to smear Vaseline over their lenses (skylight filters) to get a soft focus effect. Believe it or not, K-Y Jelly works better, and it's easier to remove. Try applying it around the edge of the filter, leaving the center clear, or spread it more evenly and then smudge the center with your thumb.

Smoke creates a layered atmospheric effect that can reveal the shape of light beams and functions something like a variable filter. It is heavily used in cinema, and also in fashion photography. Smoke is almost invisible when lit from the front, but shows up clearly when lit from the side or behind.

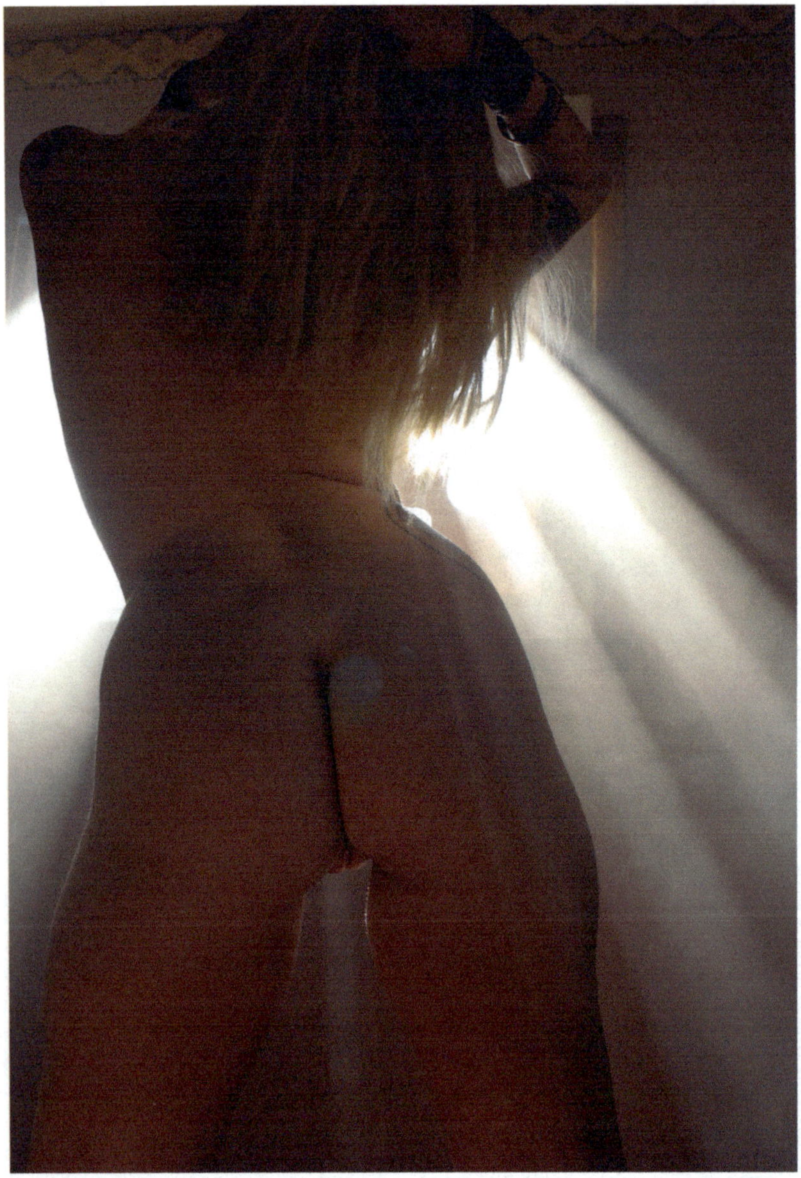

Above: © Terry Donovan. Back lighting and a smoke machine were used to produce the atmospheric effect seen here.

Facing: © Alfred Laij. Selective focus has obliterated the background details and emphasizes the sensuality of the hand contacting the breast. Nikon D3, 85mm f/1.4 lens at f/2.2, 1/200 sec, ISO 400.

Selective Focus and Lensbabies

Selective focus is a variation of soft focus. One type of selective focus can be achieved by creating a very shallow depth of field, using a fast lens with the aperture opened wide (e.g. an 85mm lens at f/1, f/1.4, or f/1.8). An example of an image using this technique might be a person holding their hands out, with the hands in sharp focus while the body is blurry. In that case the selective focus is based on foreground vs. background.

A different type of selective focus happens when the lens produces an island of sharp focus with everything else defocused. That is a bit more like the way we actually see—we have sharp foveal vision and much softer peripheral vision.

The Lensbaby Composer offers a complete, easy-to-use selective focus system based on the idea of tilting the lens to control the defocus effect, a technique that had essentially been available only through the use of expensive precision bellows attachments in the past. The manual-focus system consists of a lens barrel that holds interchangeable optics, fitted into a ball and socket joint. The lens barrel has

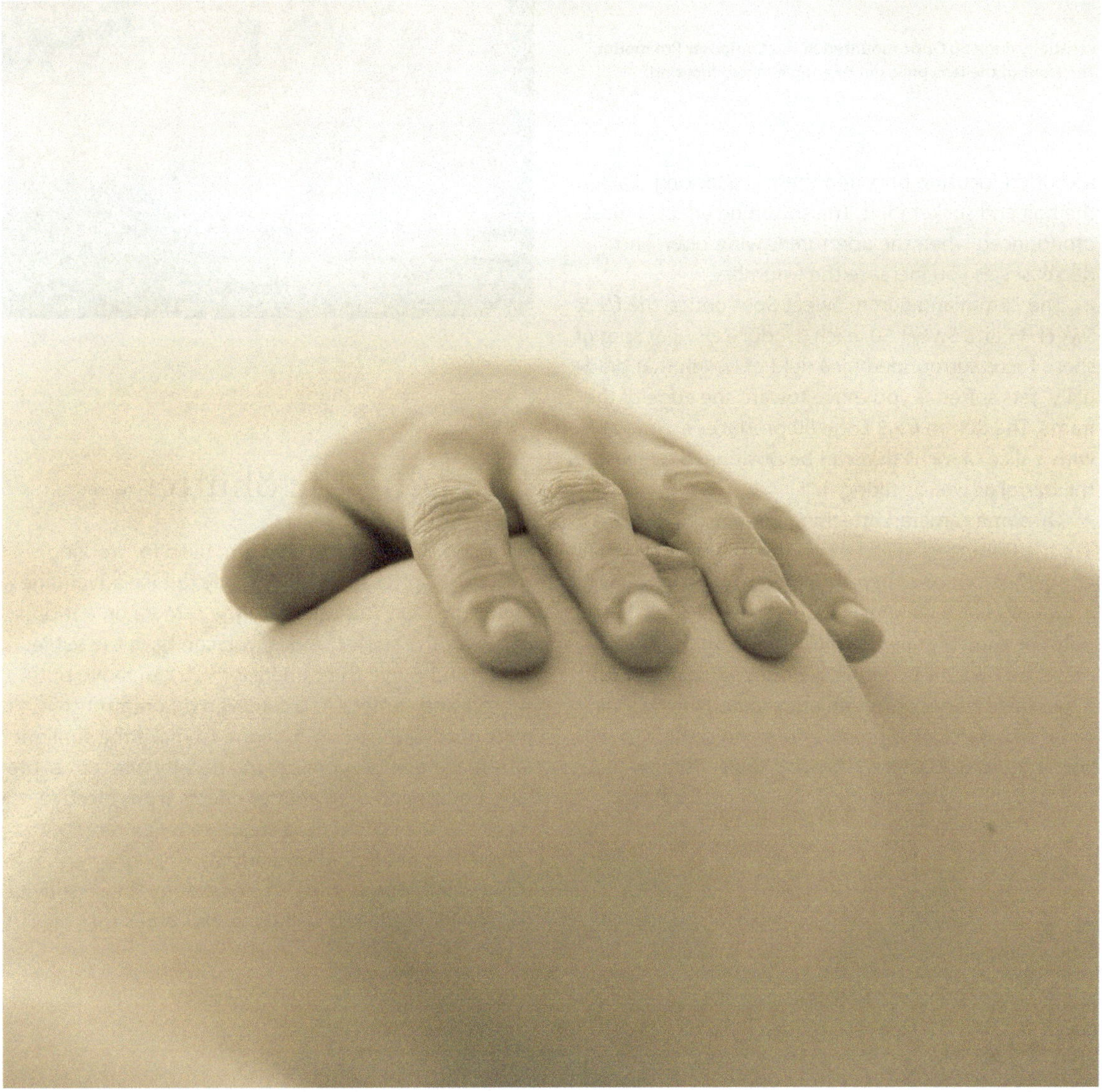

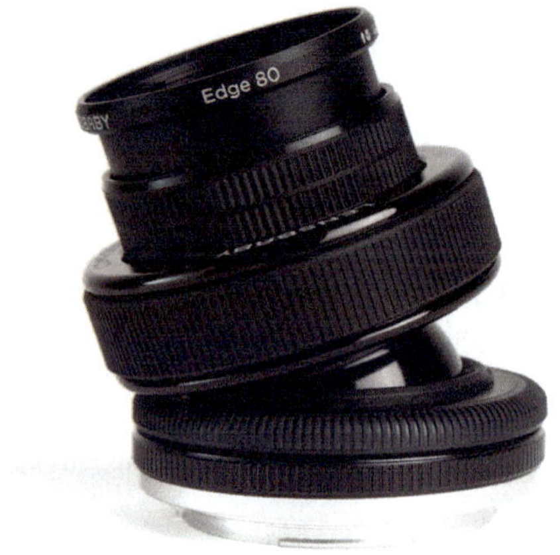

Lensbaby Edge 80 Optic mounted in the Composer Pro mount. The front of the lens pulls out to enable macro focusing.

a knurled focusing ring, and there is a locking dial for the ball and socket joint. The softening effect is most pronounced when the aperture is wide-open and decreases as you increase the f-number.

The 35mm and 50mm Sweet Spot optics, the f/2.5 Sweet 35 and Sweet 50, each produce a sweet spot of sharp focus surrounded by a field of bokeh that gradually gets softer as you move toward the edge of the frame. The 80mm f/2.8 Edge 80 produces an image with a slice of focus that can be positioned by twisting the barrel as well as tilting it.

On some cameras, attaching a manual focus lens like the Composer switches off the metering system altogether, but on others, the metering switches into a spot or center-weighted mode and indicates that only the shutter speed is under your control. If your metering becomes completely disabled, you can use a handheld meter or put an auto-focus lens on your camera to determine the aperture and shutter speed you want to use before attaching the Lensbaby.

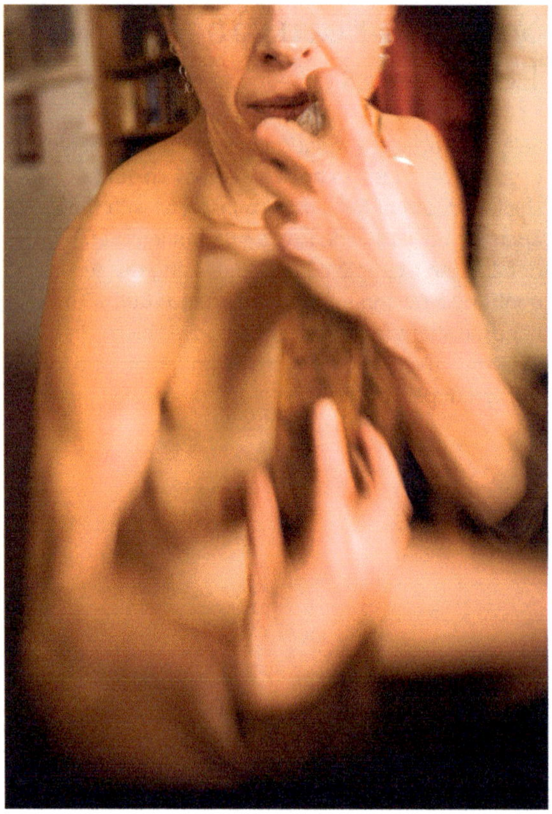

Dragging the Shutter

Dragging the shutter is the term used for working with low shutter speeds, primarily to take advantage of motion blur. You can place the camera on a tripod and have the subject move, you can have the subject sit still and move the camera, or you can move both subject and camera. You can even do drag shutter work outside in strong sunlight. To make the sunlight dim, place one or more neutral density filters over the lens. Combining drag shutter effects with selective focus has the potential to create some extremely compelling images. Many early street photographs show what appear to be empty streets. The sensitivity of early film required such long exposures that only

Above: © Lou Benjamin. Shot with a Lensbaby Sweet 35. The sweet spot was positioned to place emphasis on the model's face. The smearing effect of the lens resembles motion blur.

Facing: © Scott Foltz. A long exposure transforms flowing water into luxurious texture.

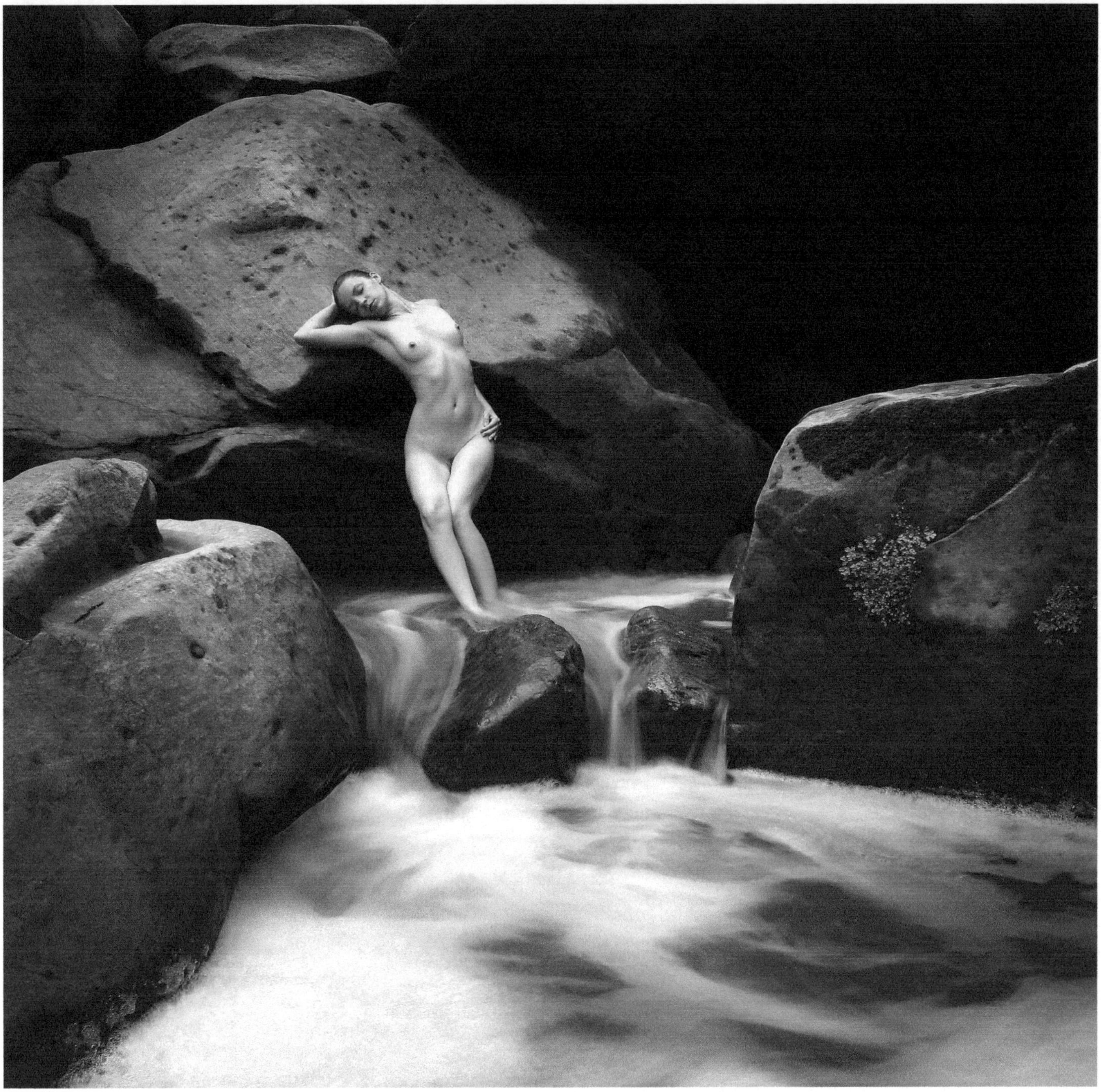

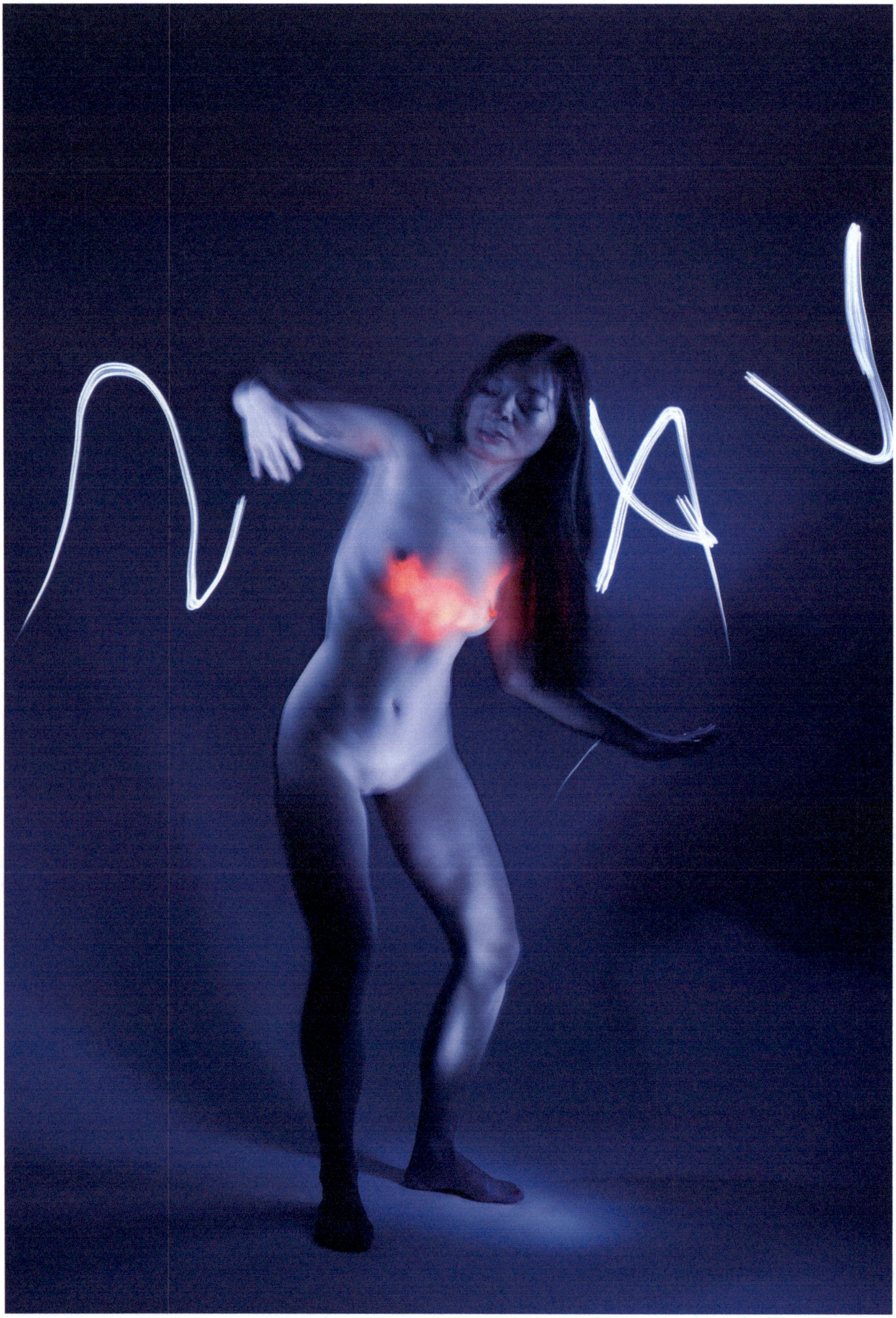

objects that remained completely stationary registered an image.

Often, high-contrast light will make drag shutter results more interesting. If you mix ambient light and flash, and have the subject move, the flash will freeze the subject and the ambient light will record a ghost trail.

Light Painting

Light painting is an interesting application of dragging the shutter. It works best if you black out the windows, place the camera on a tripod, and pre-focus the camera. Set the exposure to 30 seconds or more, trip the shutter, begin to move the flashlight around to illuminate your subject from different directions. The results of this technique are extremely variable. To succeed with it requires a willingness to give up control to some degree, and experiment. Even successful results are hard to duplicate, making it a process that is artistic at its very heart.

Be careful about standing too long in one place, or you may be recorded in the image. If you let the light stay for a while in one place, you'll get a hot spot. Diffusion material and colored gels can also be used to modify the look and output of your flashlight. You can also use cardboard or Cinefoil to make a snoot that keeps the flashlight beam narrow. The light source can be shaded to prevent light trails from showing up in the image, or you can intentionally allow the flashlight to register, and even point it directly at the camera.

You can have your sitter hold still for part of the time, then quickly change position and hold again, to create images that look like step-wise superimpositions. Alternately, you can have the model move slowly and constantly for a different effect. Turning the light on and off during the process can allow your subject to change position without registering a motion trail.

Web Resources

Rosco Cinefoil—http://bit.ly/1zR38On
Timothy Greenfield-Sanders—greenfield-sanders.com
Image Makers/Image Takers—http://bit.ly/1DnNlbr
Carrie Leigh's *NUDE*—carrieleigh.com
Barry Lyndon—http://bit.ly/1FhqyTk
Pictorialism—http://bit.ly/ZNdhjT
Stephen Shore—stephenshore.net

Facing: © Lou Benjamin. Inspired by Matisse's *Icarus* from the *Jazz* series. The model's pose relaxed slightly over the course of the 30-second f/13 exposure, to create the ghosting effect. The model was illuminated with an LED flashlight with red and white beams. The spacing of its LEDs created an effect that resembles brush strokes with thick bristles. The blue color in the background is from the LED light on a nearby piece of equipment. White balance was set to tungsten, so as not to neutralize the blue.

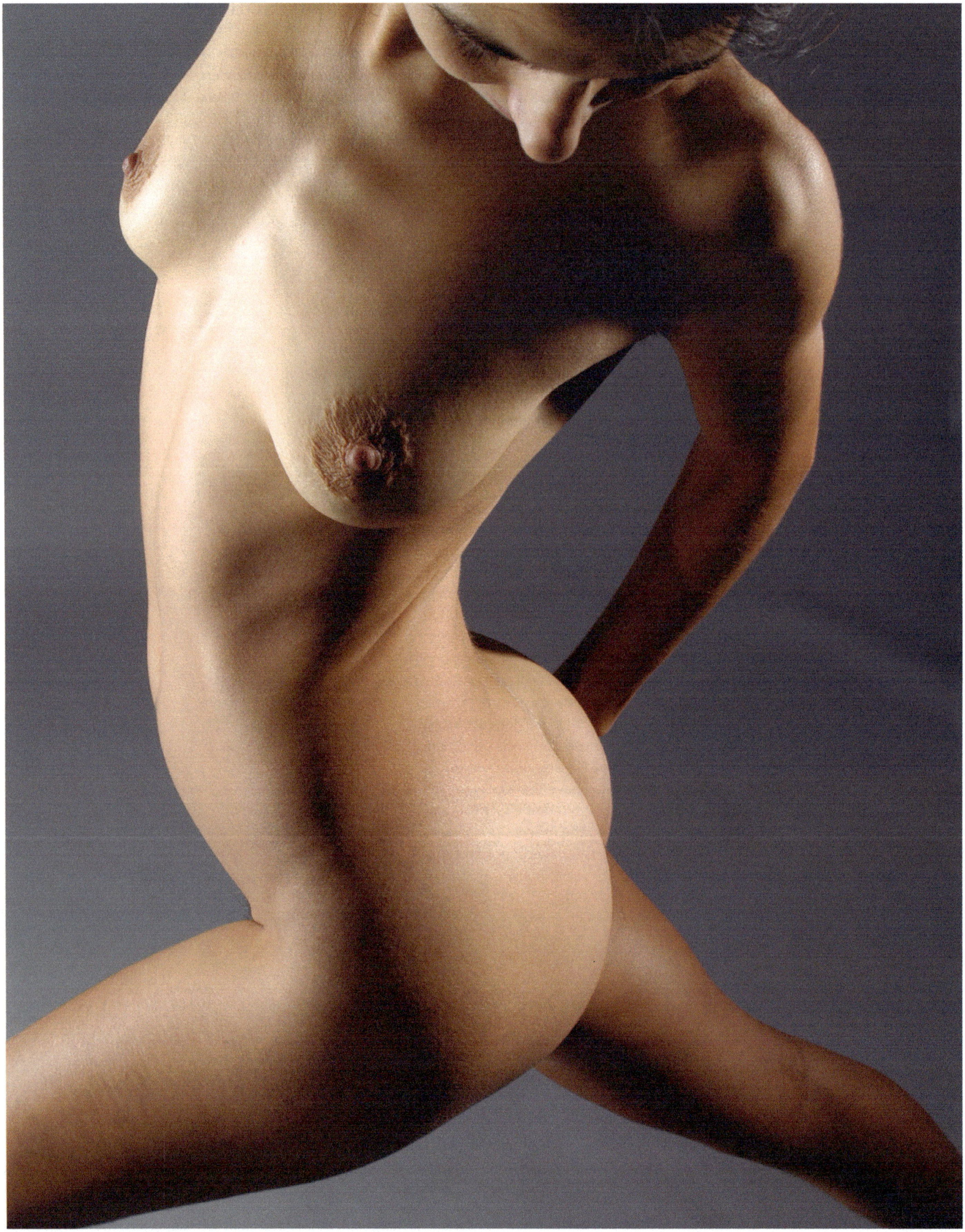

Chapter Six | It All Starts with Light

"What makes photography a strange invention is that its primary raw materials are light and time."
John Berger

GIVEN THAT photography means "writing (or drawing) with light," it makes sense that understanding light and exposure can make a tremendous difference in the kind of work you produce. Light is more than the substrate of photography; it can be a principal character. It informs the visual language of a photo even as it imparts the image upon a light-sensitive surface. Light can be shaped and augmented to make your photos more powerful without the need for elaborate manipulation in post-production. It can inject drama, create mystery, and profoundly affect how we perceive the sculpture and spatial qualities of a subject. Light also gives us color—from the cool blue of the sky to the warm yellow-orange of candlelight—and color often conveys emotional overtones or symbolism.

A broad range of options in image-making come from taking advantage of differences in the intensity, duration, and qualities of various light sources. You can learn to distinguish qualities of light and the ways that they affect a photo in much the same way that skiers distinguish snow: they don't just see snow; they see hard pack, moguls, powder, crud, crust, slush, corn snow, loose or wet granular snow, fresh snow, spring snow, and ice; and they know how each will affect

Facing: © Lou Benjamin. Model: Béu Tornaghi.

the skiing experience. A similar awareness of different kinds of light will give you a significant advantage in making more effective photographs.

Light can be diffuse and "soft" or directional and "hard." Bouncing light off surfaces or shining it through diffusion material softens it, reducing contrast and color saturation as well. Lenses and grids can harden light. Midday sun is high-contrast, directional, and hard, capable of making your subject squint and turning their eye sockets into black holes. Daylight through a window tends to be soft because it has bounced around before it enters the window, and is often diffused further by curtains. The light on a foggy day is flat, low-contrast, and so diffuse that it is often shadowless. Lamp light through a shade is far softer than the light from a bare bulb. Standard umbrellas bounce light while shoot-through umbrellas diffuse it. A silver umbrella produces light with more contrast and color saturation than a white umbrella. Light bounces inside a soft box before passing though diffusion material.

Anything that emits light can be used to illuminate an art photograph, and you can choose a light source for its distinguishing characteristics. Some shooters might exploit the look of on-camera flash, while others insist on natural lighting. In the studio, photographers often choose among window light, continuous light, strobes, or a mix of light sources. These choices affect both the process of shooting and the look of the image. They can also impact the psychology of the interaction between the artist and the subject.

If you're looking for inspiration good places to start are cinema and painting—especially the classics. There's a lot to be learned from Renaissance painting, German Expressionism, and the masters of cinema. That's not to dismiss the masters of photography. They are something of a given, but also there's a kind of visual inbreeding that comes from only looking at photography. (Yes, that statement does have a certain irony in a book that's chock-full of photographs for you to look at.)

Ridley Scott, who directed *Blade Runner* and *Alien*, as well as *Thelma & Louise*, is known for using light to create texture and tone. One of his signature techniques is to stream bright lights, often colored with gels, through fog or steam to create brilliant bands.

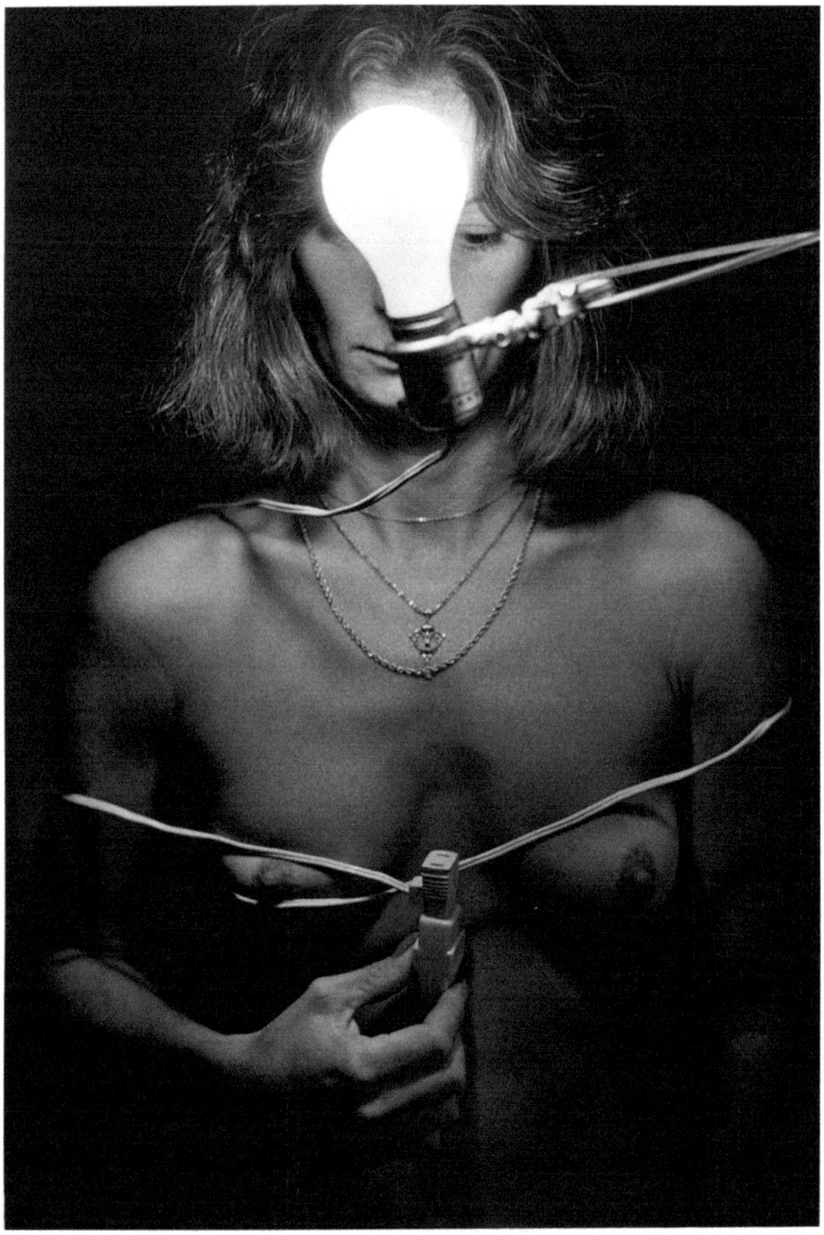

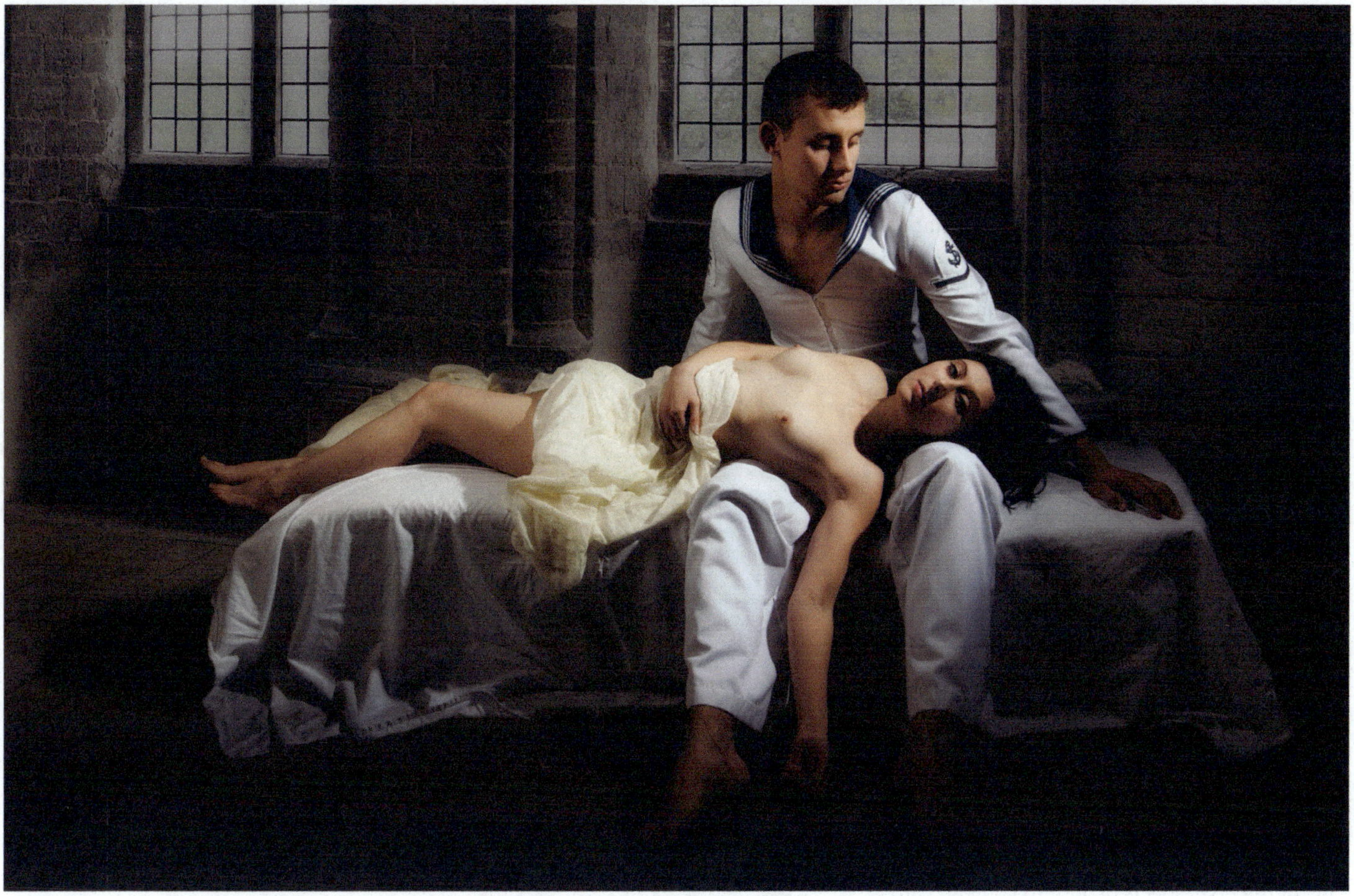

Facing: © Harvey Stein. Correct exposure was critical for this low-key image. Light from a bare bulb can produce stark, harsh shadows, yet it works perfectly in this image.

Above: © Terry Slater. The lighting design is a key element of this photo, which references Michelangelo's Pietà more literally than does the photo by J. D. Yezierski in Chapter Three.

A number of acclaimed photographers, as well as cinematographers and movie directors, have taken much of their inspiration from Renaissance painting. Much of Robert Mapplethorpe's work reflects the work of the Mannerists and the engravings of Albrecht Dürer. Martin Scorsese has acknowledged that Caravaggio's work influenced *Mean Streets* and *Taxi Driver*.

Caravaggio was the first to shape and stage lighting in his distinctive and influential manner. At one point he was thrown out of his apartment by his landlord for damaging the roof—he had cut a hole to light the scenes in his studio. He essentially documented his lighting technique in the painting *Martha and Mary Magdalene* (c. 1598), which shows a rectangular highlight reflected in the mirror—the hole he cut in the ceiling produced the dramatic light, and the reflection from the mirror opened the shadows to reveal Mary's face.

As you study a photo, you can often read the lighting arrangement by looking at the eyes and where the shadows fall. The size and shape of the catch lights can be a clue as to the type of lighting instruments used, while the shadows can indicate their direction and angle.

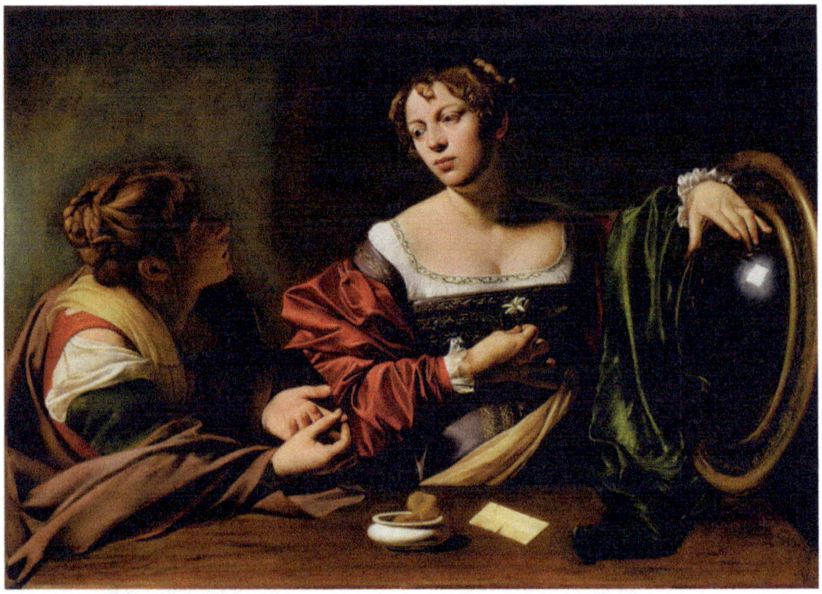

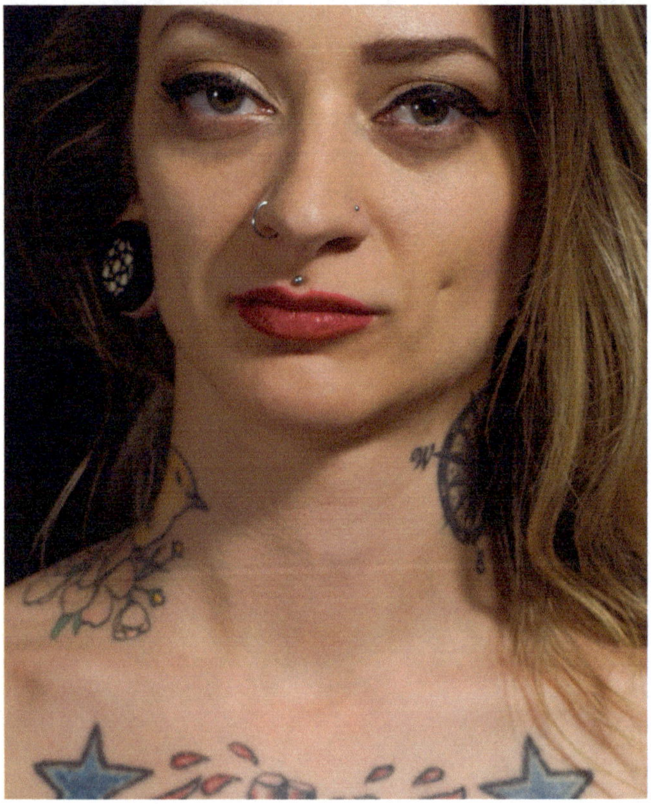

Hard and Soft

One of the first aspects of light to contend with is how shadows are rendered. Hard light creates hard-edged shadows, while soft light creates shadows with a diffuse, feathered edge. In hard light, the rays of the beam are traveling in more or less the same direction. In soft light, the rays are scattered. There is a continuum between hard and soft light, and the art of working with these qualities is figuring out when to use each, and how they can be combined to best effect.

Hard light is sometimes called specular light, because it tends to create bright, "hot" highlights. The shadows produced under hard lighting tend to be dense and show very little detail, with a crisp, distinct edge. Shadow play in front of a projector works because the light from the projector lamp is focused into a hard beam. Hard light comes from relatively

Above (top): Michelangelo Merisi da Caravaggio, *Martha and Mary Magdalene*, c. 1598.

Above (bottom): © Lou Benjamin. Catch lights in the eyes can hint at the lighting setup.

Facing: © Lou Benjamin. Hard light from the model's left was produced with a grid, while the soft light from the right comes from a soft box. The light on the left is about three stops brighter than the light on the right.

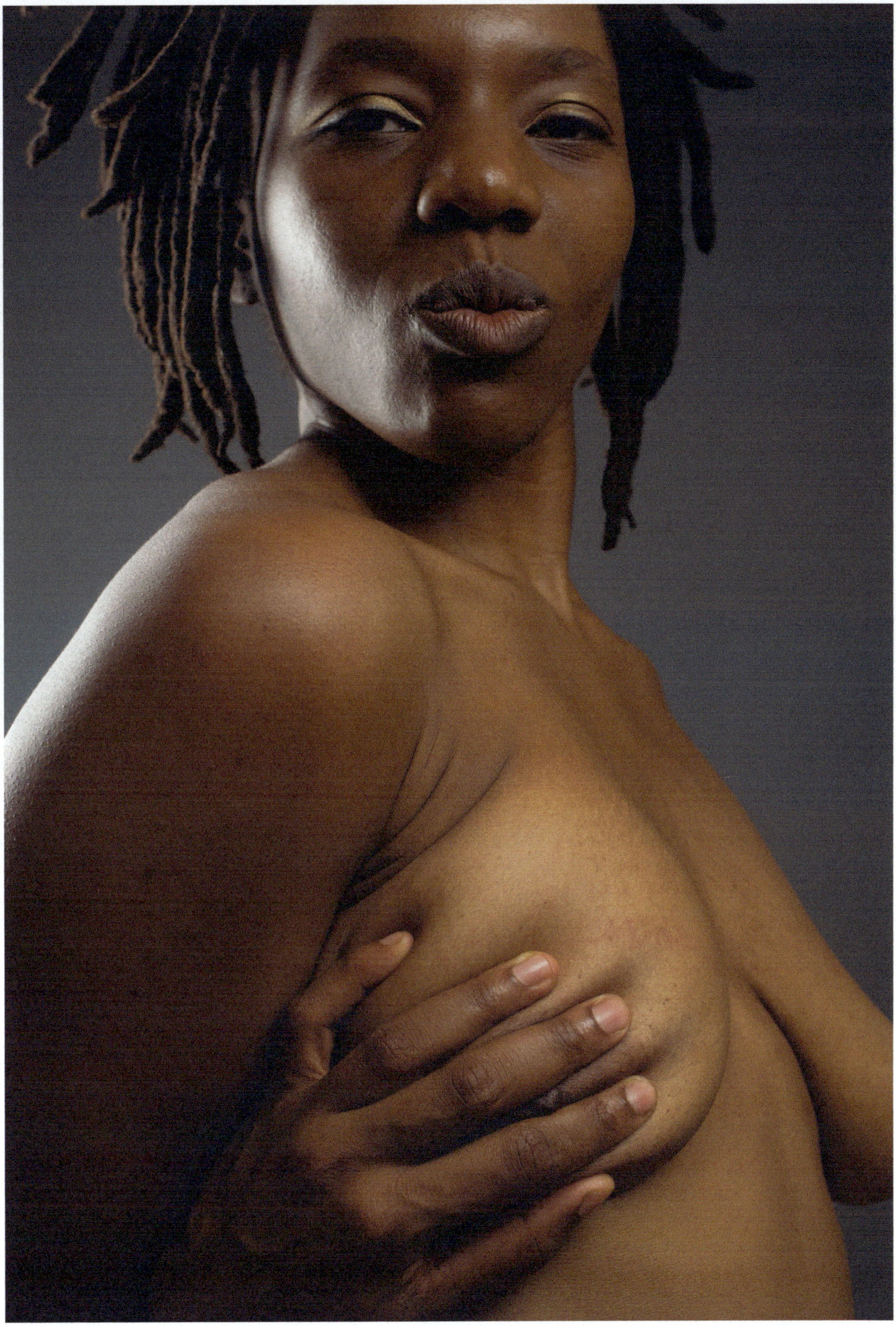

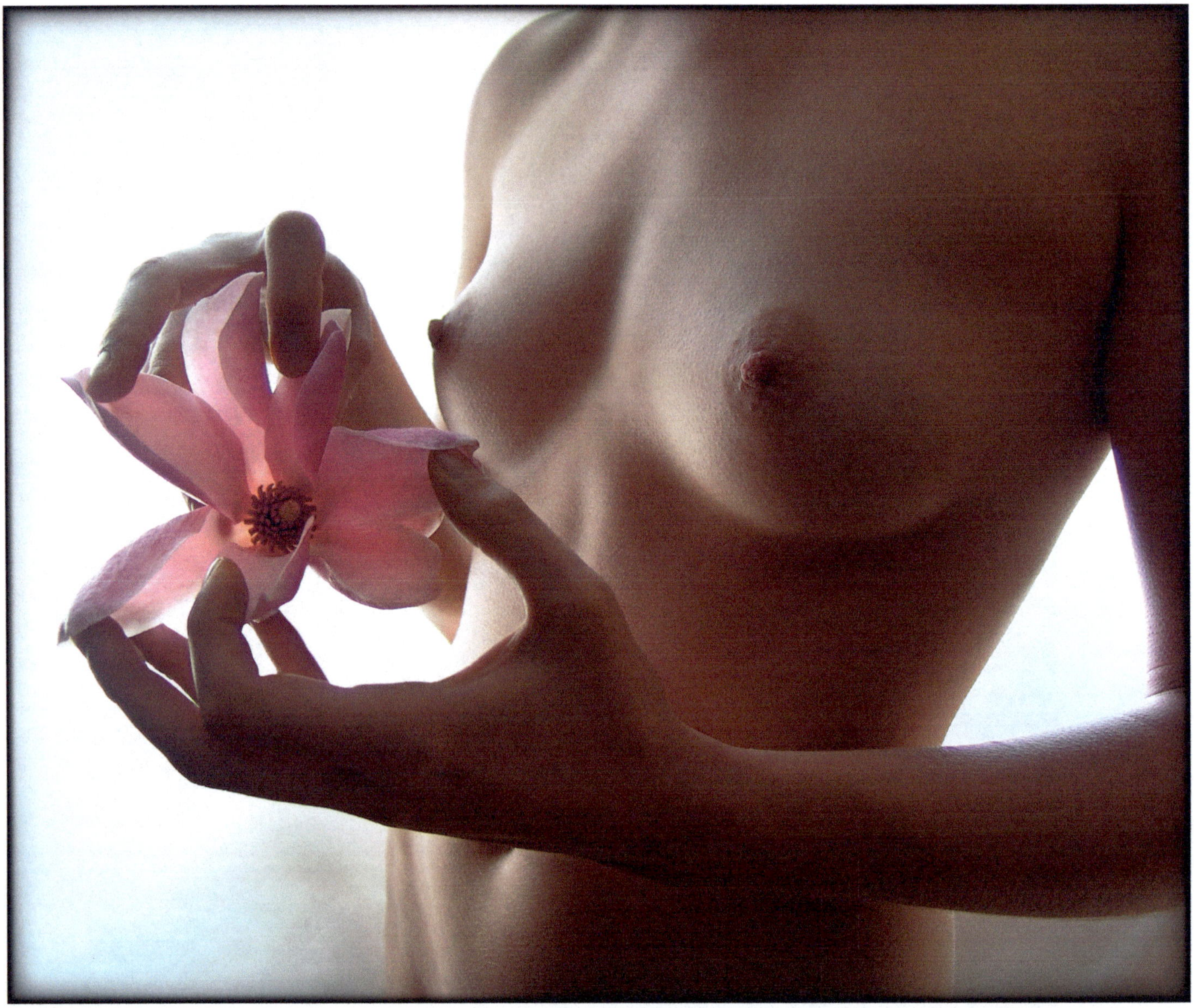

Above: © Pascal Renoux. Back light from a window is further softened and diffused by a sheer curtain. The light wraps around the figure to show body contours. The figure is not in silhouette because of fill light from the front, most likely reflected off the walls.

Facing (top): © Lou Benjamin. Model: Lauren Babree. Soft light that wraps around the figure can show sculptural contours with subtle shadows. A window, approximately seven feet square with a white translucent shade, has the same lighting effect as a soft box. The window faced northeast and the model stood about seven feet from the window, the optimum distance for a soft box of that size.

Facing (bottom): © Lou Benjamin. Model: Sie Ist Idaho. The model is approximately 13 feet from a 5½ foot tall window with no diffusing shade. However, this light is not nearly as hard as the light from a grid.

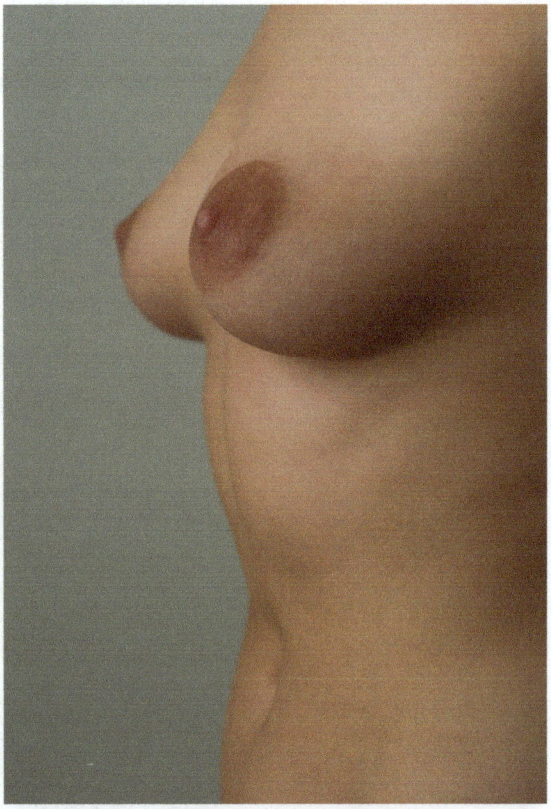

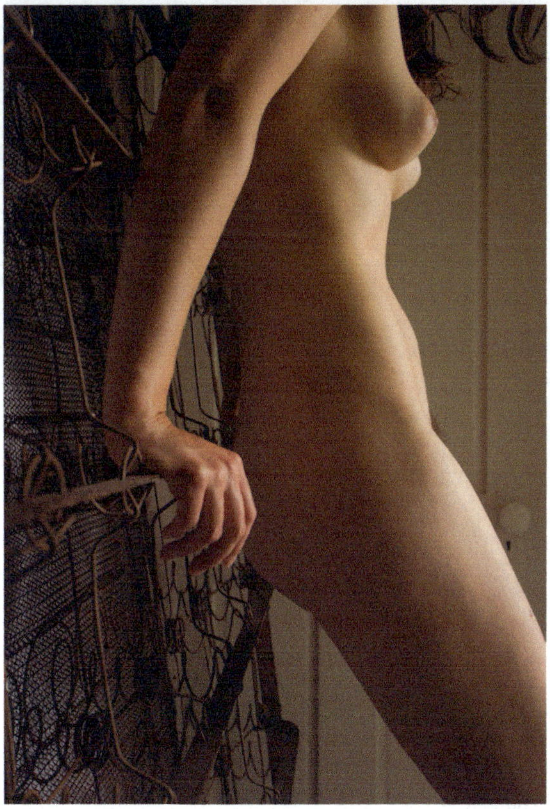

small light sources. On a clear day, the midday sun is a high-contrast pinpoint light source that creates hard shadows that can be very difficult to deal with.

Light can be softened by shining it through material that diffuses it or by bouncing it off a surface. Under soft lighting, if the edge is diffuse enough, shadows can be nearly undetectable. Soft light also tends to make colors look less saturated.

The larger the surface of the light source relative to the subject, the softer the light. Relative size will decrease and the light will gradually become harder (and dimmer) as you move the light away from the subject. Multiple lighting instruments can be arranged behind a large piece of diffusing material to create an expansive soft light source that casts a singular, diffuse shadow; without the diffuser, each light source would cast its own distinct shadow.

Windows, especially large ones, can be a great source of soft light. The softness of the light depends on the conditions outdoors and the direction the window is facing. North light is a favorite among sculptors because it is extremely consistent in intensity throughout the day. Light from the east or west is the most variable, and light from the south is hotter and harder.

When hard, direct sunlight is too intense and contrasty, you can seek open shade on the shadow side of a large building or under a canopy of trees. Under open shade, filtered light reflects down from the sky, giving the light a high color temperature. You can get interesting catch lights in the eyes by having the sitter face out of the shadow. This light can still have some direction to it, so you may get interesting shadows, and color saturation is not a problem the way it is with extremely diffuse light.

On overcast days, cloud cover can diffuse the sun's light to the point where shadows are undetectable. This omnidirectional light can be used to create great portraits, though it can also lack contrast and make colors look washed out. When that happens, a bit of fill flash, especially off axis, and kept to a minimum, can add dimension and put a sparkle in the eyes. The light on overcast days is also extremely blue, and imparts a cool tone to everything if it isn't compensated for.

Direction

Where the light is coming from has as much impact on your image as the hardness of the light. Even with simple flash photography, moving the light off-camera can substantially improve the look of the image. We have an expectation that natural light will come from above for the most part, firelight (which comes from below) being one exception.

Because a hard light source throws distinct shadows, there is a creative opportunity in positioning the lights so as to place those shadows within the frame. You can make the shadow loom large or fall away. If you don't want shadows to show, you can angle the light downward and frame so that the shadow falls outside the frame. You can also pull the sitter away from the wall. You can also minimize the shadow with a soft light source so you don't have to deal with it.

Placing a hard light at an oblique angle to the skin will bring out its texture. The harder the light, the more pronounced this effect will be. Oblique lighting also causes parts of the body to throw shadows, emphasizing the spatial and sculptural qualities of the body. The shadows produced by soft light can still have enough contrast to bring out sculptural forms while minimizing the texture.

When a hard light source is positioned at an extreme angle beneath the subject, the upward shadows can be very unsettling. This is known as "horror" lighting. Some lighting teachers declare that you should never direct light upward at your sitter, but there are exceptions. As one example, angling a smaller lighting instrument slightly upward and focusing a pool of light on just one part of the body can produce a striking and unusual visual counterpoint or accent that is aesthetically pleasing.

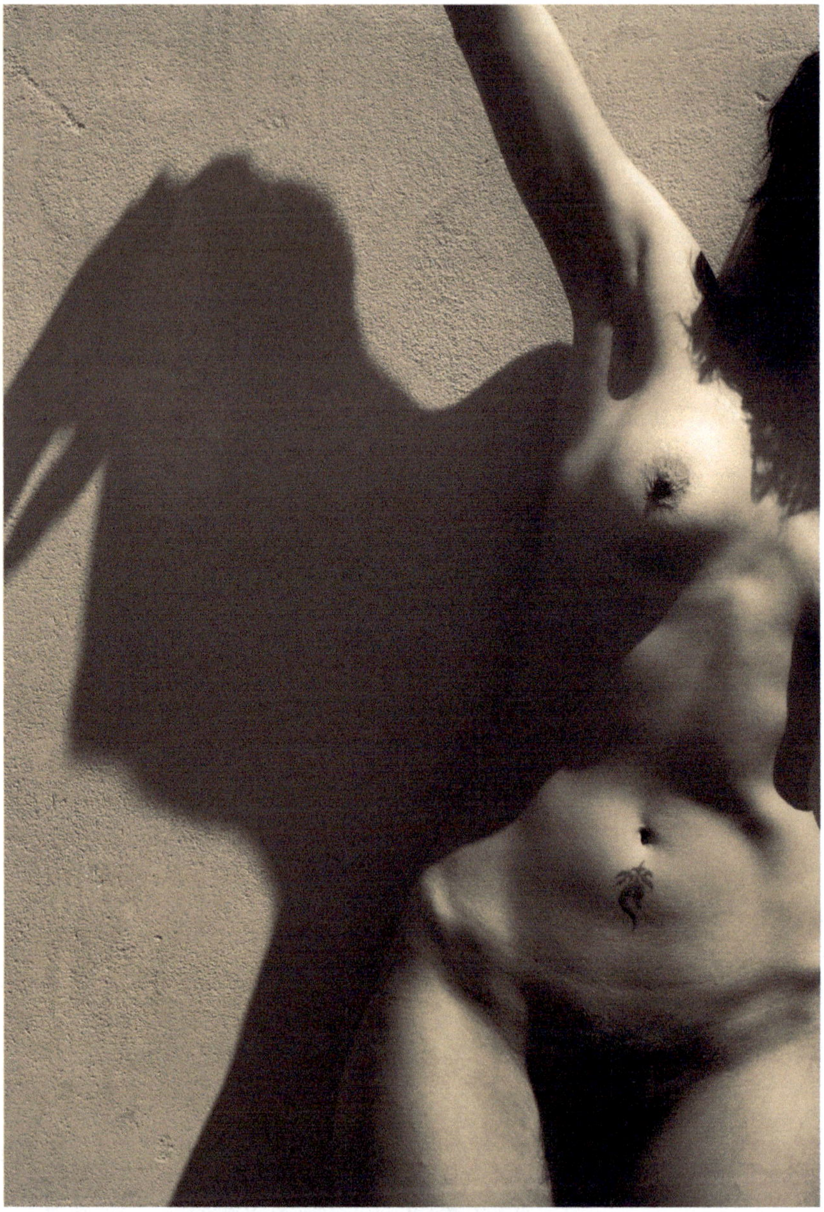

Above: © Lou Benjamin. Model: Béu Tornaghi. Afternoon sun in July projects hard shadows and brings out texture and contours. The angle of the sun projects fascinating distortions.

Facing: © Lou Benjamin. The shadows under the arms and the right shoulder blade give an indication of where the moderately hard light source is located. The angle of the light is such that the contours of the body are brought out without overemphasizing skin texture.

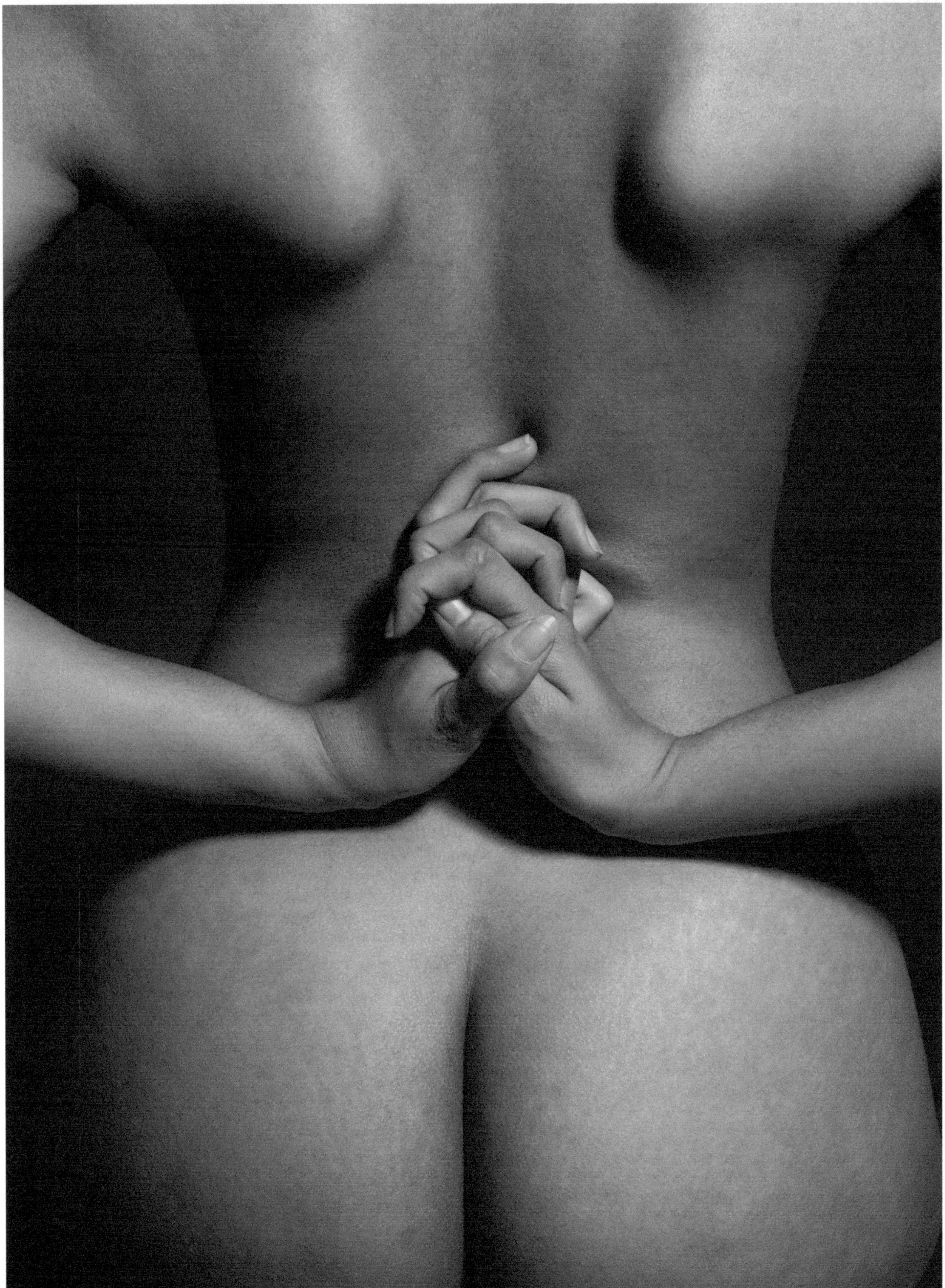

Intensity

As soon as you start working with light from more than one source, you're likely to be concerned with the relative intensities of those sources. We compare intensities of light in powers of two—each twofold increase or decrease in intensity is a stop—and your camera's ISO sensitivity, shutter speed, and aperture are all calibrated in stops. Thus, doubling the ISO value or cutting it in half is a one-stop change in sensitivity. Like ISO, doubling or halving the shutter speed is a one-stop change in exposure. And increasing or decreasing the power output of a flash or strobe twofold produces a one-stop change in exposure.

You can adjust the intensity of light from a continuous source by moving it. Because light intensity increases or decreases by the square of the distance, doubling the distance to the subject or cutting it in half produces a two-stop change. If you only need a one-stop change, dim it by moving it back to 1½ times the distance, or make it brighter by moving it closer by ¼. If you've maxed out the power on your strobe and it's still not bright enough, you can move it closer, too.

On lenses, each major stop down from the maximum aperture lets in half as much light as the previous stop, but f-numbers are based on fractional powers of the square root of 2 so they don't progress in nice, even values. To use aperture effectively, it helps to memorize the f-number sequence. If your memory isn't that good, you can purchase an inexpensive bracelet imprinted with the f-numbers online. You can also count clicks—most camera aperture controls are calibrated in ⅓-stop increments.

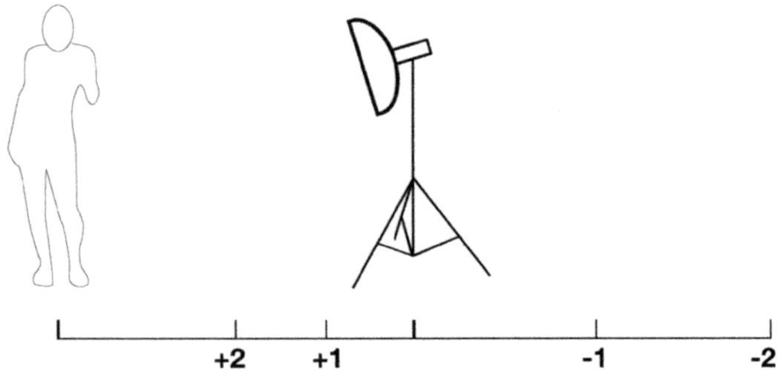

Moving the light source for a one-stop or two-stop change in intensity.

Color

Of particular interest to the photographer working with nudes is the class of colors that are referred to as memory colors—sky blue is one, and healthy skin is another. When these colors are off, it can send a strong signal about the picture we are viewing. There is even a cultural component to these memory colors: The color used to represent healthy olive skin in Western print magazines is considered dark and cadaverous in many Asian cultures.

Colors also interact—surrounding one color with another can change how we perceive the first color. This phenomenon is known as simultaneous color contrast. A practical result of this is that surrounding your model's warm skin tones with a cool background (e.g. blue sky or green foliage) will make his or her skin look even warmer. It works the other way, too—your sitter's skin will look cooler when set against a warm colored background such as a bright red backdrop.

Our perception of color arises in the nervous system, so it makes sense that there would be a psychological aspect to color. In fact, one branch of psychology studies the impact of certain colors upon the emotions and their value in the treatment

1	1.4	2	2.8	4	5.6	8	11	16	22	32

The major aperture values for 35mm cameras, in one-stop increments. An f/1.2 lens is ½ stop faster than an f/1.4 lens, while f/1 lenses are rare and extremely expensive. Fast telephoto lenses typically have a maximum aperture of 2.8. Most cameras actually let you select apertures in 1/3-stop increments, so you may see other values in your viewfinder (e.g. f/4.5 and f/5 between f/4 and f/5.6, or f/9 and f/10 between f/8 and f/11).

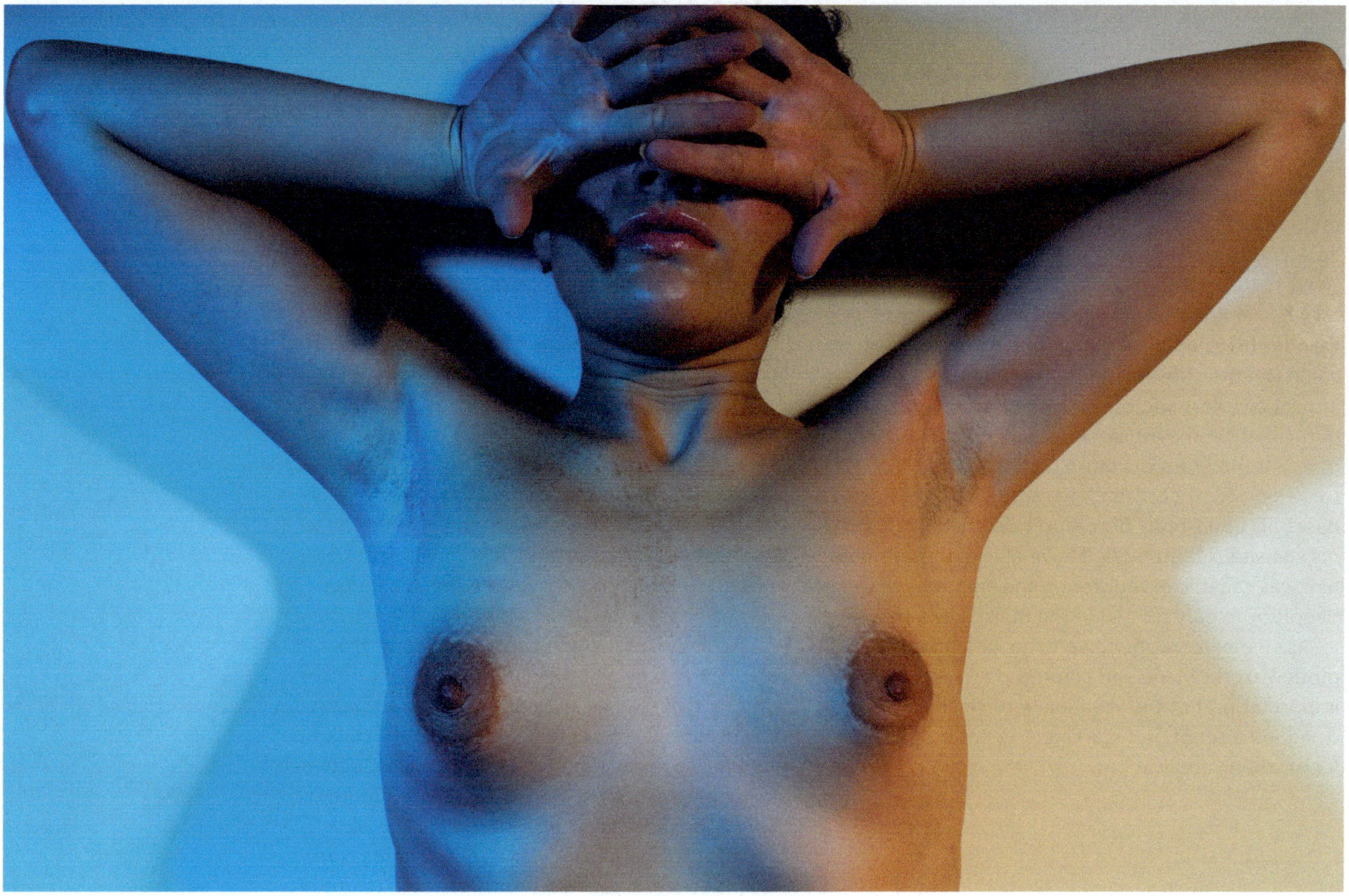

© Lou Benjamin. Playing on warm/cool color contrast, a blue gel was applied to the light that is filling the shadow on the left side of this photo. White balance was adjusted to make the "white" tungsten light source appear a moderately warm yellow. Colored lights lose saturation and become washed out as you increase their intensity, so they work best in low-key or shadow-side applications.

of psychosomatic illness. We have favorite colors and phrases that describe states of mind, such as "got the blues," "green with envy," and "painting the town red." During Picasso's famous "Blue Period," he painted in blues and blue-greens, colors that are described as "austere." Black and white photographers tacitly acknowledge the psychological impact of color by toning prints and selecting photographic papers based on their warm or cool tonality.

In 1810, Johann Wolfgang von Goethe (probably better known for his literary contributions than for his scientific work) published a theory of color. Goethe's observations about the emotional impact of colors and optical effects still carry weight, particularly in the art world. Master cinematographer Vittorio Storaro (whose credits include *The Last Emperor*, *Apocalypse Now*, *Reds*, and *Dick Tracy*) bases his philosophy of color on Goethe's work. On his website, Storaro says, "I have always thought that film was capable of registering the emotions of the people who participated in the making of a movie ... As cinematographers, we write with light and motion, using shade and color to punctuate one important part of the vocabulary of cinema." Storaro designed a set of gels marketed by Rosco specifically for aesthetic applications.

One Light or More

Many well-known portrait photographers' signature looks are based on using a single light. It's a simple, unconfused way of lighting. One successful strategy is to use a very large, soft light source situated behind the photographer. A big soft box or skylight directly above the model is a very effective way to light bodyscapes. A completely different look can be achieved by placing a hard source above and to the side of the model.

When more than one light is used, the dominant light is known as the key light. The other lights are typically placed for effect—to open the shadows (fill) or to separate the subject from the background, or to create highlights (kickers). A strong light from one side of the body may leave the other side in shadow. In that case, it can be useful to throw light into the shadow areas with a second light or with a simple reflector. This technique is referred to as filling or opening the shadows.

When working with fill, nuance is often the essential difference between an everyday photo and one that really stands out. The shadow areas provide a sense of depth, which is lost as you add more fill. The challenge is to find a balance between showing detail in the shadows and making the subject look too flat or indistinct from the background. The relative intensities of the lights come into play here. If you use a light meter to read the light, you will quickly find that you need a difference of at least one f-stop for the difference in brightness to register clearly, while four or more stops creates a high-contrast look. Even though you need a substantial difference to clearly register lighting contrast, opening or closing the aperture on the camera by as little as ⅓ stop can make a significant difference in the overall exposure.

We're talking about lighting ratios here. These are sometimes expressed in terms of relative intensity, such as 1:2, 1:8, etc., but it is generally a lot easier to work directly with stops. If you want a second light to be three stops dimmer (a 1:8 ratio) than f/8, your meter should read f/2.8. Your camera has a dynamic range of approximately ten stops between pure black and pure white. That means black is four to five stops

Facing: © Donna Feldman Lasky. The extremely short duration of strobe light freezes motion. Lasky prefers unfussy lighting and generally lights with just one large overhead soft box. Her approach was inspired by early experience photographing in a space illuminated by a skylight.

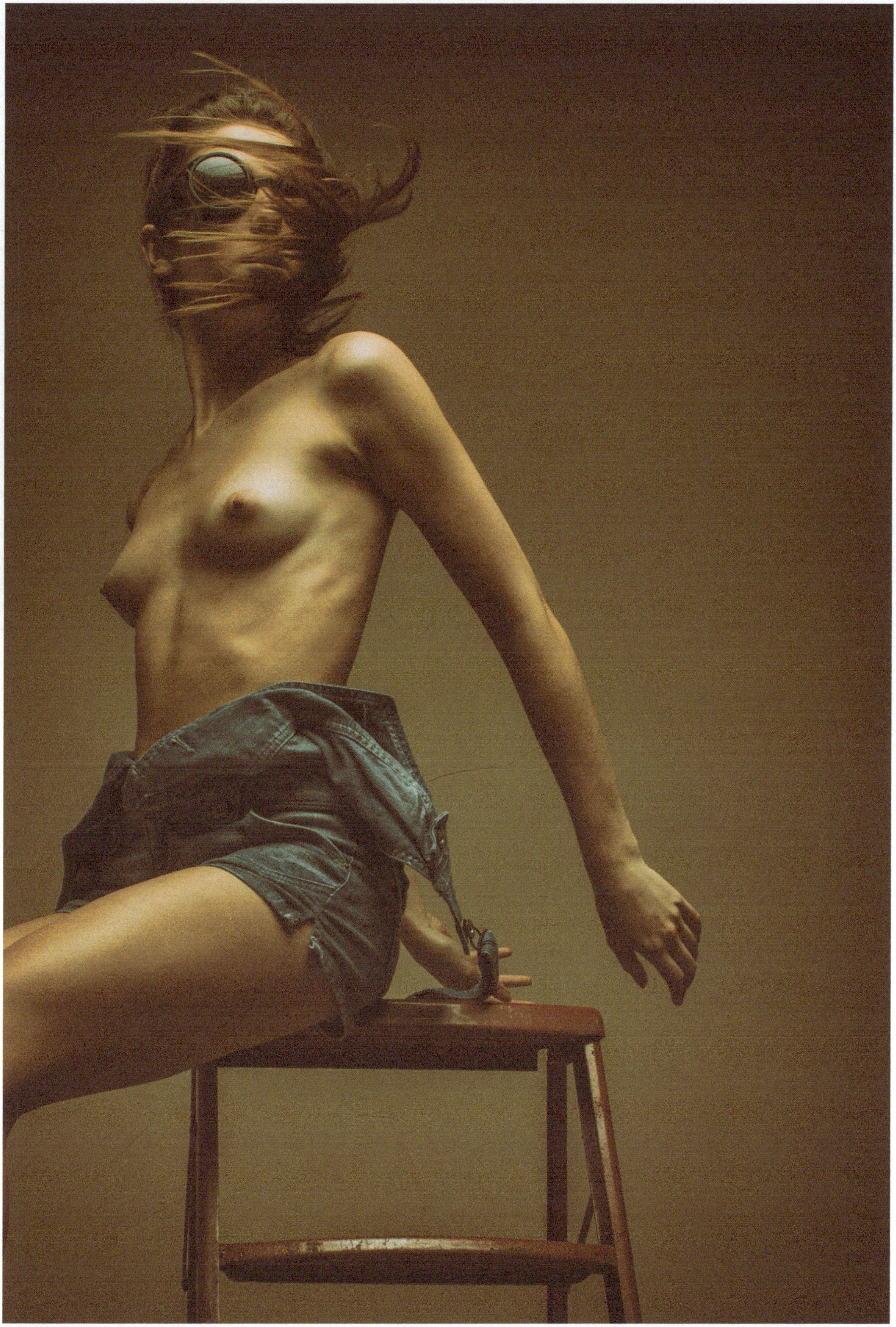

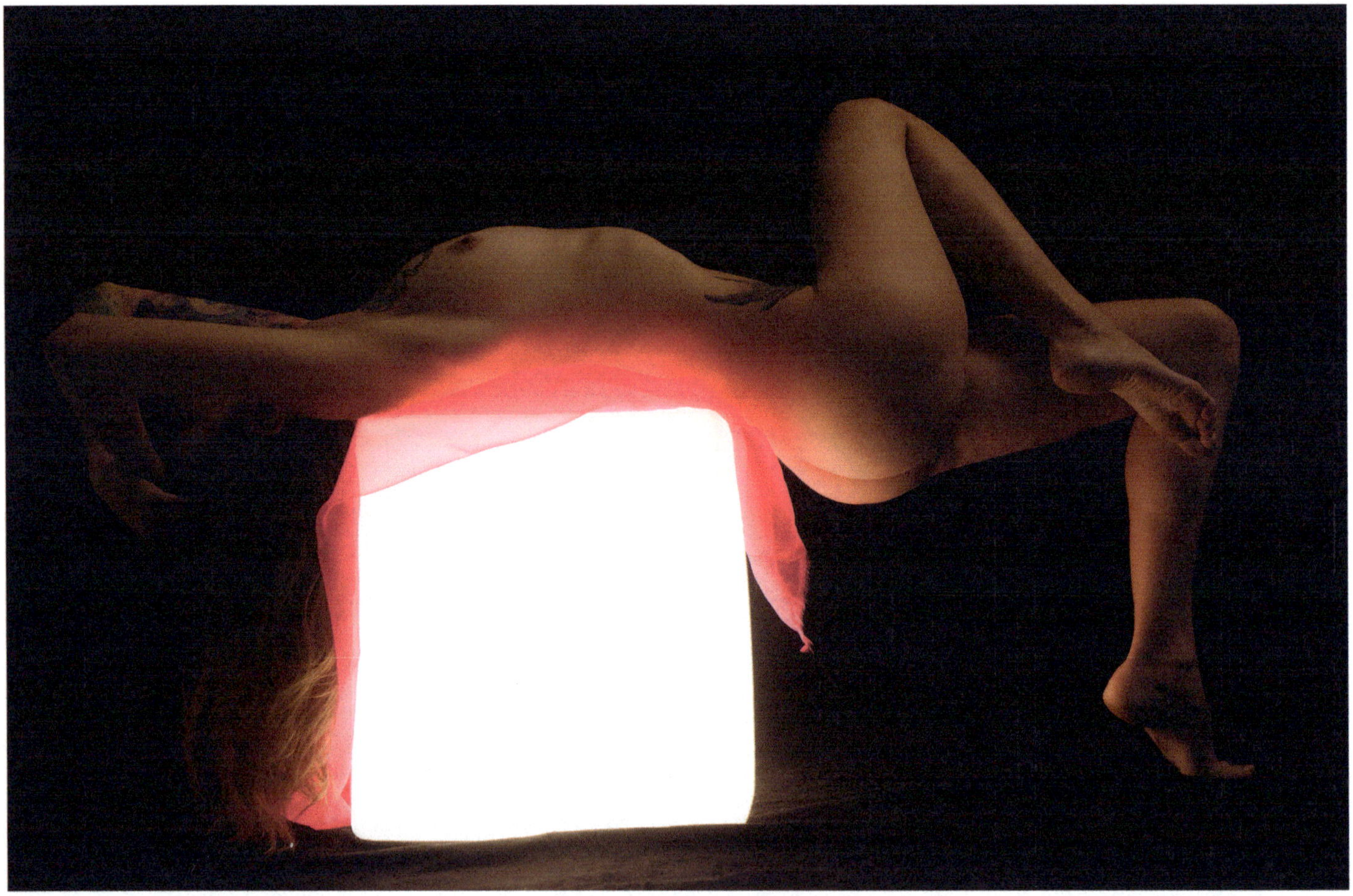

© Lou Benjamin. Model: Theresa Manchester. The key to exposing this shot was making sure that the light cube was bright, but the color of the draped fabric was not washed out. Over-exposing the scene could have flooded the rest of the scene with light, too. The fill on the model's shadow side comes from a dimmed light fixture on the ceiling. When the model sat upright on the cube, a 2' x 3' white foamcore card was placed against a light stand to bounce the ceiling light and fill the left side.

below middle gray, and it's rare that you'll want or need lighting ratios much greater than four or five stops apart.

Difference in f-stops	*Lighting ratio*
(Same intensity)	1:1
1 stop	1:2
2 stops	1:4
3 stops	1:8
4 stops	1:16
5 stops	1:32
6 stops	1:64

The camera's built-in meter comes up short and hand-held meters come into their own as soon as you start dealing with measuring and controlling multiple light sources. This is true when dealing with strobe lighting ratios, and also when blending flash with ambient light. Many hand-held meters have a flat disc mode that allows you to measure the light from each light source separately. This can save you from having to turn off one of your lights to measure another.

A hand-held meter measures light intensity and displays the aperture and shutter speed settings needed to produce a standard exposure. When measuring continuous light sources, you will use both readings to set your camera, but with flash and strobe you will select a shutter speed at or below the maximum sync speed (more on that later) and only use the indicated aperture. That's because the strobe delivers all of its light in a pulse that finishes long before the shutter closes. When you are mixing ambient light and strobe, the aperture controls the strobe exposure and the shutter speed controls the ambient light. So, if your flash meter reads f/8, shooting at 1/250 (maximum sync for many cameras) might not register anything lit by ambient light at all, but shooting at 1/60 would record parts of the scene illuminated by the ambient light two stops lighter.

Contrast, Chiaroscuro, and Noir

The word "chiaroscuro" is Italian for light/dark, and it is often used to describe high-contrast, low-key, images. Sixteenth-century Baroque and Mannerist painting made heavy use of chiaroscuro, and Caravaggio is particularly well known for employing it. It is a useful technique for adding drama to a portrait that has been widely adopted by photographers. Shadow also creates a sense of mystery. In nude photography, dense shadows are often used to create a draping effect for the genitals. Slightly opening the shadows, so that we get just hints of detail, can pique the viewer's curiosity.

"Rembrandt" lighting is a specific application of chiaroscuro. Cecil B. DeMille is credited with the first use of the term, somewhere around 1915. The key characteristic of this style of lighting is that one side of the face is illuminated and the other side is dark, except for a triangular area beneath the eye. The triangle is produced by the intersection of the shadow extending from the nose and the shadow on the cheek. Ideally, it is the same width as the eye and no longer than the nose. The light is placed roughly 45 degrees to the side, and at an elevation of about 45 degrees, though this will vary, depending upon the shape of the subject's face and the attitude of their head. When the subject is facing away from the camera, the shadow side is closest to the camera. The effect is most dramatic with hard, high-contrast lighting. Grids and barn doors (discussed later in this chapter) are two light-shaping tools that can be used to enhance the effect by hardening the light and preventing it from spilling onto the background.

The opening shot for this chapter shows an example of rim lighting. Placing two strip lights (tall, narrow soft boxes) slightly behind the subject on each side and facing each other will produce this effect. The soft light wraps around the figure, gradually fading into shadow in the middle. As you move the model toward the camera and away from the lights, the shadow area in the middle expands until you have a silhouette with bright edges. "Egg crate" grids will harden the light from a soft box. A harder light makes

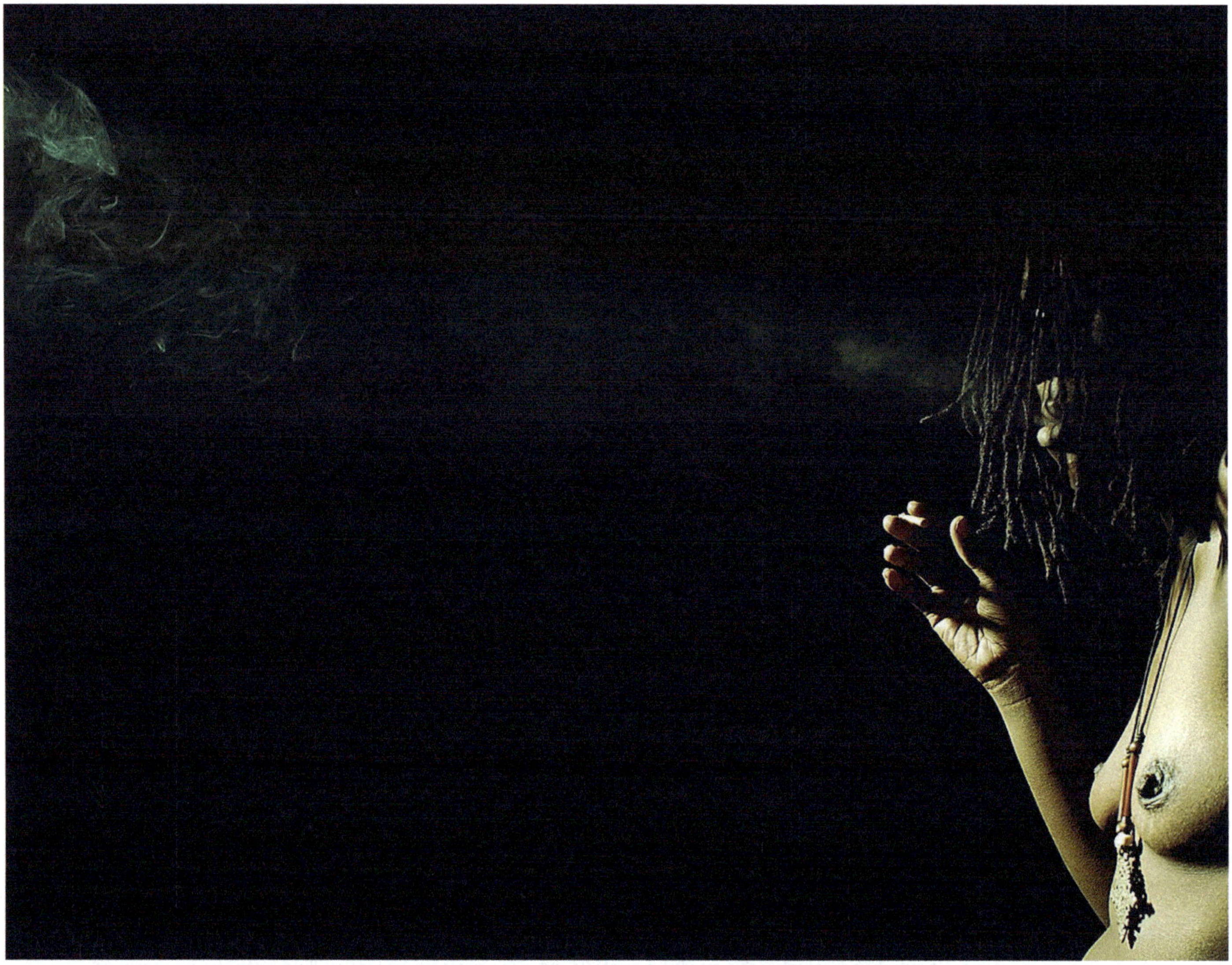

© Jafar M. Pierre. Light from the left illuminates the column of smoke in this asymmetrically balanced portrait. The intentional green cast adds to the mood.

the illuminated areas hotter and transitions more quickly to shadow, which tends to emphasize edges and make the figure more abstract. Rendering a rim-lit image in black and white tends to emphasize the form and space of the figure.

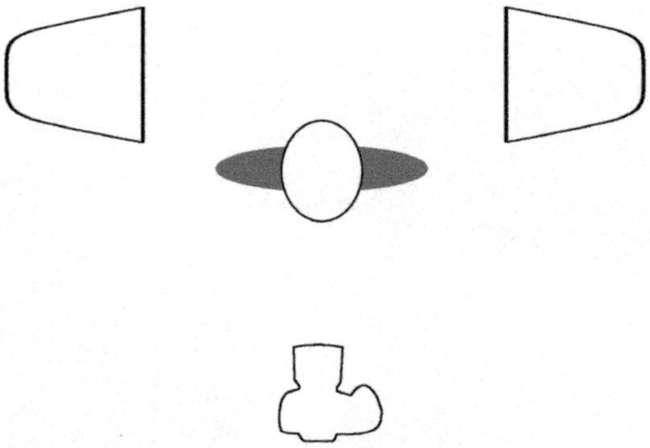

Lighting arrangement to create the rim lighting effect. Vary the effect by moving the model forward or backward relative to the lights.

A popular technique in cinema lighting is to light the front of the subject with a soft light source, and light the back with a hard light source to create a bright edge. Depending on how moody you want the shot to be, you can position the lights so that the face is partially obscured in shadow. With this lighting style, there is contrast in both the tonality and the qualities of the light.

Film noir (French for black film) is known for its low-key, high-contrast, black and white look. A classic example of the genre is Roman Polanski's *Chinatown*. The visual style is a descendant of German Expressionist cinema of the 1920s and 1930s (e.g. *The Cabinet of Dr. Caligari*, Fritz Lang's *M*). Scenes are often lit from the back or the side, with harsh shadows. Hard light sources, such as Fresnel spots or grids, are typically used.

Avedon Lighting

Richard Avedon's signature portrait look isolated the subject against a plain white background. The plain white gives us nothing to work with, not even color or tone, and so we look that much more closely at the subject. The evenness of that white background and the fact that it registers as white in the photo are two clues that the look is not as simple to achieve as it appears.

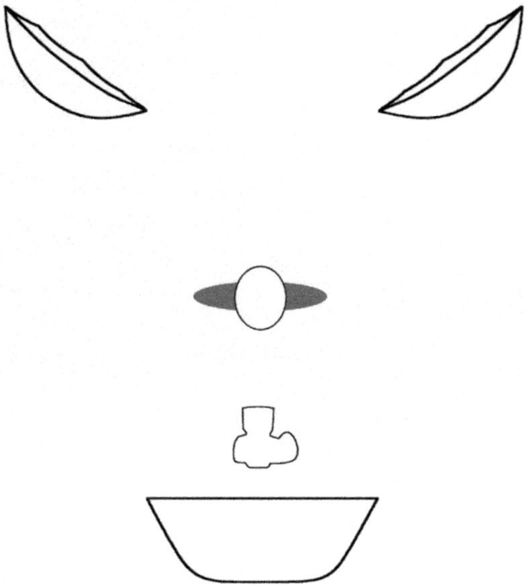

Set-up for Avedon lighting.

The lighting works by illuminating the background separately from the sitter. For best results, you need some distance between the sitter and the background, so that you don't have to contend with spill light from the background wrapping around the sitter.

Avedon himself typically used a large soft box to light the model, but your variation on that look could use any instrument you like—a grid spot in the Rembrandt position, for example. The light on the

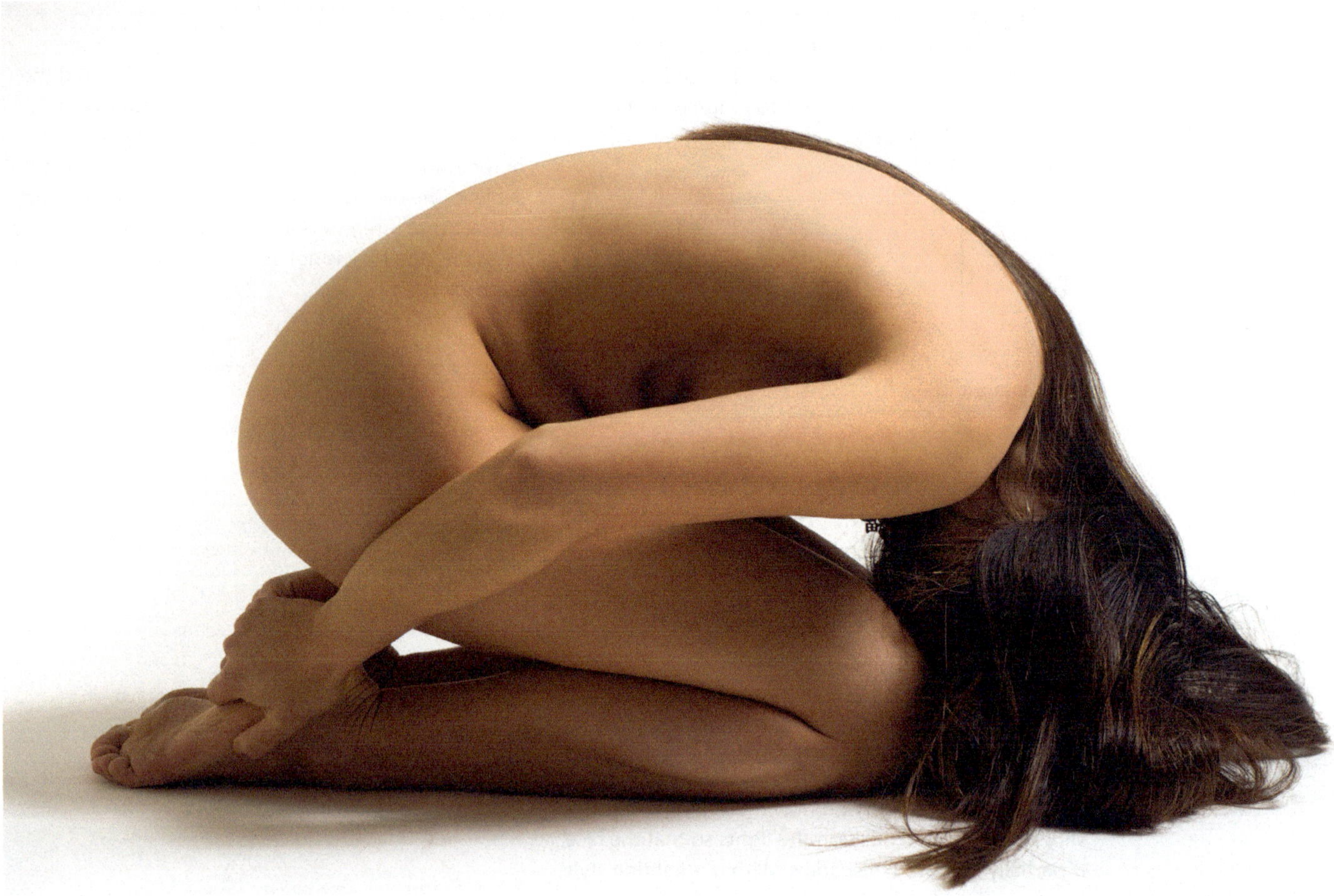

Above: © Lou Benjamin. The white seamless paper background is lit Avedon-style with two umbrellas. Instead of using flat, frontal light, a medium soft box was placed above right. The shadow on the floor indicates the location of the soft box.

Facing (left): © Lou Benjamin. Model: The Red Pill. Shooting into the shadow, with lighting from two light sources. A hard light source is positioned behind at camera left. Note the highlights on the hands and the spill across the thigh from a soft box positioned above right, in front.

Facing (right): © Lou Benjamin. Model: Béu Tornaghi.

background should be even, and should read approximately two stops brighter than the subject. Meter the background first, then light your model. For example, if you can get your background evenly lit at f/11, you want your sitter's reading to be f/5.6 for a two-stop difference, or f/4 for three stops.

Other lighting styles use uneven lighting on the background to isolate the subject. For example, you can use a spot or snoot to shine a circle or oval onto the background, and place the sitter inside the vignette to produce a result similar to burning the edges in post-production. With "checker boarding," one or more lights are shined onto the background to create alternating light and dark areas.

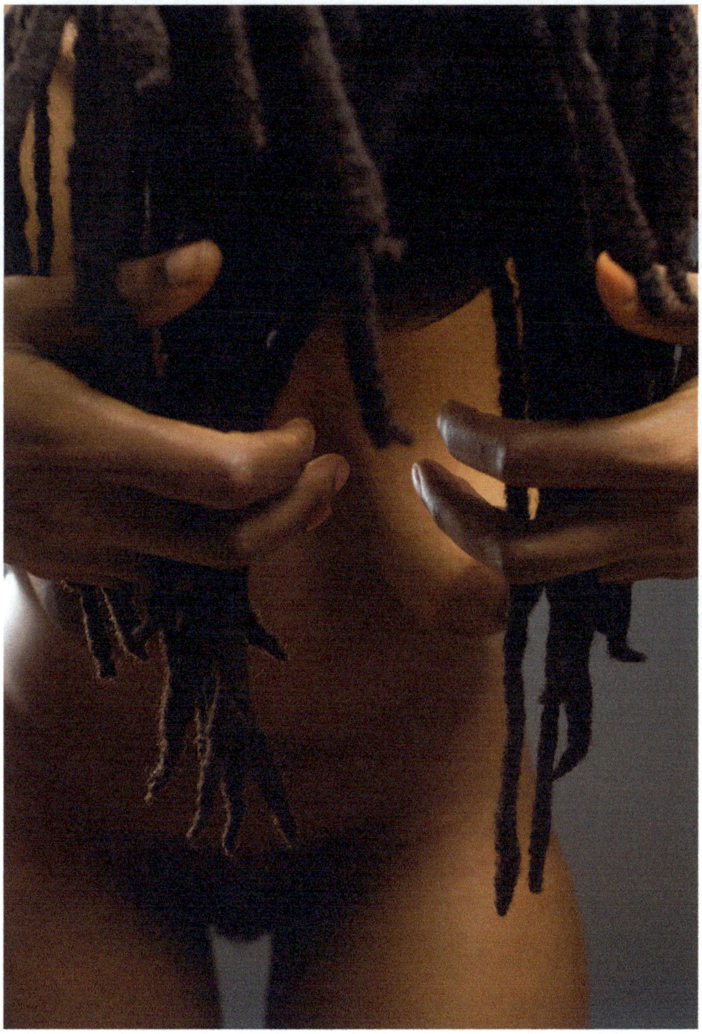

Silhouettes

To make a strong silhouette, it's often necessary to actually light the background. When you illuminate a light-colored background, a fair amount of light can bounce around the room and that bounced light can be strong enough to fill the shadows in the foreground and diminish the effect. You can use a "black bounce" in front of the model and around the shooting area to control the unwanted reflections. Black bounce can be a matte black cloth material that is taped or draped over walls and surfaces or large sheets of foam core with a matte black surface. Some studios even paint the ceiling black. Of course, you can amplify the effect of the lighting with post-production in Photoshop, but it takes skill to make the result look convincing.

Pulling the figure away from the background keeps light from spilling around the edges of the figure. Conversely, placing the figure close to the background can give the effect of the figure merging with it.

The technique that photographer and educator Frank Franca calls "shooting into the shadow" is an extension silhouetting. The subject is placed between the photographer and the lighting instrument so that some light spills over onto the camera side of the shot. The effect can be very moody, featuring large, dark areas punctuated with small pools of light.

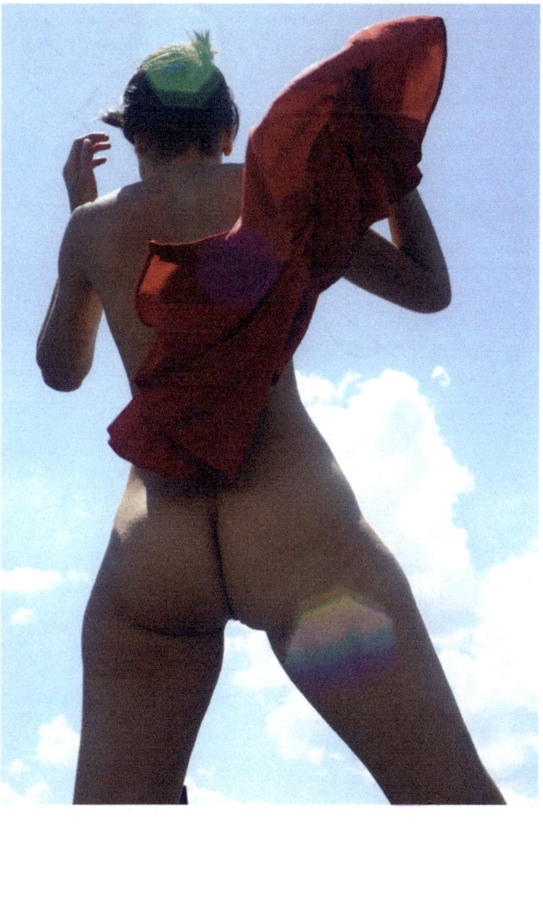

Working with Spill, Flare, and Halation

When you place the sitter between a light source and the camera, there is always the potential for some light to travel directly from the light source into the lens. If the light is strong enough, you will get a colored flare pattern in the image. If not, you will generally get a soft, foggy, reduced-contrast look known as halation. The shorter the focal length (the wider the angle), and the more wide open the aperture, the more you'll have to contend with it.

You can intentionally produce this effect and use it artistically, but if you don't want it, your first line of defense is a lens hood. In more difficult cases, the important thing to recognize is that these effects are caused by light that is not illuminating the scene, but spilling into the lens instead. You can find the offending light source and "flag" it by blocking its light from the lens. A flag can be a notebook held in your hand, or it can be a piece of cloth or plastic made for that purpose and attached to a stand. You can also make your own flags out of Cinefoil, a heavy aluminum foil painted flat black.

Often, it is easiest to put the flag close to the lens, but sometimes it is sufficient to place the flag on or near the light source. How do you figure out where to place the flag? If you can look into the front of the lens, you'll see the offending light source reflected in the front element of the lens. Just position your flag so that the reflection disappears.

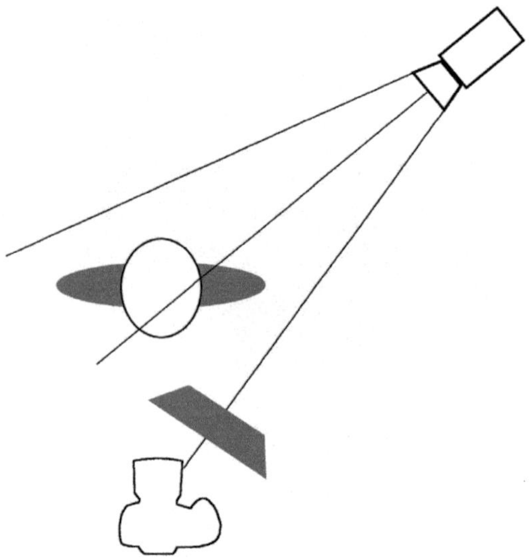

Flagging a light source to prevent flare.

If the lighting instrument you're using spreads light, there is always the potential for spill, meaning light that is falling onto surfaces that you didn't intend to illuminate. Aside from flare and halation, the problem can be as simple as too much light falling onto the background. The trick is to position the light, the camera, or both so as to minimize unwanted spill.

A creative use of spill is to intentionally bounce light off walls. Cinematographers often create soft lighting for large areas by bouncing lights off a pebbled foam surface called bead board. It's important to consider the color of the surface you are bouncing the light off of. It can substantially change the color of the illumination with some unpleasant results.

Daylight

Many photographers swear by daylight, natural, or "available" light. Paolo Roversi, known for his elegant nudes, has shot mostly with window light throughout his entire career, and Irving Penn used window light for most of his portraits. Daylight studios often have north-facing windows because the light changes the least during the course of the day. The light is as blue as open shade.

Photographers who regularly work with natural light are keenly aware of how it changes and moves throughout the day. Helmut Newton did a series of diptychs contrasting "naked" and "clothed," part of which he shot at a villa in northern Italy in 1981. In one of his first diptychs, he shot the same woman clothed and undressed (except for high heels, which he thought was essential for distinguishing nude from naked). He shot each panel of the diptych in the same location, using similar poses, but he didn't try to perfectly duplicate the poses. He realized that the light would change, and didn't want light to be the only difference between the two panels. In doing so, he was embracing and exploiting the constantly changing character of natural light, while emphasizing that these were two distinct moments.

Facing (top): © Pascal Renoux. "Golden hours" light is very warm and contrasts with the cool blue of the sky, which is not yet fully illuminated. The elongated rectangular framing of this photo also emphasizes the gesture of the outstretched arms.

Facing (bottom): © Saddi Khali. Shadows cast by Venetian blinds create a distinctive dappling pattern that adds to the visual interest in this environmental portrait. Man Ray produced a number of well-known photos using blinds. Lace curtains can also create striking dappled effects.

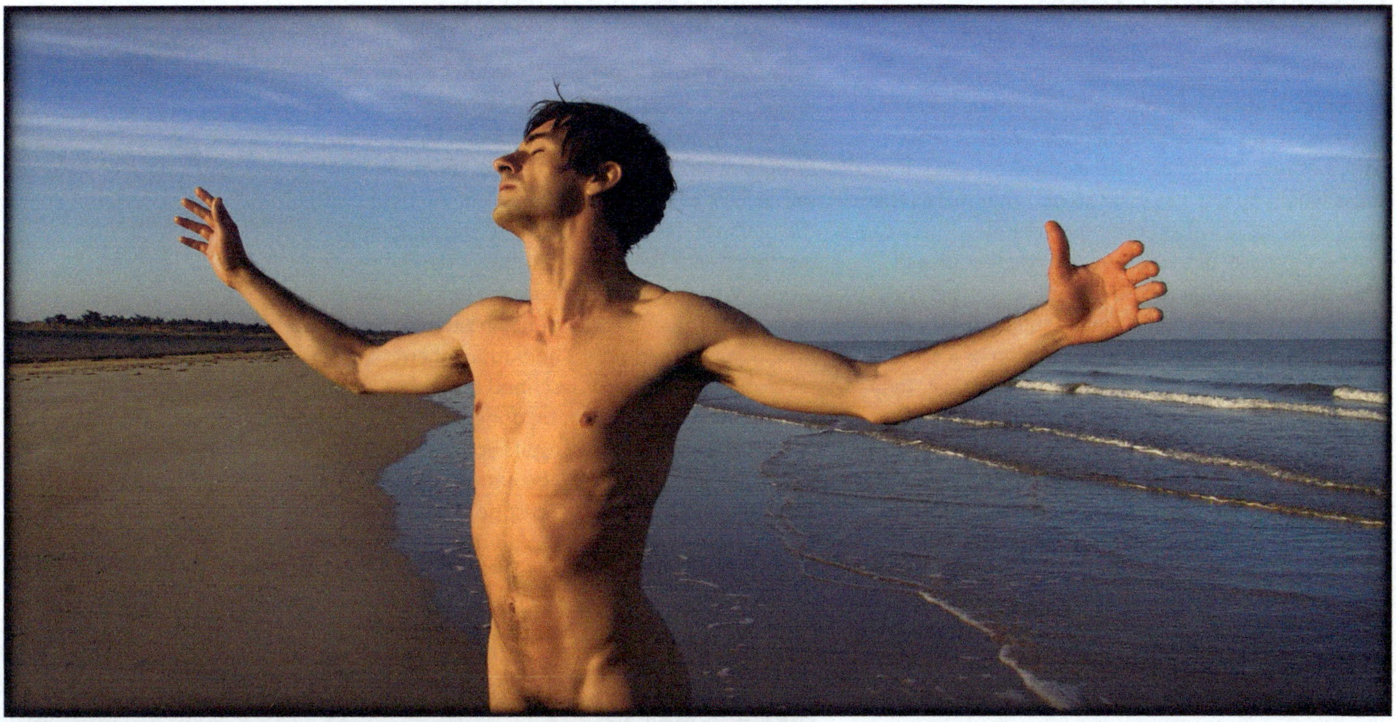

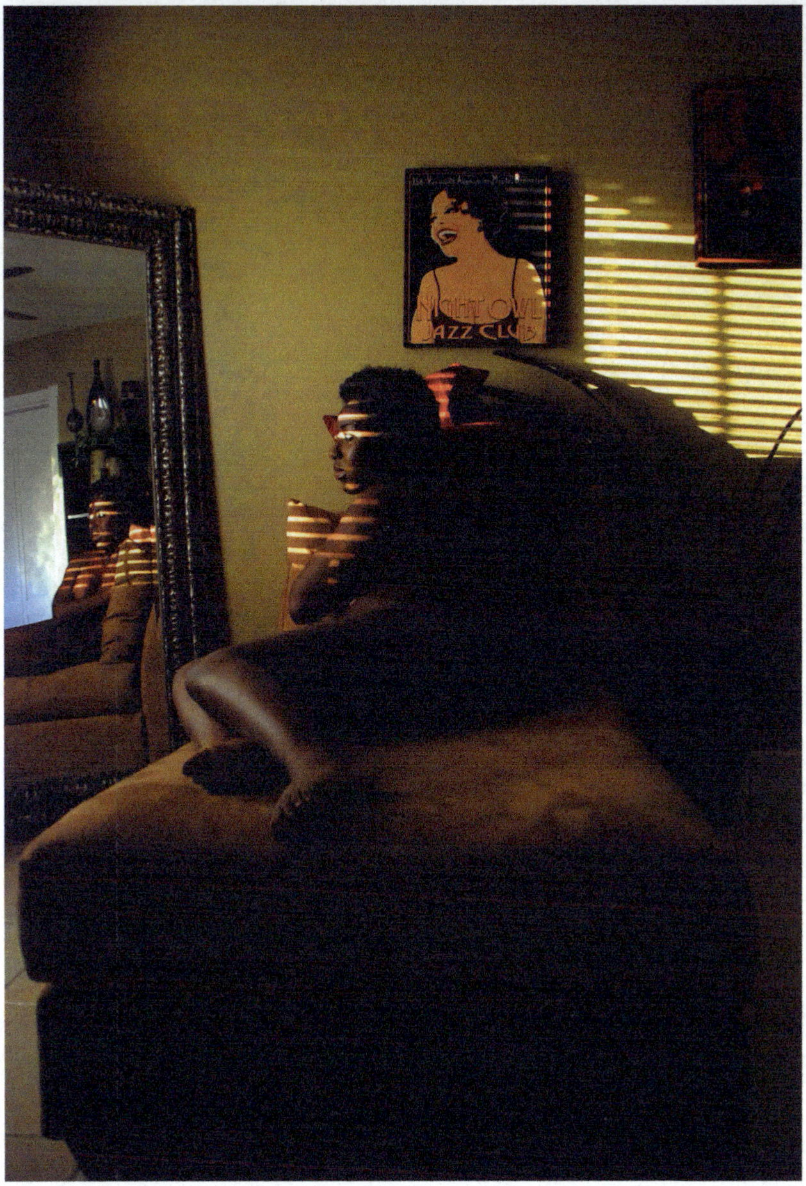

Many who shoot outdoors prefer the "golden hours" near the break of day and sunset, when shadows are long and the light takes on a warm color. That color is an important quality. If you're shooting digital, it's important not to wash out all that beautiful color by using auto white balance or even a custom white balance that neutralizes the color of the light. Instead, you want to shoot with a standard daylight white balance. That way, the warm color of the light will register.

If you duck under a canopy of trees, you may well get dappled light—an irregular pattern of highlights that falls on your sitter. Exposure settings can be challenging in this often beautiful and dramatic light. If your white balance is set to daylight, the leaves will also create a strong green color cast in your image. If you shoot raw, you can photograph a gray card to sample the white balance during the initial editing stage, or you can compensate for the green by moving the Tint slider toward magenta. It might also be possible to tame unruly highlights in Lightroom or Camera RAW.

Continuous Lights

Continuous lights used be called "hot" lights, but newer sources such as LED lights do not get very hot. These lights are the most straightforward to work with, because they're as close to WYSIWYG ("what you see is what you get") as you can get. That makes them great tools for learning lighting techniques. There can still be surprises, but you have a fairly clear idea of what the camera will record as soon as you set them up and turn them on. And, unlike sunlight, they don't change characteristics over the duration of a shoot.

LED light sources have come into their own. They offer the benefit of low power consumption and relatively cool operation. LEDs also typically have high CRI (color rendition index) values of 80 or more, which means their mix of wavelengths compares favorably with sunlight, strobes, and tungsten.

Halogen bulbs are tungsten (incandescent) bulbs that burn brighter and at a higher color temperature than household tungsten lights. A chemical reaction inside the bulbs causes the tungsten to be deposited back onto the filament instead of adhering to the glass the way it does in standard tungsten bulbs, so halogen bulbs do not shift color as much as they age. Halogen bulbs emit a high amount of UV light, and should always be used with protective glass or a diffuser in front of the bulb. Fixtures employing halogen bulbs can be simple affairs with just a reflector, or a more elaborate design with a focusing mechanism such as the Fresnel (pronounced "fruh-nell") spots from companies such as Arri. The beam from a Fresnel spot can be dialed between a tight spot pattern and a very wide flood.

Alternative Lighting

Projected images can be used to create layered images in-camera. The colored elements of the image being projected interact with the skin coloration, often producing surprising results. The three-dimensional form of the body distorts and interferes with the reading of the projection and the projection interferes with the reading of the body. The relatively dim light of the projector requires long exposures and opens the possibility of having the subject move intentionally to add blurs and atmosphere.

Light painting (also described at the end of the previous chapter) can be done with flashlights and long exposures. The results you get from the trial-and-error process can be extremely variable. Reducing the ISO to the lowest possible settings can maximize exposure times. Colored gels or diffusion

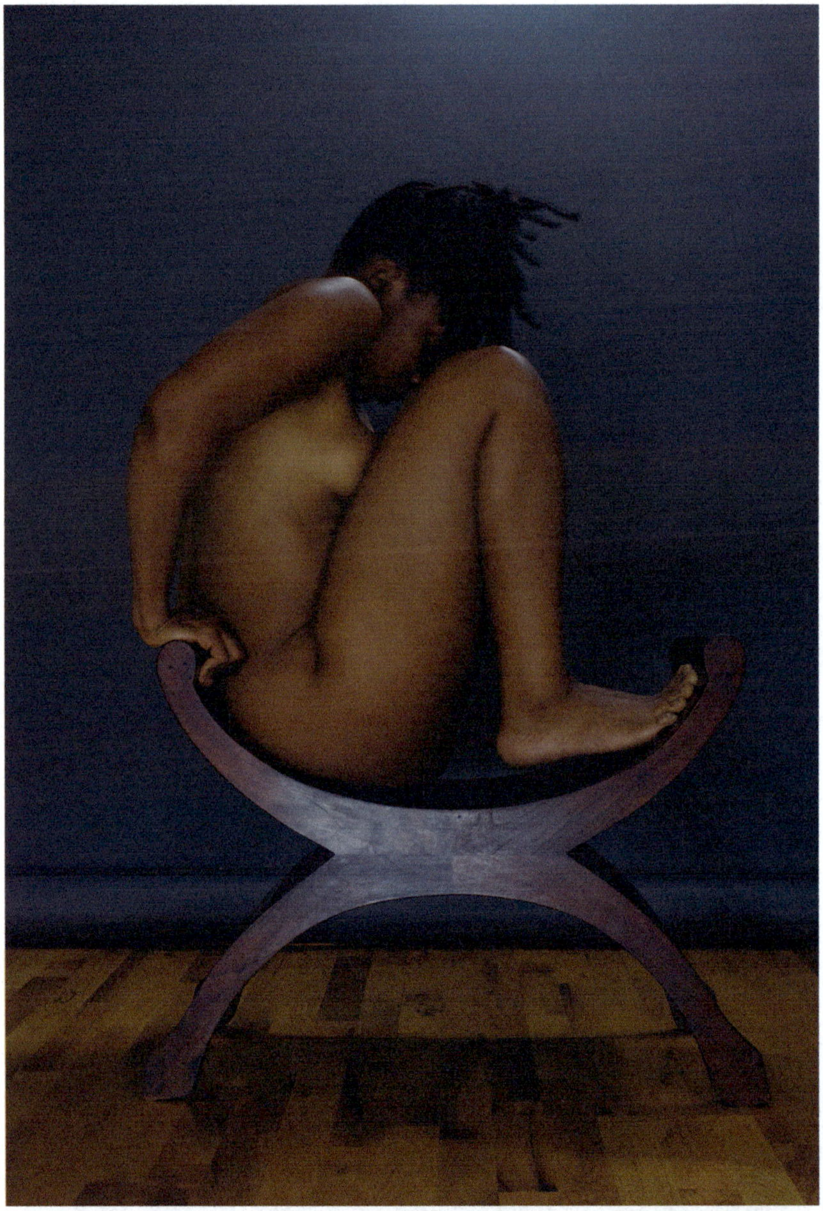

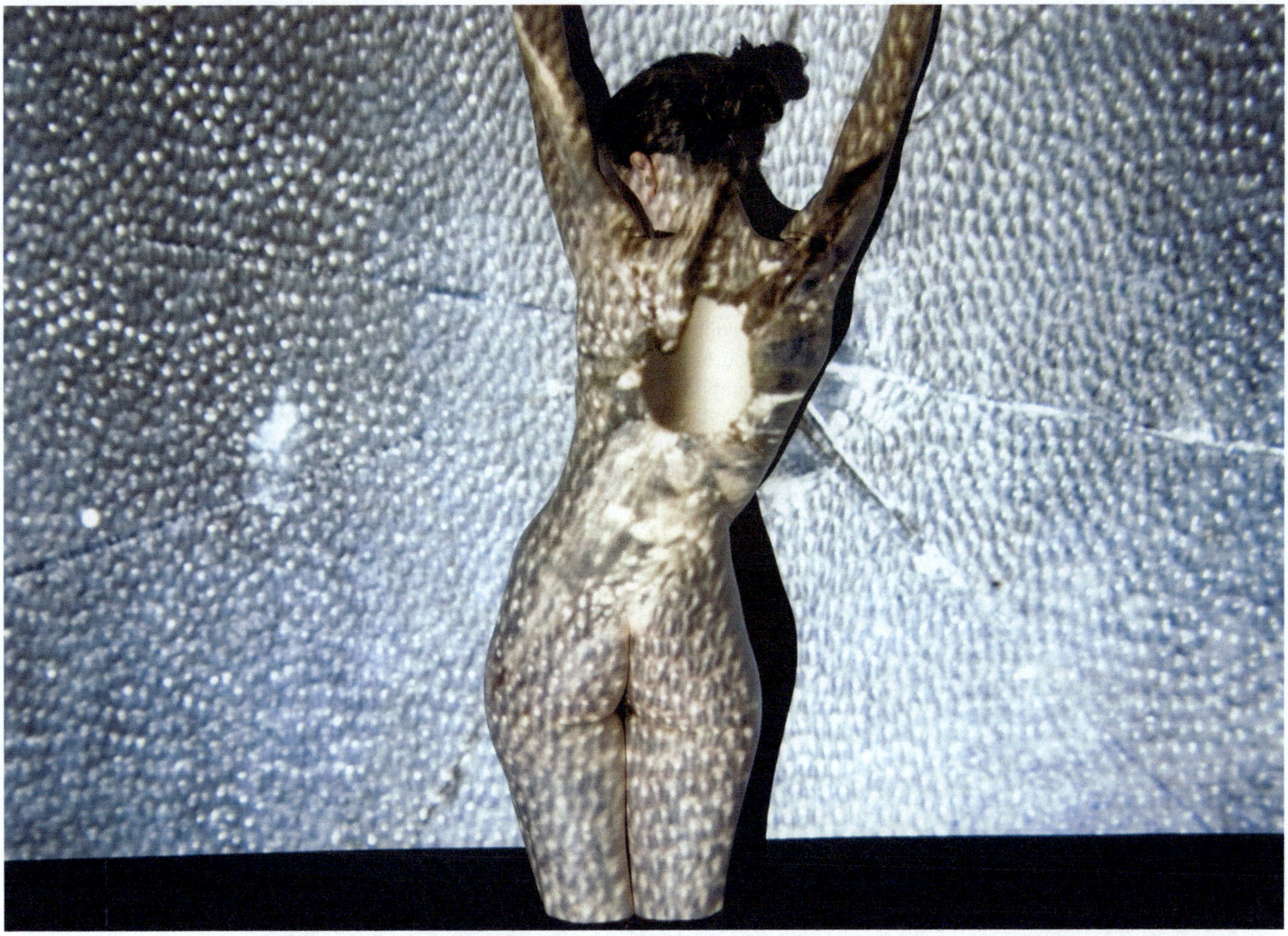

Above: "Shattered" © J. D. Yezierski. Model: Bitsy. The expressive figure of the model fuses with the projected image of a broken window. Note how the skin color affects the bluish color of the projected glass.

Facing: © Lou Benjamin. Model: The Red Pill. A scene lit entirely with a flashlight. Exposure was 30 seconds at f/10, ISO 400. Diffusion material was placed over the light, which was waved across the model from the right, left, above, and in front. The confused shadow beneath the seat hints at how the light was applied from multiple directions. The camera was a Nikon D200 with a 35mm f/2 lens (equivalent to 52mm field of view).

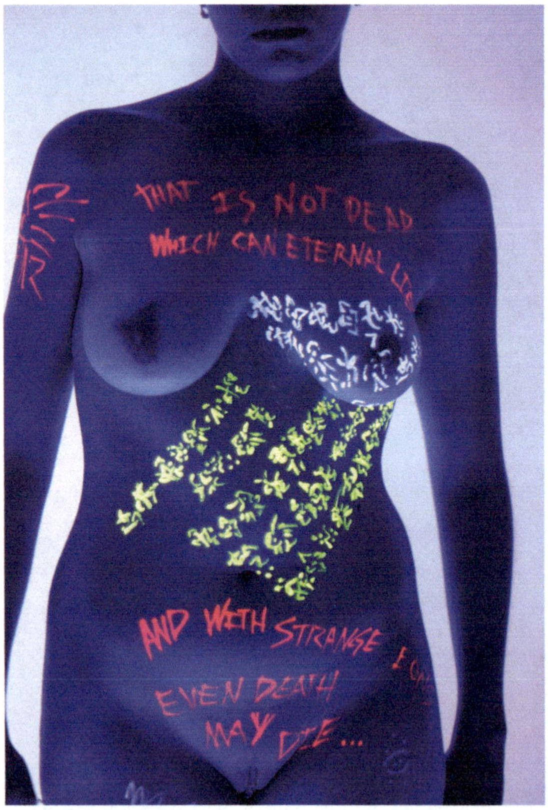

material can be placed over the flashlight to change the appearance of the beam. Pointing the beam away from the camera can ensure that the light source itself does not register. If you don't want yourself to register in the frame, wear dark, non-reflective clothing and try not to stand in one place for very long.

Another lighting approach is to drape lights on the body. If the lights are colored, you need to carefully control the exposure to capture the color of the lights. Some of the light will illuminate the body, but much more of it will illuminate the room, making the body a light source. You can also turn the body into a light source by applying fluorescent paint to the skin and lighting it with a black light. Some black-light nudes aren't even recognizable as bodies. If you work with this technique, take proper precautions—ultraviolet light is damaging to the eyes.

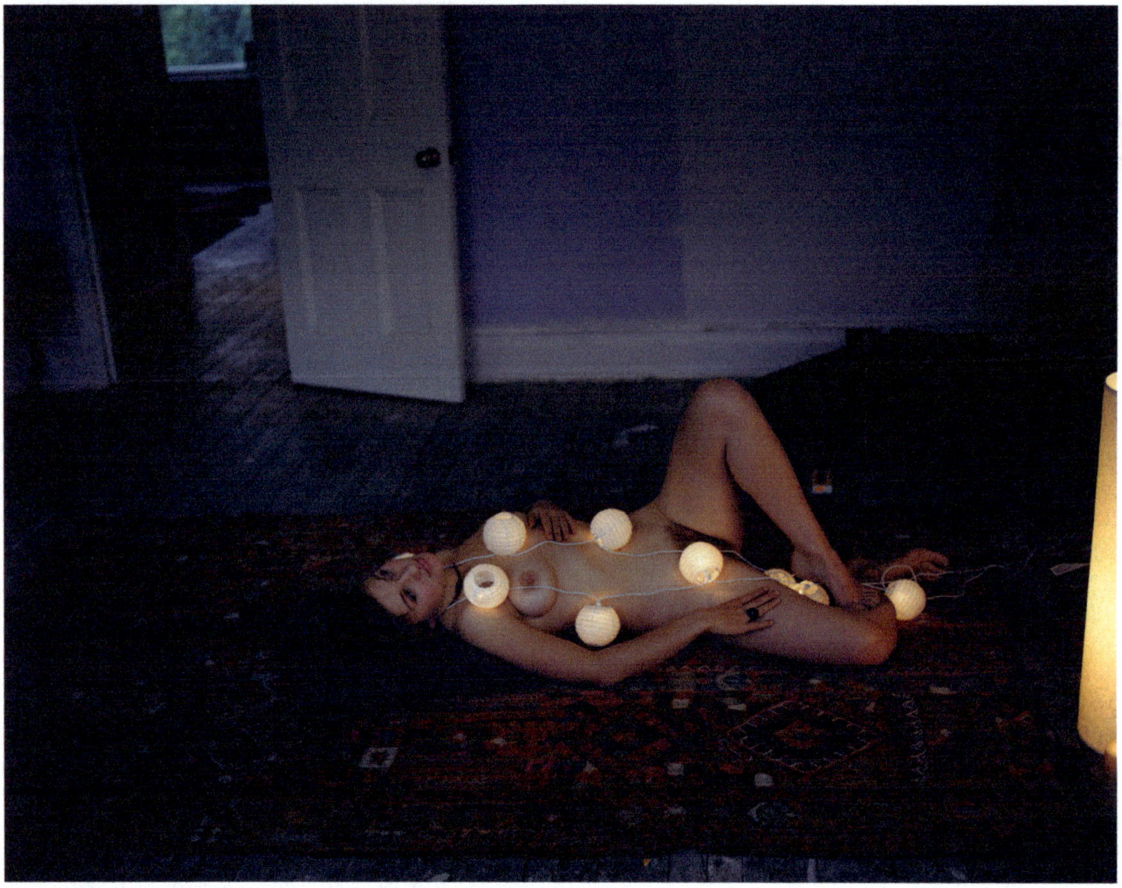

Strobes and Speed Lights

Strobes and speed lights are based on the same principle: Substantial amounts of energy are stored in capacitors which release a burst of high-voltage, high-current electricity into a tube filled with xenon gas to produce a glowing plasma. The resulting flash of light is very bright, and can last from 1/2000 second to as little as 1/12,000 second. The flash tube design used in speed lights and strobes today is essentially the same as Harold Edgerton's design from the 1940s. Because the pulse from strobes and speed lights is so brief and intense, they cannot produce the smooth, impressionistic blurring of continuous lights, but a number of pattern effects can result from repeatedly firing the device while the shutter remains open.

Strobes can produce substantial amounts of light and are typically charged from the wall. Most strobe systems feature light modifiers such as soft boxes and grids to control and add character to the lights. The array of light-shaping tools available for strobes is much wider than for any other type of lighting instrument.

Speed lights are compact designs with much lower power capabilities than their bigger siblings, the studio strobe. Speed lights generally use lenses that operate in a fashion similar to a Fresnel spot to either focus the light into a narrow beam that travels farther, or spreads to produce a flood light.

Strobes

The high output of strobes means that you can keep the ISO setting low on your digital camera, and even stop down the aperture for greater depth of field. In many cases, you won't need to use the strobe at full power, which means its recycle time will be faster still. Once designed mainly for use in the studio, strobes are becoming lighter and easier to use. A number of models are now powered by long-lasting rechargeable batteries, making them excellent for location work.

There are two main designs for strobes: monolights, and pack and head systems. Monolights are self-powered heads which have become increasingly convenient and popular. Their integrated design makes them convenient to travel with. They also tend to be more affordably priced than pack and head systems. The Profoto D1 monolight has some of the best specs of any strobe on the market, regardless

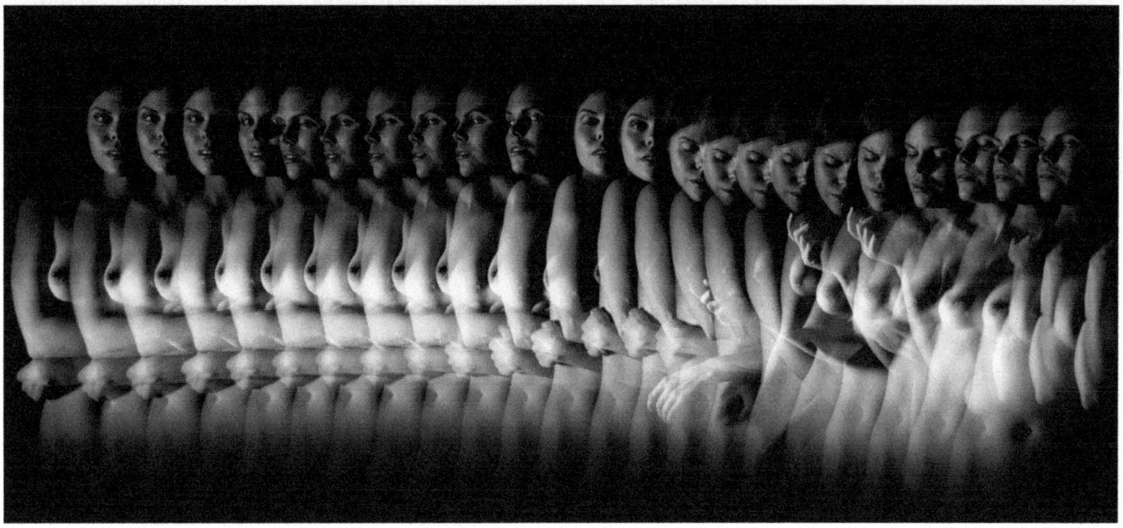

Facing (top): "Cthulhu's Canvas" © Richard Rasner (Unique Nudes) of Nakayama Studios. The glow on the body comes from fluorescent paint under UV light.

Facing (bottom): © Barney Cokeliss. Globe lights create pools of light on the body, while ambient light brings out the details of the figure and the setting.

Above: © P. J. Reptilehouse. An example of the photographer's early work. For his chronophotography, P. J. Reptilehouse uses a system he designed and built, consisting of a motorized camera mount and LED strobes, both controlled by a microprocessor. To create images, he essentially choreographs lighting and camera movement. He often choreographs the model's movement as well.

of design: Its output is adjustable over a seven-stop range in $\frac{1}{10}$ stop increments, while many strobes have a smaller range and are only variable in $\frac{1}{3}$ or $\frac{1}{2}$-stop increments. Recycle time is fast—about a second at full power, and even faster at lower settings.

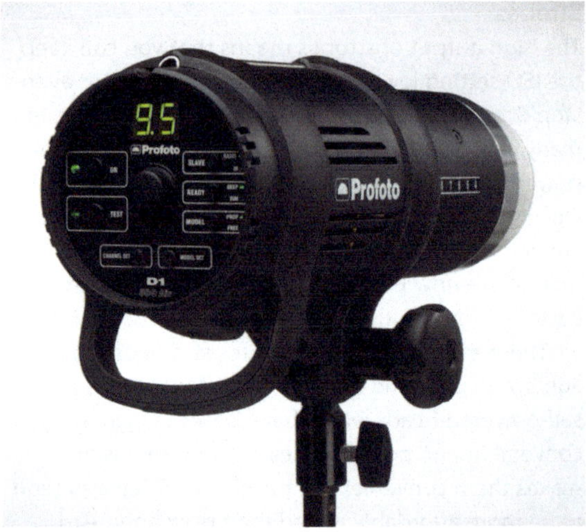

The Profoto D1 Air monolight is a compact design with great features and construction. All of the functions on the back panel can be controlled from the camera via the Air wireless remote system.

With pack and head systems, a power pack (sometimes referred to as a generator) houses the capacitors and controls, and separate heads are attached to the pack by a power cable. Most packs can control two or three heads, and are designed so that the power can be divided evenly or asymmetrically between the heads. One advantage of this design is that the heads are lighter than monolights. Packs can also be built with capacitors that store a lot more energy than the capacitors that fit into a monolight. With only one head connected to the pack, prodigious amounts of power can be delivered to the head.

Packs rated at 1200 ws are capable of delivering 600 ws to each of two heads simultaneously and are good for most digital applications. They are also substantially smaller and lighter than 2400 ws packs. On the other hand, the extra headroom of a 2400 ws pack can be useful, especially when used with power-hungry light-shaping tools or in outdoor applications. Still there are times when that amount of power is too much, especially when working in a small space.

The reason to be concerned with the power output of strobes is not raw power in its own right, but how much light is available after some of it has been absorbed by light-shaping tools and bounced around on its way to the subject. If the full power of a 1200 ws pack gives a reading of f/5.6 for a particular setup, substituting a 2400 ws pack at full power will give f/8. If you need f/11 from that 2400 ws pack, it's time to move the head about 1/4 closer. So, you'll want a lot of power when you want to do day-for-night effects, but when your concern is how dim you can make the light, a low-power pack is best, because the high-power units cannot be attenuated enough.

Most strobes have a 150 to 250 watt modeling light. That's barely enough intensity to be visible through some light-shaping tools, but it is usually enough to tell you if you're aiming the light in the right direction, and you can also use the modeling light as a continuous light source. To see what the strobe light is really doing, you need to take a test shot. Most strobes temporarily turn off the modeling light when the flash fires and turn it back on when the unit is fully charged. In cheap systems, this is the only indication that the system is ready to fire. Better systems have the option to switch the modeling light off altogether and beep when the system is ready. This can be important in applications when you are using a slow shutter speed to mix the strobe with ambient light and you don't want the modeling light to affect the scene.

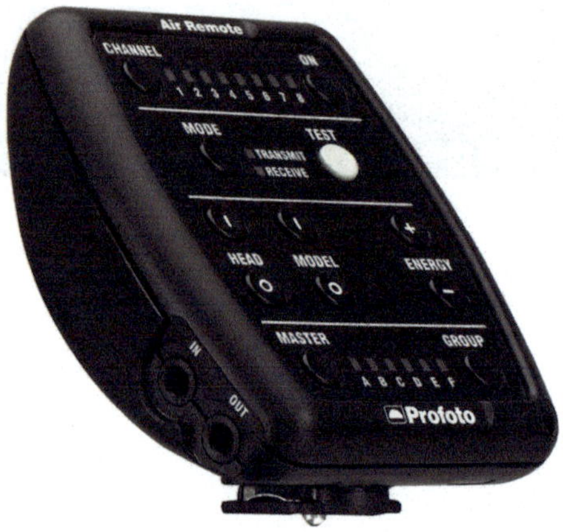

The wireless remote module for the Profoto Air system plugs into your camera's sync shoe. The radio trigger also controls all of the functions for multiple heads, across multiple frequencies and channels.

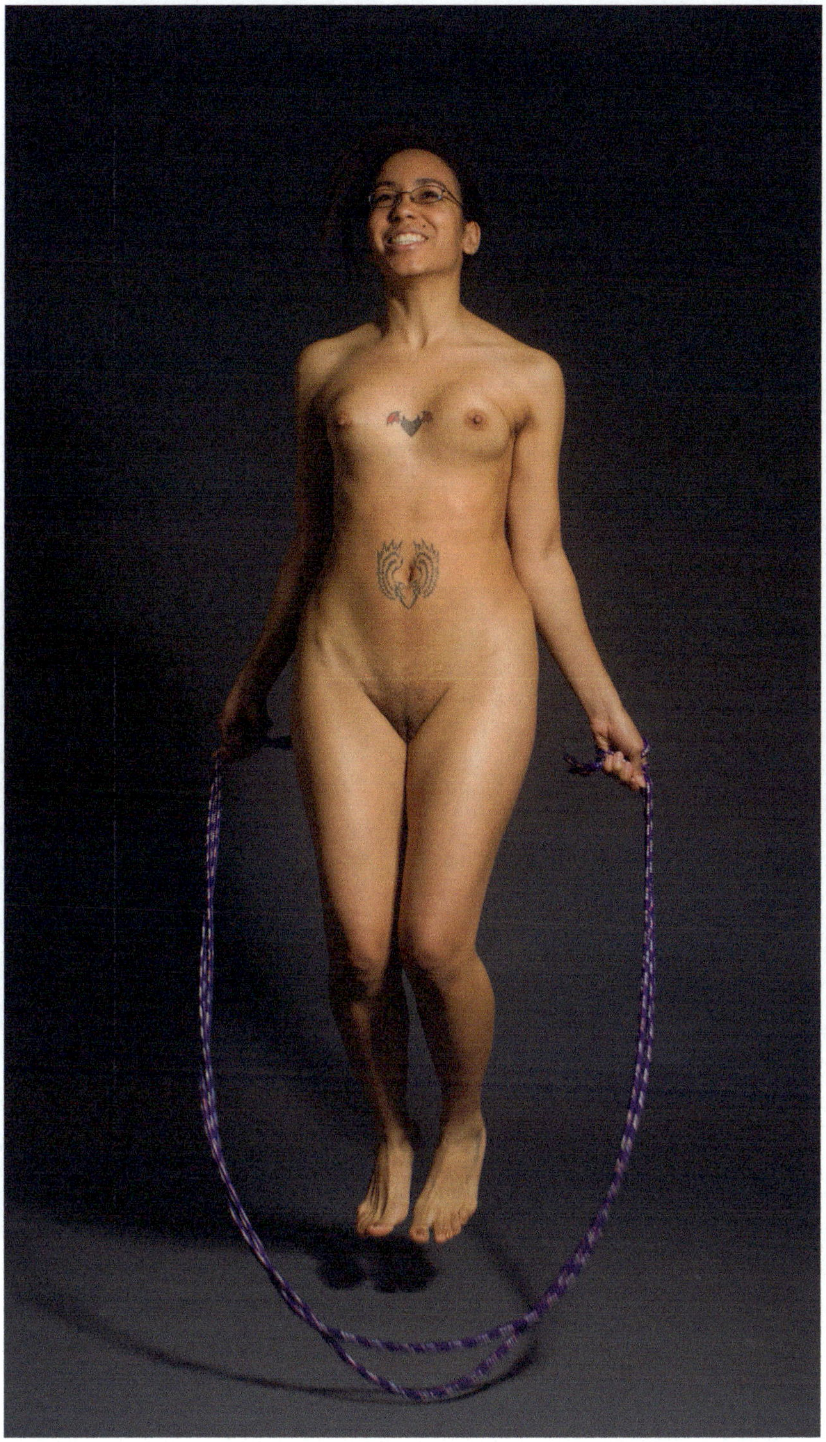

Sync cables have been the standard way of triggering strobes since their invention, and they have rightfully earned a notorious reputation for failing at the worst possible moment. The tiny connection that fits into the camera is fragile, and so are the wires inside the cable itself. If you use sync cables, be sure to have a spare handy. Pocket Wizard is one company that makes radio triggering devices to replace cables. You plug a transceiver into the flash shoe on your camera and plug a second into the strobe. The Pocket Wizard Plus III can trigger strobes or speed lights, and can also be used as a relay or a wireless remote shutter release.

Several manufacturers make strobes with built-in Pocket Wizard receivers, and others have their own radio systems. For example, the Profoto Air system remote also fits into the camera's flash shoe, and can adjust power levels, modeling lights, and even switch heads off and on independently. When used with their monolights, that means no more climbing ladders to adjust settings. The unit has a range of 1000 feet, and can manage six groups of lights over eight channels.

Speed Lights and Off-camera Flash

Canon calls them speedlites, while Nikon calls them speedlights. Regardless of spelling, speed lights are designed to be plugged into the sync shoe on your camera. The automation built into speed lights can make certain lighting tasks easy, as long as you can make sense of the manual. The battery powered units are relatively small and lightweight, which makes them very useful in outdoor and location settings where you can't easily connect to a power supply.

When connected to the camera's hot shoe, high-end pro models communicate directly with the camera, allowing them to be adjusted via the camera's controls. The connection also allows them to take advantage of the camera's TTL metering to automatically adjust power output for the correct exposure. Fill flash becomes as simple as pressing a button. If you need more or less fill, flash compensation works just like exposure compensation. Top of the line models are packed with features, but can be expensive. If you need a simple workhorse flash without all the bells and whistles, mid-range models may be sufficient at a fraction of the price.

© Lou Benjamin. Strobe light freezes action, while an aperture of f/10 provides depth of field in case the subject bounces forward or backward.

On-camera flash produces a very recognizable, flat, frontal light that is often unflattering and easily causes red eye. Getting the flash off the camera can make a huge difference. Speed lights can be placed on light stands or clamped to structures and triggered remotely. Umbrella mounts and speed rings let you attach one or more speed lights to umbrellas and soft boxes (discussed in greater detail later in this chapter).

To trigger your speed light off-camera, you can use Pocket Wizard radio triggers instead of proprietary IR-based triggering systems built into some cameras. The MiniTT1 and FlexTT5 units combine to extend your camera's TTL metering off-camera. The Plus X and Plus III models can be used with the flashes in manual mode. The experience is not unlike working with basic monolights.

As tempting as it might be to think of these small powerhouses as equivalent to studio strobes, low light output, slow recycle times, and a voracious appetite for batteries are significant limitations. Boosting the power by using multiple speed lights can become a complicated and pricey proposition.

Profoto has introduced a new category of lighting instrument that it calls off-camera flashes, which combine capabilities studio strobes and speed lights, making them excellent for location shooting. The battery-powered Profoto B1 and B2 units are triggered by a radio-based control unit that plugs into the camera's hot shoe and features TTL. High-speed sync capabilities and high power output make it possible to shoot day-for-night or open the aperture wide for shallow depth of field effects in bright light. The 250 ws B2

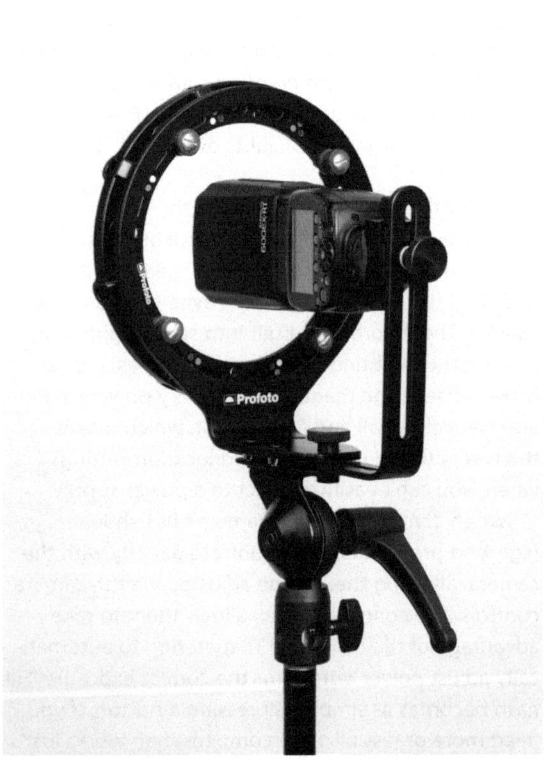

The Profoto RFi Speedlight Speedring lets you use their full range of RFi soft boxes with speed lights. Two speed lights can be attached together for use with larger soft boxes or greater output.

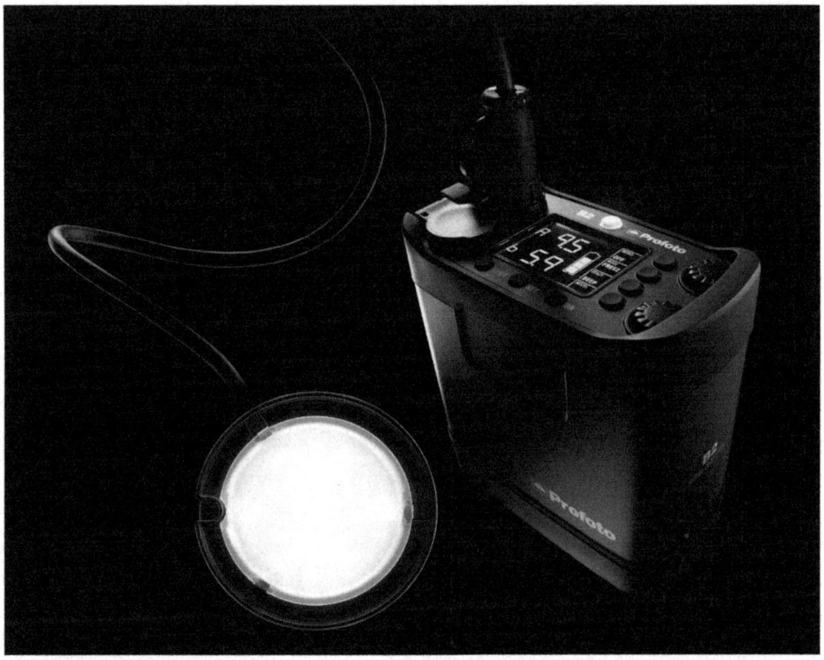

The Profoto B2 is a lightweight, powerful, battery-powered pack and head system with TTL.

ABOUT SYNC SPEED

The focal plane shutter used in 35mm format dSLRs works by opening a front curtain to uncover the sensor and then closing the rear curtain to cover the sensor after the appropriate delay. The flash fires once the front curtain fully opens. At speeds up to the maximum sync speed (typically 1/250 second or 1/125 second), the sensor is fully uncovered and the flash fires before the rear curtain begins to close. But at speeds above that, the rear curtain begins to cover the sensor before the flash can fire. The result is a black band where the rear curtain blocked the exposure, and the higher the shutter speed, the bigger the band.

High-speed synchronization (HSS) uses multiple flash pulses to enable you to use much higher shutter speeds, which can be combined with wider apertures to create shallow depth of field effects in bright sunlight, or with high-power settings to create day-for-night effects. Each maker implements HSS in a different manner, with varying results. HSS on dedicated speed lights generally only works at low power settings. Pocket Wizard's MiniTT1/FlexTT5 system can sync Canon and Nikon cameras with a broad range of strobes and speed lights, though they acknowledge that clipping and uneven exposure—which can vary by as much as two stops across the area of the photo at high sync speeds—are potential issues. Profoto's TTL-based HSS system for the B1 and B2 off-camera flashes produces consistent exposure with shutter speeds as high as 1/8000 second, and is available for Nikon and Canon.

(guide number 32 2/10 @ 2m/ISO 100) is substantially more powerful than a hot shoe flash, but its compact head is still small enough to be attached to the camera with a bracket. The B2 has a separate, compact power pack that can be slung over the shoulder. The B1 is a 500 ws monolight (guide number 45 2/10 @ 2m/ISO 100) similar to their D1 studio monolight.

Ring Lights

The ring light, or ringflash, is a special type of strobe that attaches to your camera and surrounds the lens. It's part flash head and part modifier, and is mainly used in the studio. It was invented for medical photography and has been widely adopted by fashion and art photographers. Because the light comes from equal distances around the lens, most shadows are canceled, and the illumination has a distinctive look. Helmut Newton pioneered its use in fashion and the light was a staple of his style for several years.

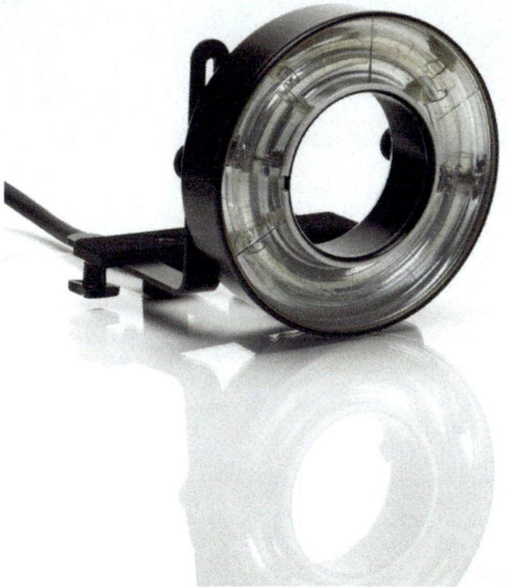

The Profoto Acute/D4 Ring is a ring light designed specifically for Acute and D4 power packs.

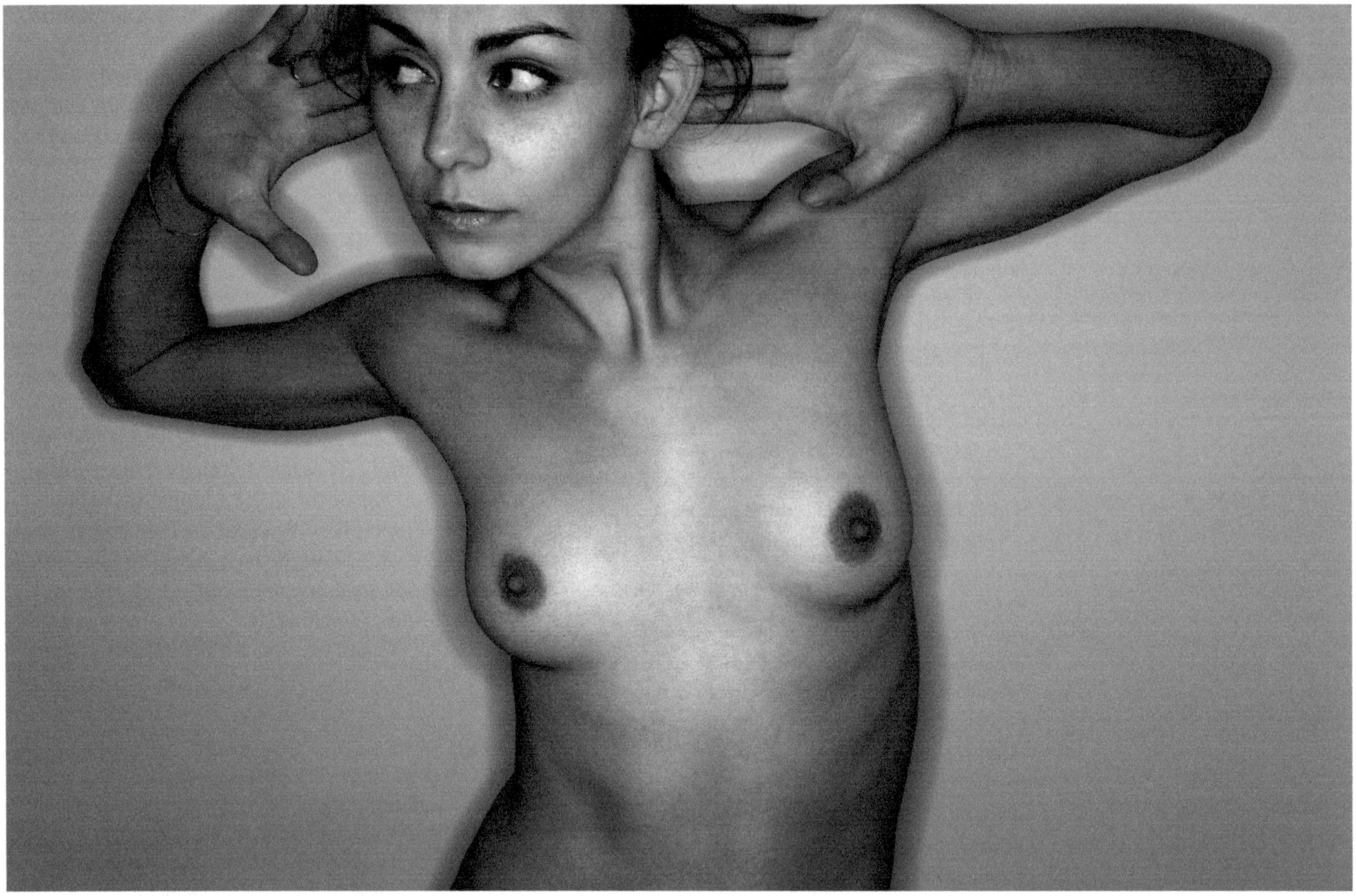

"Portrait of a Muse III," 2009 © Tobias Slater-Hunt. From the *Most Beautiful Woman in Town* series. Early digital shoot with ringflash in Justyna's apartment, 2008.

When your subject is close to a wall, ring light will create a shadow that looks like you outlined him or her with a thin, dark marker. The outline expands to some degree as you move away from the wall. If your room is dark, and your subject's pupils are dilated, the flash will switch on and off faster than they can constrict, causing red-eye. A number of photographers have used this fact to their advantage, intentionally inducing it. Others have either removed the red-eye in post-production or converted to black and white, where it's not as obvious.

The trickiest thing about working with a ring light is handling exposure. You can't vary the distance to the subject too much without over-exposing or under-exposing. Cut the distance in half, and you've increased the exposure fourfold (two stops). If you were ten feet away and step back another three, your light is now one stop dimmer.

The original ring light design was a special flash head powered by a pack. Profoto, Broncolor, and Elinchrom all make versions of this design. The basic design is essentially a bare doughnut, but different manufacturers offer a range of diffusers and soft light reflectors that further shape the light. A number of companies now sell devices that attach to speed lights to turn them into low-powered ring lights, and several manufacturers make hot shoe ring lights that are primarily designed for macro photography. While these designs are generally limited to relatively close work, they support TTL, which means you're more likely to have good control over exposure if you do move around.

Light Modifiers

Light modifiers dramatically expand the expressive potential of working with light, allowing you to harden, soften, focus, constrain, color, and shape light.

Umbrellas soften and spread light over a wide area. They are extremely simple to use, and are also among the least expensive of the light-shaping tools. A silver-lined umbrella gives a light that has brighter highlights, more saturated color, and a slightly harder look than the light from a white-lined umbrella. There are also convertible umbrellas with a translucent interior and a detachable black cover that easily switch between bounce and shoot-through use. The light becomes softer as the size of the umbrella increases and the distance to the subject decreases. Still, it is possible to have too big an umbrella, and it is possible to move the instrument too close to the subject. Some manufacturers make heat-resistant umbrellas designed to work with high-temperature lights.

Umbrellas produce spill that can be hard to control, but which also makes them excellent for illuminating backgrounds, floors, and large areas. The feathered edge, or penumbra, of the light from a bounce-style umbrella has a softer, less specular quality than the light reflected from the middle. Lighting your subject with the feather has the additional benefit that it throws less light onto the background.

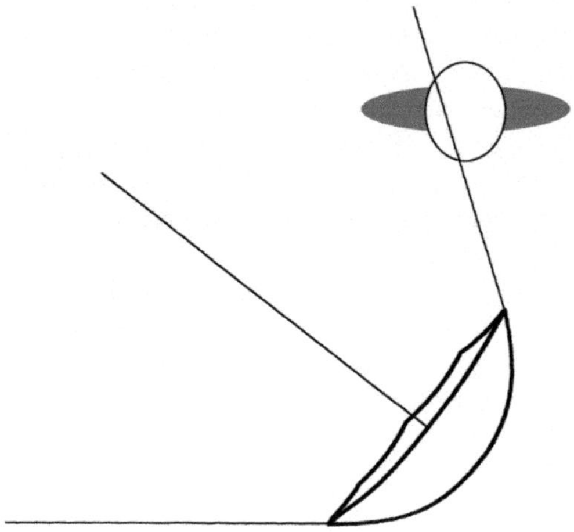

Feathering the light from an umbrella.

You will generally get better, more controllable results with an umbrella if you don't tilt it down toward the subject. Instead, draw an imaginary line between the tips and across the opening of the umbrella, and keep that line parallel to the vertical pole of your light stand. To adjust the light, just move it from side to side or vertically until you get the look that you want.

To use an umbrella with a speed light, you need an umbrella swivel adapter with a cold shoe. The foot of the flash slips into the shoe and locks in place. Watch out for metal shoes—some of them do not have insulation and can short the contacts on your flash. The shoe fits into the swivel in turn, and the umbrella fits into an angled hole in the swivel and is held in place with a thumbscrew.

Soft boxes, sometimes called light banks, are a relative of umbrellas, and some even retain the parabolic shape of an umbrella. They achieve greater softening by bouncing the light around the inside of the box and then passing the light through translucent diffusing material. Many soft boxes have the option to install a second layer of diffusion, known as a baffle. Soft boxes create a pool of light that falls off more quickly than the light from an umbrella, and colors are less saturated under this kind of light. The soft box attaches to a lighting instrument with an adapter called a speed ring, which allows you to attach the same soft box to a wide array of fixtures. Several manufacturers make soft boxes out of Nomex, a heat-resistant material that can be used with high-temperature continuous lights.

They are typically described as small, medium, and large, though the dome-type soft boxes are often specified by their diameter. Octas have eight sides, with a deeper dish. They can be very large, and are sometimes used without the diffusion material across the front. The shape of the light source shows up in the catch lights of the sitter's eyes, a boon to photographers who do not like the look of rectangular catch lights. Some octas even have a bezel with a circular cutout that attaches to the front of the diffusion panel to make the catch light perfectly round. Strip lights are tall and thin soft boxes that create a narrow plane of soft illumination with very limited spill. They are very useful for creating rim lighting effects with the figure.

Larger soft boxes produce softer light, and a good rule of thumb is to place the surface of the soft box at a distance from the subject equal to the longest dimension of the soft box. So, a 36 × 48 inch soft box looks best at about 48 inches from the subject.

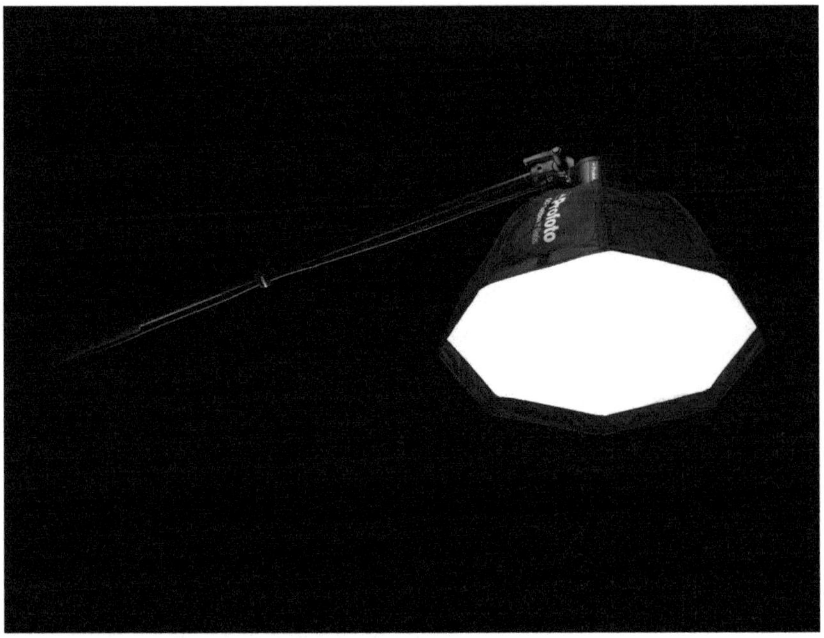

A small Profoto octa soft box attached to a B2 head and supported by a hand-held boom arm. On location, an assistant can hold the light over the head of the subject while you shoot. Wireless TTL means you, the model, and the light can move around without having to worry about exposure settings.

The beauty dish, sometimes called a soft light reflector, attaches to a strobe. It is a hard metal parabola, usually painted white inside, with a reflector suspended over the center. Light from the strobe bounces off the center reflector and back into the dish before it is radiated out toward the sitter. The light has a very soft, luminous quality, especially when used close to the subject—roughly the same distance as the diameter of the dish. It creates distinctive catch lights in the eyes.

Gels are thin sheets of translucent material that are used to color a light source. Diffusion material of various types also comes in sheets that you can purchase where you buy gels. Multiple layers can be used to make lighting softer, and of course, the diffusion can be used along with colored gels. Many gels are heat-resistant and work with either strobes or constant lights; just be careful not to put the type that is not heat-resistant onto a high-temperature light. There are holders for gels, but many photographers simply use clothespins, box clips, or gaffer tape to hold the gels in place. Under-exposure works better when you want the color to show. Color becomes desaturated and blows out as you increase exposure, so use gelled light as a fill on the shadow side or shoot your image low-key.

Neutral density (ND) gels allow you to decrease light output without moving your lighting instrument. They are neutral in color and soak up light. You can build up multiple layers of ND gels to increase the attenuation. Scrims work like neutral density gels, but are often made of metal screen to resist the heat from hot lights. Full scrims cut one stop, and half scrims cut half a stop. There are also scrims that physically cover only half the light implement. These are good for taming the light in one part of the scene when everything else is lit just right. Because they are made out of mesh, they do not produce a hard shadow line.

Reflectors, also known as bounces, are used to fill shadows. They are commonly made of fabric stretched over a flexible circular frame that twists and collapses into a smaller shape for easy transportation. Reflectors are typically white, silver, gold, or zebra colored. Some companies make a frame with interchangeable coverings. The gold and zebra colors add more warmth to the reflected light. Bead board is a foam material with a pebbled surface that is also used widely used in movie production for bouncing light, especially from a light fixture.

Both reflectors and bead board can be used to bounce light into the shadow areas of a shot, to open a face, for example. When the light is coming from above, placing a bounce at the sitter's feet can reduce the severity of shadows. Bounces are especially useful in natural light settings where fill flash is not available or not wanted, but they work great in a studio setting with flash, too.

Black bounces absorb light. Place them in front of a white wall to keep light from bouncing back onto the model and filling the shadows. You can hang commando cloth from a support to make a black bounce, and commando cloth is also excellent for blacking out windows when you need the room to be dark for light painting, projections, etc.

Grids focus and harden light. They work by soaking up light beams that are not heading in a more or less straight path from the light source to the subject. Grids are usually sold in sets, and are graded in degrees for the amount of spread they allow, typically 10, 20, 30, and 40 degrees. The tighter the angle, the more light that will be soaked up, and the harder the beam. Because grids restrict the spread of light, they are useful for controlling spill. Egg crates and louvers are essentially grids designed for soft boxes. They further reduce the spill of light, and have the additional effect of making colors more saturated, while retaining much of the soft quality of the light. There are adapters and reflectors designed specifically for grids, but in a pinch, you can attach a grid to a standard reflector with gaffer tape.

Snoots are funnel-shaped devices that fit onto the front of a lighting device such as a strobe. The small aperture allows just a narrow, circular beam of light to pass through. This can be used to create a bright highlight, isolating or emphasizing one part of the body. The edge of the circle of light produced by the snoot can be made harder by putting the snoot over a grid. There are also snoots designed to fit over Fresnel hot lights like the Arris.

Barn doors are more commonly seen on lighting equipment like the Arri Fresnel spots and movie lights, but they are available for strobes and other types of lighting equipment. They generally have either two or four wings that swivel to allow you to block the spill of light in one direction or another. With the light source above the camera and pointed down toward the subject, you can position the barn door so that the subject is lit while much of the background is in shadow, isolating the subject from the background. This technique works well with head and shoulders and even ¾ portraits.

Cookies (short for cuculoris) can create the effect of dappled light in the studio. You can make or buy these. They're essentially a piece of plywood, foam core, Cinefoil, or other opaque material with shapes cut out to let some light pass through and produce a pattern of shadows. Alternatively, you can attach shapes to a piece of window screen. These can simulate the way light spills through trees, or be cut to more specific geometric shapes. The harder the light source, the more defined the projected shapes will be. When you're working with high-temperature light

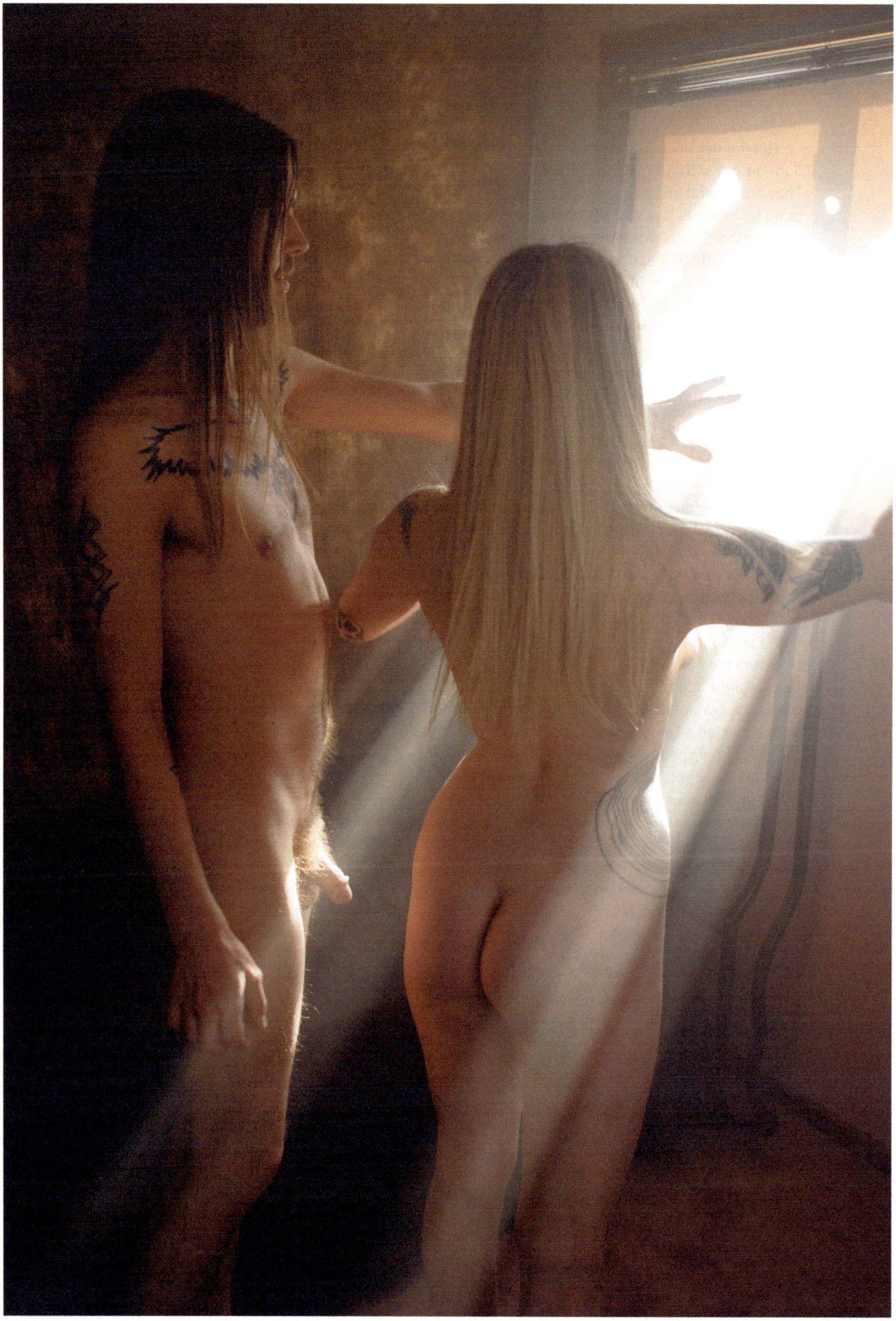

sources, make sure the cookie is fire resistant, or place it on a stand a bit farther from the source.

Light Stands

The two major types of stands are tripod stands and c-stands. C-stands, also called century stands or grip stands, are sturdier and more stable than tripod stands. Tripod stands are generally smaller and lighter than c-stands, though c-stands, which have a "turtle" base, have a smaller footprint. Rollers have the upper parts of c-stands with a tripod base and wheels. Casters are also available for some tripod stands. Booms are arms that can be extended horizontally away from the base, to place a light above your sitter without the stand being in the shot. Autopoles are vertical floor-to-ceiling supports with rubber feet on either end that are held in place by pressure. They lock into place with an adjustable lever.

Tripod-style stands are most stable when the stays that hold the legs in place form a right angle with the vertical tube. To reduce the footprint, the stays can angle downward from the legs, but they should never angle upward. C-stands are most stable when you position the arm so that the weight leans over the long leg. There's no need to over-tighten the knobs—finger tight will do. Be sure to insert the arm into the gobo head so that the weight of the arm pressing down makes it tighten. If you find yourself tempted to crank down on the knob to keep the arm from rotating, it's likely that the gravity is loosening it. Pull the arm out and switch it to the other side.

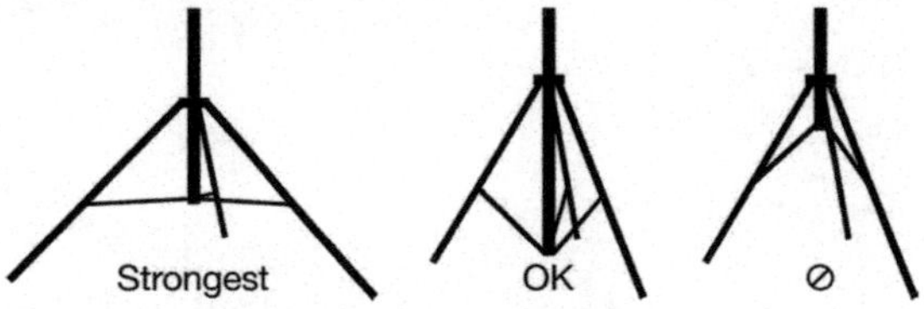

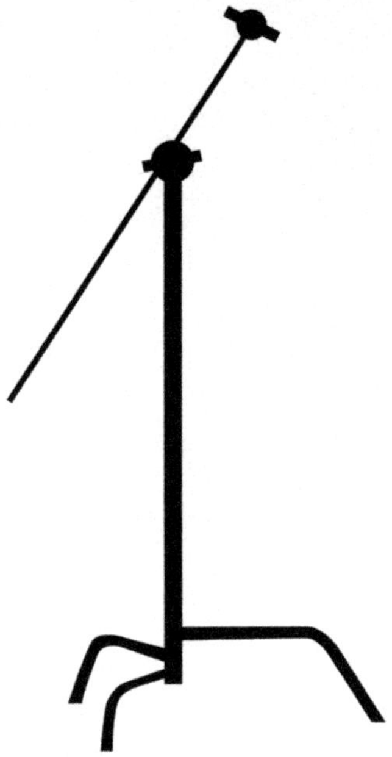

C-stands come with a mini boom called a Hollywood arm or gobo arm, which attaches to the vertical support with a swiveling clamp called a gobo head. The arm has a bare end and a clamp on the other end called a knuckle. The knuckle can be used to hold reflectors, flags, or cookies, and the bare end easily holds a strobe head or monolight.

It's a good idea to weight the bases of light stands with sandbags. The bottom leg of c-stands are even designed to hold them. With booms, it's important to make sure that the head is securely attached, properly counterweight your light, and sandbag the base. Pay attention to the maximum loads—many can only support up to 11 pounds.

You can tape small backdrops to the wall or hang larger ones from a dowel supported by C-stands, tripod stands, or autopoles. Backdrops can be seamless paper, muslin, or other types of cloth. You can also get creative and use anything from newspaper to shower curtains to bubble wrap. Black velour or commando cloth reflect very little light and are excellent for creating solid black backgrounds. You can also make or purchase painted canvas backdrops that look like the brushwork of artists like Modigliani. Muslin can be plain or dyed in different ways.

Plain muslin can be especially interesting if you crumple it so that it has lots of wrinkles and texture. Sometimes, it makes a tremendous difference to add just a touch of illumination for the background itself. Lighting it from the side will then drive up the texture. Pattern-dyed muslin backdrops have been used for so long that they can easily impart that department store portrait studio look. Shooting at f/8 or f/11 is likely to render the background in sharp detail. The fabric looks best if you keep the depth of field shallow so that the background is rendered slightly out of focus.

Facing: © Terry Donovan. The window shade acts as a cookie to illuminate the output from a fog machine. Note the circular holes and irregular bottom of the window shade.

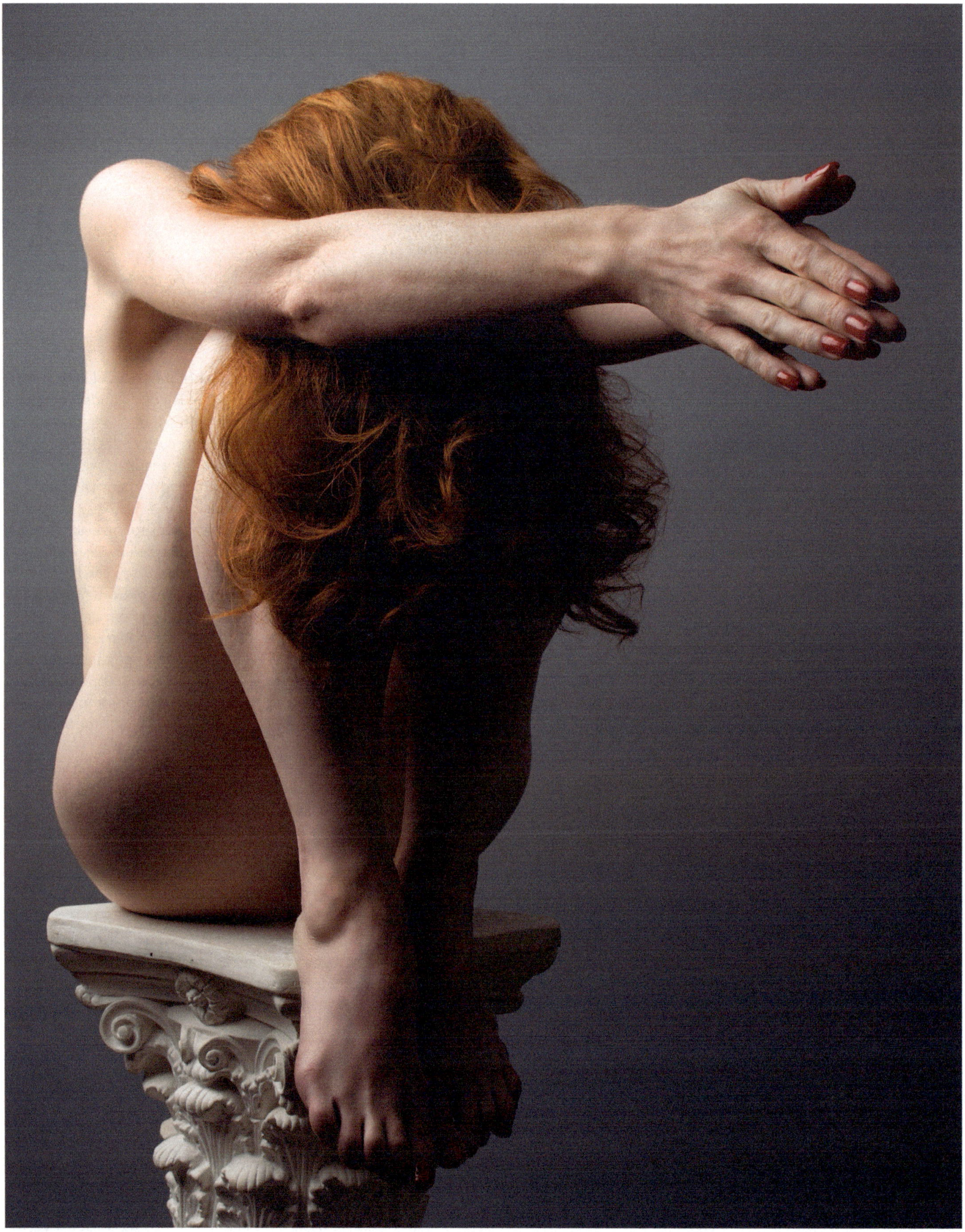

Chapter Seven | Inside the Frame

IN PHOTOGRAPHY, composition begins with an act of exclusion—pointing the camera imposes the camera's frame onto the scene, omitting everything that falls outside of its view. From there, the scene being photographed can further be framed in terms of selective focus and timeframe—the duration of the exposure. Each of these additional frames is a compositional choice. In some cases, the photographer can direct some of the action and move people or objects on a set to construct the scene in a way that is somewhat akin to what a painter does, but probably more often, it is the photographer who stands on tiptoe, squats, climbs a ladder, or rolls onto his or her belly to find a compelling view. This is the photographer's first, best shot at composition—what appears in the viewfinder before you squeeze the shutter release. Once the shutter falls, the process of in-camera composition is complete.

If we think of a photograph as a kind of dialog between the photographer and the viewer, composition is a mechanism for telling the viewer where to look. We explore principles of composition as a way of philosophizing about what makes a picture work, but these principles should be taken as suggestions, not immutable laws. With that caveat in mind, we can look

Facing: © Lou Benjamin. Model: Sienna Aldridge.

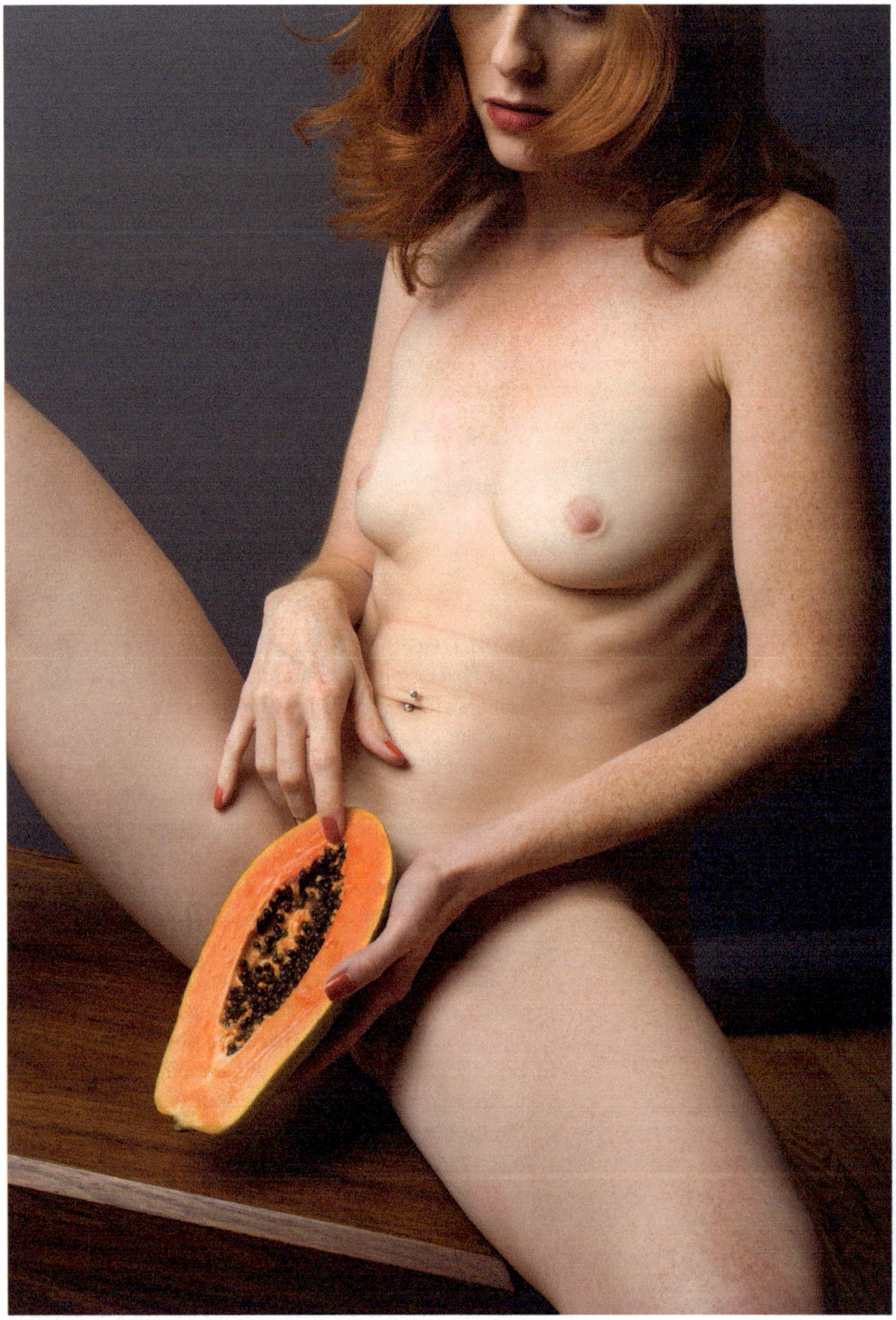

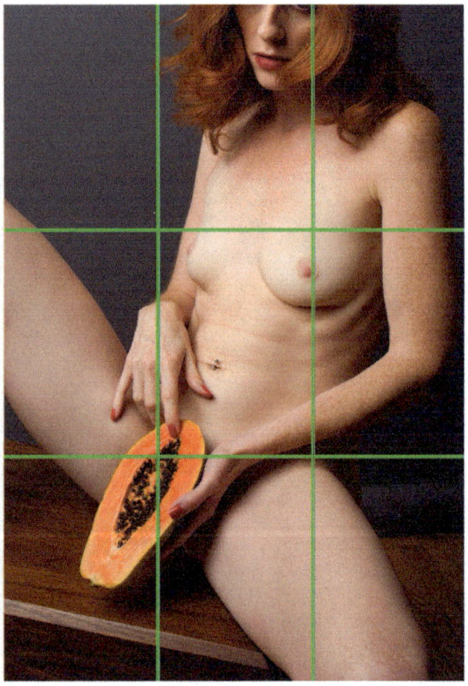

© Lou Benjamin. Model: Sienna Aldridge. A composition demonstrating the rule of thirds.

at ideas of composition that are drawn from graphic design as well as photography.

One of the constant questions in the mind of the viewer is "what is this picture about?" Techniques such as selective focus isolate the subject, direct the viewer's attention to salient details, and begin to answer the question. Selective focus works because the eye gravitates toward the sharpest part of the image. Another way to compose is to take advantage of the way viewers pay more attention to certain areas of the frame, relative to its height and width.

Students of basic graphic design are taught the "rule of thirds." While the principle generally works, calling it a rule gives it more weight than it deserves; it's just one workable way of assessing the relationship of elements within the frame. To apply the principle, you divide the frame into thirds, both vertically and horizontally. The points where the dividing lines meet have additional visual weight; you could call them pressure points. Placing an element of your composition on one of these points will focus attention upon it.

You can also treat the image segments, whether vertical or horizontal, as containers. If your sitter is in an outdoor setting, you might frame the image so that the sky occupies the top two-thirds of the frame and the ground occupies the bottom third. Or, looking left to right, the sitter could be positioned so that most of the body is shifted off-center with the axis of the body aligned with one of the vertical thirds.

Cropping in postproduction is a way of rethinking (second-guessing) compositional decisions that you made when you shot the image. You are literally restating the visual problem you're setting out to solve. Cropping also reduces the resolution of the image. The tighter the crop, the smaller the maximum print size. Pulling one side in to eliminate a problematic element from the frame is cropping for the wrong reason. Cropping done in this way usually does not respect the proportions of the image, and you end up with a composition that lacks integrity.

The shape of the image frame can have a profound effect on how the viewer relates to the nude figure, and the body's relationship to the space imposed

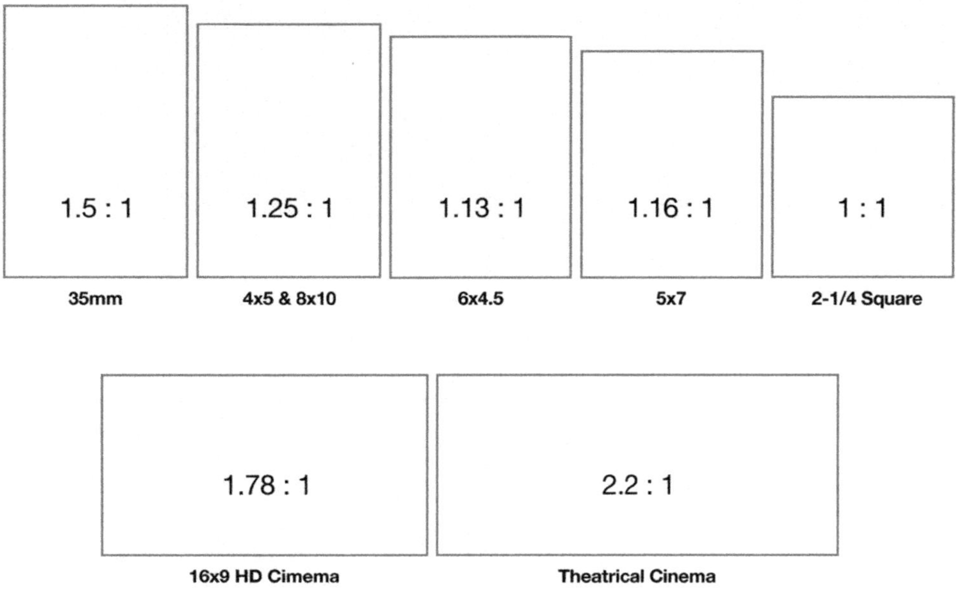

A comparison of well-known aspect ratios.

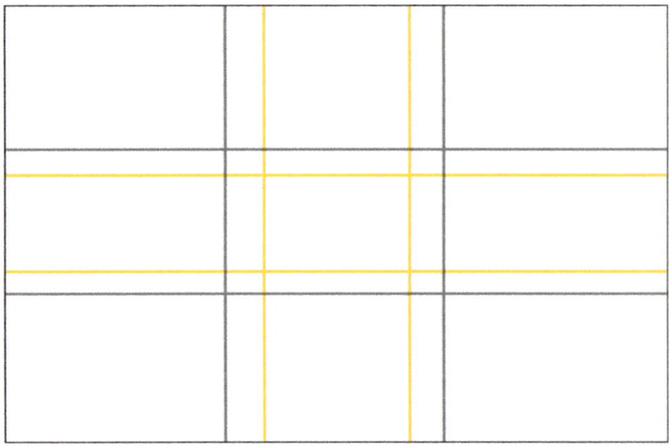

The proportions of the Golden Ratio hug the center more than the rule of thirds.

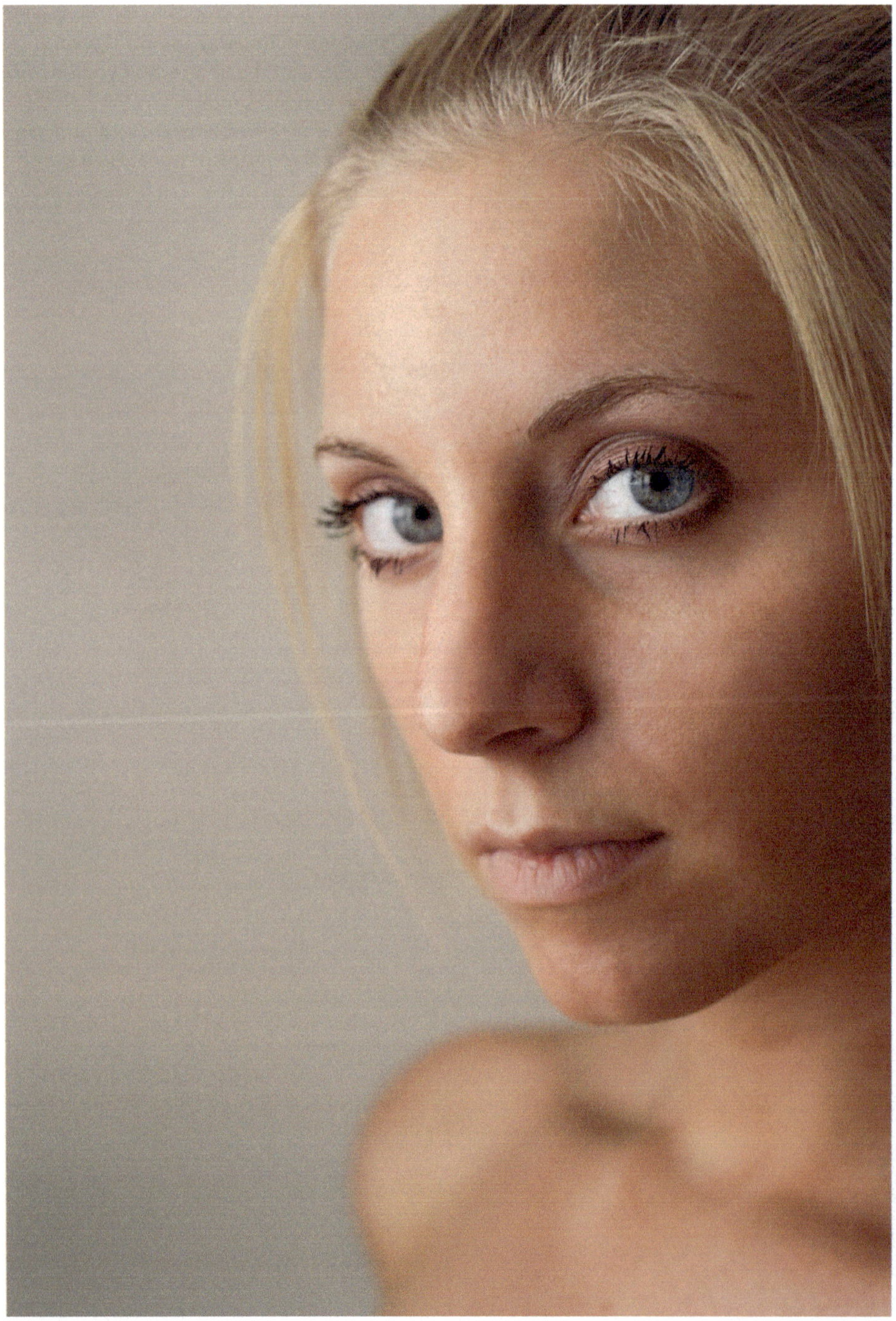

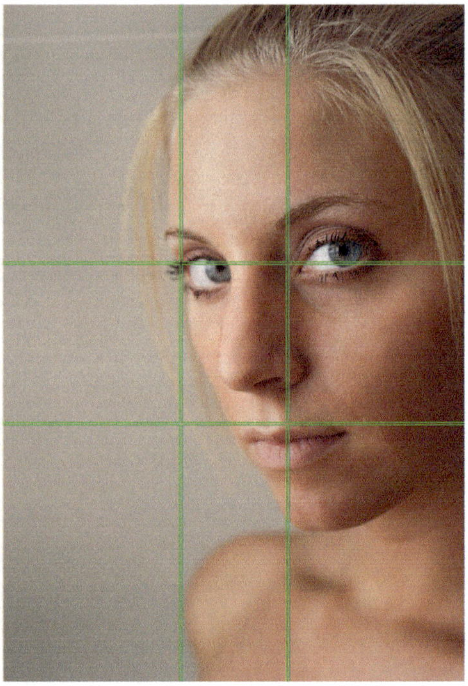

by the frame is often critical to how the overall image works. With that in mind, it is sometimes best to reframe in a way that retains the original image proportions (2:3 for 35mm format). If you prefer a different shape, consider using one of the proportions from other camera formats, such as 1:1, 3:4 (probably better known as 6 x 4.5), 4:5, and 5:7, or something cinematic, like 16:9 or 2.2:1. Beyond that, research has shown that people tend to see rectangles of certain proportions to be more "correct" or visually pleasing than others. If you crop arbitrarily, you are likely to find it harder to get groups of photos that exhibit well together. It will certainly require custom mattes and nonstandard frames for your prints.

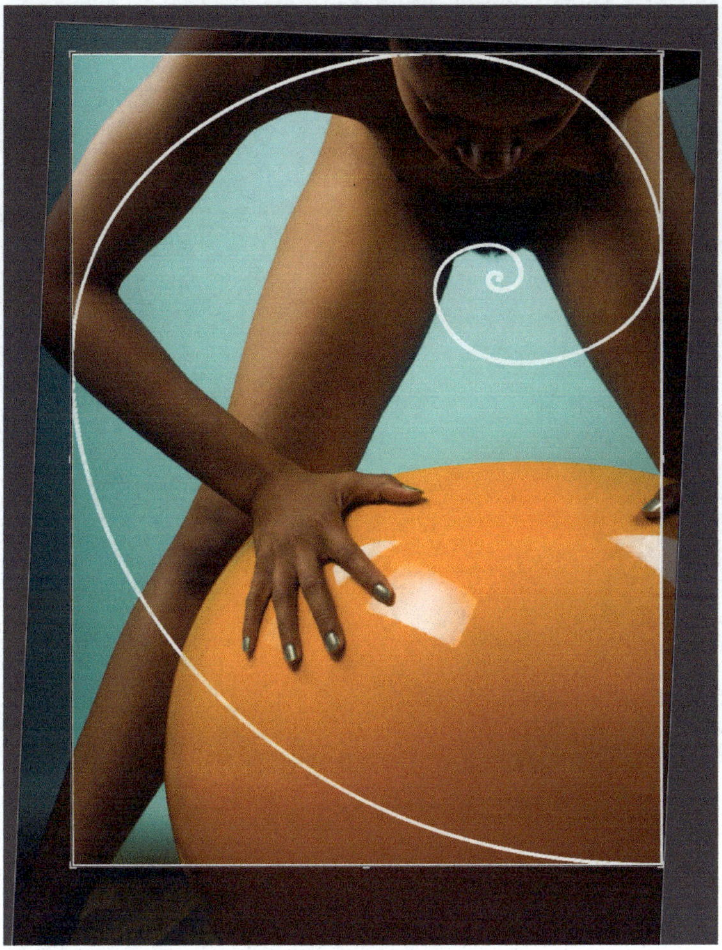

The Crop tools in Lightroom and Photoshop have overlays that you can turn on to assess the composition according to various design principles. The rule of thirds is an option, but the regimental evenness of 1/3 divisions can make compositions a bit staid.

Good alternatives for some compositions are the Golden Ratio and Golden Spiral, which are based on the Greek ratio phi (1.618). Renaissance artists and architects, including Leonardo da Vinci, used the proportions of the Golden Ratio to beautify their compositions. Applied to the rectangular frame of a photo, the Golden Ratio lines hug the center more than do the rule of thirds lines. The Golden Ratio also defines an elegant spiral. Analyses show that the proportions of the Mona Lisa are based on the Golden Section and Golden Spiral.

In addition to the rule of thirds, the Crop tool overlays in Lightroom and Photoshop include Golden Ratio, Golden Spiral, triangles, and diagonals. When the Crop tool is active in Lightroom, you can tap O to cycle through the overlays and Shift + O to rotate the current overlay inside the frame. If you do crop, you can crop non-destructively in Lightroom, or un-check the Delete Cropped Pixels box in the Options bar of the Photoshop Crop Tool.

The absolute center of a picture is often referred to as "dead center," and from a perceptual standpoint, placing something in the center deadens it. As we move the point of interest away from the center, visual tension increases. Lead room is related to visual tension. If a person is facing right, that is generally interpreted as the direction the person is heading. Directing the model's gaze in the same direction strengthens the sense of intent. If we place the model's nose against the right edge of the frame, it will seem as if she or he has run out of room, but if we place her or him on the left side of the frame, not only is there tension, there is lead room. The viewer looks for open space in the direction that the character is expected to move.

Facing: © Lou Benjamin. Model: Lauren Babree. A composition based on the Golden Ratio. The shot is as it was framed in the camera, not cropped in post-production.

Above: © Lou Benjamin. Model: Moon Marie. An example of using the Golden Spiral overlay to compose while cropping down to 5:7 aspect ratio from 2:3 (35mm). The image also shows examples of trapped space and a number of geometric primitives. The color palette exhibits a warm/cool color contrast.

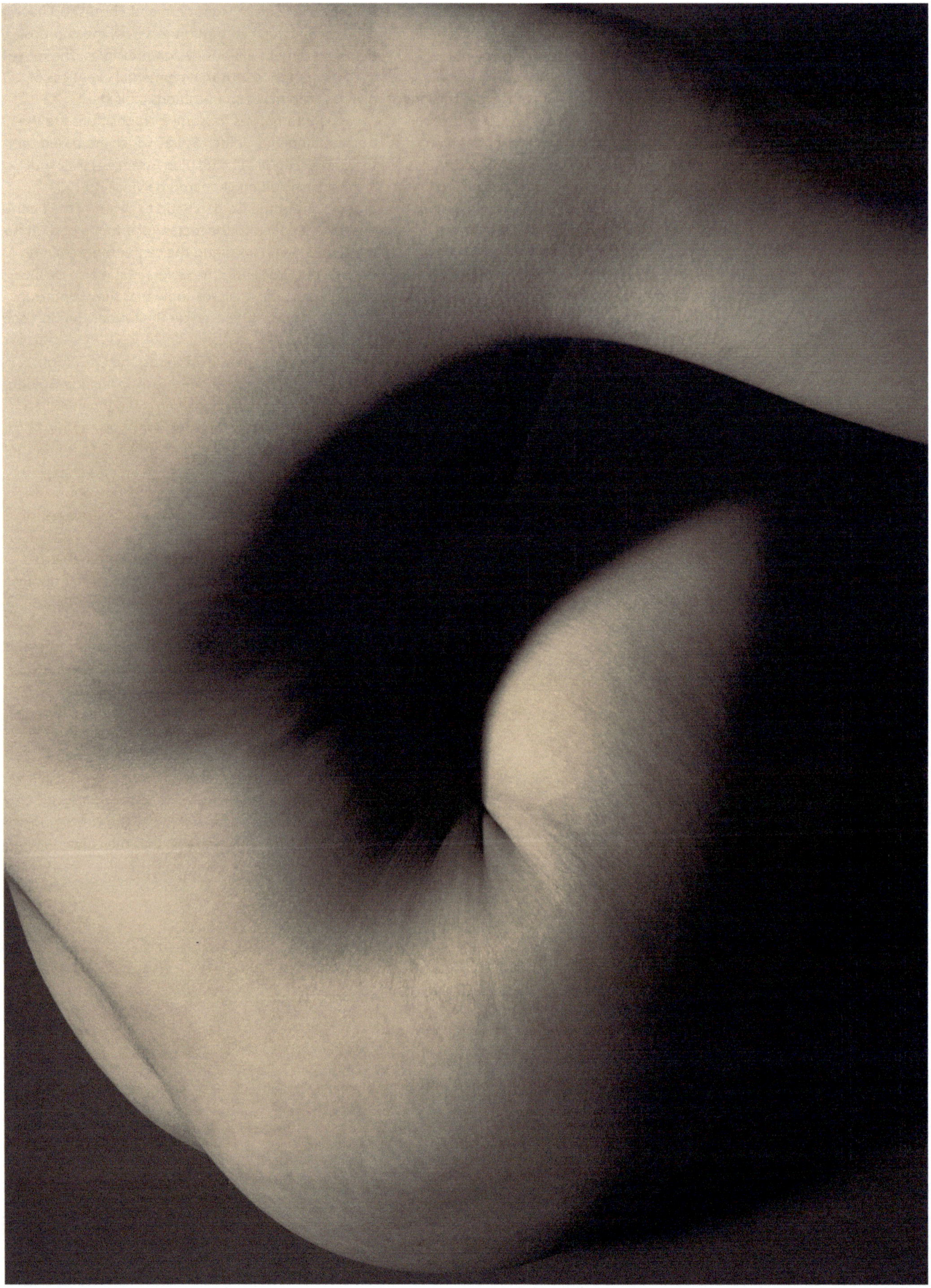

Closeness can be read as either intimacy or abstraction, depending on how close the framing is and whether the face appears or not. If the model's face is not visible, the shot will tend more toward the abstract or the erotic.

If you are interested in creating intimacy, an eye-level angle or slightly below is a very powerful way of inviting the viewer to relate to the person in the photo and creates a sense of involvement. Many classic intimate portraits have been shot with the lens positioned somewhere between the eyes and the solar plexus. Cutting the top of the head with the frame can accentuate the emotional dimension of an image, especially if the sitter fills most of the frame. It imposes a view that is akin to looking the sitter in the eye. Having parts of the sitter's body extend beyond the boundaries of the image can also emphasize the imposition of the frame itself.

Sometimes, a hand, foot, or some other part of the body collides with the frame so that just a part of the extremity is cut. Such framing usually looks like a painful amputation and is distracting. The viewer's attention is focused upon the missing body part, instead of whatever else you are hoping to put across. Such unfortunate framing can be avoided by intentionally running your eye around the edge of the viewfinder before you trip the shutter.

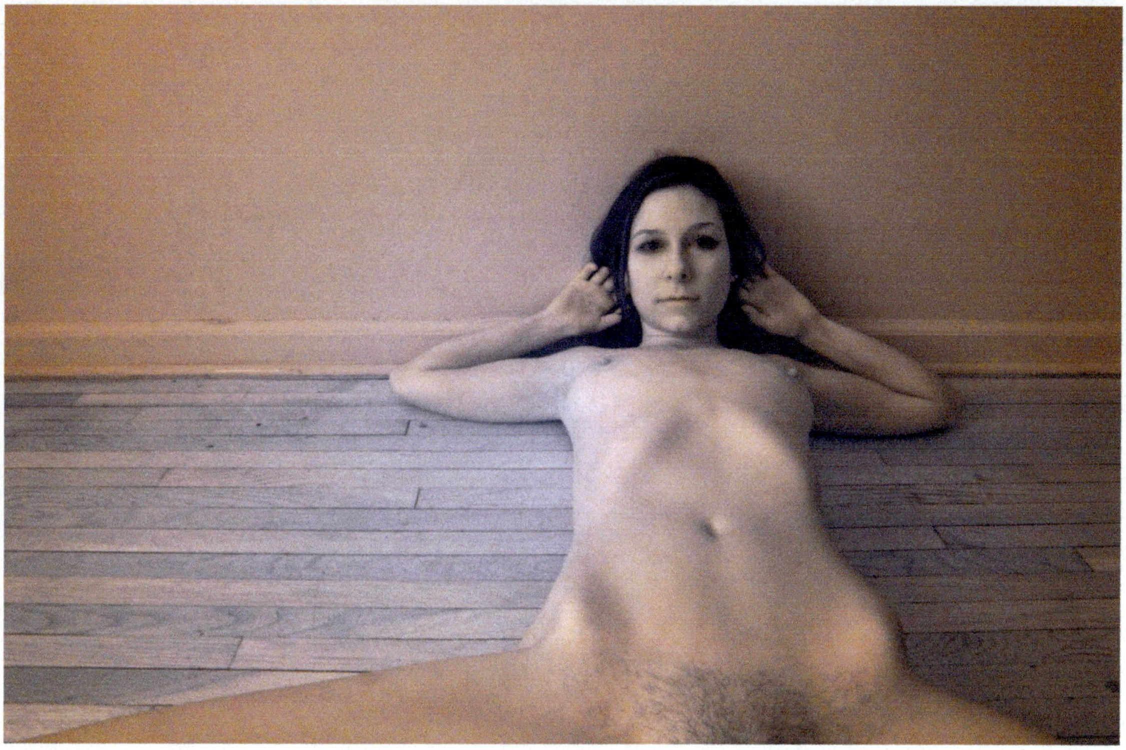

Facing: © Lou Benjamin. Tight framing and shadowy light remove contextual cues and emphasize form.

Above: © Alan Fresco. Flirting with the edge of the frame emphasizes the parts we can't see. Wide-angle distortion and infrared color add to the intrigue of this photo.

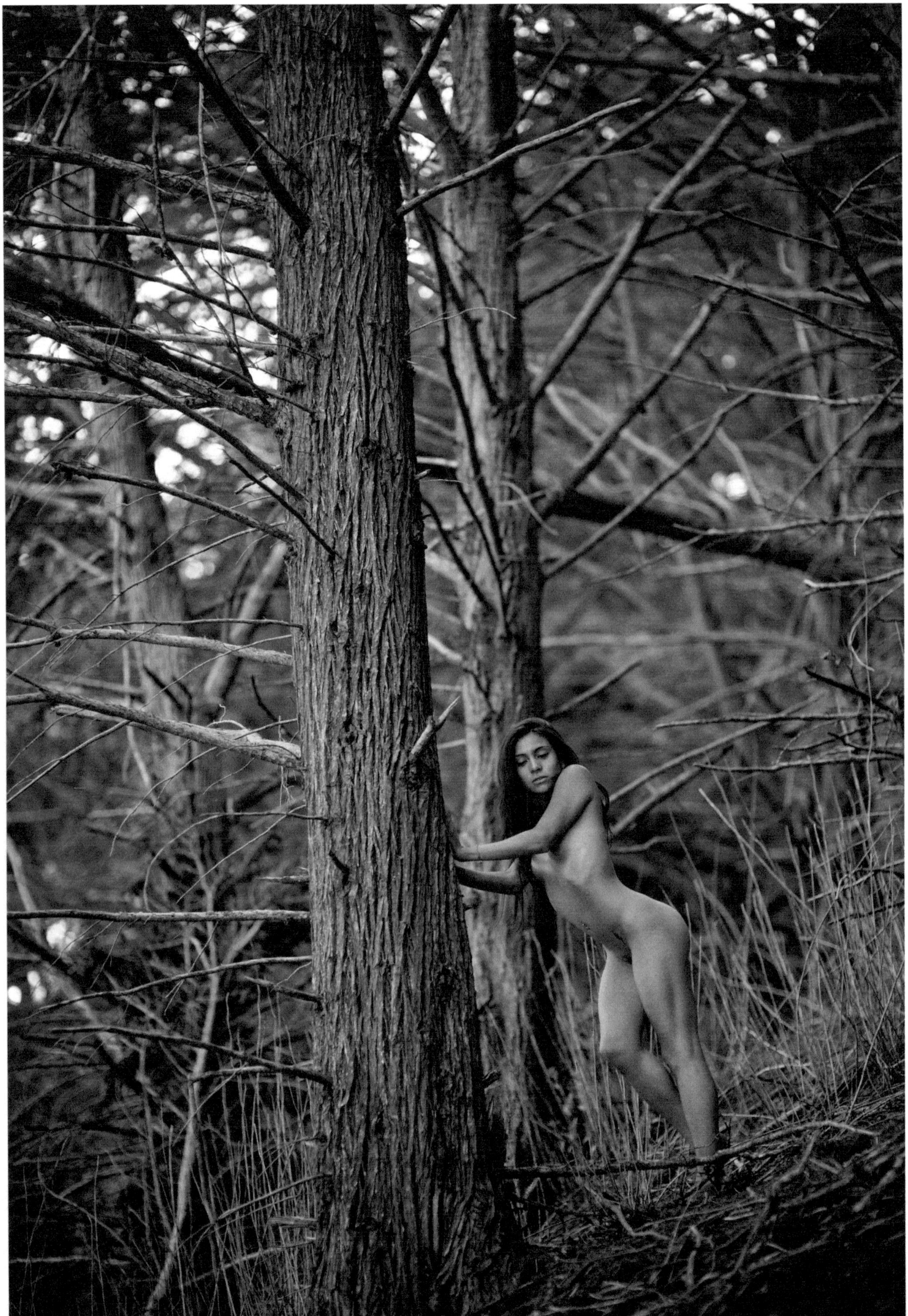

When the full body is shown, we often relate to the image as a complete person, not an abstract body. If the face is visible, that aspect is even stronger. It is challenging to create a sense of intimacy with a full-body view. In most cases, that framing puts the viewer in the position of the detached observer. If there is a lot of space around the figure, the body can be read symbolically, and the image often takes on overtones about the relationship of humanity to the larger environment.

When we view the subject from a high angle, it can come across as dominating or victimizing the subject, especially if the model is a woman in a prone position. However, as you elevate the camera, the viewer's perspective also becomes increasingly detached. When you elevate the camera enough, the point of view becomes the omniscient bird's-eye view of cinema and graphic novels. When you are shooting from a low angle, the model moves by degrees from being heroic, to menacing, to dominating. At some point, you get a worm's-eye view, which can be detached and omniscient or pervy and pornographic.

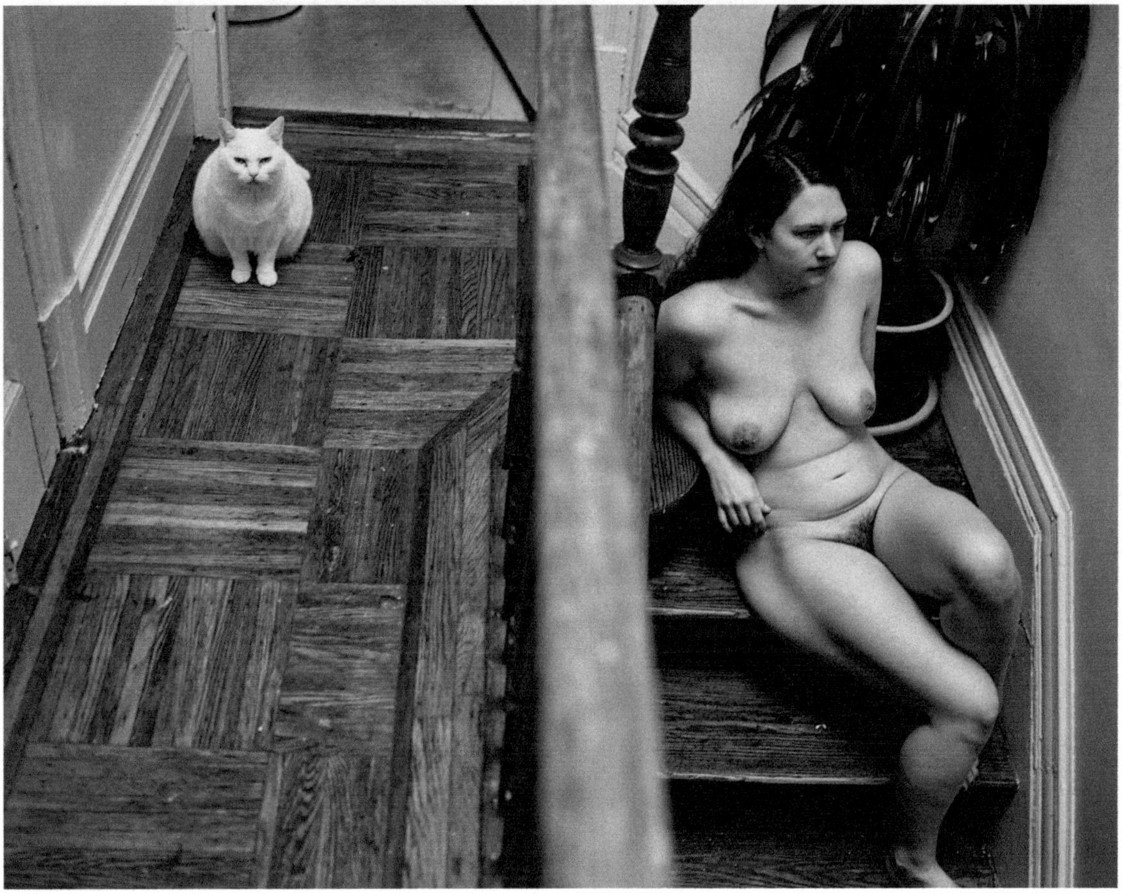

Facing: © Alfred Laij. The nude in nature is a resilient trope. The model's sculptural pose, reminiscent of modern dance, emphasizes her muscular physique.

Above: Zizi and Kate © 2014 by George McClintock, with Kate Collins. Bird's-eye view provides an unusual perspective, while the bannister creates a powerful spatial divider. We have the cat's full attention but the woman is completely detached. The divided frame depicts two very different psychological spaces and functions much like a diptych.

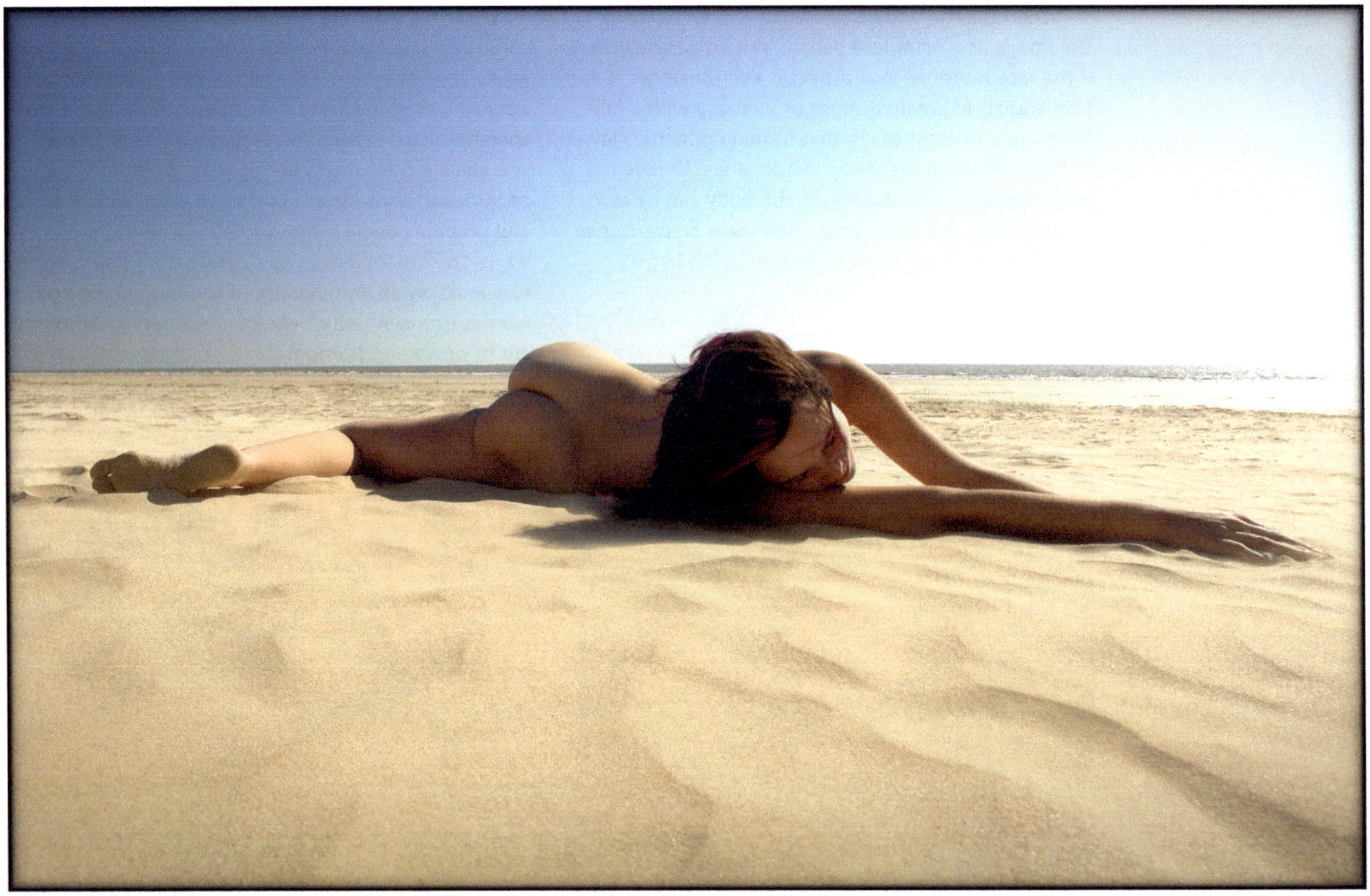

Above: © Pascal Renoux.

Facing: © Alfred Laij. Quite literally, a frame within the frame.

Portrait (vertical) and landscape (horizontal) orientations tell different stories. Our natural perceptual field of view is landscape, and so it should be no surprise that cameras create landscape images in their normal orientation. There are also practical aspects: If your work is to be published in a standard magazine, portrait images are optimal. Landscape photos either have to be run at reduced size, or spread across the pages with the "gutter" cutting through the middle, often disrupting or obscuring valuable details.

If your intent is about the person, portrait orientation can isolate the sitter from the environment and hint at their own "inner landscape." If the subject is standing, you can pull back to shoot the full body in portrait. The body will fill much of the frame, and even though the shot includes the environment, the emphasis tends to stay with the figure.

With landscape framing, head-and-shoulders views can fill the frame nicely, especially if you are willing to cut the top of the head. Landscape generally compels us to either shoot that way, or to pull way back and place the figure in a tableau. In landscape orientation, the environment naturally dominates the full-body figure.

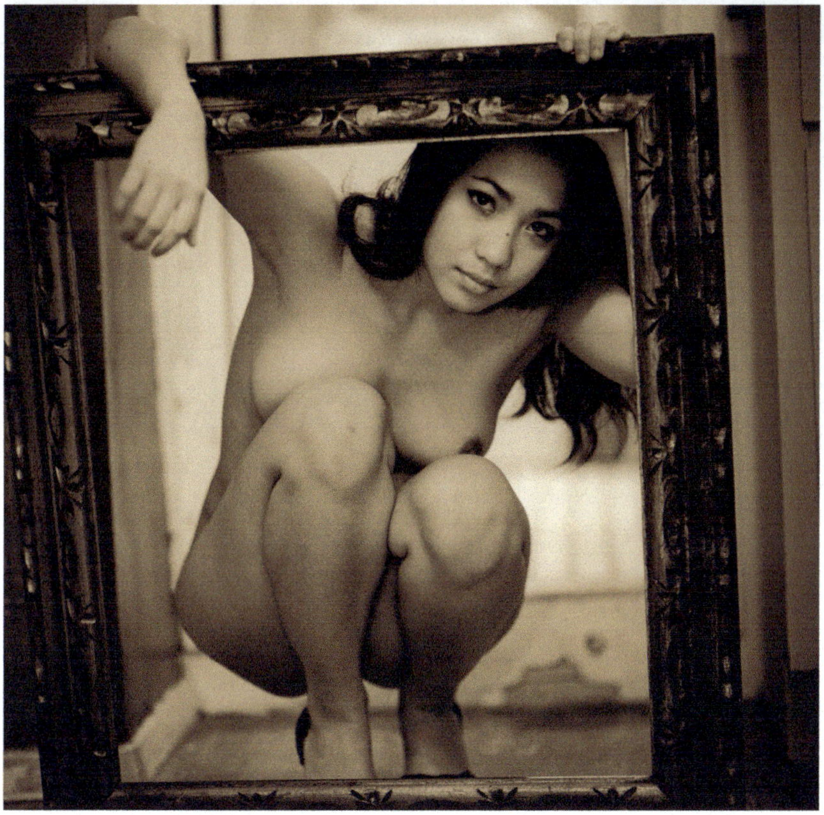

Looking Deeper into the Frame

The emphasis of the early part of this chapter was the perspective of imposing the photographic frame on the scene. In the remainder of the chapter, we'll shift the emphasis and look at additional ways to think about what happens inside the frame.

In a word, simplify. That is an important (and often challenging) mantra. Be clear about what your image is about, and try to distill your compositions down to the elements that express that. Some models react negatively to a seamless background because of the way it functions. It is a powerful simplification tool that creates a quiet, relatively unobtrusive background and focuses attention on the model.

Windows, doors, and mirrors in a shot can all have the effect of creating a frame within the frame. A framing element does not have to be a literal frame. It can have as few as two sides and consist of a striking color, texture, or shape. Portrait photographers often project a circular or oval pool of light onto the background behind the sitter to create a framing element. The frame within a frame can be a powerful compositional element, because it doubly focuses attention on the subject. For fashion, portrait, and glamour photos, models often create a framing effect by surrounding their faces with their arms. The mirror is especially interesting when used as a frame, because it can show two perspectives on the same scene, perspectives that may even seem to disagree. When shot so that you cannot see the mirror's frame, mirrors can be particularly disorienting. Burning (darkening) the edges of the frame in post-production also functions as a framing element.

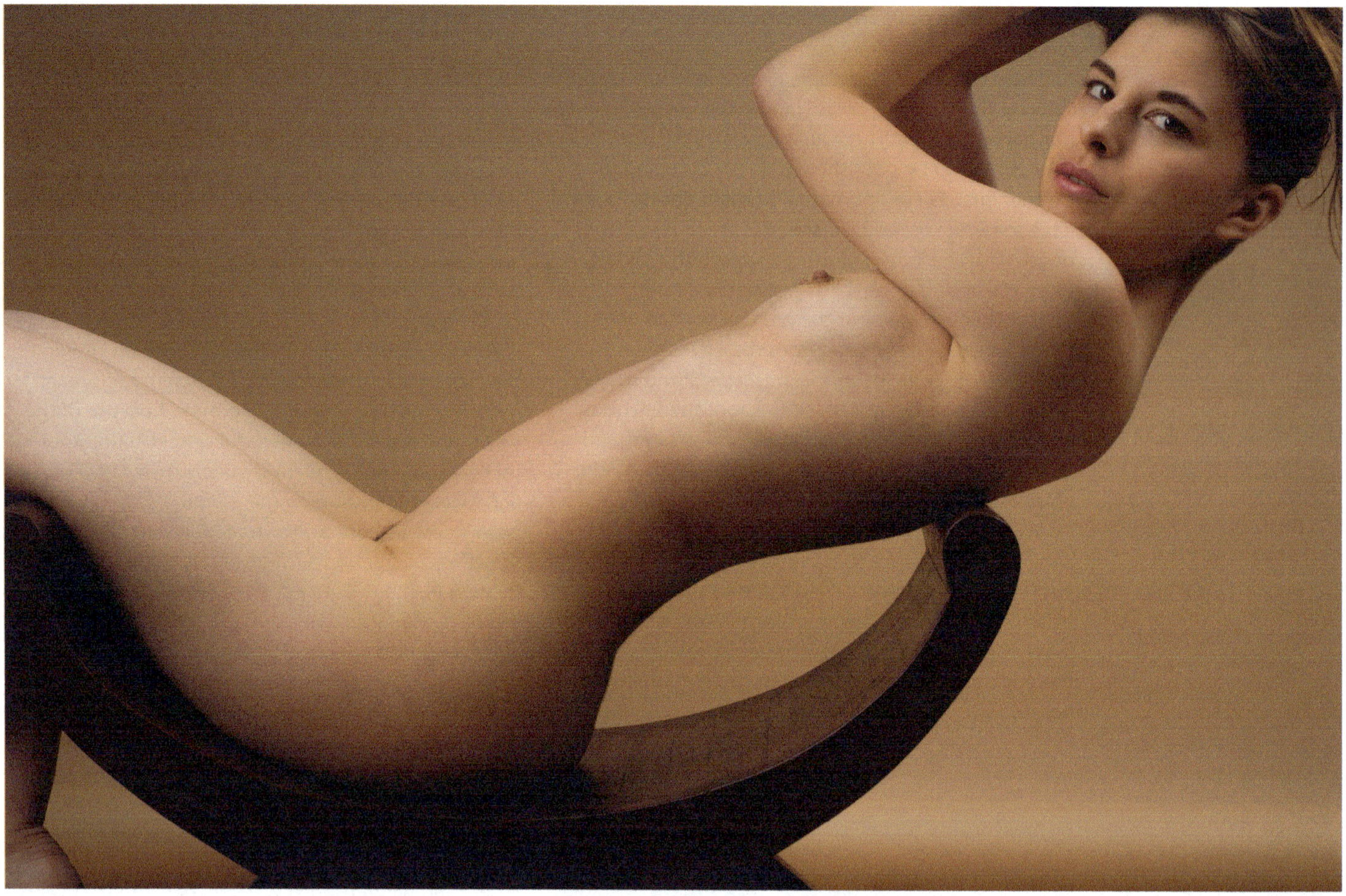

Above: © Lou Benjamin. Model: Aubrey. Eye contact and a strong diagonal draw the viewer in.

Facing (top): © Lou Benjamin. Model: Aubrey. The triangle is a fundamental element of this composition, however the presence of the lips and the highlight on the breast add touches of sensuality.

Facing (bottom): © Lou Benjamin. Model: Aubrey. Sweeping lines and contours characterize this figurative shot. The angle of the light from above left casts shadows that emphasize contours. The lighting comes from a studio strobe fitted with a grid.

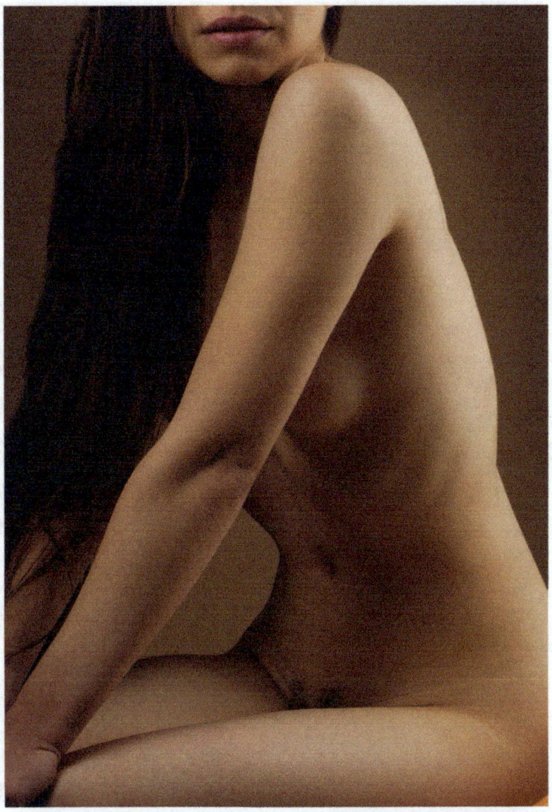

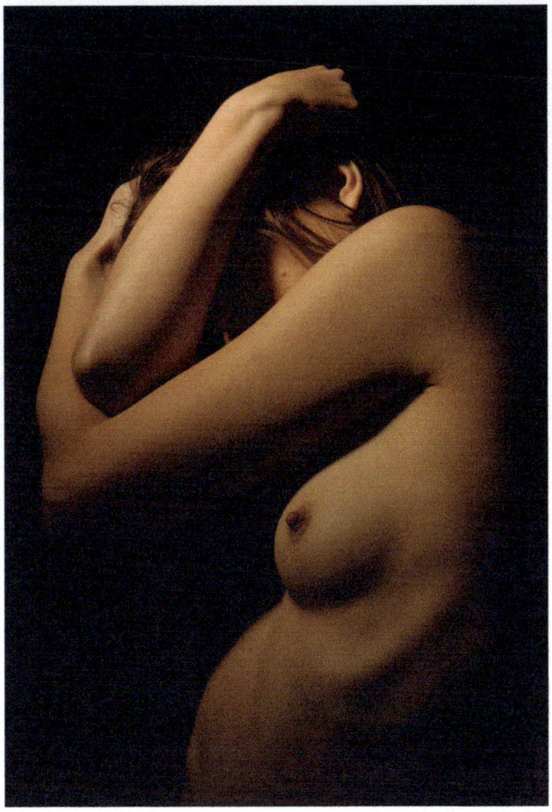

Our eyes are particularly attuned to finding lines, especially verticals, horizontals, and diagonals. Any pronounced line in a photo, such as the edge of an object, will lead the eyes somewhere. Objects inside the frame can function as start and end points for imaginary lines (such as the line that connects the pupils, the line that connects the nipples, and the vertical from the forehead to the chin) that provide structure to the image and keep the eye circulating inside the frame. When used strategically in a composition, we refer to them as leading lines. They often direct the viewer's attention to the sitter, but they can also help to describe the space around the sitter. For example, a model sitting on a road can be shot so that the sides of the road act as leading lines that emphasize a vanishing point. The key thing to watch out for is that you don't capture or emphasize lines that lead the eye completely out of the frame.

Sloping, curved, and bent lines are particularly good for adding a sense of energy and motion to an image. André Kertész produced a dramatic series of distorted nudes, photographed with the aid of a funhouse mirror. These images make lyrical use of curved lines. The nude offers many compositional opportunities to isolate and emphasize curved elements of the body. Gentle curves can have a particularly sensual quality. S-curves, Z-curves, and zigzag lines inject increasingly more energy and edginess into your image. Triangles, diamonds, circles, and squares are all primitive, flat shapes that our eyes are particularly attuned to find. These shapes can be based upon imaginary lines. Many Renaissance paintings were composed on the basis of triangles.

Spatial dividers are lines that separate a picture into two parts. The division can be foreground/background, right/left, above/below, or anything else. A doorway (inside/outside) is one example. The water line of a stream and even a shadow can function as a spatial divider.

Patterns and texture are related. Lighting effects like louver slats and dappled light are examples of patterns, but artists such as Spencer Tunick are able to make patterns out of whole bodies. Using shallow depth of field, backgrounds can be reduced to patterns of repeating soft forms.

Negative space is another term that comes from graphic design. Emphasizing negative space can create powerful sculptural effects, or enhance the abstract qualities of an image. When the model places her hand on her hip and pushes her elbow away from her body to create a diamond-shaped space between her torso and her arm, we are dealing with trapped space, a specific type of negative space. Tension is related to negative space—as you push the figure toward the side of the frame, you increase negative space and tension as well. The composition becomes increasingly asymmetrical, and yet many of the most effective of such images will still be balanced.

Balance is perceived primarily along the horizontal axis and works on the basis of visual weight. Symmetrical balance is the easiest to understand and the most straightforward. With symmetry, the balancing elements are equally distributed on either side of the vertical centerline of the picture. It's no muss, no fuss, but can be boring. Asymmetric balance is often unexpected and can be compelling. A small object with a lot of visual weight can balance a large object that is not as visually dense. Think in terms of a lever. If the centerline of your image is the fulcrum and you place the sitter slightly right of center, a pillow, placed to the extreme left can balance the image. Asymmetric balance is something that is accomplished by feel. Once you get it, you will find it relatively easy to do.

Color in photography is relatively "new school" and was not taken seriously in art circles until the late 1970s, when artists such as William Eggleston emerged. It is also one of the most powerful and confounding elements to compose with.

Compositions can be based on color contrasts and color harmonies, and there are essentially three types of color contrast. The first type of color harmony is based on warm/cool color contrast. Warm colors are on the redder end of the spectrum (think fire), and cool colors tend toward blue or blue-green (think water). One method of split toning is to apply a warm

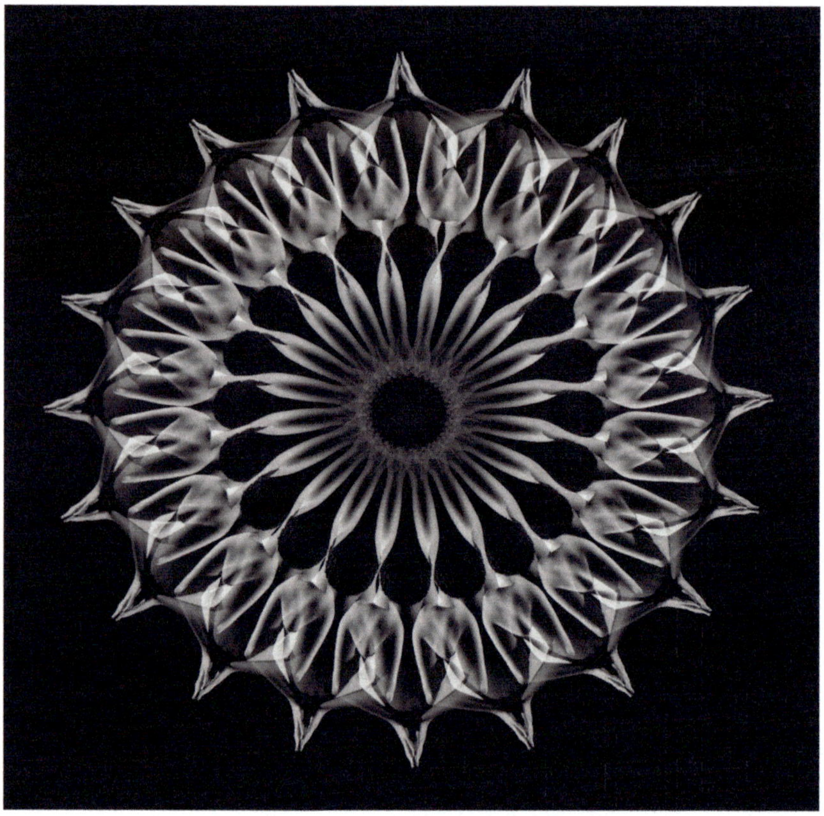

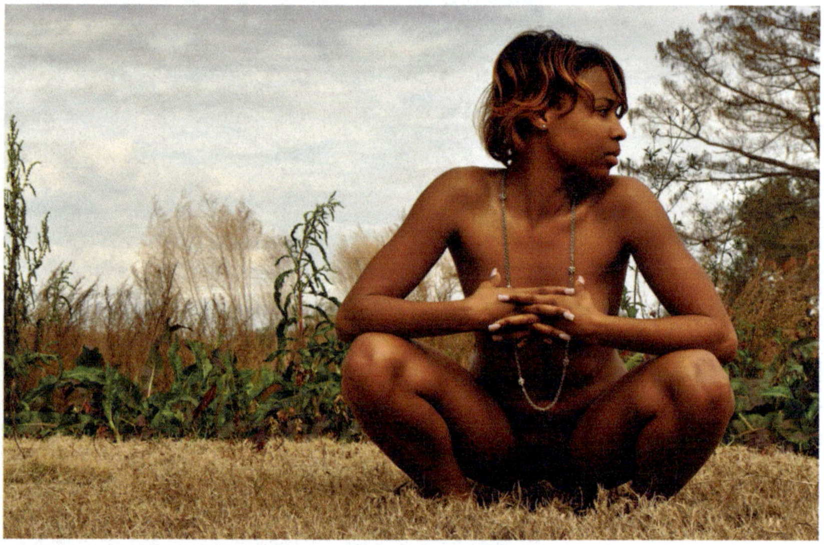

Above (top): © P. J. Reptilehouse. The repetitive pattern was created in-camera and results from spinning the camera around an axis in a single ten-second exposure. Light was provided by multiple flashes from LED strobes and camera motion was controlled by a microprocessor.

Above (bottom): © Saddi Khali. If the model were turned to look as though she were moving to the right, she would be out of lead room. Instead, she is clearly stationary. Her gaze emphasizes the imposition of the frame and suggests that something is going on outside the frame. The asymmetrical composition still feels balanced.

Facing: © Ned and Aya Rosen. Even with tight framing, the body is not completely abstract. Subtle cues, such as color, allow us to recognize that we are dealing with a figure.

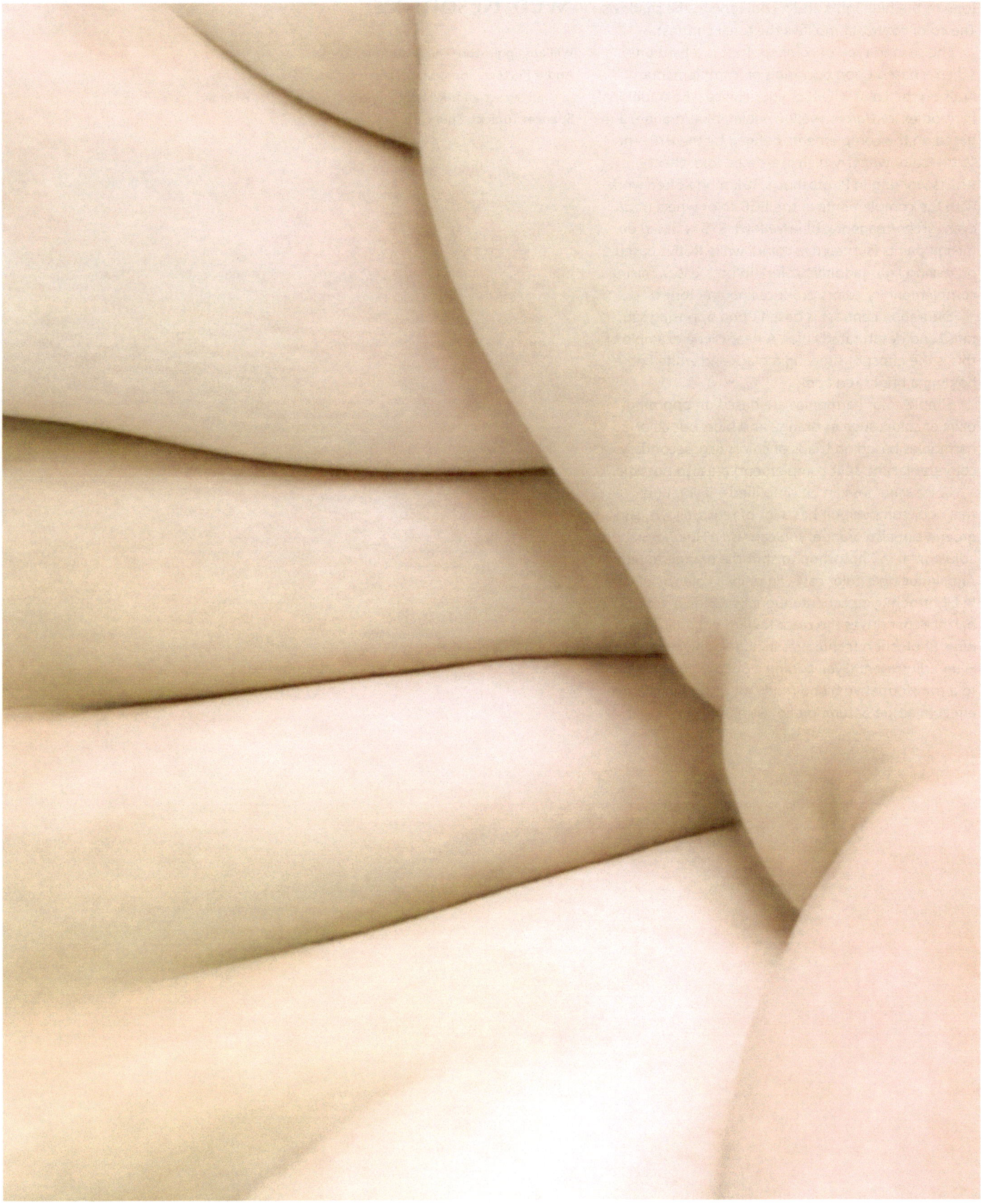

tone to the highlights and a cool tone to the shadows. The color contrast amplifies the tonal contrast.

The second type of color contrast is a harmonic scheme based upon opposing or "complementary" hues on the color wheel of your choice. The traditional harmonies (red/green, yellow/violet, blue/orange) are based on the complements defined by the RYB—or "art"—color wheel, which pre-dates color theory. Artists working in Photoshop's RGB mode often work with the complements of the RGB color wheel (red/cyan, green/magenta, blue/yellow). RYB is based on mixing paints (subtractive color), while RGB is based on mixing light (additive color). In both cases, mixing complementary colors produces neutral tones.

Saturation contrast is based upon opposing saturated and desaturated color. A near-cliché example of this is the effect of showing a black and white figure holding a bright red apple.

Simple color harmonies are based on opposing pairs of colors such as orange and blue, but color harmonies based on triads of colors (e.g. secondary colors, adjacent, split complement) are also possible.

Color schemes can be simplified—if you find that your composition has a lot of reds, yellows, and greens, but also orange, you can use a Hue/Saturation adjustment in Photoshop to shift the orange to red. And, inducing a color cast can unify a color palette. In Lightroom, you can intentionally assign a white balance that drives the color toward either amber or blue. Photoshop techniques include applying a Photo Filter adjustment layer, adding a Solid Color layer set to a transformative blend mode, or using the colorize effect in a Hue/Saturation adjustment layer.

Web Resources

William Eggleston—egglestontrust.com
André Kertész—brucesilverstein.com/artists/estate-of-andr-kertsz
Spencer Tunick—spencertunick.com

Facing: © Terry Donovan. The composition features an analogous color scheme (adjacent colors—red, orange, and yellow) plus contrast between saturated and desaturated (black and white). Motion blur adds atmosphere.

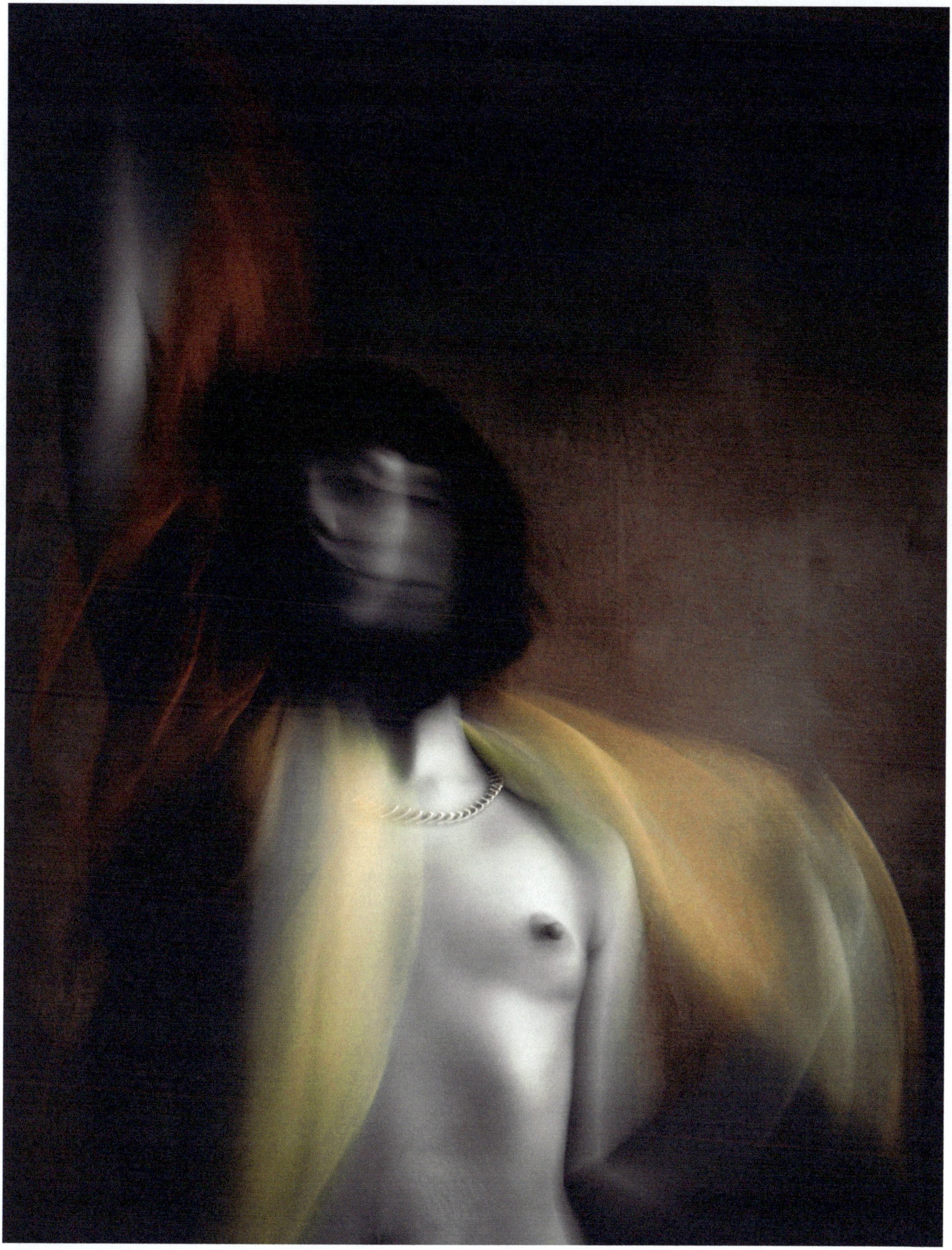

Part III
Making Nudes

Celebrated photographer Gregory Crewdson describes his process of making photographs in terms of pre-production, production, and post-production phases. The first two parts of this book have been mainly about pre-production. In this part, we will look at production and post-production. We will also look briefly at showing your work, which can actually be an important part of any artist's process.

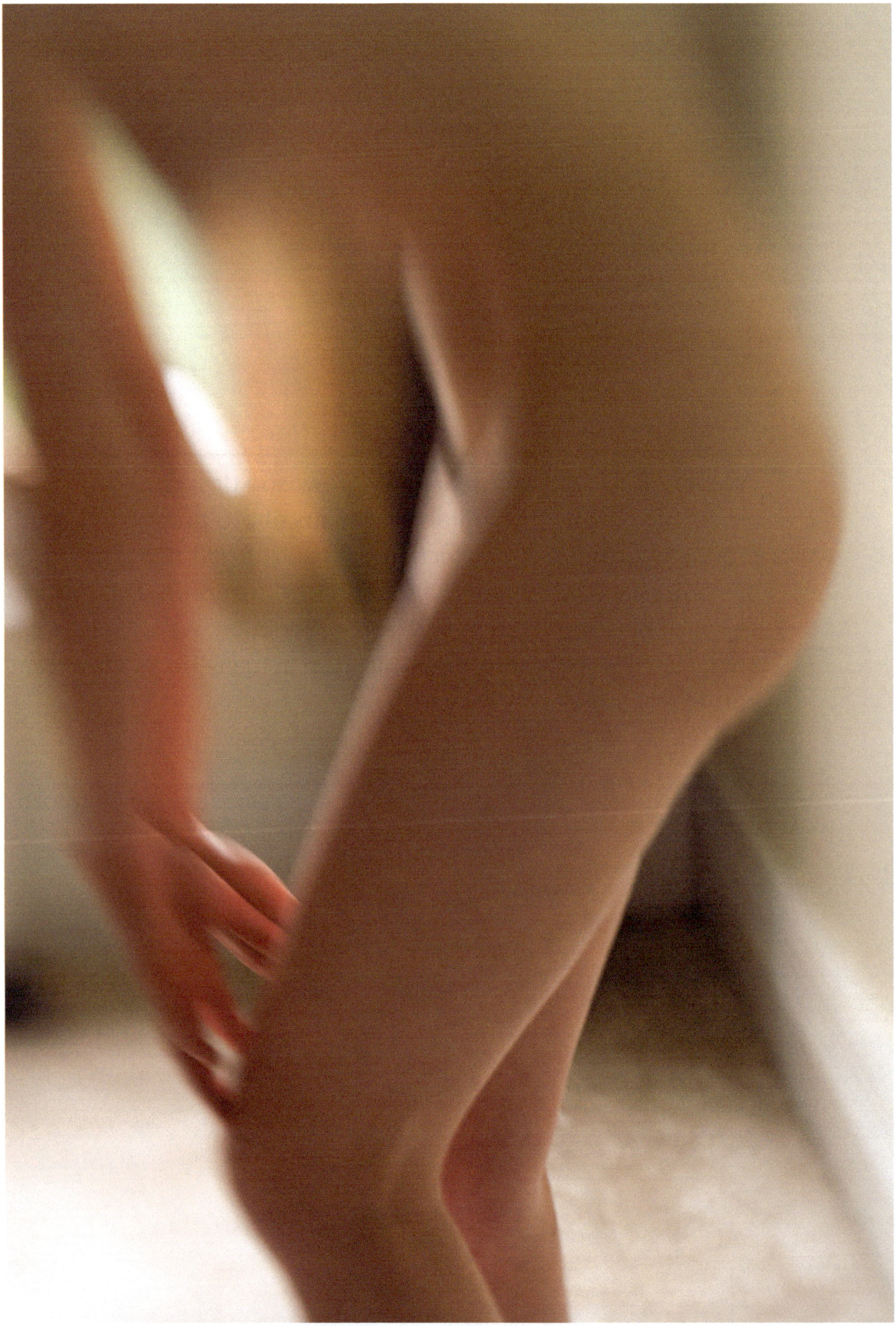

Chapter Eight | Tripping the Shutter

IT FINALLY comes down to the moment of actually making photos. There can be a lot to think about, prepare, and manage before, during, and after a shoot. But a shoot shouldn't be overly stressful, and even if it's not giddy fun, it should be enjoyable. This is your time to be in the creative flow.

Your Choice of Setting

The first logistical question you'll address is whether to shoot on location or use a studio. Each has its plusses and minuses. Location shooting is essential for environmental portraiture and it offers ready-made scenery, but the settings can sometimes be problematic and the light can be challenging. The studio is an unshaped lump of clay, but far too many photographers simply show it as the bare (and potentially boring) space it is.

Both the benefit and the challenge of the studio is that it starts as a blank canvas. Many photographers simply put up a muslin or seamless paper backdrop and shoot in a minimalist style with a light or two, but a studio can be more akin to a movie sound stage—a

Facing: © Lou Benjamin. Model: Sie Ist Idaho. Lensbaby optics can create evocative blurring effects. This image was produced with the double glass optic.

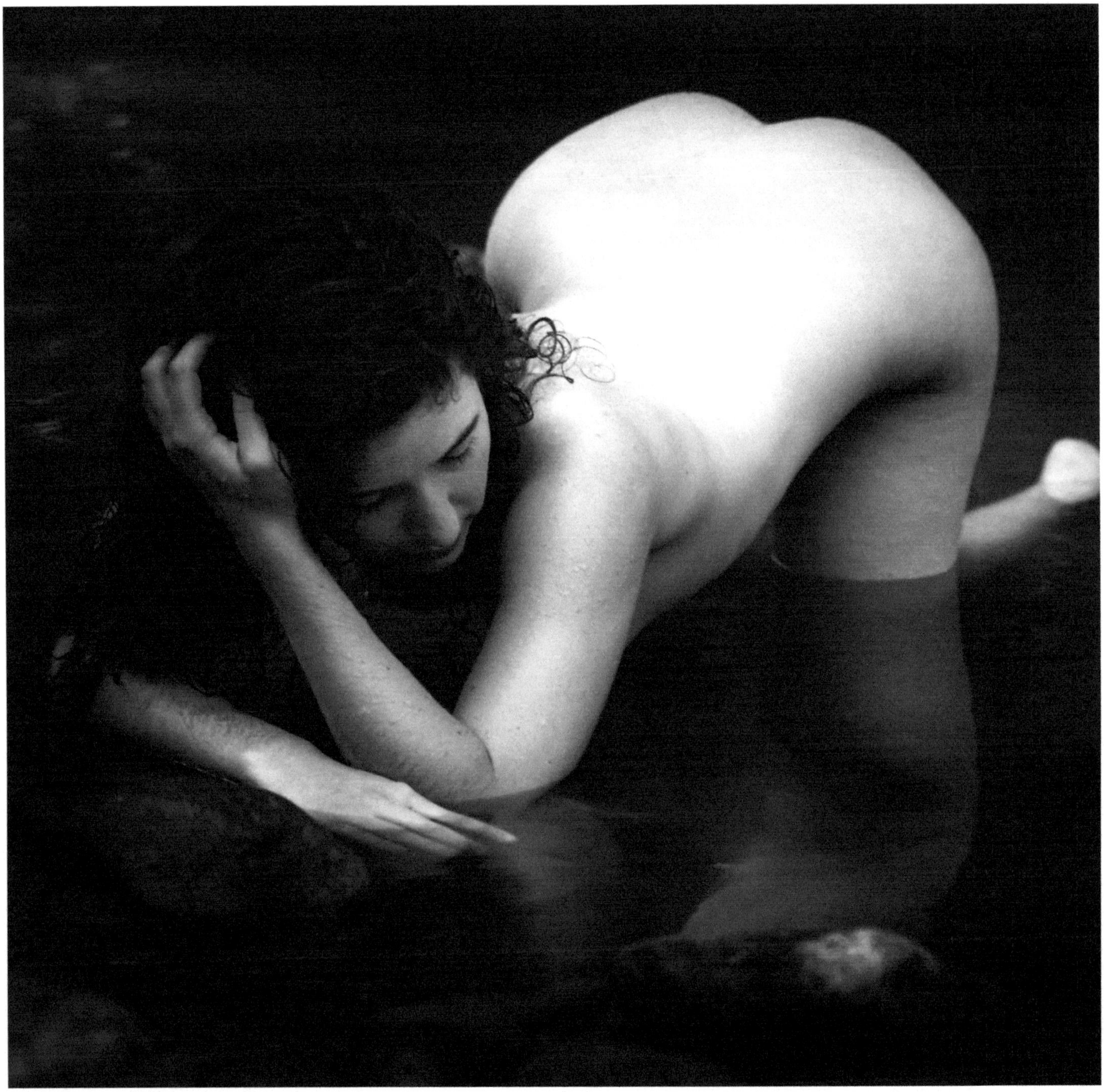

© Scott Foltz from the series *Waterscape Nudes*. This high-contrast black and white photo emphasizes form. Foltz, who specializes in landscapes and nudes, began the series in 2005 and most of the photos from the series have been shot in northeast and central Ohio.

place where you build illusions. Some photographers construct sets inside the studio. A bit of wainscoting and some vintage-looking wallpaper on a piece of sheetrock with a support can transform a bare white-painted cinder block space into the wall of a country cottage.

Early in his career, David LaChapelle found creative ways to work within the confines of a very small apartment that he converted into a studio. After he had gained a degree of success and moved into a much more expansive space, he felt compelled to build a small set that approximated the tiny space he was used to working with. He fed creatively off that constraint. In contrast, Helmut Newton preferred shooting on location because he felt that a woman cannot come to life in front of a white background. His work was a form of environmental portraiture that was about showing the rules of a segment of wealthy society and how the woman "of a certain milieu" lives.

Spencer Tunick creates spectacles with hundreds of naked bodies sprawled across expanses of terrain, populating famous locales, or filling the voids of striking architecture. The studio setting is far too restricted for the kinds of images he is interested in creating. His is location shooting in the extreme.

Whether shooting in the studio or on location, happy accidents do happen, but you can increase the likelihood of getting satisfactory results by preparing ahead of time. In the studio, that means setting up lights and equipment before the model arrives. For location shooting, that means scouting out your settings in advance of working with the model. If you plan to use available light on location, you will probably want to visit several times, at different times of the day, to see how the light plays across the setting. Being prepared and familiar with the location allows you to keep momentum going during the shoot, which keeps the model engaged and energized.

Safety First

If you are shooting on location, you may need to hike to the site. Make sure the model wears appropriate shoes and clothing to get there—vegetation can grab and cut at clothes and skin. Once you get there, make sure the area is clear of glass, splinters, nails, or other sharp objects, particularly if you are shooting in dilapidated structures. You want to make sure that wherever a model is going to position herself, that it's a safe environment. Check the area for "critters" that might disturb or harm a model and make sure the flooring is sound, so that no one will fall through it. The same goes for rocks by streams, which can be slippery, and cliffs or other elevated areas. It's a good idea to pack a small first aid kit for location shooting. Think through how you will deal with an emergency or injury, but do whatever you can to avoid accidents in the first place.

Many models want to please, and will take extraordinary risks to get you the shot. Emphasize safety, and let the model know that you do not want them to do dangerous things. You may need to manage this during the shoot and reign in any daredevils who might tumble from an unstable structure or find themselves sucked into rapids or dangerous currents. If it is just you and the model, make sure you can see each other at all times. Don't let yourself get wrapped up in dealing with the camera or technical things so that you lose sight of the model. Your priority should be safety; the camera and the shot are secondary. No image is worth someone's life or health, not to mention the lawsuits.

Hoisting lighting equipment above the ground can be risky stuff, for both people and equipment. The higher you hoist things, the more unstable they become, and the more important it is to properly sandbag the base. Be sure to take precautions. Tungsten hot lights, and even the quartz modeling lights on strobes, can put out a lot of heat. Snoots and grids get hot, even on strobes. Handle carefully. It's a good idea to have work gloves, oven mitts, or some kind of heat protection when you're adjusting such lights. Strobe heads often have plastic protection covers for transportation. Be sure to remove those covers before firing up the head, or the modeling lamp could end up melting the cover or even starting a fire.

Wires are a tripping hazard. Route them carefully, and it's a good idea to tape them down in areas that will receive a lot of foot traffic. If you run the power cable for a strobe under the leg of your light stand, kicking the cable is more likely to make the stand slide than tip over. If you have something with an end that juts out, such as a boom, mark it with something brightly colored, so that no one accidentally walks into it. As the old saying goes, it's all fun until somebody loses an eye.

How Much Gear?

The more you can make the equipment and process disappear, the stronger your connection to the subject. Some photographers always work with a minimalist camera and lighting arrangement as a way of keeping the equipment from dampening the interaction. Richard Avedon would set his camera on a tripod and never look through the viewfinder (or at the ground glass of his view camera) while he was shooting, because he felt it imposed too great a separation. He used a remote shutter release, moved around the room, and often used psychology to provoke responses from his sitters.

Time spent swapping lenses is a lost opportunity as well as an opening for getting dust on your sensor. Pro photographer and blogger Ken Rockwell argues cogently that you generally need to carry just two or three lenses. For example you could carry three primes—20mm, 50mm, and 85mm (Cartier-Bresson only shot with one—a 50mm). A good two-lens assortment might be a 35mm prime, and a 70–200mm zoom. Notice the intentional 100 percent gap between 35mm and 70mm—you can take a step or two forward or backward instead of trying to change lenses.

Rockwell also suggests that you don't need a dedicated macro lens, as most modern zooms have good macro capability. If you do pack an 85mm macro, there's no need to carry a second 85mm lens without macro. Fast lenses (e.g. f/2.8 zooms or f/1.2 primes) were designed for the lower sensitivities of film and are mainly necessary for beautiful bokeh in digital. Many digital cameras have good to excellent performance at ISO 800 and higher, so an f/3.5 zoom may well be sufficient.

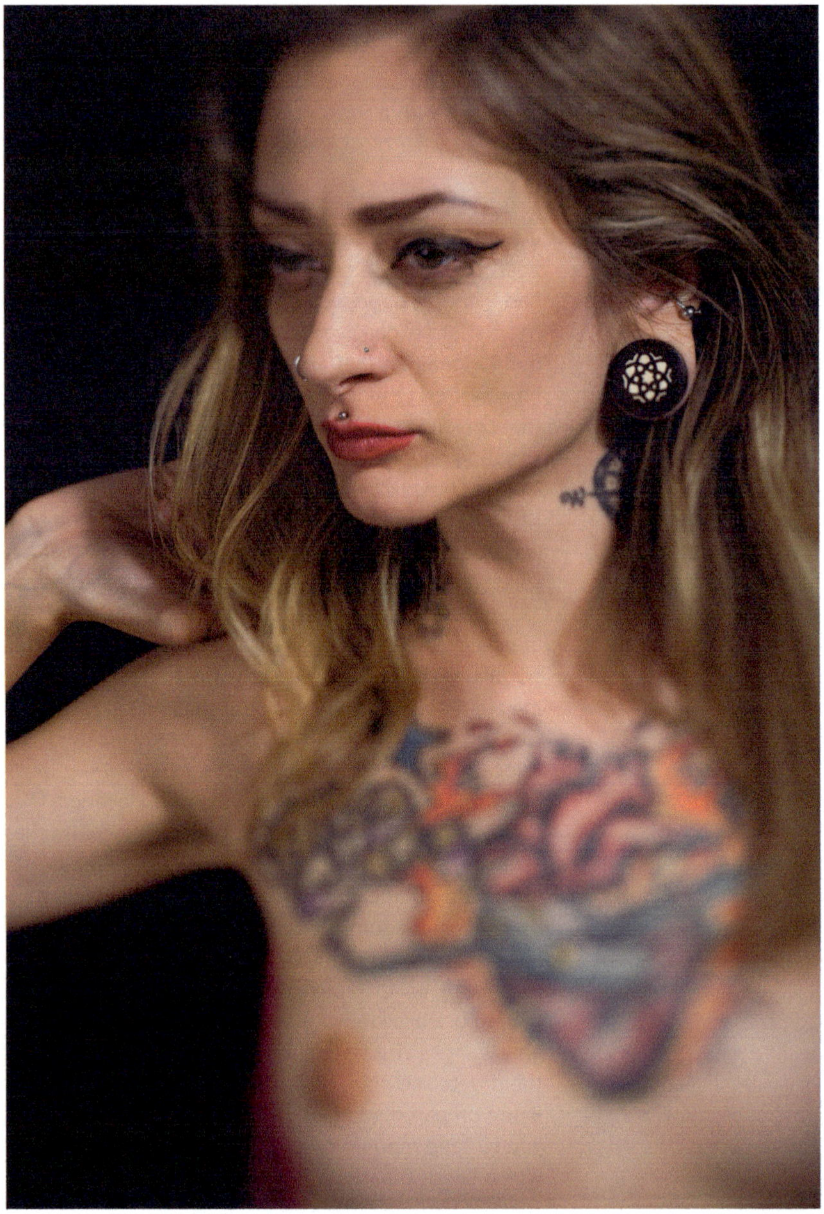

© Lou Benjamin. Model: Theresa Manchester. Along with your small complement of standard lenses, you might consider something like the Lensbaby Edge 80. In this shot, the slice of focus is oriented diagonally across the face. The background is black commando cloth, and the scene is lit by a pair of Profoto D1 Air 500 monolights with small white umbrellas.

Optimizing Color

For optimum color performance, it's a good idea to shoot reference targets for each lighting condition. Color temperature can change as you change the power setting on your strobes or vary the mix of lights. If you plan to shoot with colored gels, be sure to take your reference shot with the gels removed. You can shoot a gray target for white balance only, or use a ColorChecker Passport to sample white balance and also build custom camera profiles. Even if you plan to sample a custom white balance in post production, it's a good idea to avoid auto white balance and select a standard white balance or use a gray card to pre-set your white balance in-camera.

It's best to grab a shot of the ColorChecker whenever the lighting changes (for example, from daylight to fluorescent) as well as when you change lenses. Be careful not to over-expose the test shot. In bright sunlight you can take one or two additional bracketed shots at -1 EV and maybe -2 EV to make sure that the software can read the gray ramp on the ColorChecker. We will look at camera profiles in more detail in Chapter Ten.

Shooting in raw gives you the greatest latitude in post-production. Use it if you can. It's probably counter-intuitive, but when you shoot raw, you'll get more accurate colors on your camera's display screen if you set the color space to sRGB. If you choose Adobe RGB, that preview will probably look yellowish and washed out. This is because the display screen assumes that your previews are in sRGB. The same thing happens to your colors when you post Adobe RGB files on the web. Choosing sRGB will have no adverse effect when you process your photos in post-production because your raw processing software ignores the camera's color space setting when you process the file.

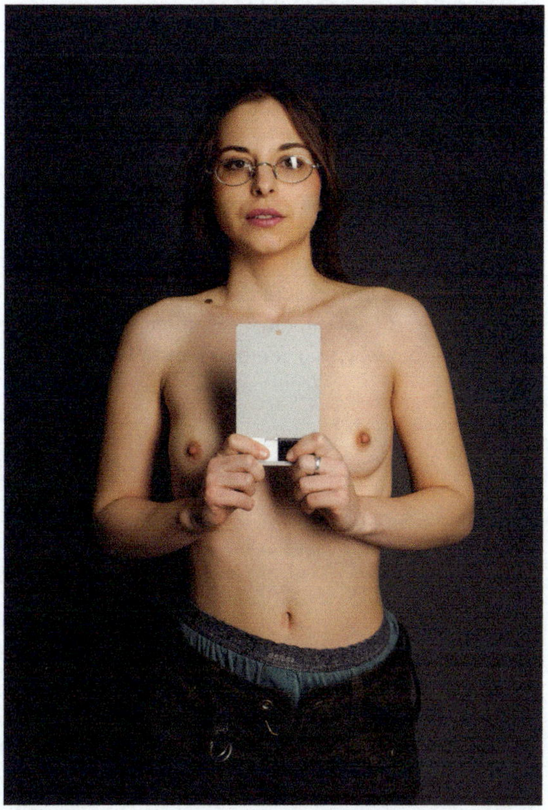

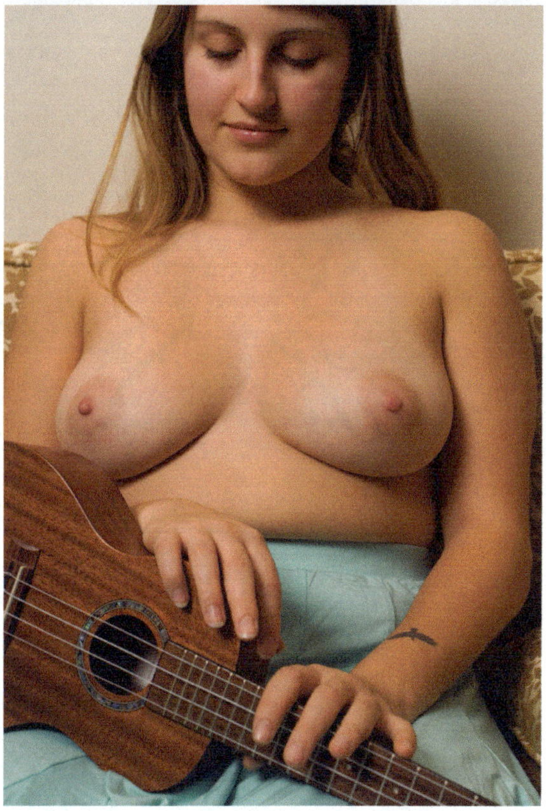

Above (top): © Lou Benjamin. Model: Aubrey. In post-production, you can sample a gray card for more accurate white balance and then sync the setting to the other photos shot under the same light.

Above (bottom): © Lou Benjamin. Model: Julie Vee. Using a ColorChecker Passport, a custom camera profile was made for Nikon D200 fitted with a Nikkor 35mm f/2 under strobe lighting. The celeste green skirt, the sitter's skin, and the gold pattern in the couch, along with the overall tonality of the photo, are more accurate and look substantially different with the custom profile, compared to the result with the default Adobe Standard camera profile.

Selecting Tonality

Your exposure determines how your camera records the overall tonality of the scene. For a standard exposure with matrix metering, the overall tonality of the scene will average out to a medium gray, and that's why white walls and snow look gray instead of white when you photograph them. You can intentionally over-expose such scenes by one or more stops (labeled EV on the exposure compensation controls for most digital cameras) to lighten the overall tonality. In that way, you can make snow look whiter, intentionally blow out the highlights in a window, or reveal details in the darker parts of the scene.

You can also under-expose significantly (for example, by 2 EV or more) to create moody images with pools of light in an expanse of darkness, or simply to preserve the details in brightest parts of the scene. If your meter reads f/5.6 at 1/250, you can select either f/11 or 1/100 for a -2 EV exposure. If you're shooting raw, your camera actually records more shadow and highlight information than what you see in the histogram or the raw file's preview. You can often recover highlight detail that looks blown

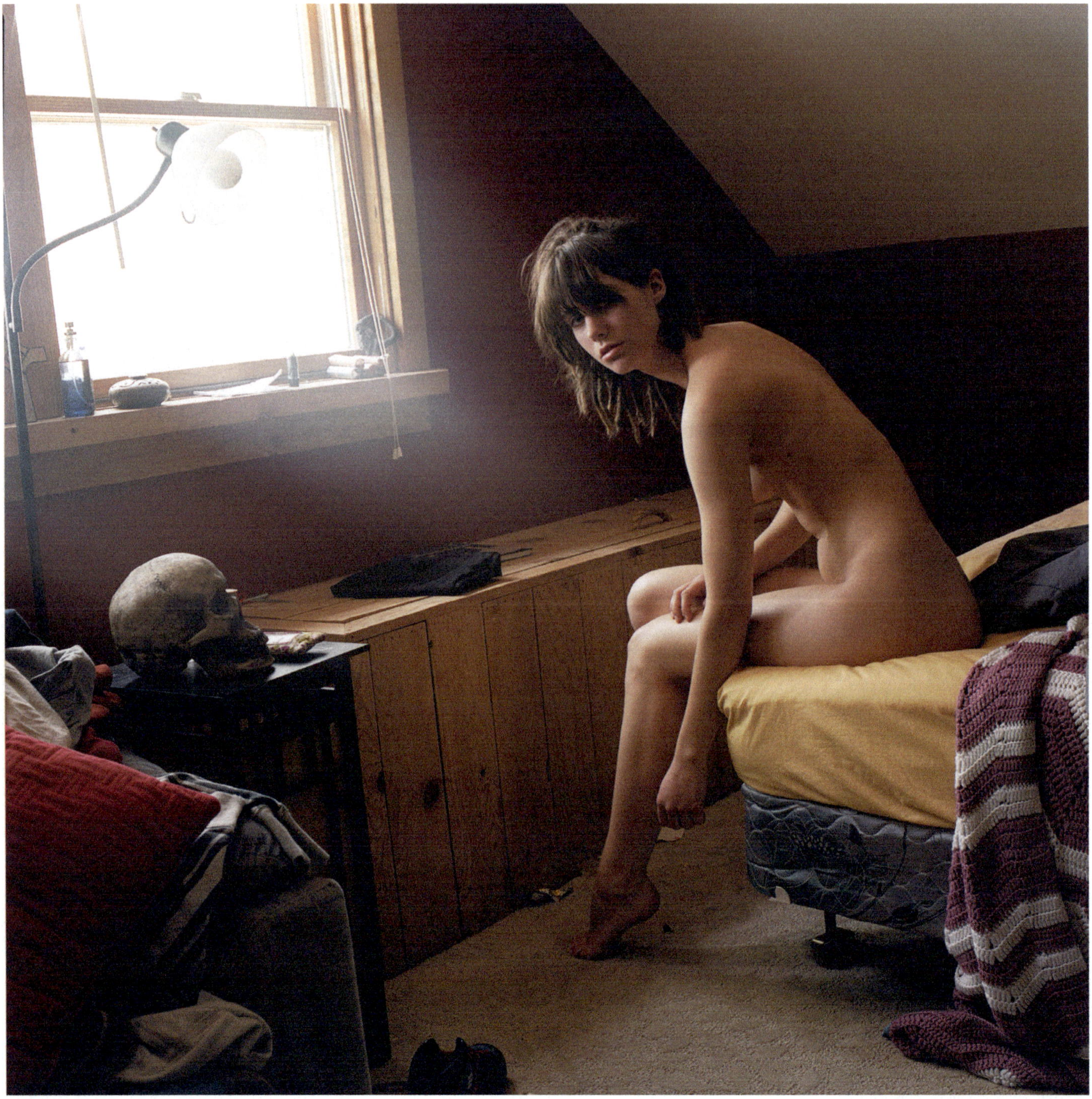

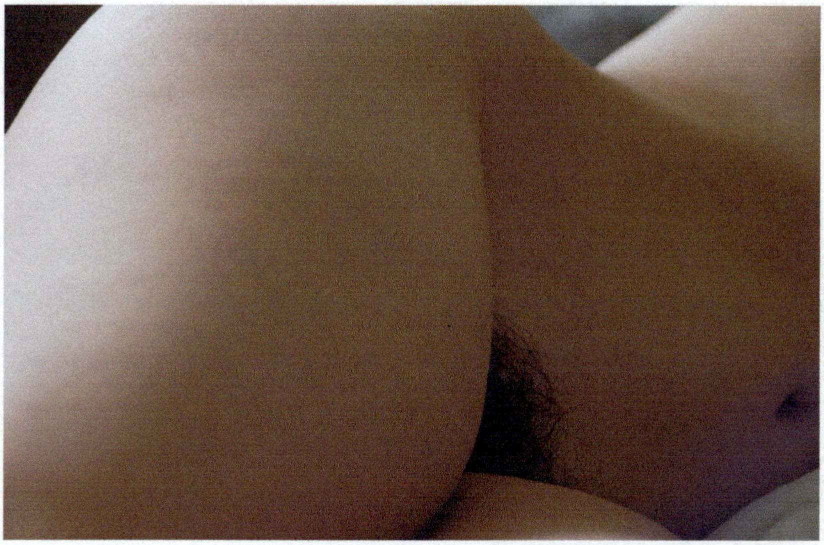

when you process the image, but you don't have as much latitude to recover shadow details if you under-expose too much.

With center-weighted metering, the edges of the scene are ignored. This can be useful if you're shooting into a dark area surrounded by bright highlights that you don't care about blowing out—perhaps you're in a back-lit situation and you want to focus on a face. The center weighting will calculate the exposure based on the average of the tones in the narrower area. Spot metering does the same, but for an even smaller area. In each case, the metering system is calculating the exposure needed to make that region come out medium gray. If you need it to be whiter, you may want to use Exposure Compensation to offset that exposure by +1 EV or more. In manual mode, your camera's metering system shows over- and under-exposure in EV units (stops). When working with continuous or natural light, you can center the area that you want to meter in the viewfinder, hold down the exposure lock button, and then recompose before tripping the shutter.

In particularly challenging lighting, the histogram on a digital camera works as a kind of after-the-fact light meter. You can make a test shot and look at the histogram to see if biasing the exposure setting up or down will make the scene look more like what you envisioned. As you increase or decrease the exposure, the peaks in the histogram will move accordingly. While a "normal" histogram should not show spikes, or clipping, at the blacks or whites (the extreme left or right), it can be totally appropriate to have such spikes in low-key and high-key images.

When you use the histogram as a light meter, remember that the histogram represents the distribution of tones in the preview image you see on the back of the camera, rather than the linear raw data. While that might sound like a problem, it's not. The preview and the histogram will be influenced by any contrast or scene settings you may have applied, and can indicate that your highlights are blown out or your shadows are blocked up, when you actually have the highlight and shadow information in the raw file.

Of course, by the time you begin to concern yourself with exposure settings, the model will already be in front of the camera. We'll look at working with models in depth in the next chapter.

Web Resources

Richard Avedon—www.avedonfoundation.org
Caravaggio—www.caravaggio.org
David LaChapelle—www.lachapellestudio.com
Irving Penn—http://bit.ly/1klGlgP
Ken Rockwell—http://bit.ly/1CvKQ5a
Spencer Tunick—www.spencertunick.com

Facing: Photo by Osmyn J. Oree, from the series *Honesty*. Shot on film, Oree uses the environment to tell stories and give insight into the people depicted. He also intends to "make the nudity less about eroticism or shock value, and more about the universal sense of rawness and honesty." The careful choice of exposure reveals details in the shadows while allowing the window to blow out. The window light illuminates particles in the air, rendering the atmosphere palpable.

Above: © Lou Benjamin. Soft back light from a window wraps around body contours in this photo. With back lighting, you often have to boost the exposure to be sure the shadowed foreground areas get enough light.

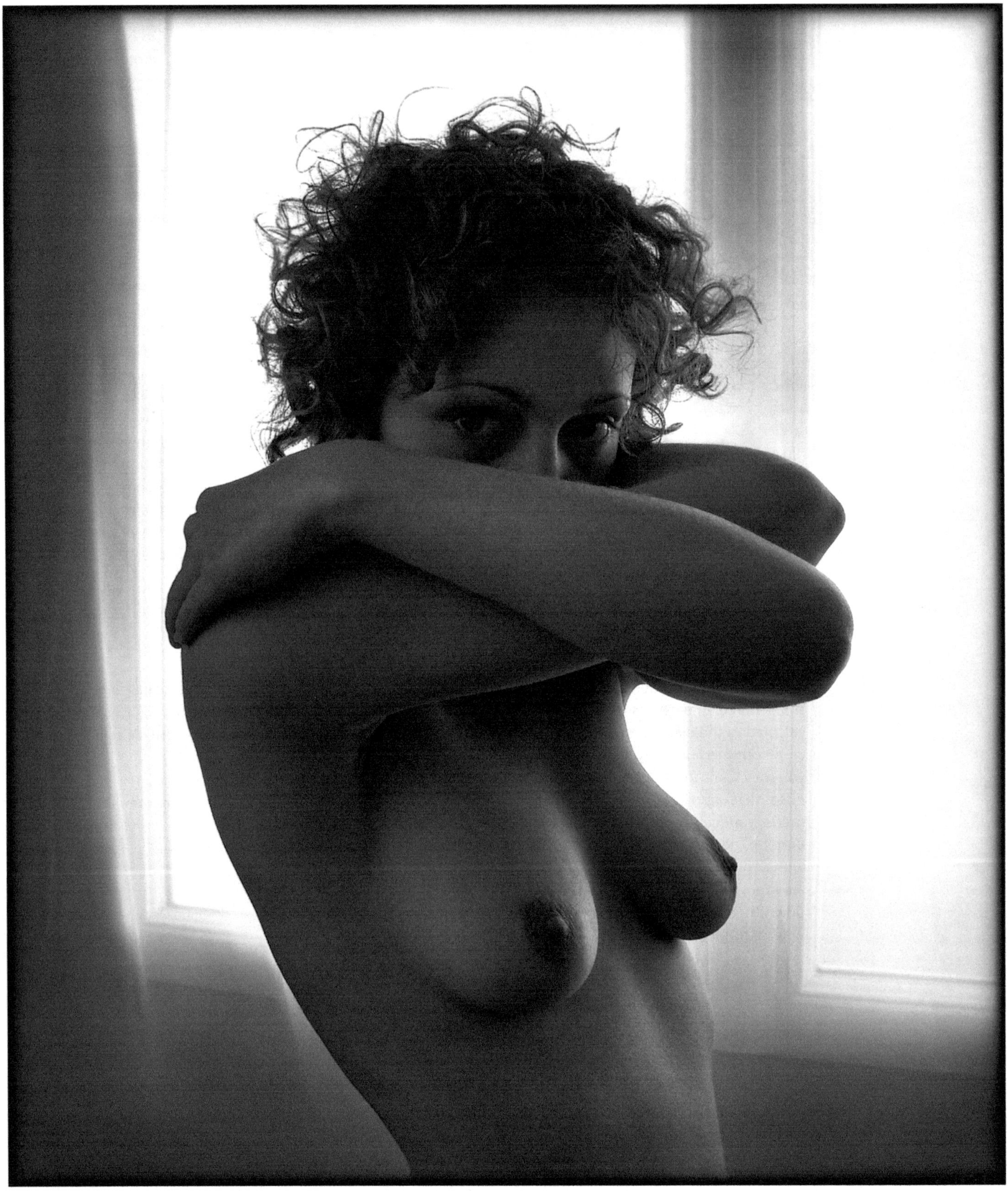

Chapter Nine | Collaborating with Models

THE PEOPLE in front of your lens aren't simply light reflectors, they're literally the embodiment of your ideas or the personification of the characters in your narrative. Their ability to convey a feeling in body language and expression may be the essential ingredient in a successful image. In short, modeling (for lack of a better word) is performance, and it's a good idea to think about what level of performance you're looking for before you start selecting models to work with.

Consider that the terms "model," "subject," and "sitter" are all somewhat problematic ways of referring to the person who will be in front of the camera, because each implies a certain power relationship and almost constrains the nature of the ways in which the people on either side of the camera will think about the collaboration. Even thinking in terms of the model "posing" has its own built-in limitations. The model can be far more than a poseable plastic figure, as Saelon Renkes demonstrates in the following interview.

Facing: © Pascal Renoux.

Interview with Saelon Renkes (saelon.com)

"My photos are most often about the kind of world I want to live in. Photography gives me a way to connect to this world—a world with quiet places of beauty, places of wonder, places that make me want to drink them in deeply—and to share them with others. I'm in love with the natural world, with the diversity in all its forms of life (both plants and animals), and with all the real people and real shapes within it. I'm fascinated by the emotional range of the human temperament, and by finding its reflections in the poses and expressions that people take on naturally.

Ruth Bernhard has been one of my strongest influences, and I've been particularly affected by the theme of one of her books, *The Gift of the Commonplace*. In her work this often refers to commonplace objects, and in the workshop I took with her she challenged us to find something beautiful to photograph within a limited number of feet of our meeting room. I love working this way, and I love to take this same approach with photographing the human body. Like many feminists who came of age in the 1970s, I came into photography with my own biases about nude photography, and from the beginning I wanted to pursue work that affirmed the beauty of ordinary human bodies, rather than contribute to a process that would further the insecurities the average woman has about her own body. Perfect bodies are beautiful, and they are lovely to photograph, but when I can find expressions of extraordinary beauty in a completely real-world body is when I feel that I am doing my best and most significant work.

I've studied photography, painting, and printmaking with David Bayles, Ruth Bernhard, Lucien Clergue, Steve Kiser, Alan May, Ted Orland, Holly Roberts, and Brian Taylor, in private workshops, at UC Santa Cruz Extension, the Pacific Art League, and at Foothill College. I've taught workshops for UC Santa Cruz Extension, St. Mary's Art Center, and privately. I've been exhibiting my work since 1994, on the Web and in galleries, and it has been included in many private collections. I'm currently living in Los Gatos, California (about 25 miles south of San Francisco), with my husband, Steve Fend (a USGS stream ecologist). I'm represented by The Main Gallery in Redwood City, and I exhibit my work in other places when the opportunity presents itself."

What impact do Uelsmann and Bernhard have on your work today?

▶ Both are (or were, in the case of Bernhard) absolute masters of printing, and both have been incredibly generous to students of photography, sharing freely of their techniques and insights. Both have provided considerable inspiration—Uelsmann with working beyond the normal constraints of reality, and Bernhard with the art of finding beauty in the commonplace. Bernhard gave especially good workshop assignments, such as to find a number of good images within 25 feet of the classroom, or a number of good images without getting out of bed, things like that. These are excellent exercises, and ones I repeat frequently on my own. There are incredible photographs right under our noses all the time!

How does being a feminist affect your work?

▶ It took me a bit longer to gravitate towards nudes because of my concern with exploitation of the female body. I struggled with that one for a little while, but I was especially interested in the timelessness that one can get with the nude figure. My feminism surely has guided some of my approach in how I work with the models. For instance, my insistence on providing what they need for their own comfort, both physical and emotional. I don't want to make a photograph that either of us is not comfortable making. It is always a collaborative effort and the model has as much say as possible. Originally I put some effort into finding male models as well, as part of a feminist urge to keep things equal. I didn't really keep this up very long though—since I do prefer working with friends or friends of friends, and those males very rarely are willing to model. To my mind it is still a bit odd, but men are often more shy about being photographed nude than most women.

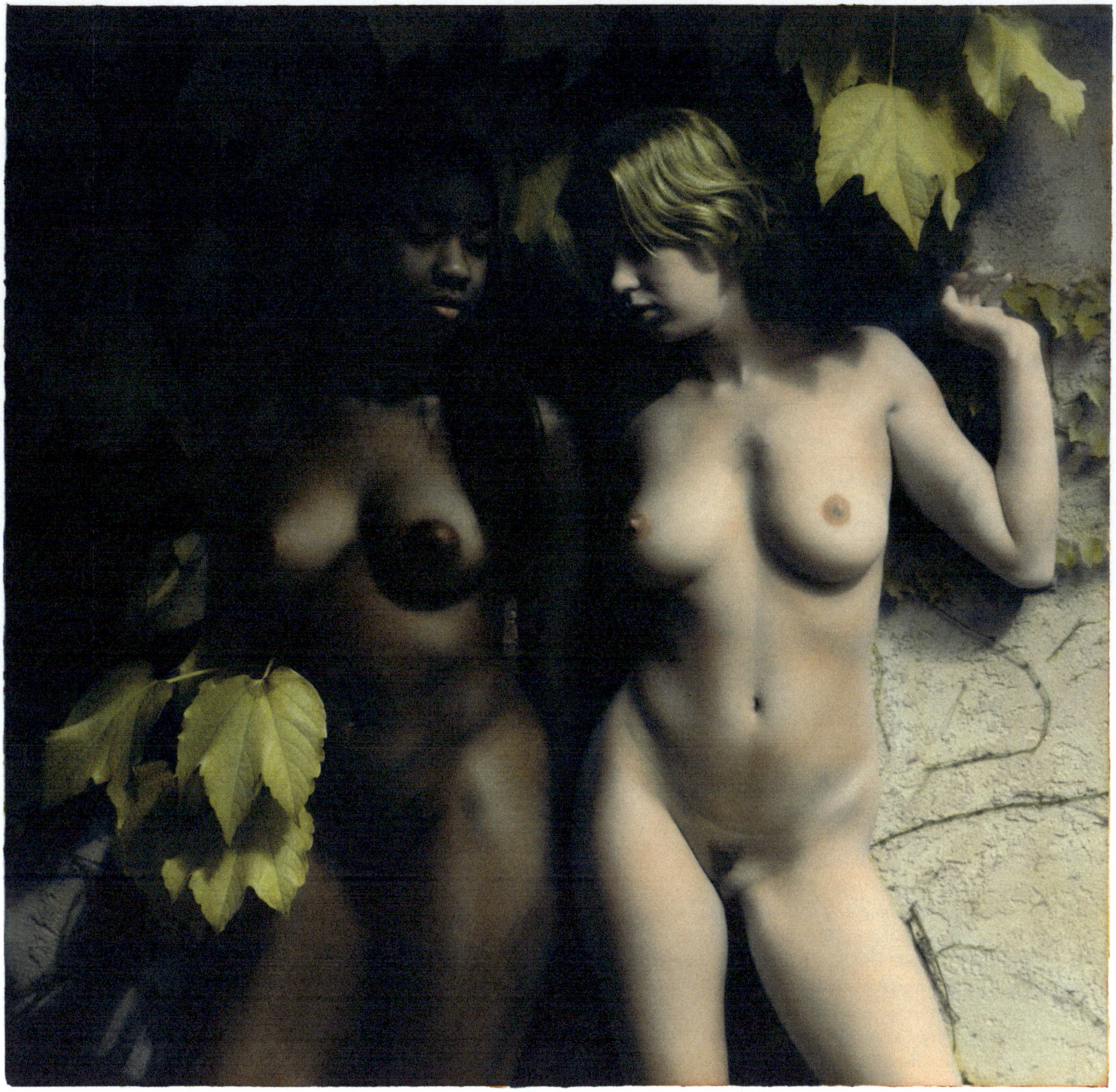

"Sun Shadow" © Saelon Renkes.

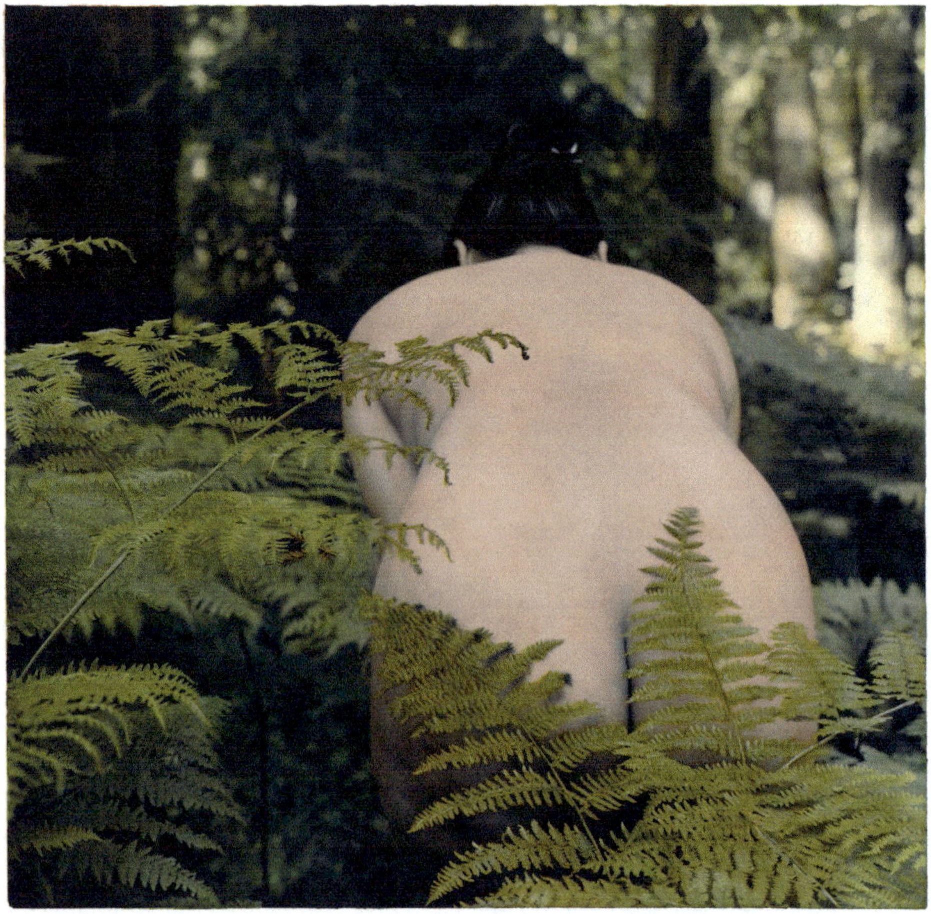

How much do you pre-visualize?

- I do a lot of pre-visualization in the field and in the studio. It is an extremely useful process that saves time by making it far easier to get the best print in the darkroom or at the computer, and also prevents a lot of garbage from ever making it to the proof sheets (or folders full of digital files). So much of good photography comes down to severe and careful editing, and pre-visualization is the first step in that process. Even in the digital age, with so many image adjustments possible, the final images are always better if they've been created with the right values in the first place. On the other hand, I still do a fair amount of post-visualization too, and refuse to take on any sort of guilt over that. The creative process doesn't stop with the click of the camera shutter. If I can create a final image that works, I don't care if it is the same thing I pre-visualized or not.

How would you describe the relationship between you and the sitter. Can you say something about how you interact during a shoot?

- I especially enjoy working with non-professional models—friends or acquaintances—because they tend to bring more spontaneity to the photo sessions, and they are less likely to offer me a repertoire of the same old poses. They also tend to be more nervous

"Nude Ferns" © Saelon Renkes.

about the sessions at first—they may not be comfortable with having me really look hard at their body, or they may be shy about offering up poses or thoughts. I work hard to establish some level of comfort; I really don't like to make people uncomfortable in the first place, but also the kinds of images I am trying to make almost always require relaxation on the part of the models. This is where the photographer really needs to know what they are trying to achieve though, as I have one photographer friend who is completely the opposite—he is particularly interested in capturing that very same discomfort that I am trying to banish.

As a general rule, I prefer to have models in poses that are natural and comfortable to them, and to be as at ease as possible. Photographs always have a lot of the photographer in them, and while I feel that when the model is ill-at-ease the photograph becomes even more about the photographer and less about the model, it is also possible that my preference has more to do with my own search for emotional comfort. At any rate, I do try to help the model feel comfortable and relaxed, and I like to sort of experiment slowly until we find the poses that come most naturally to the model.

My usual process is to try to have a few simple ideas planned out to start the session, where I just tell them what I want them to do, as a means of breaking the ice and giving me a chance to see what their bodies are really like. If I haven't worked with the model before, these are almost never the images that work best, but they do serve an important function in getting things warmed up.

For those models who stay nervous a little longer and are still somewhat stiff while being observed with the camera, I find that it can work wonders to stop to change film (or change the memory card or battery). Tension is fatiguing, so those particularly nervous models often sigh a great sigh of relief when the camera is finally turned away, and really relax. A few glances in that direction while fussing over the camera can sometimes reveal a really great pose, and I've often done an abrupt shout of "Wait, don't move at all, that's a fantastic pose." Most models are even more relaxed once they've seen that you are really happy with what you are getting.

Do you have advice for beginning nude photographers?

▶ Yes indeed! I strongly believe that anyone who wants to do nude photography should experience being on the other side of the lens as well. This is the very best way to learn about working effectively with a model. I think it's most effective as a learning tool if you model nude for another photographer, but it is also good to practice by using yourself as a model. What do these suggestions bring up in your mind? This in itself is useful to know, as it may offer a little insight into the things that come up in a model's mind. Do you think your body isn't attractive enough? Try to find innovative ways to use only parts of your body—there are many ways to make a beautiful photograph with a human body. Are you concerned with being recognized in ways that might be embarrassing? Think about ways to make it not recognizable by using only part of the body, or by manipulating the lighting or the focus, or by cropping to the point of abstraction. More tips to make this exercise more successful: Use a tripod for the camera and place a large mirror behind it to get a better idea of what your layout is looking like. A second tripod can be used as a stand-in for yourself, to give you something to focus on, while also marking exactly where you need to place yourself when you get back on the lens side of the camera. A self-timer can be used to release the shutter, but it sometimes is difficult to get everything completely arranged quickly enough. In that case a very long cable release cord or a remote control can be a blessing. This whole process can be a bit complex and sometimes frustrating, but it is really an excellent way to learn and get some practice without the pressure of worrying about another person who might be getting impatient or bored.

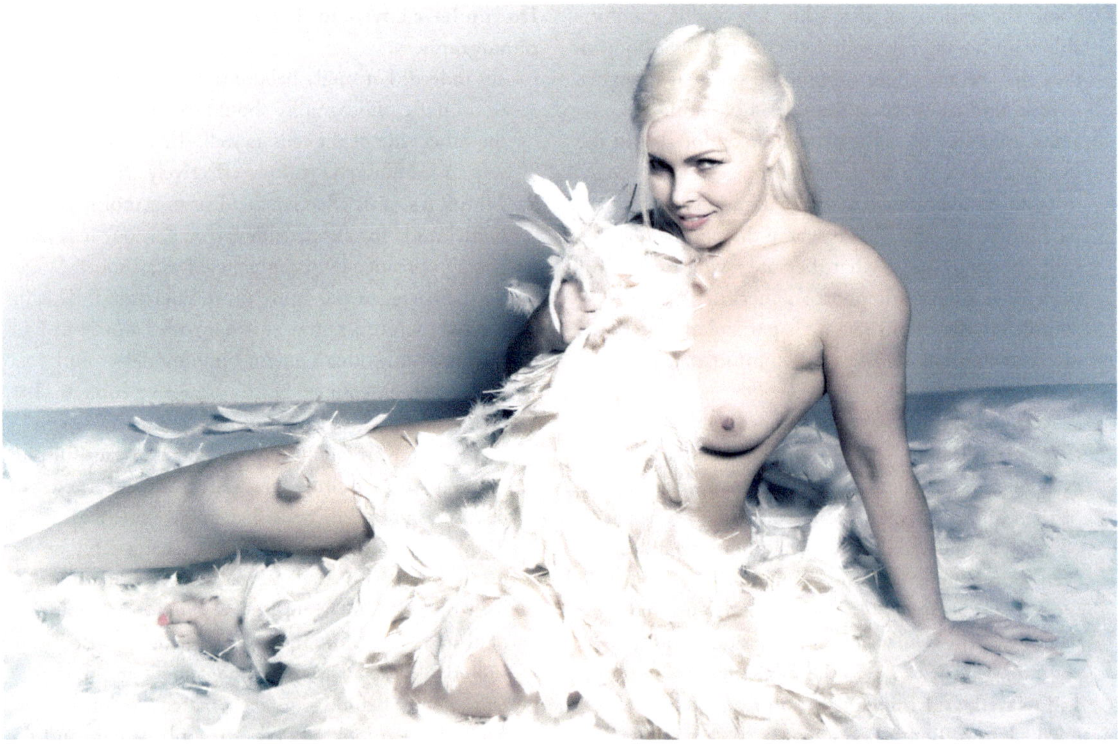

Muses

In Greek mythology, the muses were the nine daughters of Zeus and Mnemosyne, the personification and inspiration of the arts, literature, and science. Throughout art history, the term "muse" has signified a deep personal (and often romantic) relationship between the artist and sitter. However, what is most important to us in all of these pairings is not whether the relationship was sexual, but the profound connection they had in the creation of their art. Today, the term muse also applies to a model who is particularly charismatic and works largely without direction from the photographer. The idea is that they improvise, spontaneously generating attitudes and poses that are the ideal raw material for a photographer. Professional muses have often been modeling for a good amount of time, and really understand how to deliver the poses and presence that make for strong images.

Famous artists' muses often motivated them to pick up their brush, pencil, sculpting tools, or camera and make work. Harry Callahan's wife Eleanor was a source of pure inspiration. In the beginning, he photographed her out of necessity—he couldn't afford to hire models. She has said that she never initiated any of the poses, but granted him full permission. Harry fully conceived the shots, knowing she would never refuse. Some muses even informed the artists' creative direction. Such was certainly the case for Man Ray and Lee Miller. Edward Weston drew inspiration and direction from both Tina Modotti and Charis Wilson. Modotti and Weston influenced each other's work significantly.

Above: © Terry Slater.

Facing: © Pascal Renoux.

Finding Talent

Your selection of model has a lot to do with the results you get. Think of movies—a director's casting choices have a profound effect on the film that results. Even in a portrait, you're telling a kind of story. Part of the casting process is reconciling the image that you want to make with the way the model wants to be seen, and not everyone can express the qualities that you're looking to show. Thus, it helps to be clear about what you're looking for and be selective.

If you are just starting out with art nudes or want to improve your work, it can be valuable to hire a muse or an experienced model/photographer, and let them know you want to learn from them. Beyond giving you great poses and teaching you about working with models, they can give you guidance about lighting and shooting. Chances are, their confidence will also reduce any nervousness you might have. Working with better models will result in better quality work for your portfolio—something that other models will look at to gauge whether they are willing to work with you. The process of casting models is not a one-way street, and the better your portfolio, the more access you will have to better models. In fact, once you have a strong portfolio, good models will contact you about the possibility of working together. Of course, modeling and studio rental fees can add up quickly. Workshops and group shoots are another way to work with better models at a more reasonable cost,

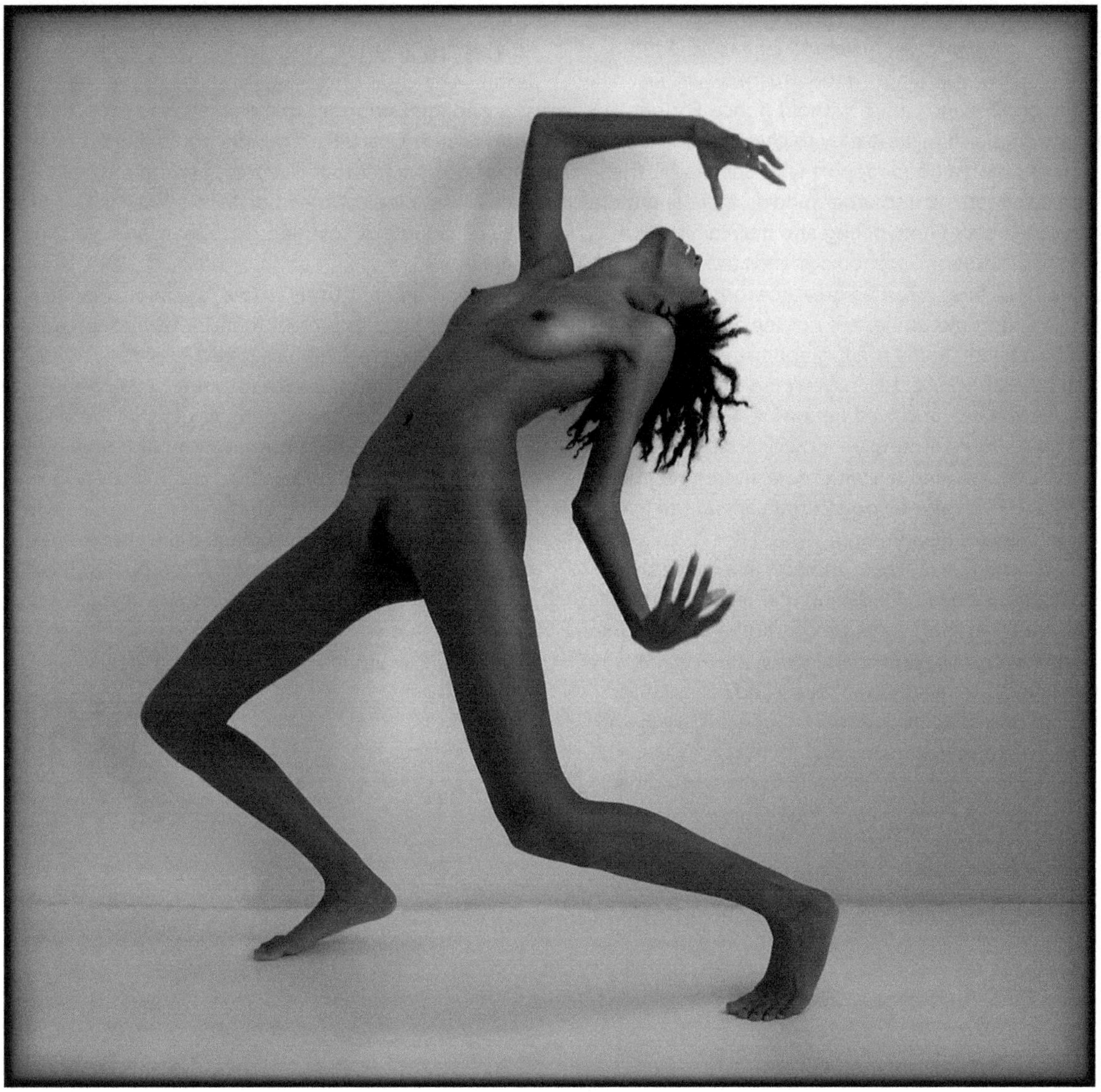

although you aren't likely to have full control of setup and lighting, and your shooting time will be more limited.

There are numerous online networks for casting models as well as other talent such as makeup artists and retouchers. With over 900,000 active profiles, one of the best known is modelmayhem.com. Purpleport.com is currently making an effort to expand its presence in the US. iStudio.com is owned by OneModelPlace.com. PureStorm.com is another option, and in the US, there's also Craigslist. This is hardly an exhaustive list. Each of the sites has its pros and cons, including differences in functionality and culture. Most have free or low-cost membership options as well as premium memberships.

Networking sites can put you in touch with a lot of models fast, but that doesn't mean that you'll get the best results. Expect no-shows, last-minute cancellations, and awkward novices among the good connections. Some models may seem enthusiastic at first, but somehow never manage to schedule a shoot. Other seemingly good prospects will just delete their profiles and vanish without notice. Fortunately, these sites also make it easy to check references. Once you establish a good rapport with one model, they can often refer you to other models. More and more models are also networking and maintaining connections through Facebook. Friends (even Facebook friends) of friends can be great to work with.

Online communities are not the only option for finding talent. Some photographers prefer novices or amateurs, because they haven't developed ingrained habits and preconceived notions about how to model. Finding sitters through your own social circles can often put you in touch with more interesting people who will even afford you a certain amount of trust from the very beginning.

You can literally meet subjects in a coffee shop or a bar. Justine Kurland, who is known for her idyllic tableaus featuring nude, earthy mothers in wilderness settings, describes prospecting for subjects this way: "I hang out in health food stores and playgrounds with a box of prints and talk to strangers, try to show them pictures, tell them what it's about. The ones who believe in the vision are the ones who come." For the series *Poughkeepsie Journal, Dream America,* and *Morning Call*, Katy Grannan placed ads in local newspapers that simply read, "Art Models. Artist/photographer (female) seeks people for portraits. No experience necessary. Leave msg." After talking on the phone with Grannan and agreeing to be photographed, many of her subjects chose to pose nude.

When proposing to shoot, be up-front about shooting nudes and the concepts you're interested in working on. If you're worried about people stealing your ideas, at least give a general description of the kind of work you're looking to shoot. On networking sites, some models post disclaimers like "no pornography," "keep it classy," or "tasteful nudes only." These statements are boundary markers, and because everyone defines concepts like pornography and tastefulness differently, it's important to come to an understanding of what your potential model means by that language ahead of time. Not doing so could be a complete waste of time or worse, if a model puts out negative reviews of working with you.

Perhaps the most important thing to be aware of is that your sitter brings expectations to the shoot, too, and it is important to manage those expectations from the very start. For example, some models expect the photographer to pull a great performance out of them. Take a look at their portfolio—you can't assume they're capable of anything more than what you see there.

A condition of trust is crucial. It's unfortunate that art models need to protect themselves from predatory behavior. Many models have direct experience with photographers who use their cameras as a pretense to leer at them, grope them, or try to get them into bed. Because of this, it's not unusual for models to want to give you a "sniff test" before they commit to shooting. This might mean insisting on bringing someone with them to a first-time shoot. Others will want to meet or talk on the phone in advance. If you plan to have the model sign a release, let them know ahead of time (some ask that you send it to them to read before they agree to show up).

Facing: © Alan Fresco.

The 2257 Regulations

If you plan on shooting and publishing certain types of imagery, you may be required to maintain records under the "2257 regulations." Depictions of actual or simulated sex fall under the regulation, and an important phrase in the law, "lascivious depictions of the genitals or pubic area," can even be interpreted as applying to models in tight-fitting clothes. Though the government has signaled its intent to use the law to regulate the porn industry, some artists are nervous about the regulations because the Department of Justice (DOJ) has declined to rule out the possibility of prosecuting artists.

Let's be clear: Simply photographing someone in the nude does not mean that you need to comply with the 2257 regulations. The key question is whether your work depicts real or simulated "sexually explicit conduct." If you do crotch shots, images involving masturbation, or sex scenes, you may be required to maintain records documenting the age and names of the performers at the time the imagery was made. A cross-referencing requirement means that photographing the model holding up a driver's license next to his or her face is not sufficient. If you post those images to the Web, you also have to label the web pages in a very specific way and document the URLs that the images were uploaded to. Additional aspects of the requirements can become extremely burdensome. A detailed examination of the law can be found at www.xxxlaw.com/articles/primer5.html.

As of the writing of this edition, the government has only initiated the prosecution of one case, and it has since suspended checking the records of pornography production companies under the Obama administration, but as long as the regulations remain on the books they could be enforced under a future administration. Because the law allows the government five years from the date of any violation to begin prosecution, people who violate the regulations today could still face prosecution in the event that the next administration resumes enforcement.

If you have doubts, you should consult a lawyer who specializes in these matters to determine your level of risk. In addition to consulting legal professionals, it may be worthwhile to engage one of a number of companies that specialize in record keeping compliance.

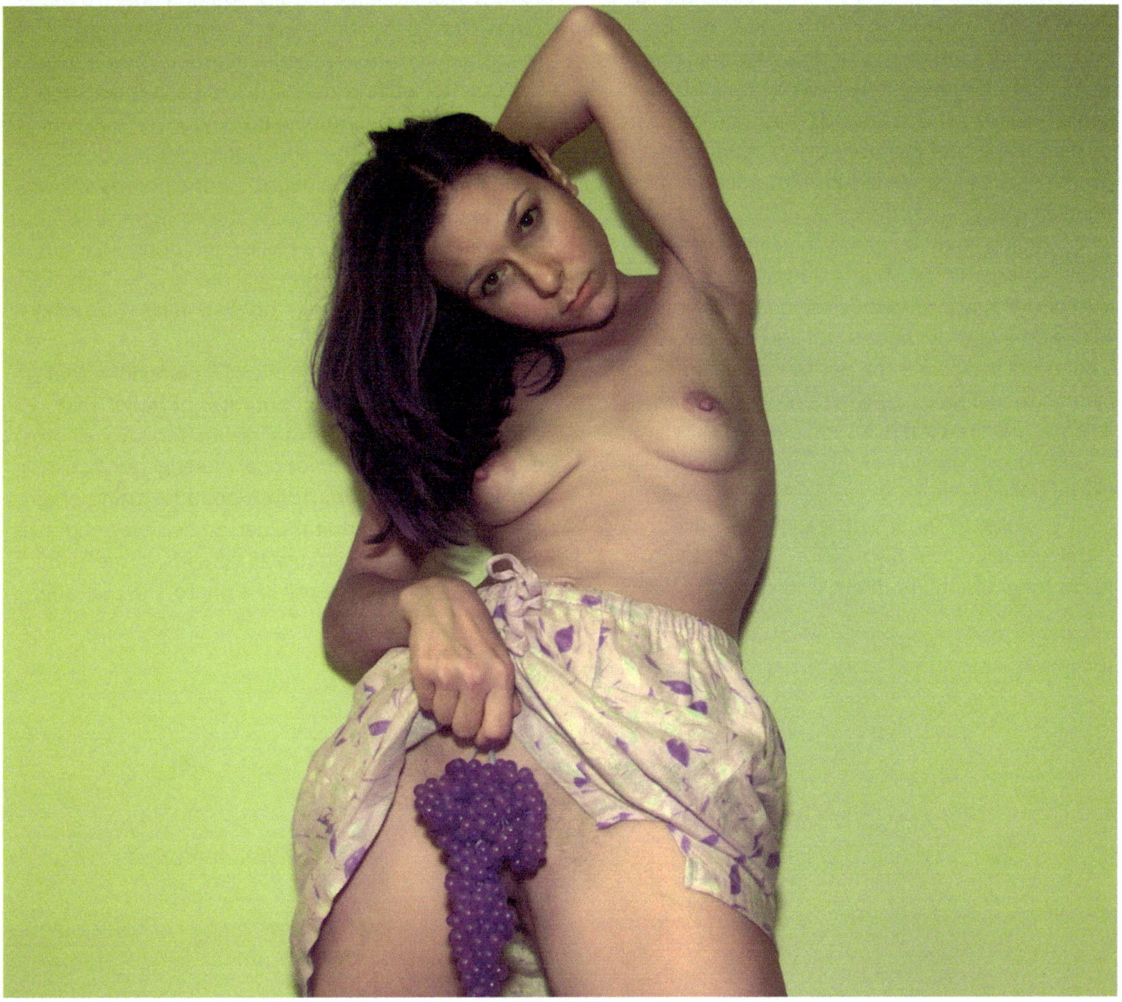

Compensation

You can expect to negotiate the terms of compensation every time you book a shoot. There are professionals who make their entire living from art modeling, there are hobbyist models who just do it for the love and adventure of it, and there are novice models who hope to be paid well in the future, but are willing to trade time for usable portfolio shots.

Lee Friedlander paid the then-unknown Madonna $25 for a 1979 photo session. That's equivalent to about $80 in 2013, still well below what professional models in the Tri-State area typically ask for today. Many good models ask between $100 and $150 per hour to shoot nudes. Some also have a two-hour minimum, and ask for travel compensation, and some give a price break for three or more hours. Many are negotiable, and will work out a reasonable arrangement based on the nature of your project and what you can afford.

Another form of compensation in use is abbreviated TFCD or TFP, sometimes referred to as trades, or shortened to TF or TF*. The abbreviations mean Time for CD and Time for Print, respectively. The idea is that the model gives time in exchange for quality images that they can use for their portfolio and self-promotion. People have widely differing approaches to doing trades, and the practice has been misused by photographers as well as models. Many models see it as "working for free" and will not do nude shoots (or in some cases *any* shoots) on a TF basis. It's only a good deal for the model if you're able to provide quality photos that can generate future business, and for many, nudes won't suffice.

Modeling agencies generally refer to trade arrangements as test shoots, and often send models out for them, provided they see quality in your portfolio. Some agency models will agree to do nude or semi-nude shots after the portfolio work is done. The fashion model look isn't what every art photographer is looking for, but if it is, all you need to get started is about a dozen quality samples of your work to show the agencies.

If you plan to shoot with trade agreements, you should develop your own clear and consistent set of terms for entering into them, and state your policy up front. Helmut Newton's practice of shooting one for the client and one for himself is a workable approach. In your case, the "client" would be the model—you would shoot portfolio quality images in whatever style the model needs in addition to your arty naked photos. Spell out your turnaround time, how many retouched/finished images you will provide, and any other stipulations. And, keep your word—it's an agreement where time truly is money for both parties.

Some models expect to receive a copy of every frame that was captured during the session, sometimes even specifying raw files. That is tantamount to using your talents as a photo booth. Often, those same models will take your images and edit them. The result can be bad images attributed to you. If you are interested in promoting your work and developing your reputation based on the quality of your images, it's never a good idea to agree to that sort of arrangement.

Releases

If you plan to use a release, show it to the model before you begin shooting, but wait until afterward to have it signed. Technically, you don't need a model release for editorial use, which includes artwork published in books or shown in art galleries. You're in the clear to sell fine art prints and posters, and you can run unreleased photos inside books. That said, you may want to have the model sign a release documenting the ways you might use the photos anyway. The reason for this is because there's nothing to stop someone from finding a lawyer and bringing a suit regardless of whether they will prevail, in which case you might have to "lawyer up" to defend yourself at considerable expense.

Model releases are required by companies that publish photographs for "purposes of trade." That means you probably want a release for cover photos or photos used in promotional materials for books. Use for purposes of trade includes advertising or any usage that implies that the person depicted endorses a product or demonstrates its benefits. In the event of a lawsuit over trade use of a photo, the publisher is liable, not the photographer (unless you sign a contract that indemnifies the publisher). The release protects publishers and makes your photographs salable; they will not license your work for commercial usage without one.

Editorial use of a person's image, which includes fine art, does not require a release and is protected under the first amendment. However, even though the fine art use of an image may place you on solid legal footing, that doesn't prevent you from having to defend yourself in the event that someone brings a lawsuit over the use of their image. *Nussenzweig v. diCorcia* is a celebrated case that concluded that the fine art use of an image, even including limited edition sales of prints, is not "for purposes of trade." The case lasted from 2005 through most of 2007, when the New York Court of Appeals ruled in favor of diCorcia. The cost of Philip-Lorca diCorcia's defense had to be enormous. As an established A-list artist, he had the resources of the Pace/MacGill Gallery at his disposal, something that most of us do not.

You can find language for your model release in a number of places, including the Business and Legal FAQ on the ASMP (American Society of Media Photographers) website at ASMP.org. The language for model releases doesn't vary much between the different sources.

What's really important is the understanding you have with the model, not the signature on the paper. It's best to actually have a conversation so that you and the model have an understanding about how you might use the photos in the future. The paper only documents that understanding.

You may encounter models (usually early in their careers) who want you to sign a release form that they have prepared. It is likely that the document contains stipulations about how you can use the photos, often under the mistaken impression that they share in the copyright. It is probably not a good idea to sign such documents. If possible, you can amend your own release to address any concerns the model may have; otherwise, it's best to walk away from such arrangements. Again, it's a good idea to discuss usage before you shoot so that you and the model are on the same page.

Copyright

Standard model releases only contain language about the photographer's possible uses of the image. It is a good idea to have the model sign a second document that acknowledges you are the copyright holder and specifies the usage rights granted to the model, or add that language to the release. Many photographers state that the model has the right to use the photos for self-promotion only, and even stipulate that the images cannot be edited.

Some models believe that they are the author or co-author of a photo (and therefore copyright holder), based either on the fact that their likeness appears in the image, or on the degree of collaboration involved in creating the idea. However, that is not the law; the lead actors in a feature film do not share in its copyright. It is important to understand that the law states that the copyright automatically belongs to the photographer from the moment the exposure is made, and it is designed to protect the unique expression of the idea and not the idea itself.

If you feel generous and want to declare that you and the model jointly own the copyright, you can, but joint ownership means that either party can do whatever they like with the image, without securing the permission of the other or having to share any benefits of that usage. Instead of joint copyright, you might consider retaining the copyright and granting broad usage rights to the model instead.

Shooting

The first thing to deal with is skin. Tight-fitting clothing leaves marks. Experienced nude models often arrive at the shoot wearing loose-fitting clothing and no underwear. If your model arrives wearing tight clothes, offer her or him a robe and plan to wait somewhere around half an hour for the marks to go away. Otherwise, you'll probably have some work to do with the Healing brush in Photoshop after the fact.

You will probably need to break the ice before you do any actual shooting. This may be as much for you as for the model. Conversation can be almost anything, but it helps if you're genuinely interested in your sitter. It can be just small talk, but if you say too little, that almost guarantees that your model will be stiff and ill at ease, or just plain bored. If your model volunteers information about a girlfriend or boyfriend, it's probably okay to talk cordially about the subject, but you don't want to give the impression that you're prying or coming on to them.

Music can help to create atmosphere during the shoot, and take some of the pressure off you for creating banter. Some models insist on it. This is more easily done in a studio, but you can also take a portable player on location. Some models routinely bring music, and others will bring it if asked. You can play your own music, but be aware how it affects the sitter. If it doesn't seem to suit the sitter's tastes, or if it's too loud or distracting, turn it down, change it, or turn it off.

At the beginning of the shoot, it is often useful to show your sitter examples, sketches, mood boards, or reference material. Helmut Newton couldn't draw, but made descriptive notes on props, lighting, compositional ideas, and themes. The point is to give the model an idea of where you are going with your concept, but don't overwhelm them. The British have a lyrical phrase for giving too much information: "You're blinding me with science." You want to develop a sense of how much information your model wants and needs, and keep them in the loop without overdoing it.

No one approach works for all situations. Irving Penn's book *A Notebook at Random* shows preparatory sketches he used for some of his fashion shoots next to the finely crafted finished product. These are examples of pre-visualization and shooting with a clear end in mind, where the model almost functions as a prop. On the other hand, accounts of his "Earthly Bodies" sessions describe his interactions with his models as being highly collaborative and almost nonverbal, where Penn communicated with them in a primal way using "coos, murmurs, and supportive breathing to convey that everything was wonderful, just right in this perfect situation."

You want to give yourself permission to shoot what you envision. There is such a deep-seated cultural aura of shame associated with nudity, that photographers often reflexively censor themselves. Lots of photographers who are beginning to shoot nudes are actually nervous being around naked models. You want to be relaxed and confident. Photographers are often asked in interviews whether they are aroused by shooting nudes and many respond that shooting abstract fine art nudes can be far less arousing than photographing lingerie-clad models because the lighting and posing transforms the body into an organic form divorced of sexuality.

Directing the model during the shoot can depend on the model's style of working. Many experienced models know what sides to show, and are also aware of how light falls on their bodies. On the other hand, models can fall into rote poses. If your sitter is new to modeling, it's especially important to pare your input to small chunks, interspersed with banter. You want to use simple directives like "Turn your head a little more" or "Can you bring your chin down a bit?" For more elaborate poses, be ready to act out your idea, even badly.

Your sitter wants confident, competent direction, a sense of where your shoot is going, and an opportunity to collaborate. Paraphrasing a post from a model in an online forum, a great photographer does the following:

- Comes to the shoot with creative and innovative ideas.
- Listens to a model who is creative, but does not make the model come up with all the ideas.
- Tells a model "soften your eyes," "pop your hip," "push out your pelvis," and "twist to elongate."
- Tells a model "you have a hair out of place," then comes and fixes it.

Once you start shooting, it's important to keep the communication open. If you get lost in dealing with the camera, the lights, or any of the logistics of shooting, your chances of getting a strong image are greatly reduced. If you are shooting digital, avoid reviewing so much that it takes you away from making more photos. One way to do that is to set your camera so that it does not automatically display the shot every time you trip the shutter.

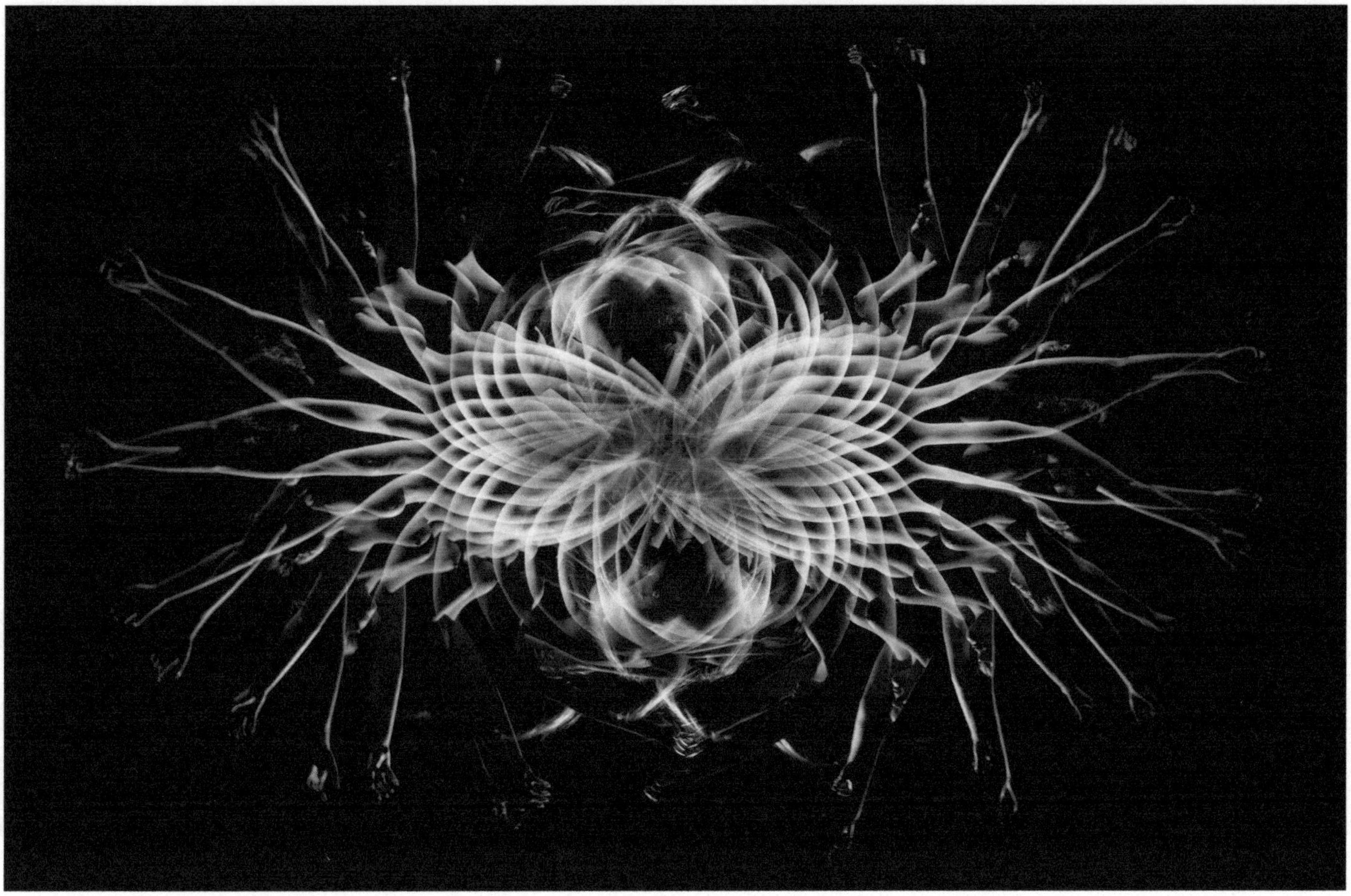

© P. J. Reptilehouse. To create this photo in-camera, the model made exaggerated gestures in front of a camera attached to a microcomputer-controlled moving mount. During the single eleven-second exposure, the model synchronized her movements with those of the camera to produce the elongated form. The pattern was produced by multiple flashes from LED strobes.

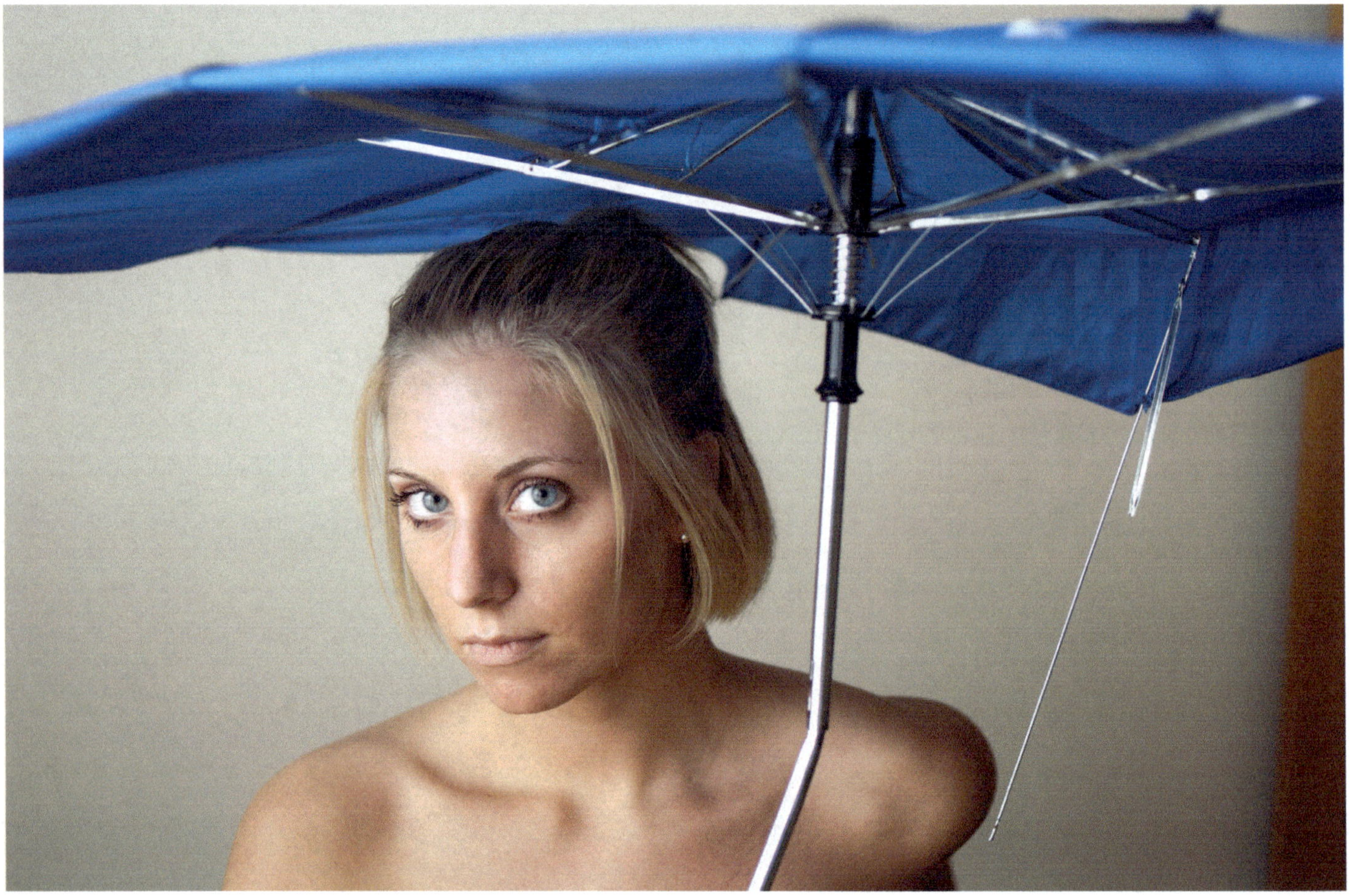

That's not to say that you shouldn't review your shots from time to time. It could save you in the case where a setting accidentally got changed. In some cases, sharing a few shots with the model can also put them at ease. If you are trying to create a specific tableau or express a particular idea, you can stop and review shots with the model after a few minutes. You can use the reviews to make adjustments to the model's posing and clarify what you are going for. You can also adjust your own position, perspective, and framing, check whether you need to zoom or move in or out, higher or lower, or more to the right or left.

You can be coach, cheerleader, or provocateur. Look for ways to coach the model to strengthen the poses, or suggest alternatives that build on their strong points. You don't have to play the detached observer/camera operator, you can interact with the model more like a stage or screen director who gives the actor what they need to elicit the best performance. But, don't forget that even without clothing, your sitter has personal space that you don't want to violate. Touching is risky and should be avoided, but if you feel you must touch in order to give direction, ask permission, and don't forget that "no" means "no."

Web Resources

ASMP Business and Legal FAQ—http://bit.ly/1CsAq69
David Bayles—www.davidpaulbayles.com
Ruth Bernhard—www.artnet.com/artists/ruth-bernhard/
Lucien Clergue—www.anneclergue.com/Artists/Lucien-Clergue/portfolio
Philip-Lorca diCorcia—http://bit.ly/1GZ9Kk8
Katy Grannan—fraenkelgallery.com/artists/katy-grannan
Steve Kiser—www.stevekiser.com/
Justine Kurland—http://bit.ly/1lkx6lX
Justine Kurland, NYT, 2/25/07—http://nyti.ms/1IDv2SI
Helmut Newton—www.artnet.com/artists/helmut-newton/
Ted Orland—www.tedorland.com
Irving Penn—www.artnet.com/artists/irving-penn/
Man Ray, Le Violon d'Ingres—http://bit.ly/1CLSWtN
Holly Roberts—www.hollyrobertsstudio.com
Brian Taylor—www.briantaylorphotography.com
Jerry Uelsmann—www.uelsmann.net

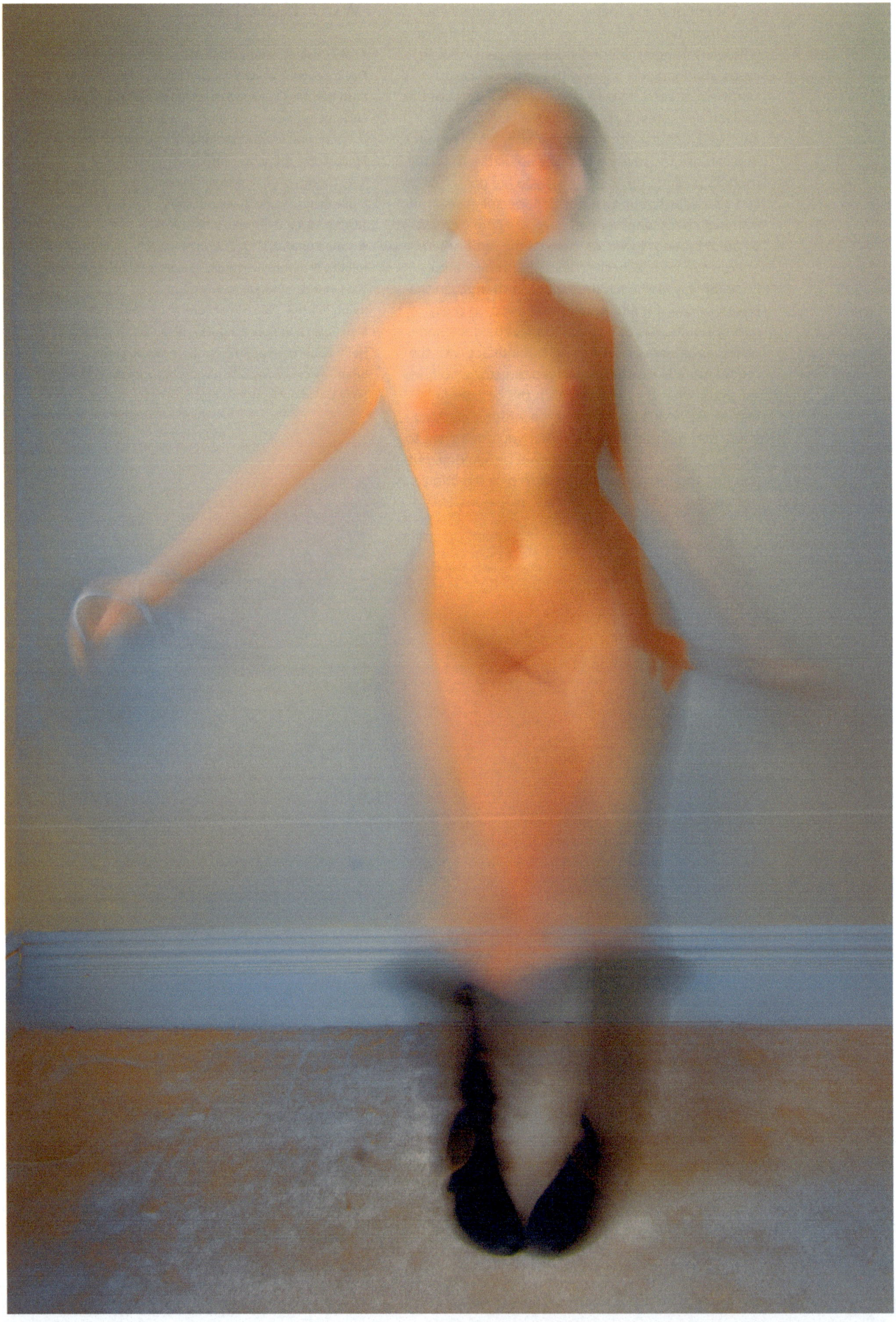

Chapter Ten | Working in Digital

A MAJOR challenge faced by photographers making digital art echoes the challenge that photography itself faced at its inception—namely the perception that the machine, and not the artist, is creating the work. Another perception is that "Photoshop" (really, all image-editing software) brought about photo manipulation. This isn't true—"combination printing" existed during the time of Fox Talbot, and was practiced by many photographers who sought to have photography recognized as an art form. Jerry Uelsmann's amazing darkroom work still challenges artists working in digital and requires high levels of skill and artistry to even approximate in Photoshop. Yet, the perception is an acknowledgment of the power of Photoshop's transformation tools, and image editing software has made sophisticated transformation more accessible. We'll look at some of those tools here.

This chapter will focus briefly on some practical aspects of working in digital related to shooting nudes, including managing (and finding!) lots of files with Lightroom, editing in Lightroom and Photoshop, and maintaining color accuracy. We'll also touch on some techniques for altering, compositing, and retouching images in Photoshop. The workflows discussed here are based on pairing Lightroom with

Facing: © Lou Benjamin. Model: Lauren Babree. Inspired in part by the work of Francis Bacon, this image began with a motion-blurred exposure. Adjustments were applied in Lightroom and color was manipulated in Photoshop to emphasize the orange/blue color contrast.

Photoshop. As much as people talk about Lightroom and Photoshop as though they are competing products, they are actually two very different toolboxes designed to work together.

Many Photoshop-only books are bigger than this entire book, let alone this chapter, and we can't cover these tools in tremendous depth. However, we will look at some topics that may not get as much attention in books specific to Photoshop or Lightroom.

Shoot or Scan

Chances are, you're likely to make a lot of digital files in the future. The single most important thing to keep in mind as you do is that every original file should have a unique name. Beyond that, there are a few preparatory steps that are worth doing to get the best results.

If you're working with film, scan to 16-bit Adobe RGB TIFF files at the native resolution of the scanner. If you have access to a Hasselblad (formerly Imacon) scanner, use it. The scanners have extremely high dynamic range and curve the film to flatten it across the path of the scan head and produce perfect edge-to-edge sharpness. The resulting files will be large, but they will give you maximum flexibility in your workflow and offer the largest possible printing size. You've probably seen photos labeled "low-res film scan" posted on web sites. These are not those. Instead, you can easily export low-res copies from your high-res original scans via Lightroom when you need them.

It's a good idea to have a consistent naming convention for your scans. You can use a date in YYYY-MM-DD order followed by a serial number to make your filenames unique and sequential. It might also be useful to add the source of the scan to the name, for example, SCAN_IMACON_2014-06-25-009.tif. This is a fairly compact and abstract file name, but if you manage them with an organizer such as Lightroom, you'll have a preview and you'll also be able to add a substantial amount of metadata to make it easily retrievable.

You can set your digital camera to assign unique names to your photos from the moment you shoot them and avoid renaming them later. Digital cameras name photos by combining a prefix (e.g. DSC) with a sequential number from 0001–9999. To make your file names unique, you can change the prefix each time the number sequence restarts. Your prefix can consist of a unique identifier for each of your cameras combined with a letter that indicates how many times the sequence numbers have iterated.

To set up the filename prefix, access *File Name* under *Setup* on Canon cameras or go to *File Naming* in the *Shooting* menu on Nikon cameras. Use the first two characters of the prefix to designate the camera and the third for the iteration. For example, D8A would be a good prefix for a brand new Nikon D800. After 9,999 frames, you would change it to D8B.

You'll need to make sure that continuous file numbering is on, so that you only have to change the prefix every 10,000 frames. For Nikon, set *File Number Sequence* (usually under *Custom Settings* or *Setup*) to ON. For Canon, set *File Numbering* under *Camera Settings* to Continuous.

Organizing Files on Your Computer

A good practice is to store your photos on your computer in a stable, logical order—you shouldn't need to rearrange them after you first transfer them into your photo archive folders. The organization scheme shown here extends from the in-camera naming scheme described above. It is an alternative to organizing files by date that still provides a sequential structure and adds a small amount of recognizable and searchable metadata to the folder name.

You can organize your original photos into folders grouped by camera on an external disk, separate from the Lightroom catalog and previews files. Each of your cameras will have its own set of folders, split out by iteration cycle (e.g. D800a, D800b, etc.). Thus, the first levels of your folder hierarchy would look something like this: [disk name]/Cameras/D800a.

Each time you transfer photos from your camera's memory card, you copy them into a new folder within

A NOTE OF CAUTION

If you're already a Lightroom user and you like the organization scheme shown here, do not try match this scheme by renaming and reorganizing files and folders via your computer's operating system. If you do, you will create a massive headache for yourself. One option is to keep the legacy organization for your older photos and continue on with the new scheme. It is possible to reorganize and rename folders from within Lightroom, but you might not even have to, especially if you use tags and collections. Read on for more information.

the folder of that camera's current iteration cycle. You name the new folder by combining the first sequence number from the photos on the card with a brief general description of the group of photos. So, if the first frame of photos from a shoot with model Theresa Manchester was D8A_2102, a good name for the folder would be *2102 - Theresa Manchester*.

Because the names of the folders and photos all begin with sequential numbers, all of your photos stay in the order that they were shot, and you can find the photos of Theresa, even if you never tag a single image, by searching for the folder name. And, since metadata in your photos contain your camera's date and time stamp, you can still find files by date without including it in the folder name.

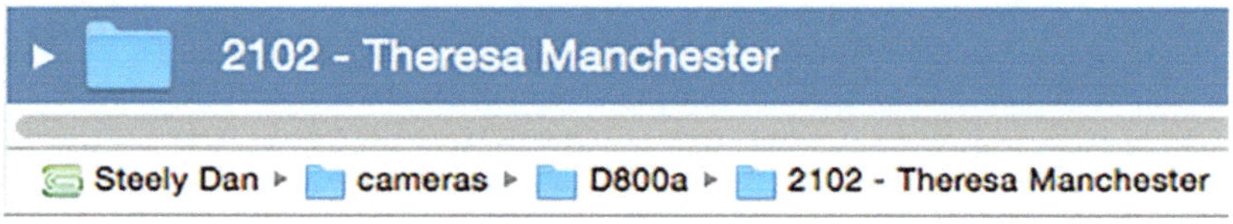

Screen shot showing the selected photo folder and the full path to it.

Shooting Raw

If you're shooting digital, the raw format will give you the greatest latitude. It's better to think of JPEG as an output medium, like a print, rather than a medium for recording your originals.

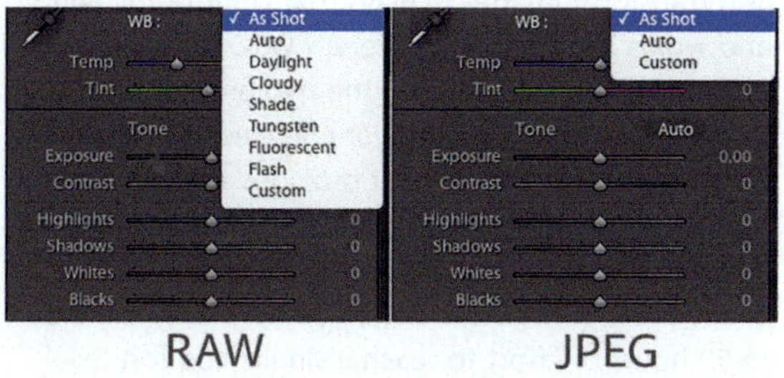

White balance options are just one place where you see differences between the processing options for 16-bit raw files vs. 8-bit JPEG.

JPEG is a compromise format that keeps the file size small, which allows you to shoot more images, but at the cost of image quality and flexibility in post. One trade-off is that you have to nail the exposure because JPEG does not retain any recoverable highlight or shadow information. And, JPEG only has an 8 bits per component bit depth (which limits the latitude you have for making adjustments). The JPEG format uses what we call "lossy" compression—it literally discards information—to keep file sizes small. That's a great solution for uses like the Web and emails, but not so good for a photo archive.

Even though you generally want to share your photos as JPEGs, they're easy to generate downstream when you need them. Only shoot RAW + JPEG if you have a specific application for it, e.g. you need JPEGs immediately after shooting and don't have a computer to process raw files. Otherwise, shooting RAW + JPEG simply cuts down on the number of shots that will fit on your card.

Lightroom Plus Photoshop

It's not an either-or proposition, Lightroom and Photoshop are designed to be paired. You can think of Lightroom as an all-round tool for both managing and enhancing photos that features non-destructive editing tools. Photoshop allows you to combine, edit, and transform images in ways that Lightroom cannot, and works in an entirely different way. One other significant difference between the two products is that Photoshop has a much longer and steeper learning curve. Its complexity is what provides so much editing power, but also makes it harder to grasp. You can reach moderate proficiency with Lightroom with five or six hours in the classroom, but it typically takes 30 to 50 hours of effort to reach a similar comfort level with Photoshop.

People who have worked exclusively with Photoshop up to this point are accustomed to organizing their files with Adobe Bridge and processing their raw files through the Adobe Camera RAW (ACR) plugin. Lightroom integrates the functionality of those tools and adds many features of its own. The Develop module in Lightroom uses ACR as its processing engine, but offers a more modern interface. However, ACR is built into Lightroom, not a plugin, so sometimes features appear in ACR well before they're included in a Lightroom update.

You manage your photo inventory in Lightroom's Library module. Perhaps the most salient difference from Bridge is that Lightroom stores information about your files in its own database, meaning that you can still search for files and preview them even if the drive containing your originals is currently offline. In contrast, Bridge is a browser, meaning that it can only show you the contents of drives that are available.

CREATIVE CLOUD PHOTOGRAPHY PLAN

One of the most economical ways to get your hands on Lightroom and Photoshop is with a subscription to Adobe Creative Cloud Photography plan. The plan also makes it easy to stay current with the latest versions. In addition to Lightroom and Photoshop for the desktop, you get a suite of Web-based services and mobile applications. Adobe has done major releases annually since the inception of Creative Cloud, and all updates and major releases are included under the subscription plan. The Creative Cloud application notifies you when updates and releases are available. You can click to install or de-install as needed.

This is a big change from the perpetual licensing arrangement of the Creative Suite (CS6 was the last version), where major releases were introduced roughly every other year at a substantial upgrade cost. Those updates also required a significant investment of time to understand and get accustomed to changes and new features, prompting many photographers to work exclusively in either Photoshop or Lightroom and to assess whether to upgrade at all. Some photographers opted not to, and may still be running versions as early as CS4 even today. The Creative Cloud Photography plan makes it almost painless to upgrade to a substantially modernized set of tools and stay current.

Initial Setup

The general workflow we'll be exploring is as follows:

1. Import photos into Lightroom
2. Tag and prioritize
3. Enhance in Lightroom
4. Further refine images in Photoshop
5. Create projects and share from Lightroom.

Before you begin, it's a good idea to set some preferences in Lightroom and Photoshop to optimize the connection between the two. We'll start by specifying the default settings that Lightroom will use when it packages files for editing in Photoshop via the Edit in Photoshop command. Start Lightroom and do the following.

1. Click *Lightroom* > *Preferences* (Mac)/*Edit* > *Preferences* (Win), then click on the External Editing tab.
2. Set *File Format* to PSD, *Color Space* to AdobeRGB (1998), and *Bit Depth* to 16 bits/component.

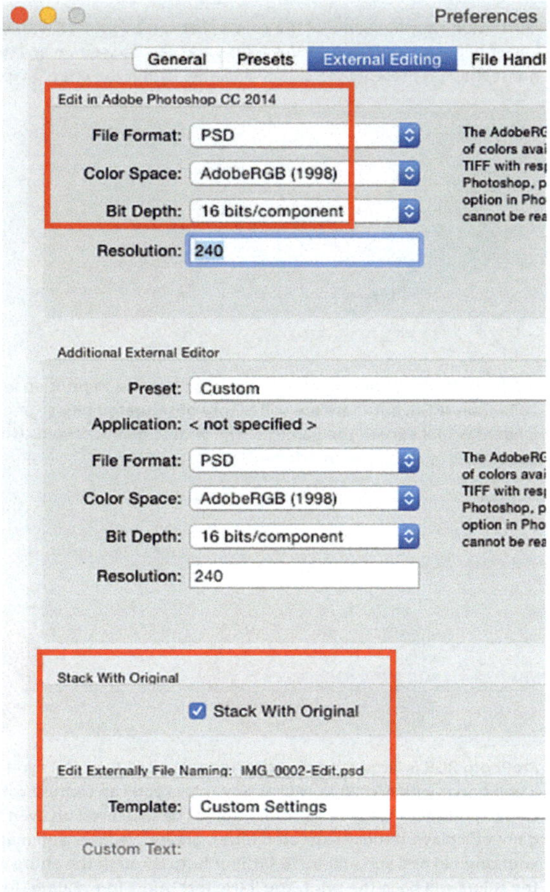

Don't worry about resolution, it only determines the default print size. You'll also see dire-looking warnings about the AdobeRGB color space and that PSD is less efficient than TIFF. In practical terms, neither of these are critical, and you can override the settings when a particular image requires it.

3. Check Stack with Original.
4. Optionally, choose Edit from the Template menu to open the Template editor and use it to set up how files will be named when they are prepared for editing in Photoshop.

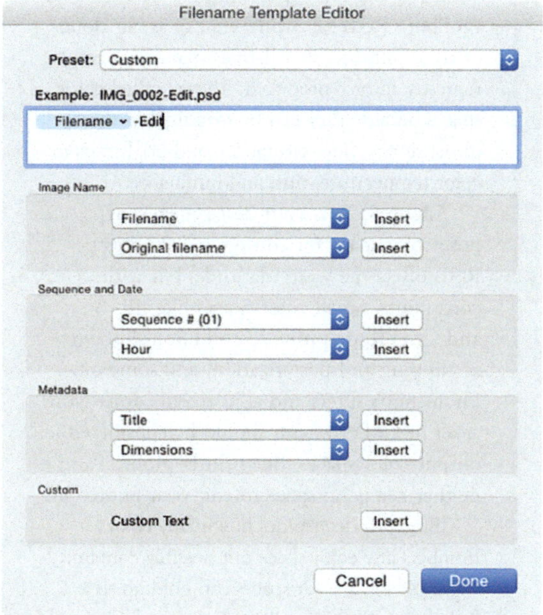

Setting up Photoshop file naming with the Template editor.

5. Close the window.

Next, you'll set up key preferences in Photoshop for collaborating with Lightroom. You'll set up color management policies to ensure that ProPhoto RGB or sRGB photos stay in their original color space when you open them in Photoshop, even though the working space (the default color space) is set to Adobe RGB.

WHICH WORKING SPACE IN PHOTOSHOP?

Your choice of editing color space affects how much latitude you have to make adjustments within an image. Digital color is based in numbers, and color spaces like Adobe RGB and ProPhoto RGB can be thought of as big clouds of color numbers that define what colors can be represented or reproduced. They're called color spaces because they can be measured in three dimensions—hue, saturation, and brightness or color temperature, tint, and luminance.

Adobe RGB is your best general-purpose color space for editing and ProPhoto RGB offers the widest latitude, but with constraints. Small color spaces like sRGB and CMYK are prone to conditions known as clipping and posterization, and some of Photoshop's filters and adjustments don't work at all in CMYK. Both should be considered output color spaces, like printer profiles, and neither is a good space to edit your photos in.

Bit depth determines how many color numbers any color space can possibly contain. Eight-bit RGB color spaces can hold up to a little more than 16 million discrete color values, while 16-bit RGB color spaces can have over 281 trillion discrete values. That's literally the square of the number of colors available in 8-bit.

The Adobe RGB color space contains millions of discrete color values, and can be used in either 8-bit or 16-bit mode, while ProPhoto RGB contains so many color values that it requires 16-bit. If the two spaces were sets of Crayola crayons, Adobe RGB is like the eight-color set, and ProPhoto is like the 64-color set. While "more is better" seems true in this case, having to stay in 16-bit mode can strain the performance of some computers. There is also a second aspect of working with ProPhoto that reduces its usefulness: many of the colors it offers are not visible on any computer display and can only be reproduced on wide-gamut printers. So, if you're not planning to print with a wide-gamut inkjet printer, you're not likely to be able to take advantage of the additional colors in ProPhoto RGB.

So, if you're working with highly saturated yellows, majentas, blues, and greens, then maybe you'll be able to make use of the wider gamut of ProPhoto RGB (but only if your intention is to print). If you're shooting skin tones against pastels, you're not likely to see any benefit. And, if you're primarily posting on the Web, those colors will be lost by the time the photo is converted to sRGB.

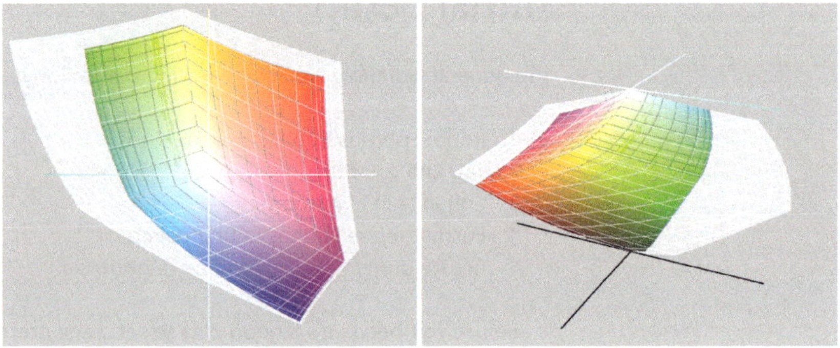

The Adobe RGB completely encapsulates sRGB.

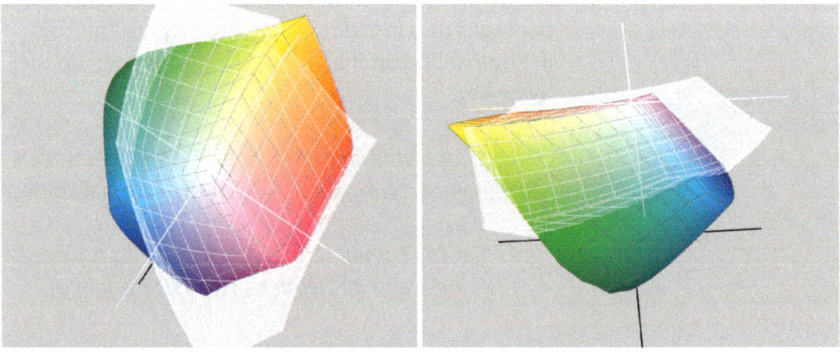

Illustration showing some of the colors that can be printed with Epson Premium Luster paper on an Epson 2880 versus what can be seen on an iMac screen. The ghost shape represents the colors available within the iMac, a typical sRGB screen.

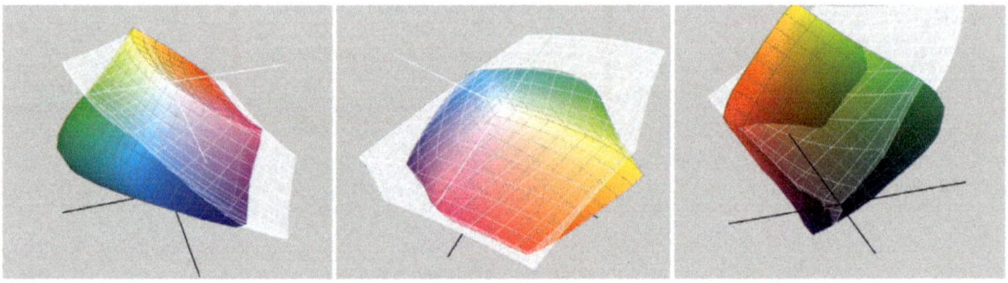

Adobe RGB can display more of the colors available to print on luster paper with a 2880 than sRGB, but there are still plenty of saturated blues, greens, yellows, and magentas that exceed the gamut of the widest-gamut screens (which can display about 95% of the colors in Adobe RGB).

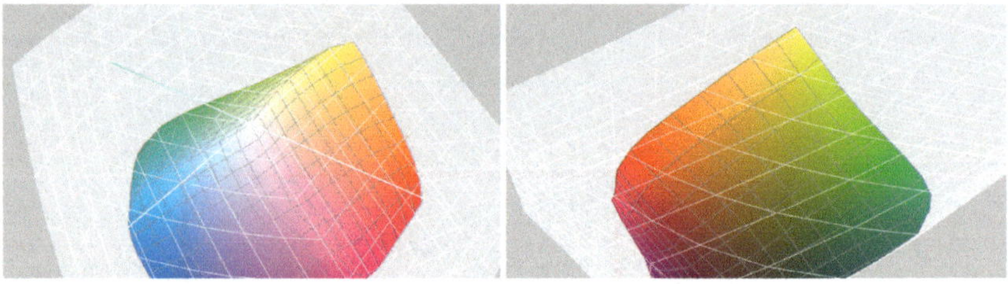

ProPhoto RGB is large enough to encompass all of the colors you can print on luster paper with a 2880 as well as any colors you can capture with a digital camera, however many of its colors cannot be displayed on even the widest-gamut displays. If those saturated blues, greens, yellows, and magentas are in your original and you edit in 16-bit ProPhoto through the entire workflow, then the colors will be in the print. You'll use test prints to evaluate the colors in the shot that you cannot see on the display.

Start Photoshop and do the following.

1. Click *Photoshop > Preferences > File Handling* (Mac)/*Edit > Preferences > File Handling* (Win).
2. In the File Compatibility box, set *Maximize PSD and PSB File Compatibility* to Always.

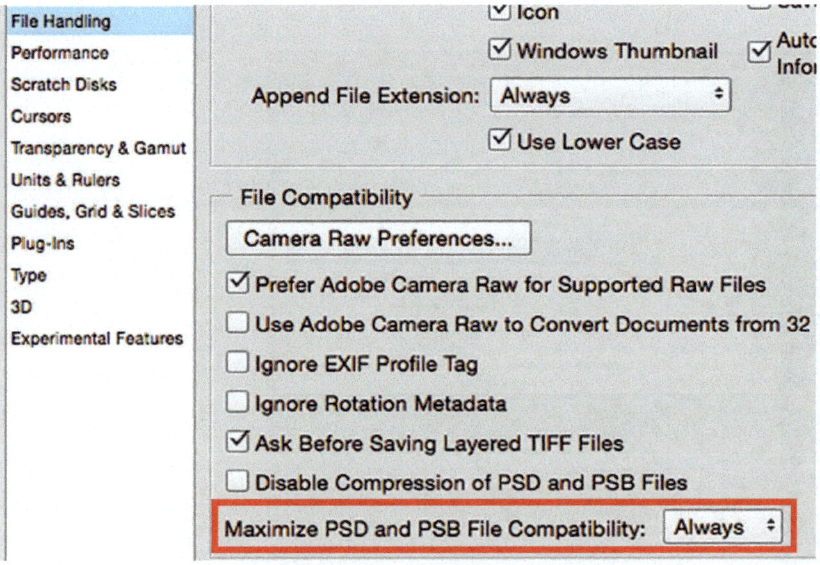

The Maximize Compatibility setting ensures that you'll be able to import Photoshop files you create from scratch into Lightroom. It will also prevent a message from popping up when you save scratch-built files.

3. Click *Edit > Color Settings*
4. Select *North America Prepress 2* from the Settings menu. This specifies Adobe RGB as your working (default) color space.

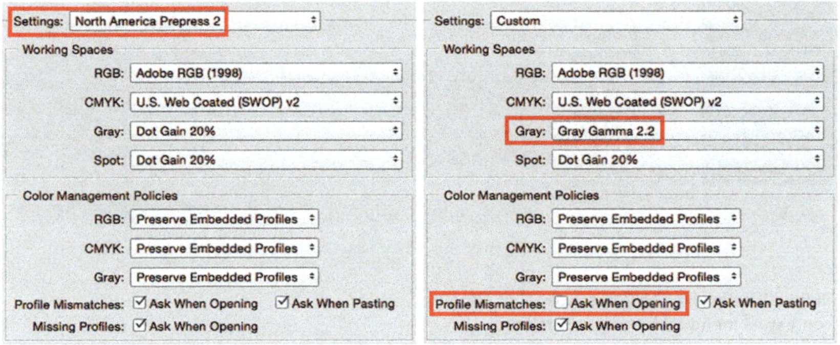

Starting with the North America Prepress 2 preset, change the Gray setting to Gray Gamma 2.2 and turn off the option to show an alert when the color profile of the image you're opening does not match the working space.

5. Change the *Gray* setting to Gray Gamma 2.2. The Settings menu will now read Custom—that's OK.
6. Uncheck *Ask When Opening* next to Profile Mismatches.
7. Click OK.

Here's a caveat: With these settings, if you open a sRGB JPEG file directly into Photoshop, you'll be editing in 8-bit sRGB. That's a recipe for problems. It will also happen if you use the Edit in Photoshop command in Lightroom and select Edit Original. Immediately after you open such files, click *Image > Mode > 16 bits/Channel*. This doesn't give you back the missing data, but it gives you more latitude going forward. You'll also want to upgrade the color space to Adobe RGB as follows.

1. Click *Edit > Convert to Profile.*
2. Click the Profile menu and then click Adobe RGB.
3. Click OK.

Once you have upgraded the JPEG for 16-bit Adobe RGB editing, you won't be able to save it as a JPEG, but you don't really want to. Best to save as a PSD. To see the file in your Lightroom catalog, you may need to import it or synchronize the folder you save it to.

Cataloging Your Files in Lightroom

When you're ready to import images, launch Lightroom and press G to switch to the Library module in grid view.

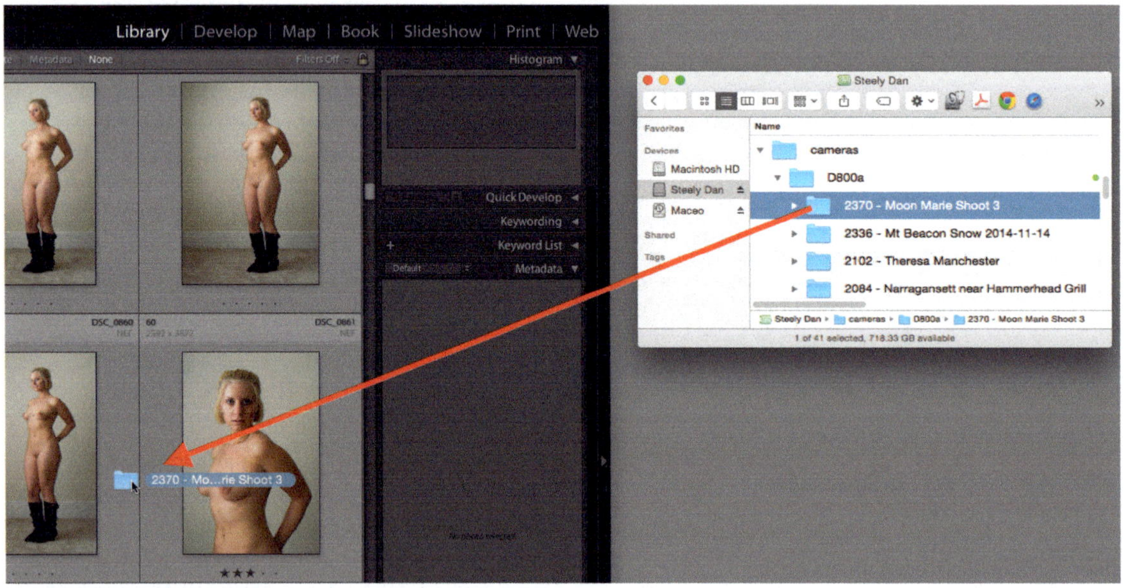

Drag files or folders from Mac Finder or Windows Explorer and drop them onto the Library grid to begin importing.

To import an existing folder from your main catalog drive, drag it into Lightroom's grid area to set it as the source in the Import dialog. The dialog will open in Add mode, which means that Lightroom will leave the originals in their current location.

If you're importing from a memory card or external drive, you'll want to use Lightroom to create a folder to receive the files before you start the import. You can do this from the Folders panel on the left side of the screen.

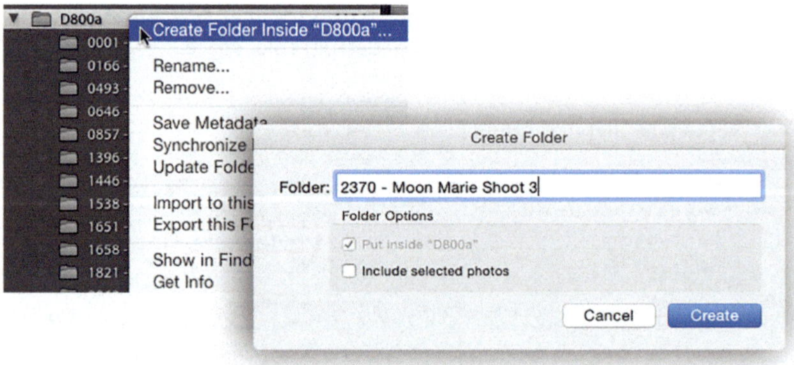

Right-click items in the Folders panel to display a contextual menu and create sub-folders.

1. Right-click (or Control-click on Mac) on a camera folder and click Create Folder Inside "[folder name]" to create a sub-folder.
2. Enter a name for your folder and make sure the box labeled "Include selected photos" is unchecked.

At this point, you might not know the starting frame number, so you can enter a partial folder name, e.g. "Moon Marie Shoot 3." When you do know the starting number, you can rename the folder. You will see how to do that shortly.

3. Click Create.

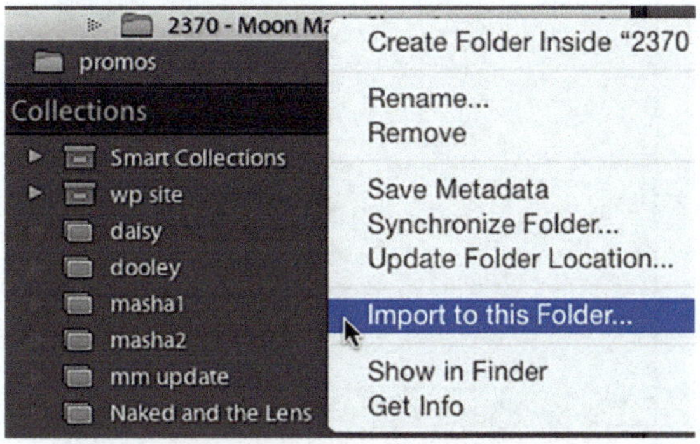

Right-click the newly created sub-folder to import items into it.

To begin importing into the newly created folder, right-click (or Control-click on Mac) on the new folder and then click *Import to this Folder* to open the Import dialog in Copy mode. You also have the option to click *Copy as DNG* instead; however, this can add substantially to your import time, and there are plenty of options for converting to DNG later in your workflow.

If needed, click *Source* on the left to expand the list and click and select your media. Camera cards will appear under Devices, and portable hard drives will appear under Files. Camera cards appear a second time under Files in case you need to drill down to a specific folder.

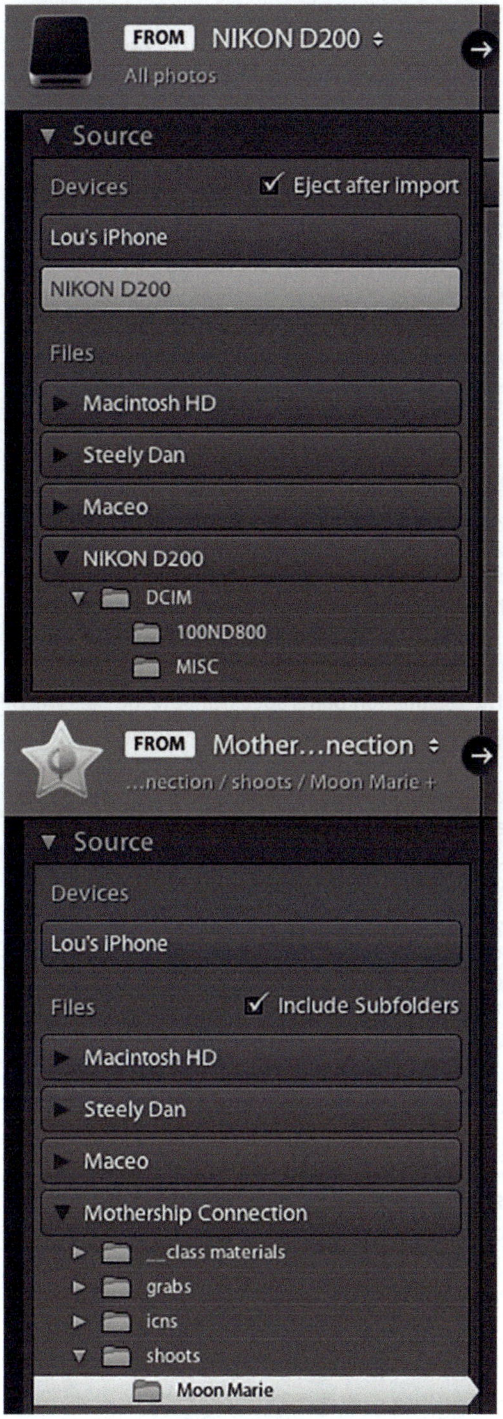

Top image shows the card from a Nikon D200 inserted. No sub-selection was necessary, so nothing is selected under Files. Bottom image shows importing from a folder on another hard drive.

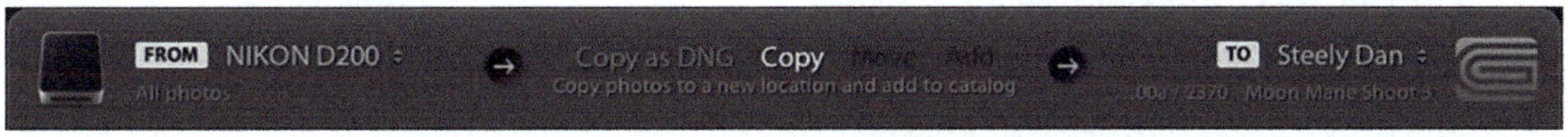

The top of the import dialog in Copy mode. The source is a camera card and the destination is the specified folder on the drive named Steely Dan.

After you've set the source, import mode, and destination, you can use the panels on the right to further enhance the import process. Note that you can click the panel headers to expand or collapse them.

Your choice of preview setting is the most critical option in the File Handling section, because it affects the time it takes to process the import. A good default setting is Standard previews, while Minimal will process fastest. The *Make a Second Copy To* option is a way of backing up your originals as you import them. In the organization scheme used here, there's no reason to rename files, because they've already been named appropriately in the camera.

Under Apply During Import, you can select a Develop Settings preset. You'll see how to create custom camera profiles and presets shortly. You can use the preset menu to choose an existing metadata preset or click New to create one on the fly. Use the Keywords box to enter bulk keywords that apply to all of the photos being imported. You'll enter keywords like "portrait," "abstract," or "erotic" to narrower selections of photos later.

The destination panel specifies how the files will be organized inside the target folder. To use the organization scheme presented here, be sure that the box labeled *Into Subfolder* is unchecked and that Organize is set to *Into one folder*.

Click the *Import* button, and when Lightroom is done, it will display the imported files in a special collection called Previous Import under the Catalog heading on the left side of the screen.

At this point, you can inspect the photos that have been imported and determine if the import went smoothly—there should be no broken previews—and get the starting frame number for your photos. If you had set the folder up with a temporary name when you began the import, you can right-click on the folder (or Control-click on Mac) and click Rename to update the name with the frame number, e.g. "2370 - Moon Marie Shoot 3."

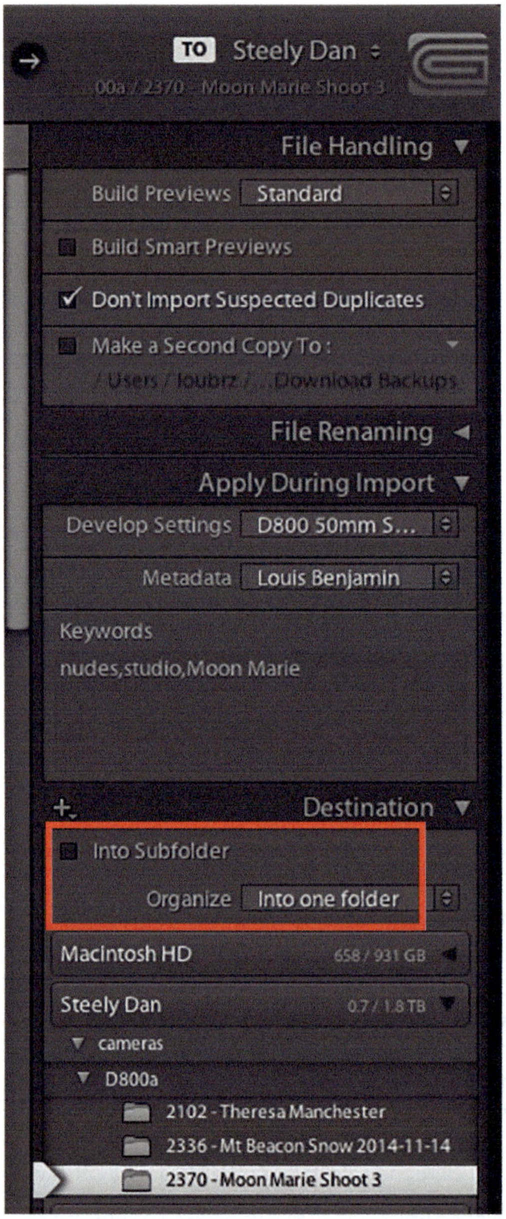

This import example applies a custom camera profile from a Develop Settings preset and copyright from a metadata preset. Since Lightroom does facial recognition, you might not want to enter the model's name as a bulk keyword.

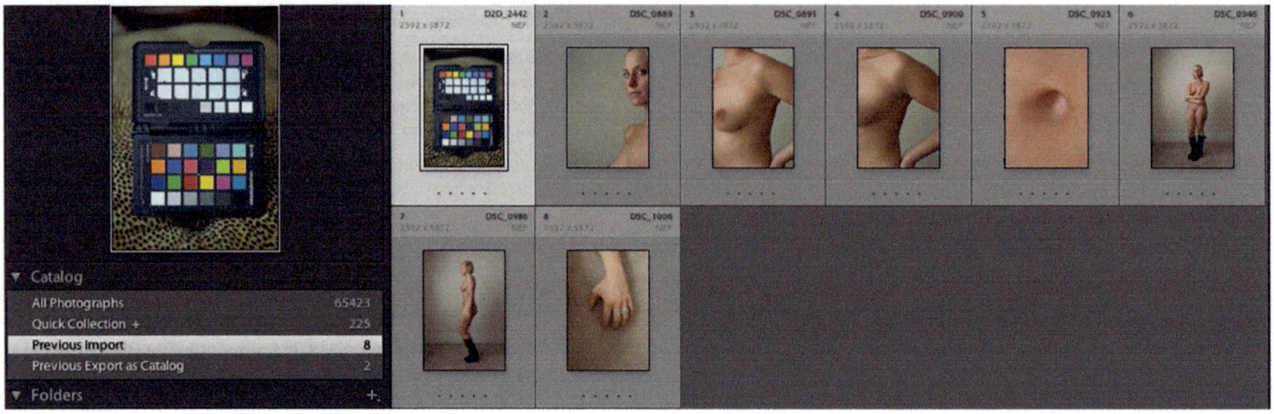

The Previous Import collection in Lightroom.

HOW LIGHTROOM STORES AND LINKS TO YOUR PHOTOS

Importing photos into Lightroom adds them to its database inside the catalog file (it ends with .lrcat). However, instead of duplicating the original file inside each database entry, Lightroom only copies camera settings and metadata, along with the name and location of the original—Lightroom leaves the actual image external to its catalog file and links the database entry to it. This is important, because if you use the Mac Finder, Windows Explorer, or some other application external to Lightroom to rename your original files or the folders that contain them, Lightroom will lose track of the originals. This is one source of the dreaded "Missing" warning.

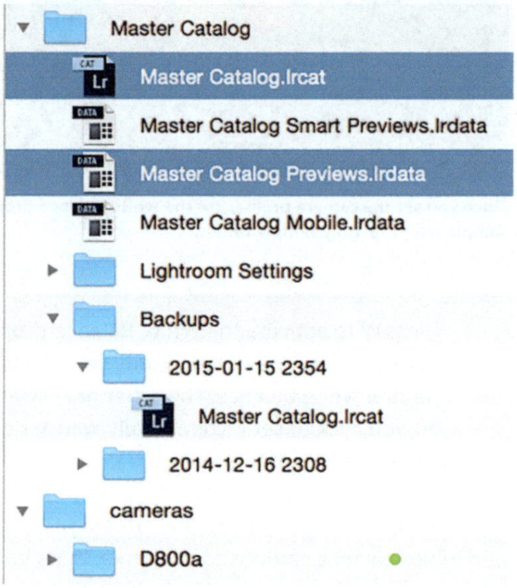

Organization of the catalog folder. The originals are stored within the sub-folders of the Cameras folder, completely outside the catalog file's folder structure.

internal drive. If your computer's internal drive is a flash drive (SSD), you will see a noticeable boost in performance compared to a hard drive. If your computer is a laptop, you can generate Smart Previews. They allow you to leave your originals at home and still make edits while you travel with the laptop. When you reconnect the offline drive, the adjustments will flow back into the originals. Smart Previews are stored in their own separate .lrdata file alongside the catalog file.

Building Smart Previews as you import can slow the process down significantly, but you can go to the grid view in the Library module, select a group of files, and then click *Library > Previews > Build Smart Previews* at any time. You can also build one-off Smart Previews by clicking on Original Photo beneath the Histogram. To discard Smart Previews and free up disk space, click Original + Smart Preview under the Histogram or select *Library > Previews > Discard Smart Previews.*

Beneath the Histogram, Lightroom displays whether your original is online and whether a photo has a smart preview. For missing photos, it also blanks the Histogram. When you select multiple files, it shows counts by status.

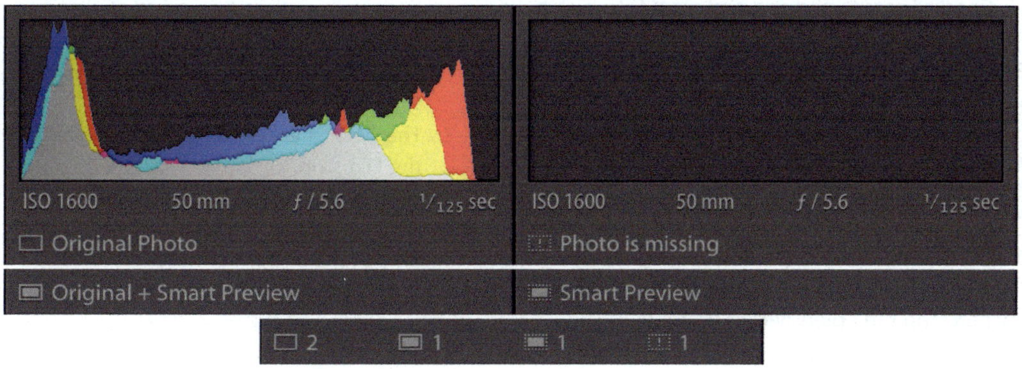

When you browse and edit your photos inside Lightroom you are working with previews. When you make adjustments to your photos, you are adjusting the preview instead of changing the original. The previews themselves are stored collectively in a separate file ending with the extension .lrdata.

Because Lightroom links the originals to the catalog instead of embedding them, you can keep your catalog file on your computer's internal drive and store your originals on an external drive. This arrangement takes up a lot less space on your

Lightroom automatically generates Smart Previews and uses them when you sync collections. When you create collections on your mobile devices, those images sync back to Lightroom desktop and are stored in the [catalog name] Mobile.lrdata file.

When you first set up a new catalog, Lightroom creates a folder named after the catalog and places the .lrcat and .lrdata files inside it. Backup catalogs are stored inside dated sub-folders within its Backups sub-folder.

Once you import, you have the option to tweak the color rendition and white balance of your shots. Choosing a camera profile other than the default Adobe Standard profile can dramatically affect color rendition, and using a custom camera profile can ensure highly accurate color and tone. It's best to apply the camera profile before setting the white balance.

Build a Camera Profile

If you shot a ColorChecker target and have the ColorChecker Passport plugin for Lightroom installed, you can generate a custom camera profile as soon as your import is done.

1. Locate the ColorChecker Passport shot and right-click (or Control-click on Mac), then click *Export > ColorChecker Passport*.

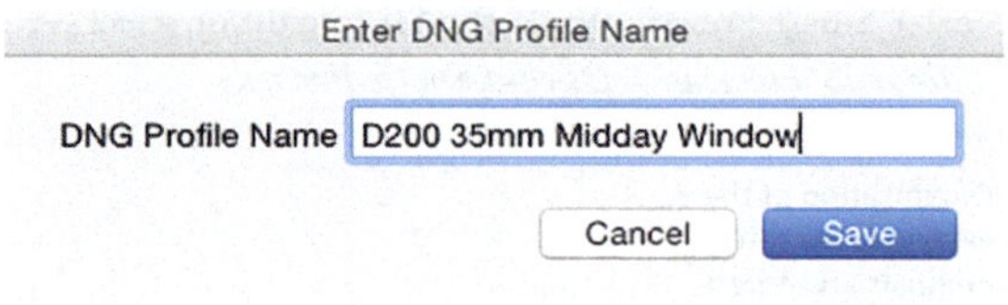

Naming the custom camera profile.

2. Enter a name for your profile. A good naming convention to follow is [camera name] [lens] [lighting condition]. Click Save. After processing, the plugin will show a message confirming that it was able to generate a profile.
3. Restart Lightroom to activate the camera profile.
4. When Lightroom reopens, select the ColorChecker passport image, and press D to switch to the Develop module.
5. Scroll to the bottom of the panel on the right to show the Camera Calibration panel. If you don't see the controls, click *Camera Calibration*.
6. Click the Profile menu and then click the camera profile you just created.

You can now override the camera's original white balance by using the white balance dropper to sample a gray patch on the ColorChecker Passport.

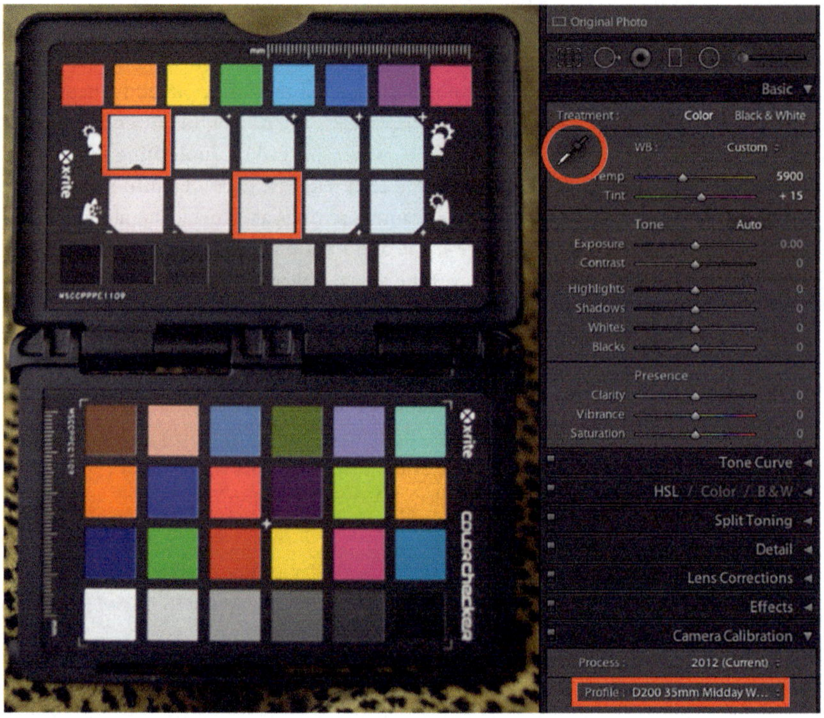

Once you set the camera profile, use the white balance dropper to sample a neutral gray sample target.

1. Press W to activate the White Balance dropper.
2. Click either of the notched gray swatches for neutral white balance. The other gray swatches let you click to set incrementally warmer or cooler color temperature.

Now, you can synchronize the camera profile and white balance settings to the other shots in this import.

1. If you don't see the Filmstrip at the bottom of the screen, select *Window > Panels > Show Filmstrip*.
2. The ColorChecker frame will be highlighted in the Filmstrip.
3. Use Command + A (Mac) or Ctrl + A (Win) to select all of the photos in the strip, and click *Sync* at the bottom of the panel on the right.

4. Click *Check None* at the bottom of the dialog, then check the boxes for *White Balance*, *Process Version*, and *Calibration*.
5. Click *Synchronize* to apply the changes.

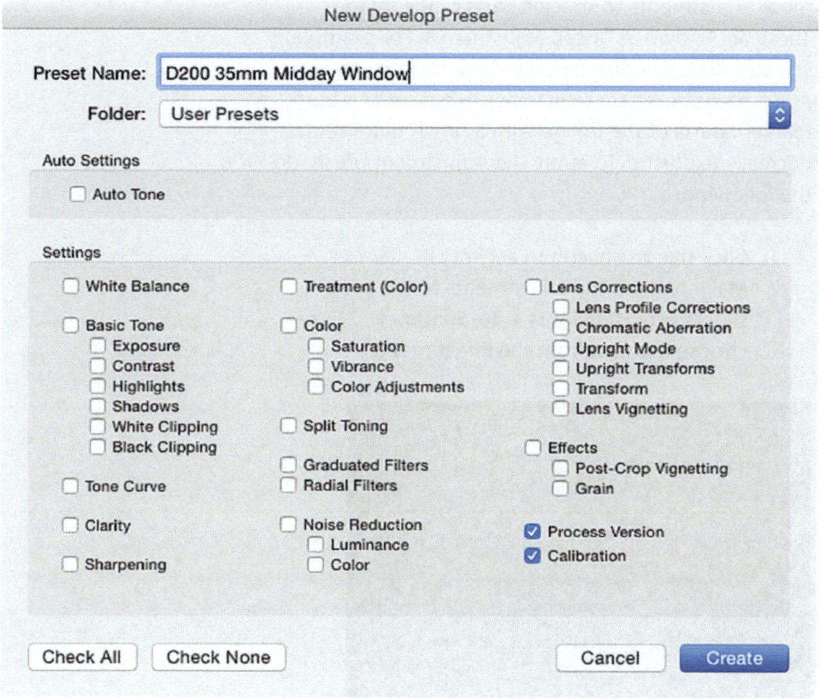

Creating a camera calibration develop preset.

To create a preset with the custom camera profile, locate Presets at the top of the panel on the left and click the + sign. Enter a name for the preset and click *Check None* at the bottom of the dialog. Check the boxes next to *Process Version* and *Calibration*, then click Create. Your preset will now be available in the menu inside the Import dialog.

Work with Photos and Make Adjustments

Let's begin this section with a couple of useful tips. First, click a photo and press F to see it full-screen and get all the clutter out of the way. Press F again to return to the previous view. Second, remember that you can create virtual copies for as many editing variations on a photo as you can dream up—different crops, different color treatments, etc.

Press D to enter the Develop module. You'll see the active photo in the Loupe view and all photos from the current folder, collection, or filtered selection in the Filmstrip at the bottom of the screen. Click a thumbnail in the Filmstrip to select another photo to work on.

Use develop panels such as the Basic panel to make "global" changes to your photos. Drag any of the tone or presence sliders to make changes that apply to the entire image. You can also hover the cursor over different parts of the Histogram to select a slider and drag inside the Histogram to adjust in finer increments than dragging the sliders directly. As you hover the cursor across the Histogram, the targeted group of tones and the corresponding slider will highlight and its name will appear directly beneath the Histogram.

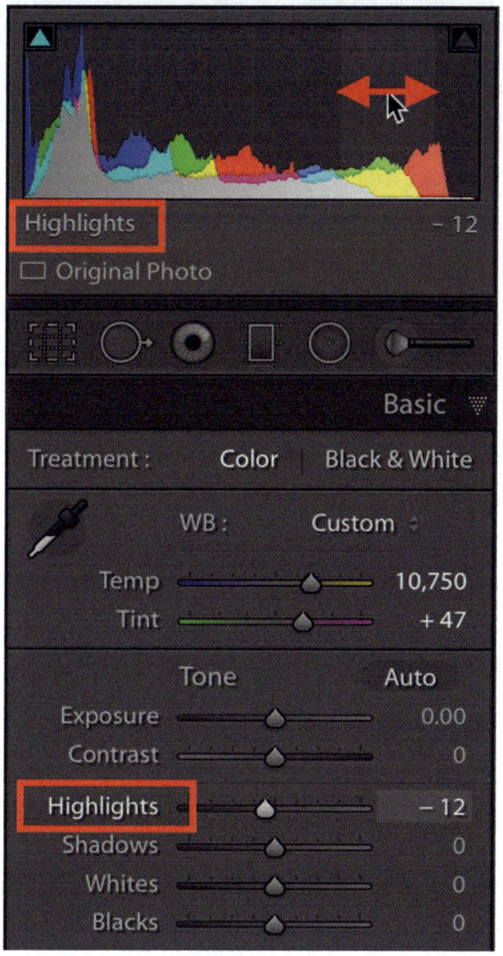

Drag in the Develop module Histogram to adjust tones in the smallest increments.

Lightroom is well-known for its develop presets. Hover the cursor over a preset in the panel on the left side to see a preview in the Navigator pane. Click to apply. If you don't like the result, you can click on another or click in the History panel to return to an earlier version.

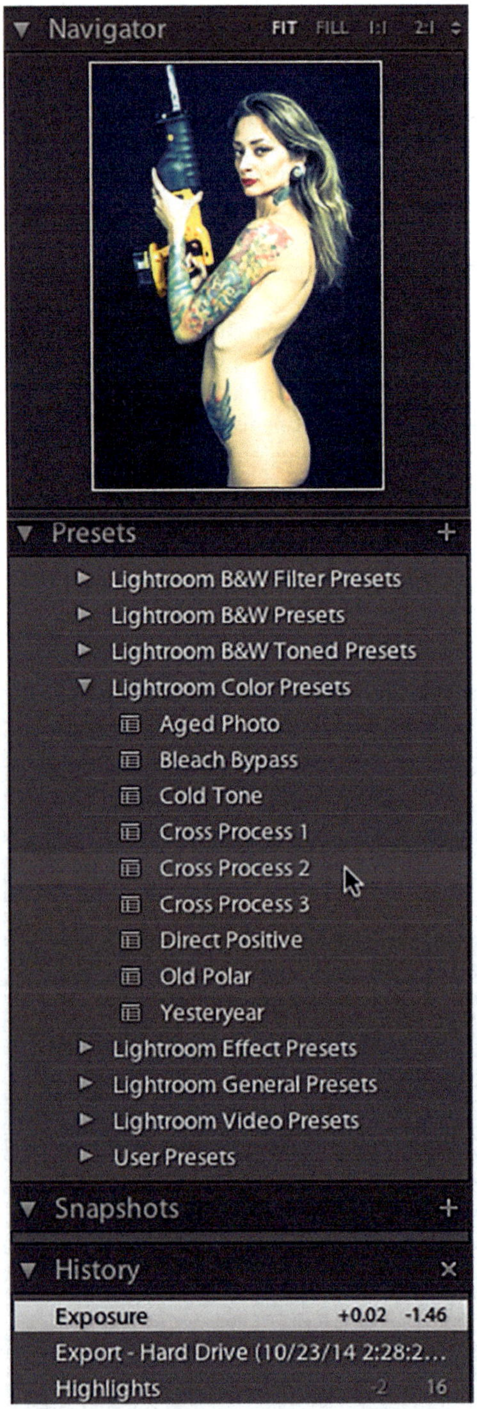

Hover the cursor over a preset to see a preview in the Navigator.

You can apply a built-in preset, adjust the settings, and save the result as your own preset—just click on the + at the top of the Presets panel.

The Adjustment brush has many of the same sliders as the Basic panel, but allows you to apply those adjustments to specific parts of the image. These are known as "local" adjustments. For example, you can dodge (lighten) parts of the image with an Adjustment brush set to increase exposure and burn (darken) parts of the image with a brush that's set to decrease exposure. To apply the Adjustment brush, do the following:

1. Click the brush icon to activate it.
2. Make preliminary adjustments to the control sliders (e.g. Highlights + 40, Shadows - 27), or choose a preset from the Effect menu.

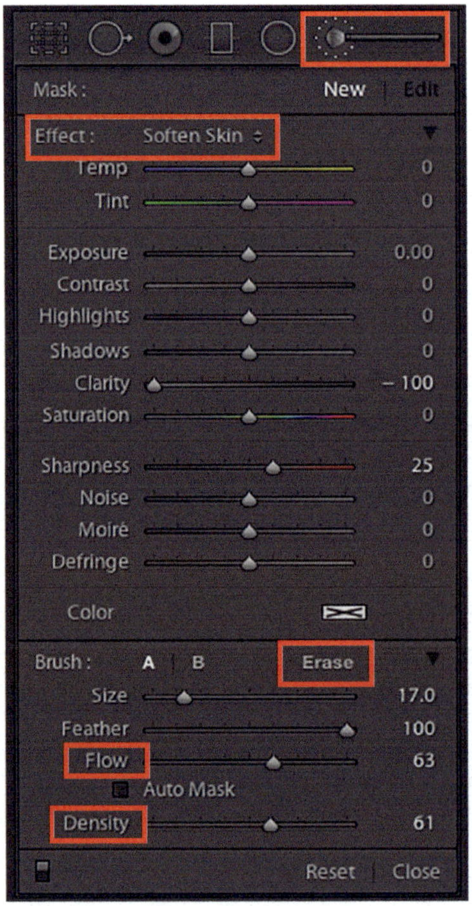

Setting up the Adjustment brush; Soften Skin preset selected.

3. Click in the image to place a control pin.
4. Paint in the image to apply the adjustment.
5. Press \ to toggle between before and after and check your progress as needed.

Once you apply the brush to part of your photo, you can readjust the sliders to refine the effect. Click *Erase* and brush in the image to remove the effect. Use the *Flow* and *Density* sliders to control how quickly the effect builds up. To place a new pin with different settings, click New. To remove the pin and start over, click the pin and then hit the Delete (Win: backspace) key.

The Radial Filter and Graduated Filter allow you to make local adjustments that have structured shapes.

If you change lenses often, you may have dust on your sensor. Because the dust spots occur in the same location on every frame, you can use the Spot Removal Tool (press Q) to remove the dust spots on one frame and sync the spot removal to other photos. To find spots more readily, press A to toggle Visualize Spots on or off. You can use the slider in the toolbar beneath the image to adjust the settings for the visualizer.

If you only want to sync settings to specific images you can copy and paste settings between photos in either the Develop or Library modules. Select a photo you want to copy settings from and use Shift + Command + C (Mac)/Shift + Ctrl + C (Win) to open the Copy Settings dialog. Select the settings you want to apply to other images, and click Copy. To apply the settings, click any photo and use Shift + Command + V (Mac)/Shift + Ctrl + V (Win) to paste the settings.

Finally, Upright can fix tilted horizons and skewed lines. It can even level images where the horizon is hidden. Open the Lens Corrections panel, click *Basic*, and check *Enable Profile Corrections* for best results; then try *Auto*, *Level*, *Vertical*, and *Full* to see which works best.

Round Trip to Photoshop

Once you've optimized a photo in Lightroom, you may find that the image you have in mind calls for some sort of transformation, such as compositing or advanced retouching, that can only be done in Photoshop. When you need the extended toolkit that Photoshop provides, it's a simple matter to transfer your work into Photoshop. And, Lightroom can automatically add your saved work back to your photo library. We'll take a brief look here at what's known as "round-trip editing" between Lightroom and Photoshop.

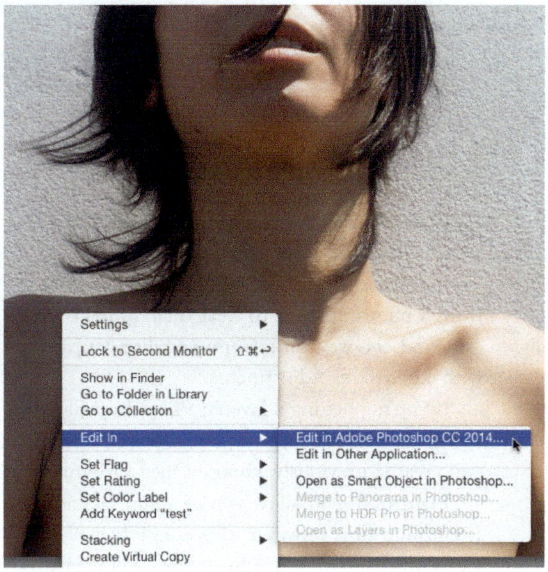

Right-click on the image to transfer it to Photoshop for further editing.

To transfer an image to Photoshop, right-click (or Control-click on Mac) on the photo and click *Edit in > Edit in Photoshop CC*. (This menu item will change to show the currently installed version of Photoshop.)

Lightroom will create a new Photoshop document and transfer it to Photoshop for editing. If you are transferring a raw file, the image will simply open in

Photoshop, but if you are transferring a rendered file such as a JPEG, TIFF, or PSD file, you'll see a dialog asking if you want to edit a copy or open the original.

EDIT A COPY, OR EDIT THE ORIGINAL?

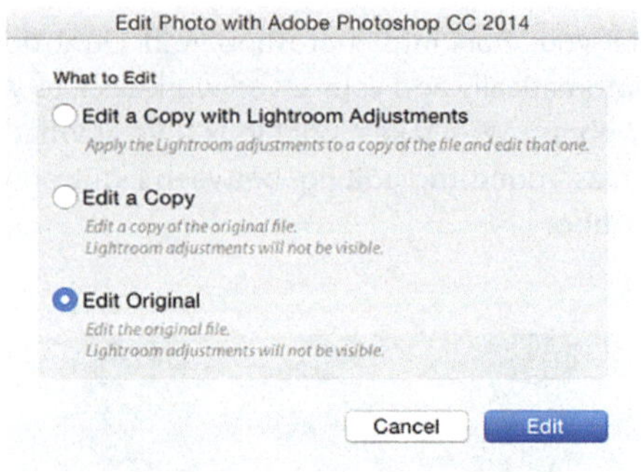

"Edit in Photoshop" options for rendered files such as TIFF, JPEG, and PSD.

Both choices that say Edit a Copy create a new file and add it to your Library.

If you're opening an original TIFF scan from a photo, it's best to treat them as read-only and choose Edit a Copy or Edit a Copy with Lightroom Adjustments.

If you're opening a layered Photoshop file and you want to keep working with the layers you created previously, choose Open Original.

Lightroom will allow you to adjust layered Photoshop files, however, choosing Edit a Copy with Lightroom Adjustments will create a flattened copy of the Photoshop file that incorporates both the changes you made in Photoshop and the adjustments you applied in Lightroom afterward. Because you're editing a new copy, you'll still have access to the layered Photoshop file.

One distinctive transformation that is available in Photoshop is the Color Lookup adjustment. It can alter the colors in a photo in extraordinary ways.

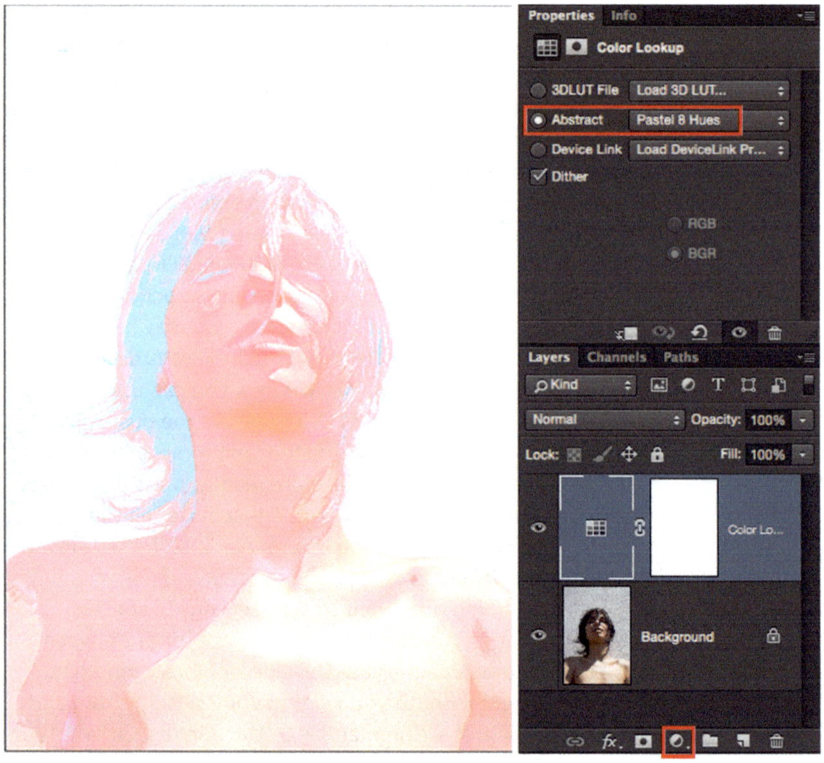

Applying the Pastel 8 Hues abstract LUT via the Properties panel. Use the menu at the bottom of the Layers panel to add adjustment layers such as the Color Lookup.

To create the effect shown here:

1. Click the black and white circle icon at the bottom of the Layers panel and click *Color Lookup*. This adds a Color Lookup adjustment layer to the top of the layer stack and opens the Properties panel.
2. In the Properties panel, click the menu labeled *Abstract* and click *Pastel 8 Hues*.
3. For a before/after, click the eye icon on the Color Lookup layer once to hide the effect and again to restore it.
4. Use Command + S (Mac)/Ctrl + S (Win) to save the file.

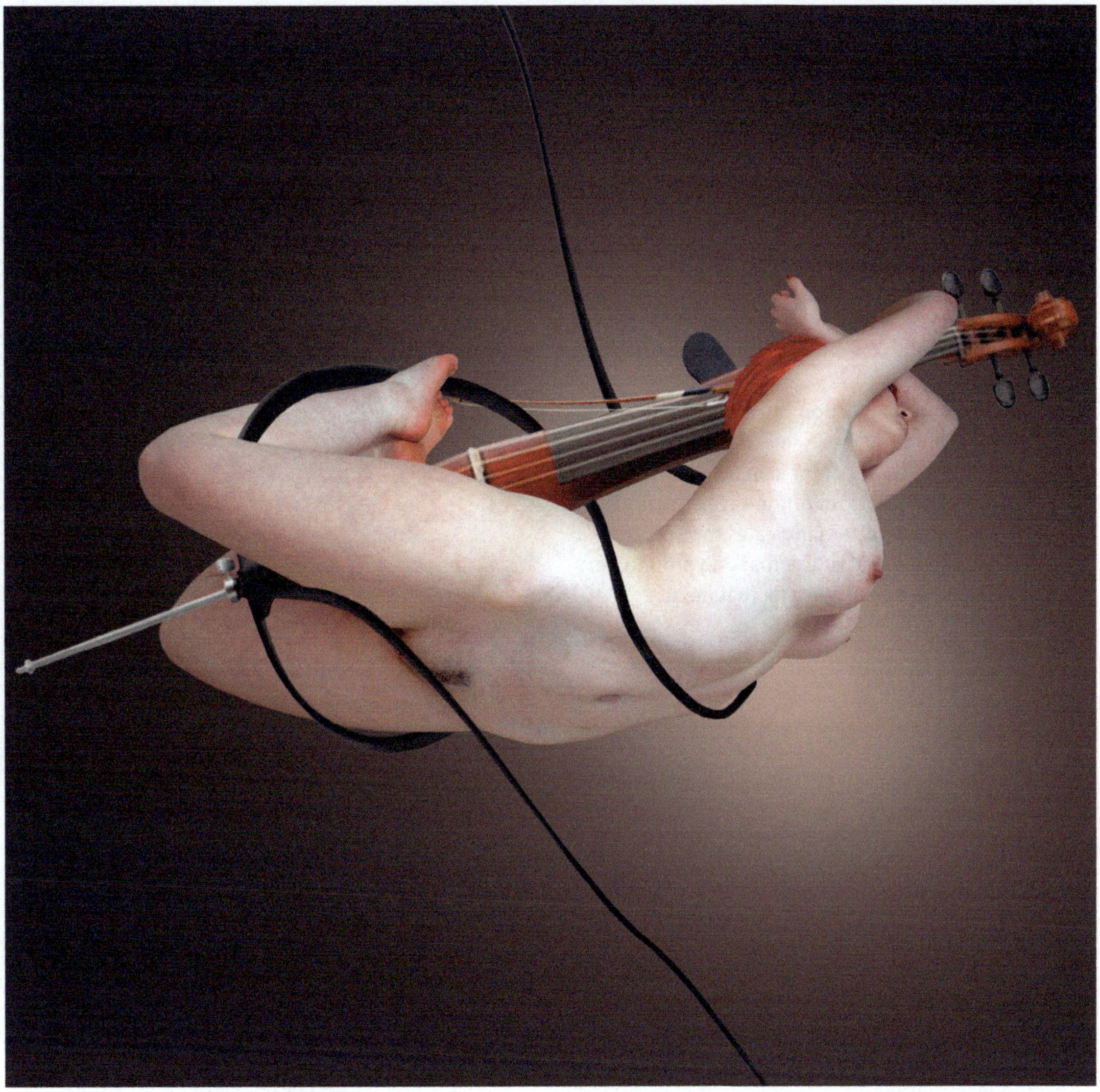

When you return to Lightroom, you'll see that the new Photoshop document has been stacked with the original in the Library, but before you do that we'll take a look at a couple of other things you can do in Photoshop.

To create the illusion of being suspended in mid-air for "Cello Player," the model literally bent over backwards across a stool that held her several inches above the ground. The photographer was on a ten-foot ladder, using a Canon 1D fitted with an 85mm lens at f/5.6. The background was white, and illumination came from two soft boxes approximately ten feet from the model.

Post-production was done in Corel 14. The model was carefully cut out—the hair being the difficult part—and then the gradient background and other elements, including the wire coil created with Bryce 5, were added.

"Cello Player" © Cheirodon.

One of the most in-demand post-production techniques is replacing the background in a photo. That's made much more difficult when the model has curly or fly-away hair. Photoshop has selection and masking tools that are designed to make that tricky task a lot easier.

1. Click the left thumbnail for the Color Lookup adjustment layer and hit the Delete key to remove the layer.
2. Click the lock icon on the Background layer to convert it to a normal layer. The name will change to Layer 0.
3. Use the Quick Selection brush to select the model. (Note the loose selection of the hair.)
4. Click the *Add Layer Mask* icon (circle in a rectangle) at the bottom of the Layers panel. The checkerboard pattern indicates transparency, and you'll notice that the masking around her hair is quite coarse. We'll fix that next.

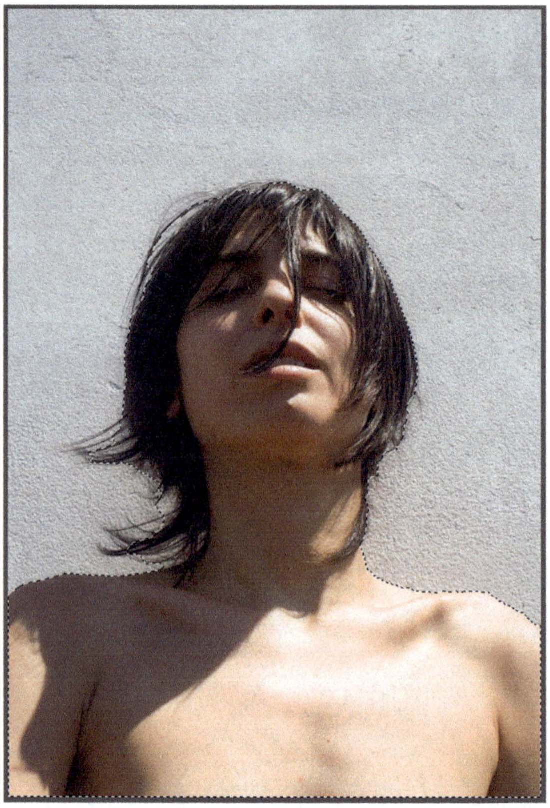

Loose "marching ants" selection does not encompass every strand of hair.

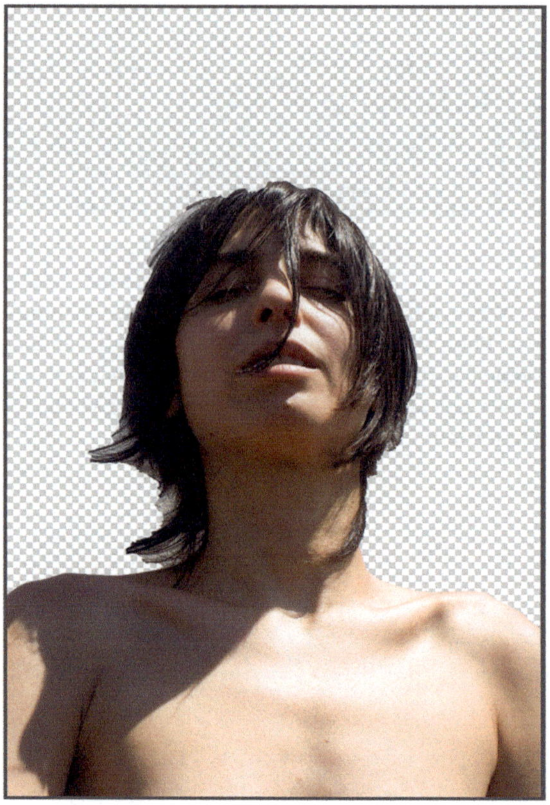

Coarse mask after converting the selection with the Add Layer Mask icon.

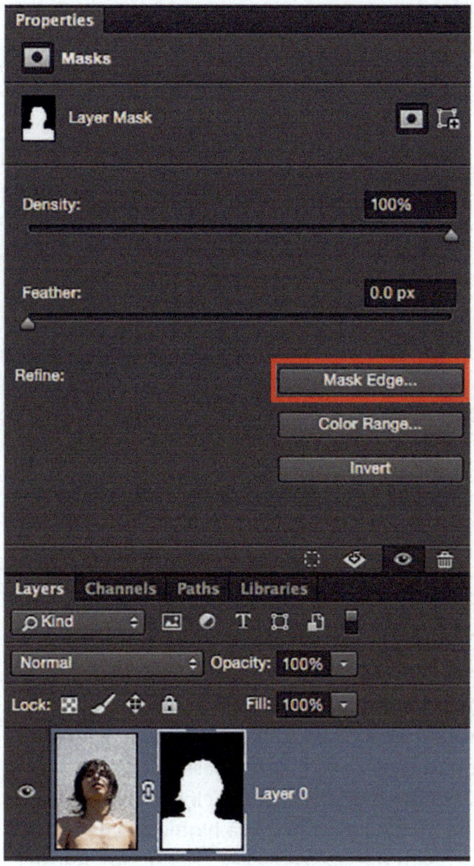

The Layers and Properties panels, including a button for access to the Refine Mask dialog.

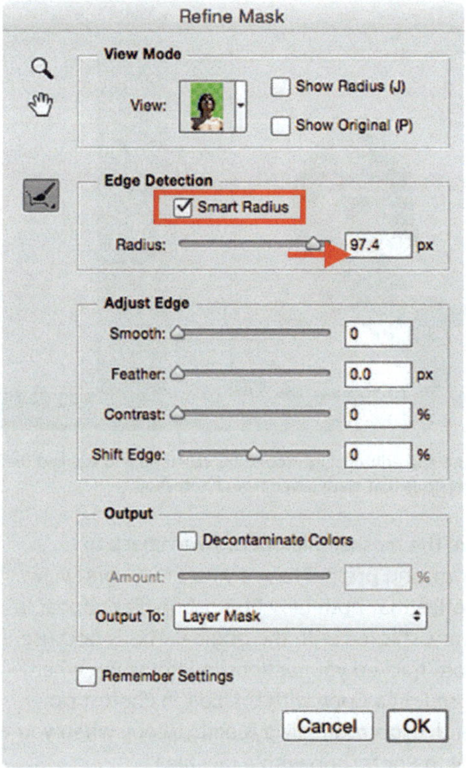

Smart Radius with a value of 100 or greater often does an excellent job of extracting hair.

5. The top of the Properties panel should be labeled Masks. If not, double-click the thumbnail for the layer mask (the one on the right with the silhouette).
6. Click *Mask Edge* to open the Refine Mask dialog.
7. Check the box labeled *Smart Radius* and increase the radius to somewhere between 100 and 200.
8. Press F to cycle through the view modes and see how the mask is resolving. You can change the radius and see whether the selection improves.
9. Click OK to apply the changes when you are ready.
10. Click *File > Save As* and enter a name that extends the filename from the right, e.g. DSC_2875-masked.psd, and click *Save*. Naming the file in that manner ensures that the derivative version appears with the original when you sort by name or search.

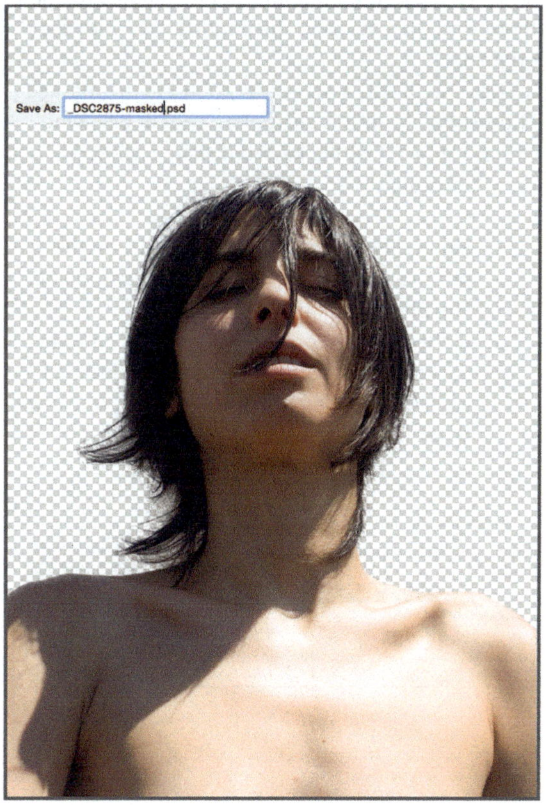

Saving the file with the improved mask.

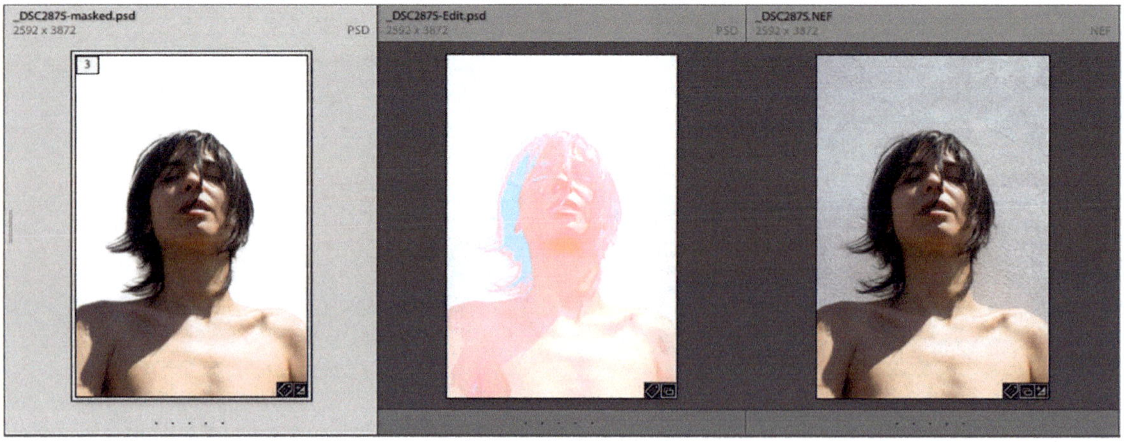

After round-trip editing, Lightroom has captured and stacked the various versions that were saved from Photoshop.

Leave the masked file open, switch back to Lightroom, and press G to see your files in grid view. You'll notice that both new Photoshop files appear in the Library, stacked with the original. This is because Lightroom tracked your actions in Photoshop when you chose Edit a Copy with the Edit in Photoshop command. (Lightroom always edits a copy when you click Edit in Photoshop with a raw file.)

If you had chosen Edit Original, you would need to add your derivative versions back to Lightroom manually. You can do that by dragging the individual files into the grid view of the Library module to import them, and then stacking the imported file with the original.

Next, we'll add a new background to the masked Photoshop file. In this example, a shot of billowing clouds retrieved with a keyword search will serve as a new background.

1. Right-click (or Control-click on Mac) on the photo and click *Edit In > Edit in Photoshop CC*. The photo will open in a new tab.
2. Right-click (or Control-click on Mac) on the Background layer's label (not the thumbnail—you'll get a different menu) and click *Duplicate Layer*.

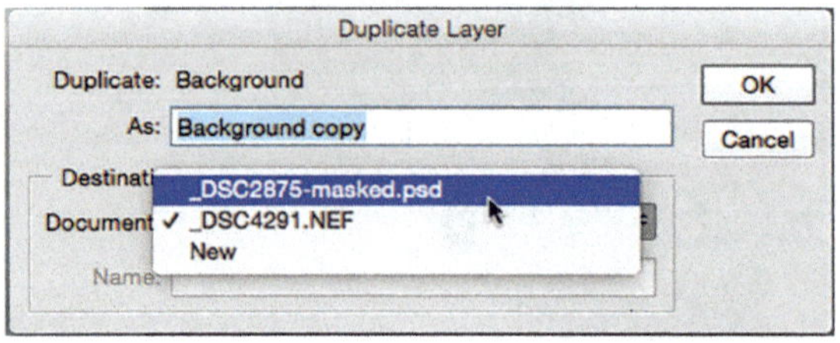

3. In the dialog, click the Destination menu and click the masked file to select it.
4. Click *OK*.
5. Click the X on the file name tab at the top of the window to close only the cloud file. If you're asked, don't save changes.
6. You'll be returned to the masked file with the cloud layer covering the masked layer.
7. Drag the thumbnail of the cloud layer beneath the masked layer. When a highlight line appears beneath the masked layer, release the mouse button to drop it below the masked layer.

That completes the initial composite. To refine the composition, you can reposition the respective layers with the Move tool—for example, moving the cloud layer slightly up and the figure slightly down. To do so, select a layer, activate the Move tool (press V), and drag anywhere in the image to reposition.

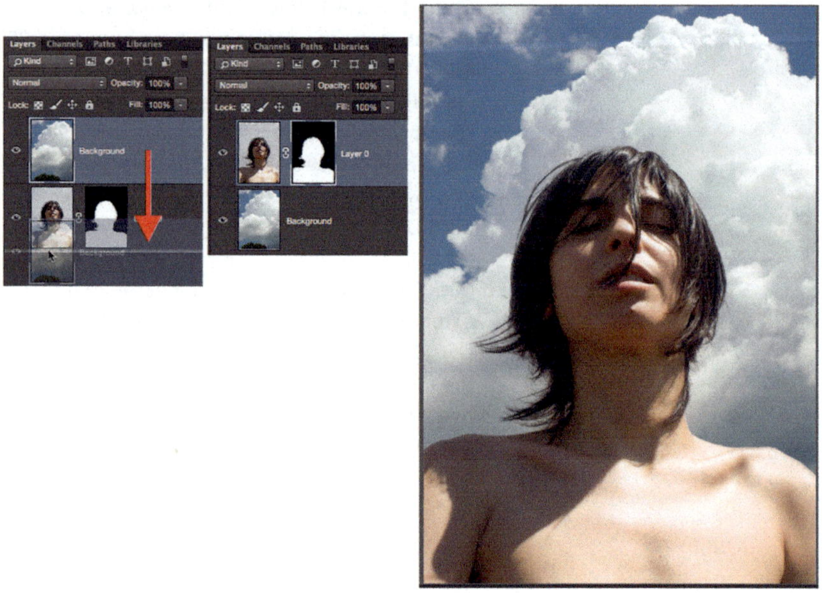

Re-ordering the layers to produce the result shown on the right.

At this point, you could use *File > Save As* to save the work under another name, or you could use *File > Save* to update the masked file that is already included in the Library. If you decide that you want to rename the file later, you can open the Metadata panel on the right side of the Library module and click on the File-name field. Enter the new name and hit Return/Enter to commit the change.

To create the composite below, Matt Barnes started by lighting the scene from the left with a magnum deep-dish reflector fitted with a grid, and added a backlight to make the smoke stand out. It was shot against a gray background with a Hasselblad 503 CW and a Phase One P45 digital back.

The initial processing was done through Capture One, and then post-production was done in Photoshop CS3. The post-production began with general cleanup and contrast. The chainsaw was shot separately and pieced in. Finally, the original background was replaced with a clean one.

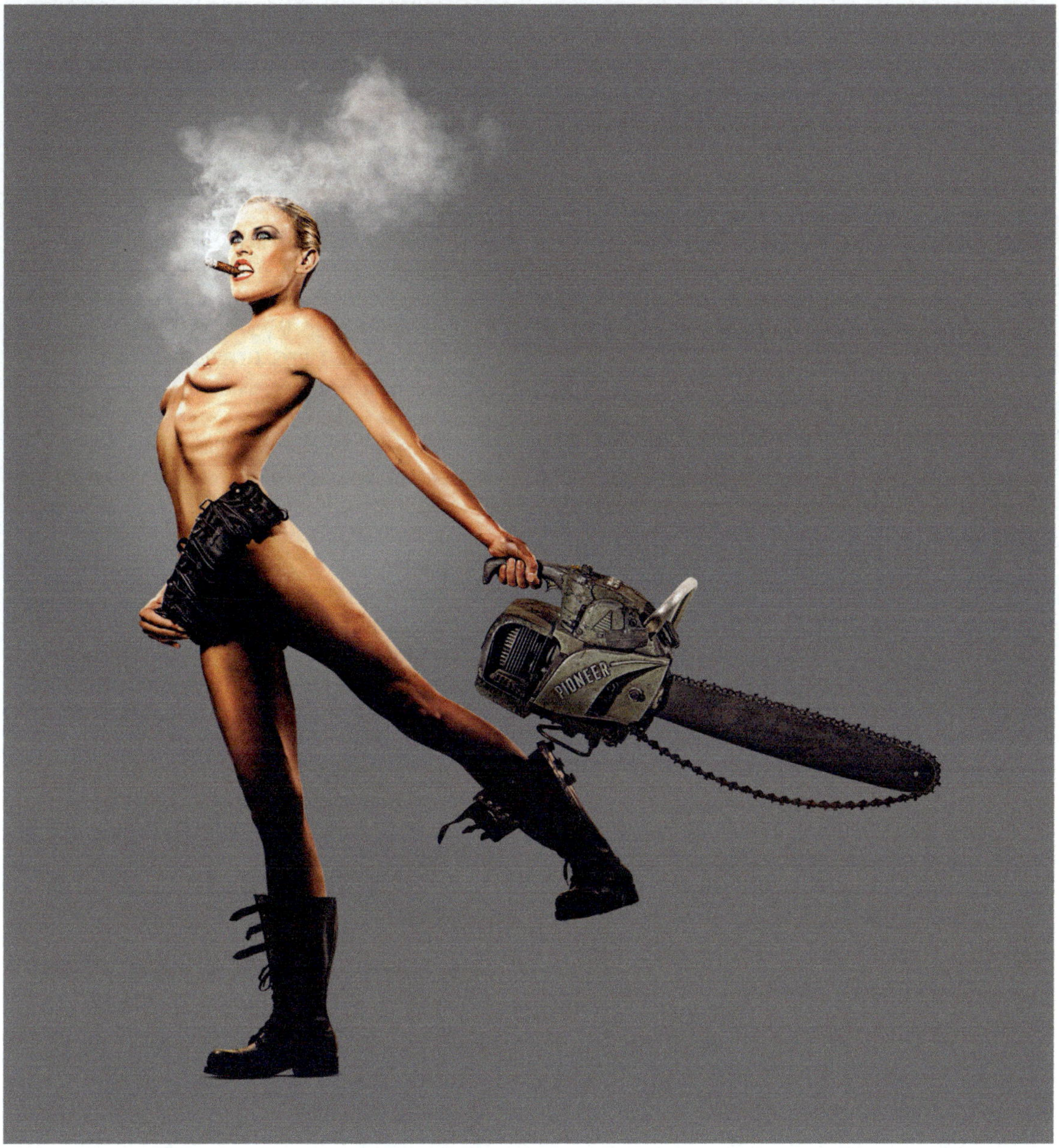

© Matthew Barnes. Model: April-Lea Hutchinson. Matt describes himself as a spontaneous person, and says he doesn't carefully pre-plan his images. He put a paper ray gun in model April's hand and they improvised from there. Matt decided later that she should be holding a chainsaw instead. Her hand was in the perfect position for it.

Frequency Separation Retouching in Photoshop

Retouching is one of the prime methods of idealizing portraits, including nudes. Unfortunately, it's often overdone, giving skin an artificial texture or the look of smooth plastic. Part of the problem is that many retouching techniques rely on blurring the image in a way that destroys real skin texture. The frequency separation technique is excellent because it allows you to retain as much natural texture as possible, while repairing problem areas and evening out color and tone in a graceful way. This is an advanced technique, but worth taking the time to master.

In applying this technique, you'll need to make feathered selections, so we'll set up the Quick Mask feature in advance to make it a bit more useful.

1. Double-click on the Quick Mask button near the bottom of the Tools panel.
2. Set Color Indicates to Selected Areas and set Opacity to 60%.

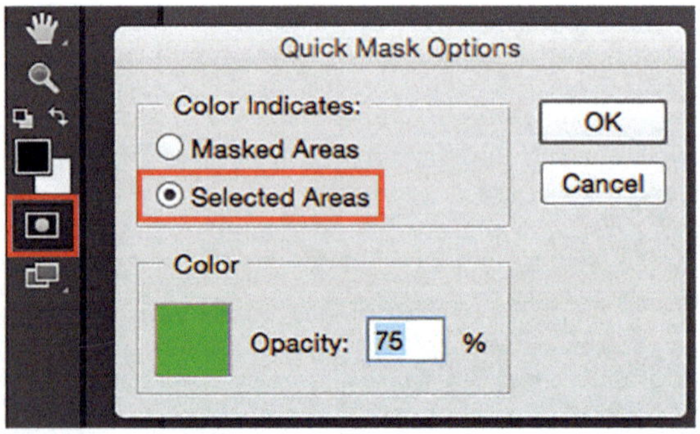

Adjusting the settings for the Quick mask.

3. Click the color swatch and enter 66ee11 in the # field at the bottom of the dialog.
4. Click OK to close the color picker, and click OK again to close the dialog.
5. After closing the dialog, you will probably still be in Quick Mask mode—check to see if the selected layer is highlighted in gray instead of a color and look at the file name tab near the top of the workspace—it will probably say Quick Mask. If so, press Q to exit Quick Mask.

Frequency separation involves splitting your image into two layers that work together. One contains color and tonal information, and the other contains texture. Once the image is broken apart that way, you can even out tone without destroying texture, and you can rearrange the texture without disturbing the underlying color and tone.

First, you'll make the layers you need and group them.

1. Open the file you'd like to retouch. To start with a photo in Lightroom, right-click (or Control-click on Mac) on a photo and click *Edit > Edit in Photoshop CC*. If you are starting from a rendered file (JPEG, TIFF, PSD) you will also need to choose whether to edit the original or create a copy.
2. When the file opens in Photoshop, select the background layer and press Command + J (Mac)/Ctrl + J (Win) twice to create two copies of the background layer (Layer 1 and Layer 1 copy).
3. Double-click on the layer name of the bottom copy (Layer 1) and change it to "Tone." Press Return (Mac)/Enter (Win) to apply the change.
4. Rename the top copy (Layer 1 copy) "Texture."
5. Click the Texture layer to select it, then Shift-click the Tone layer so both are selected.
6. Hit Command/Ctrl + G to group the layers.
7. Click the triangle on the group to reveal its layers and click the eye on the texture layer to hide it.

L–R: Layers panel as it appears when the file first opens, and after steps 2, 4, and 6.

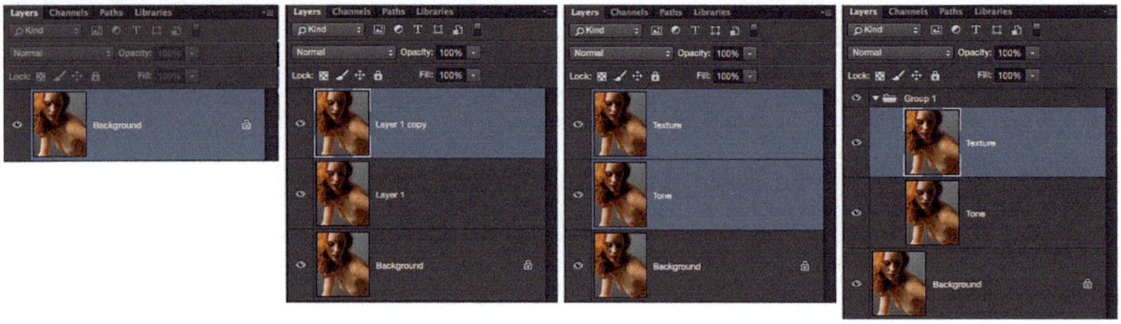

Next, you'll remove the texture from the Tone layer.

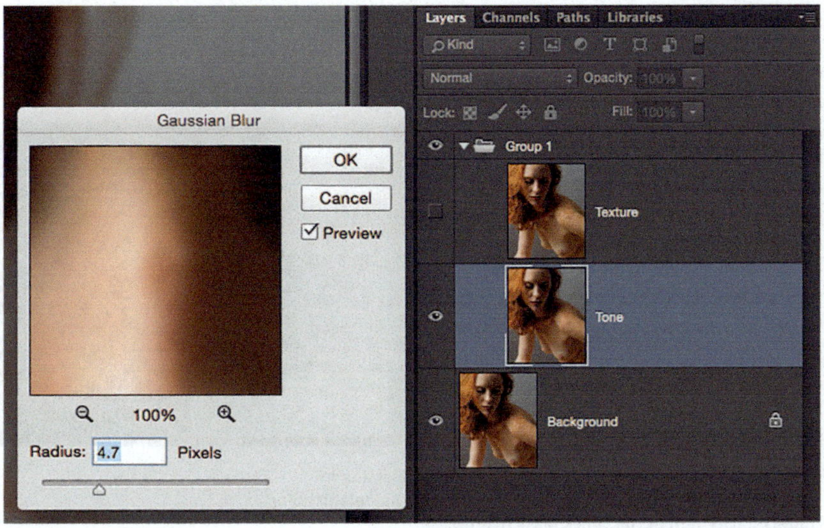

Blurring to remove texture.

1. Click to select the Tone layer.
2. Hit Command/Ctrl + 1 to zoom in to 100% and position the image so that you can see an area that you want to retouch.
3. Click *Filter > Blur > Gaussian Blur*.
4. Increase the radius to the point where fine details are smoothed away. To evaluate your progress, you can press the P key to toggle the preview off and back on.

The radius you need will vary by the size and content of the image, but images in the range of 10–12 megapixels are likely to require a radius somewhere around 5 pixels. The blurring removes the texture and reduces the layer to fields of color and tone.

5. Click OK to apply the blur.

Now, we'll perform a transformation to subtract the color and tone information found in the Tone layer from the Texture layer, leaving just texture.

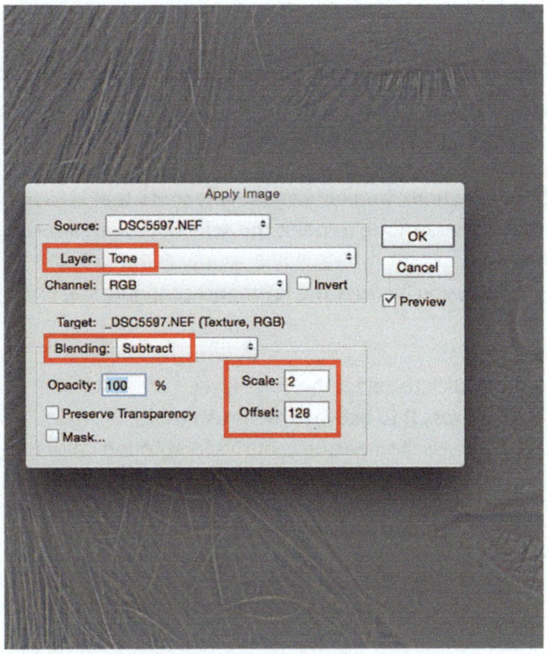

Using Apply Image to create the texture-only layer.

1. Click to select the Texture layer and click the eye icon box to make the layer visible again.
2. Click *Image > Apply image* to open a dialog.
3. Set Layer to Tone.
4. Set Blending to Subtract.
5. Set Scale to 2.
6. Set Offset to 128.
7. Click on *Normal* (the layer blending mode menu) at the top of the Layers panel and click Linear Light to change the blending mode of the Texture Layer.

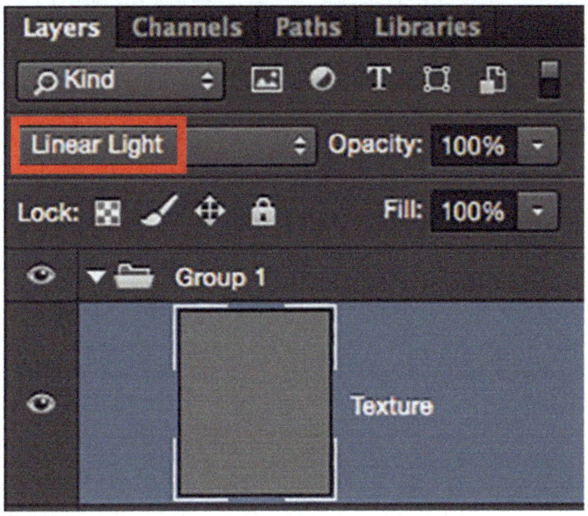

Linear Light blending mode visually integrates the tone and texture layers.

8. Click the eye on the group twice to toggle it off and back on. The separated group may be slightly brighter than the original background, but color, tone, and texture should be identical.

You smooth the tone layer by selecting and blurring areas of similar tone, such as a highlight area on the face. The key is to avoid changing the overall contours of the body or face, which would appear to reshape the surface. You want to feather the edges of the selections, and an elegant way to do that is to use Quick Mask mode to paint the selections with a soft brush.

First, you'll target the layer and configure the Brush tool:

1. Click to select the Tone layer.
2. Press B to activate the Brush tool.
3. Press D to ensure that the foreground color is black.
4. Press 1 to set the Opacity to 100%.
5. Click the well near the left edge of the Options bar to open the Brush Picker.
6. Click Soft Round and hit Return (Mac)/Enter (Win) to close the picker.

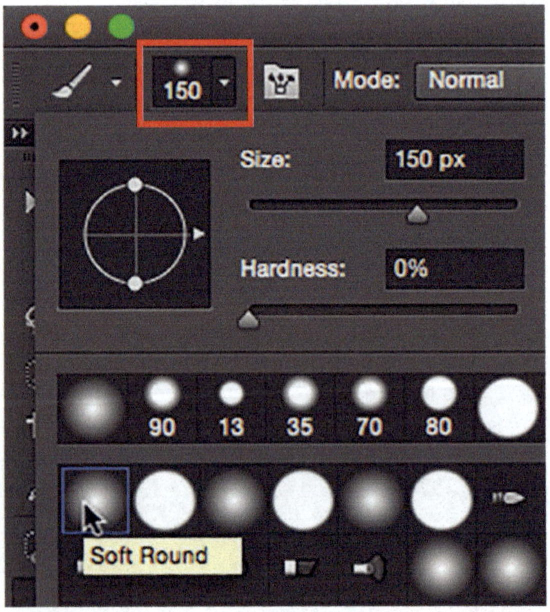

The Brush Picker is available from the tool Options bar. Select a preset from the large box at the bottom, or one of the recently used brushes in the group just above it.

Now, create a selection:

1. Press Q to enter Quick Mask.
2. Use the square bracket keys (to the right of the P key) to set the size of your brush.

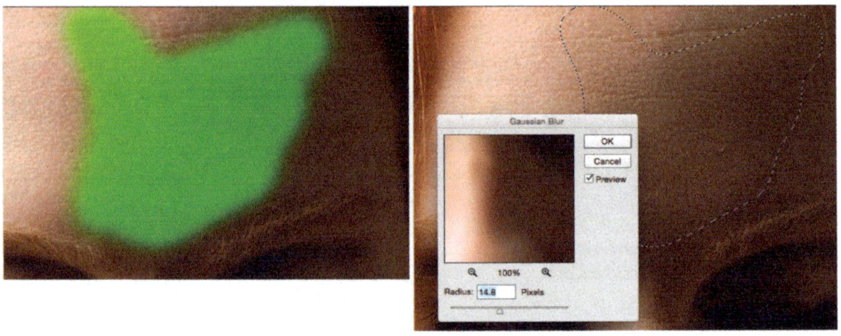

Painting with a black brush to make a feathered selection in Quick Mask. The green color comes from altering the default color (50% opacity red) of the Quick Mask overlay.

3. Paint over an area you'd like to select.
4. Press Q to exit Quick Mask. The area will be surrounded by "marching ants."

Then, apply the blur:

1. Click *Filter > Blur > Gaussian Blur*.
2. Adjust the radius as needed to smooth the tone. To gauge your setting, press P to toggle the preview off and back on.
3. Click OK to apply, then hit Command/Ctrl + D to deselect.

Now, select and blur additional areas. Repeat steps 1–3 below as many times as you need to even out the color and tone in the Tone layer. To check your progress, click the eye on the group to toggle it off and back on.

1. Press Q to return to Quick Mask and paint to select another area. Press Q to exit.
2. Hold down Option/Alt and click *Filter > Gaussian Blur*. (This works because Gaussian Blur was the last filter you applied. Holding down Option/Alt tells Photoshop to reopen the dialog, otherwise

it applies the last filter with the previous settings.)
3. Adjust the radius and click OK to apply, then hit Command/Ctrl + D to deselect.

To repair the texture, you'll use the Clone Stamp in the Texture layer to replace problem areas with "good" texture. The Clone Stamp works like Copy and Paste, in a brush. You point at an area containing the texture you want to copy and Option/Alt-click to mark a point where you want the brush to start copying from and then simply paint to apply. As you paint, the Clone Stamp tracks where you're painting, copies the corresponding area relative to the starting point, and pastes it into the location of the brush.

1. Click to select the Texture layer.
2. Click to activate the Clone Stamp tool. (Make sure you're not using the Pattern Stamp. It's under the same button and looks similar.)
3. In the Options bar, be sure that Mode is Normal, Opacity is 100%, Aligned is checked, and Sample is set to Current Layer.
4. Locate a problem area and use the square bracket keys (to the right of the P key) to size the brush.
5. Locate an area of good texture that you want to copy and Option/Alt-click to set the source for the Clone Stamp. A grayish preview will appear inside the brush.
6. Paint over the problem area to cover it, typically using small strokes or a few closely-spaced clicks.

You can repeat steps 3–5 as many times as you need to. Be sure to Option/Alt-click as you move around in the image. Otherwise, you might find that you're copying texture from someplace unexpected.

As you work, check your progress by clicking the eye on the group to toggle it off and back on for a before and after view. Though Photoshop is better able to recover than ever, it is still a good idea to save your work occasionally as you edit, and certainly at the end of your editing. If you started your frequency separation retouching in Photoshop from your Lightroom catalog, your saved changes will appear in Lightroom.

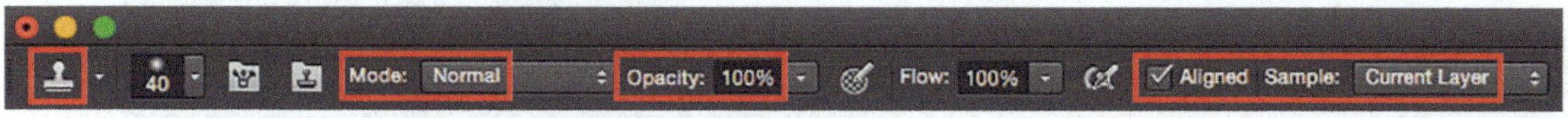

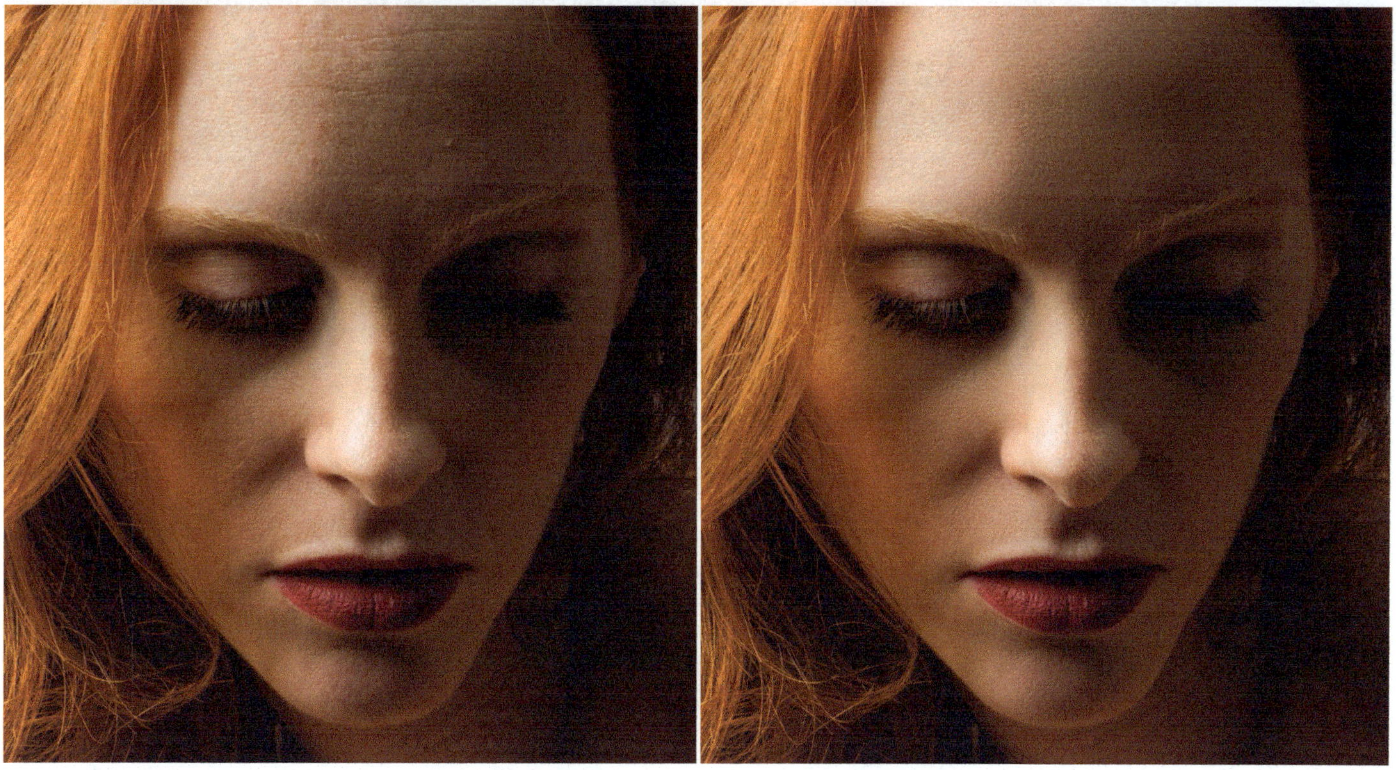

Before and after retouching.

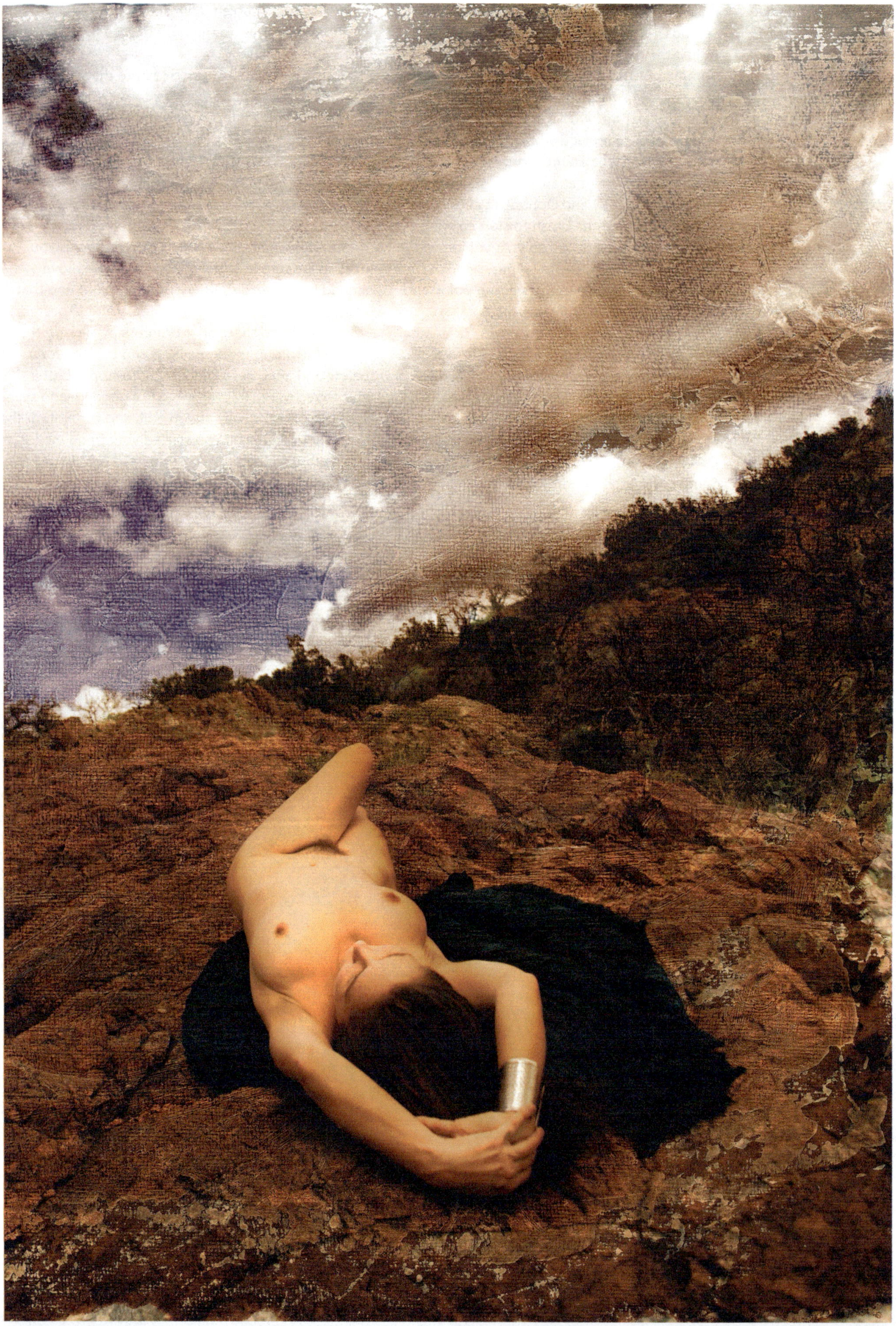

FACING
Nina Pak routinely photographs textures and maintains a digital archive of textures and photos that she combines into digital composites, using Photoshop. "For 'Nude in New Mexico and the Sky Above Her,' I made a textural layer in my painting studio. Later I photographed those various pieces of textured paper and put them into my textures file, which I use with the photographs in the layering process."

Organize Your Photos in Lightroom

The Lightroom Library module functions as an organizational hub for your photography. Its strength in managing photos lies in its ability to tag photos in a number of ways and organize them within virtual structures. When you create derivative files from the assets you manage in Lightroom, they can inherit all of the metadata tags you added to the original. Once you add photos to your catalog, you can use any of the following tools to organize them.

- *Grid view:* Press G to switch to the Library module and enter the grid view. Press = or - to resize the thumbnails. Press J to cycle through the grid view styles. Press T to show or hide the toolbar beneath the grid.
- *Rate, flag, label:* Use ratings, flags, and labels separately or together to triage your work. Click a photo or select a group of photos in the grid view and press a number between 1 and 5 to assign a star rating. Press zero to clear. Press P to flag picks or U to un-flag. Press X to reject.
- *Keywords:* Tag photos with as many keywords or keyword phrases as you like. Use the various keyword panels to build keyword hierarchies and apply keywords consistently. Keyword sets allow you to easily apply frequently used keywords.
- *Facial recognition:* Lightroom builds an index of the faces in your photos and displays them for you. Name the faces, and Lightroom suggests similar faces for you to confirm. Once you name a face, you can quickly and easily find all photos containing that face. If a face is obscured or turned so that Lightroom does not detect a face, you can draw a face region and tag the face with a name. Lightroom sometimes detects faces where there are none. False positives can be amusing and are easily removed from the face index.
- *Map module:* Find photos by where they were shot, using an interactive Google map. When shooting on location, you can grab a cellphone shot, then copy its location data and paste it onto your dSLR photos.
- *Filtering*: Select a folder or collection to show its contents, then use Command + F (Mac)/Ctrl + F (Win) to search by text. Use \ to show or hide the Library Filter bar. Click *Text, Attribute*, or *Metadata* to enable or disable each filter method. More than one method can be enabled at the same time. Click a method again to switch it off, or click *None*.
- *Smart Collections:* These are searches you can save. Their contents automatically update, based on the selection criteria you enter (e.g. raw files with three or more stars), whenever you make changes to your photos.
- *Collections*: These look like folders, but they only exist inside Lightroom. Gather photos into collections to sync with mobile devices, share with others, or work with them in the Book, Slideshow, Print, and Web modules. Drag and drop photos to add them to collections, select photos and press the Delete (Mac)/Backspace (Win) key to remove them. Using the grid view in the Library module or the filmstrip in any module, drag photos within a collection to change their sequence.

Facing: "Nude in New Mexico and the Sky Above Her" © Nina Pak.

Output and Sharing

The Create Collection dialog box includes the option to sync the collection with Lightroom mobile, or you can click an icon at the left edge of an existing collection to start or stop syncing. Synced collections appear in the Lightroom app on iOS and Android devices, where you can organize, edit, and share photos. The app has a presentation mode that hides the editing controls while showing photos on your device.

After a shoot, shared collections offer a quick and easy way to find out which photos the model, make-up artist, or other collaborators liked, or share an *ad hoc* collection with an editor or curator who needs to see some samples of your work. In Lightroom on the desktop, a toolbar with a *Make Public* button appears above the grid view in the Library module when you select a synced collection. When you click Make Public, it generates a short URL that you can right-click to copy and then paste into emails, blog posts, etc.

You can also share collections via the mobile app or a browser. Anyone who receives the link to a public collection can sign in with a free Adobe ID to view, like, and comment on your photos. You can review likes and comments in Lightroom on the desktop, your mobile devices, or the Web. If you make the collection private again, only you can see its contents.

Lightroom includes pre-installed Publish Services modules for Facebook, Flickr, and Bēhance, and others can be installed. After you set up and authorize a publish service to post content for you, you drag photos into it and click a button to publish.

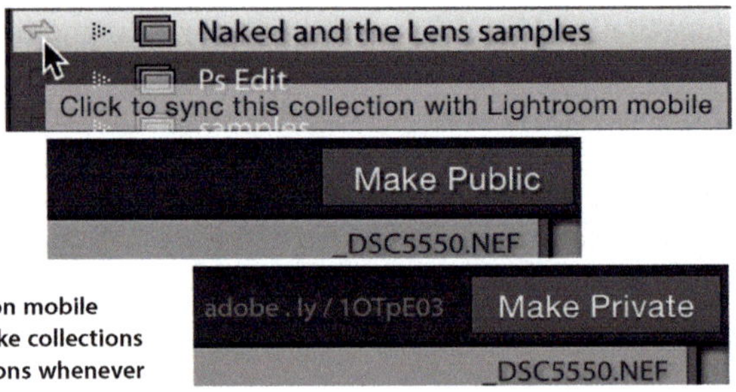

Sync collections to view and edit on mobile devices and share on the Web. Make collections private again and un-sync collections whenever you need to.

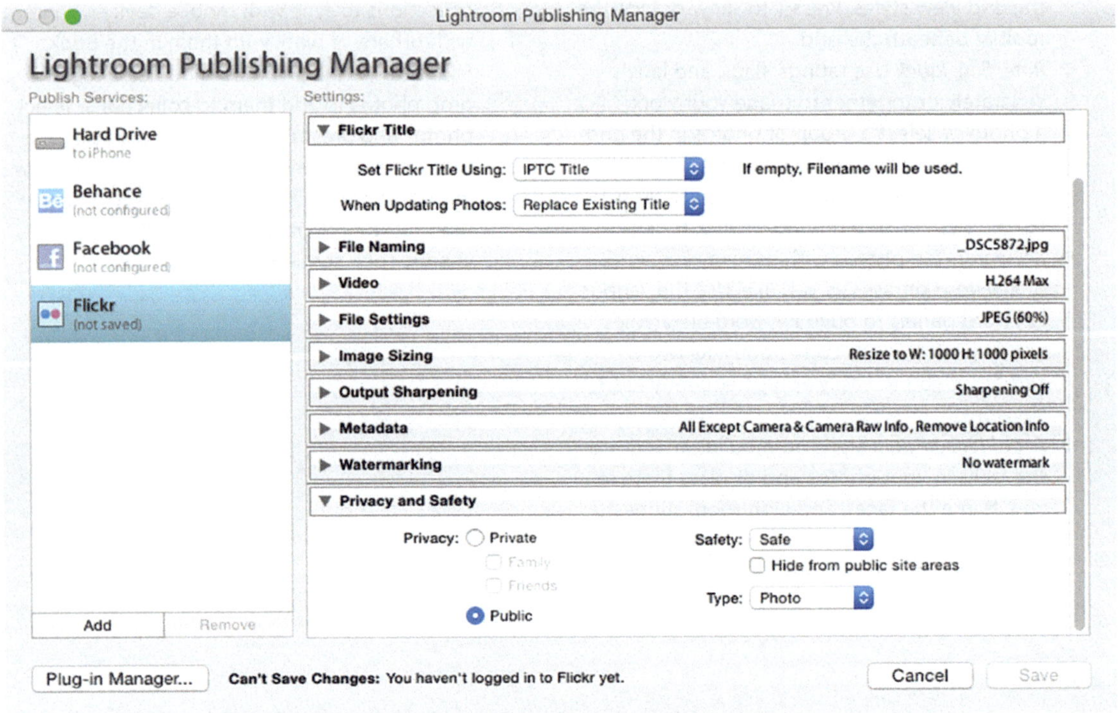

Configuring a Publish Service for Flickr.

Like Collections, Publish Services remember the photos they contain. When you add or edit photos, you can republish and the Publish Service will take care of replacing edited photos and uploading new ones. An available publish service for 500px features two-way sync, and you can see statistics and respond to comments right in Lightroom. There are several Publish Services available for WordPress.

For *ad hoc* exports, you can select one or more photos, right-click on a photo (or Control-click on Mac) and then click *Export* > *Export* to open the export dialog. To export multiple files at once, you can select photos in the grid view of the Library or in the Filmstrip along the bottom of any module.

When exporting images for the Web or email attachments, be sure to set Color Space (in File Settings) to sRGB. Your colors will render incorrectly on most people's screens if you choose any other color space. Onscreen, a JPEG quality setting of 80 is indistinguishable from 100, but the file size is about half. Lower quality settings will make the files even smaller, but will degrade the image.

Sometimes the best way to share your work is on paper, rather than on screen. Two cases are print portfolios and book dummies for potential publishers. You can use the Book module to design Blurb photo books that you can print on demand directly from Lightroom.

Organizing Files and Folders on Your Hard Drive with Lightroom

Lightroom will indicate that it has lost track of files and folders whenever you move or rename them with some tool other than Lightroom, such as the Mac Finder, Windows Explorer, or even Adobe Bridge. If you rename or relocate a folder externally, Lightroom will show it with a question mark, and any files inside that folder will show a badge with an exclamation point. This can also happen if you rename the parent folder of the folder containing your originals. To fix it, right-click (or Control-click on Mac) on a folder with a question mark and click Find Missing Folder, then use the file dialog that appears to locate the missing folder and click Choose.

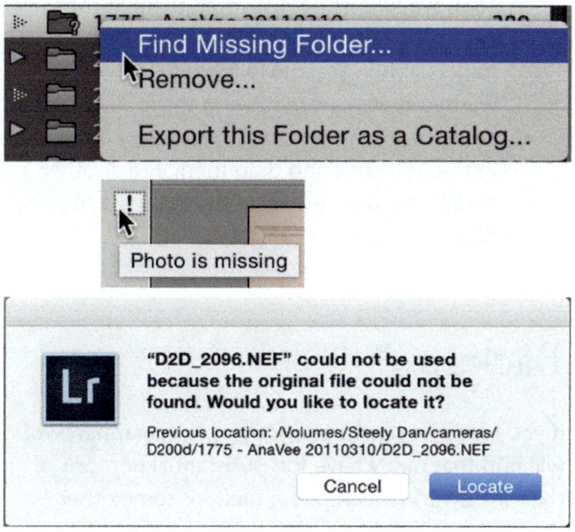

Lightroom marks missing files and folders and offers several ways to locate them.

When a few individual photos have been moved or renamed, click the exclamation point on a thumbnail (or beneath the Histogram) and then click Locate. Use the system dialog that appears to navigate to the photo and select it. Check the box labeled Find nearby missing photos to resolve other missing photos that have been moved in the same fashion. Click Select to reconnect the thumbnail to its original.

Ideally, you should be able to set up your files and folders when you first import into Lightroom and not have to change them. However, if you do need to rearrange things, you can use the Library module in Lightroom to arrange the photos and folders on your hard drive. That way, Lightroom can keep track of the changes you make to the files and folders on disk, avoiding the problem of files and folders going missing. Here are a few techniques:

- The Folders panel shows an abbreviated folder tree. If you need to reveal the folder that encloses a top-level folder in your panel, right-click (or Control-click on Mac) on the folder and click Show Parent Folder.
- To rename folders, right-click (or Control-click on Mac) on a folder and then click Rename.
- To move folders on disk, drag them in the Folders panel. You can drop folders into other folders. When you move folders, you will be warned that you are moving the folders on disk.
- To move files between folders, select them in the grid view and drag them into another folder. You will be warned that you are moving files on disk.

Backup

If you read the stories of enough photographers, you will find that many have lost substantial portions of their life's work to fire, flood, theft, or some other disaster. In the digital realm, there are the additional possibilities of file corruption and hard drive failure. Backup is your insurance against all of these and it's not a question of whether your hard drive will fail, it's a question of when. To paraphrase how essential backup is, if you don't have at least two copies of your digital images (on separate media!), it's as if they don't really exist.

You can think of the built-in Lightroom backup feature as a helper utility that ensures that your main backup software can successfully copy the catalog file onto another disk. Backup software cannot copy the active catalog while Lightroom is running, so the built-in backup creates a duplicate catalog that backup software can safely copy. Previews can easily be regenerated after restoring a catalog, so Lightroom does not consume resources backing them up.

If you set up your Lightroom catalog on your startup (internal) drive, you can use your operating system's built-in backup software to make sure that your catalog is safely backed up to a second drive. If you are running a Mac with OS X, Time Machine is an easy and effective way to backup your startup drive. Windows 7, 8 and 10 each have different built-in backup and restore features.

If your catalog or originals reside on an external disk, it is possible to configure Time Machine to backup the external drive along with your startup drive, but a cleaner approach may be to use a separate backup utility to copy those files onto another backup disk. Mac utilities include Chronosync (econtechnologies.com), Super Duper (shirt-pocket.com), and Carbon Copy Cloner (bombich.com), and there are similar products for Windows. You can also use those utilities to clone your startup drive onto a portable drive that you can boot from in the event that your computer fails. While your machine is being repaired, you can connect the cloned drive to another computer and boot from it to recreate the working environment of your main computer, including all of your applications and settings.

To protect against file corruption, Time Machine always archives the files it backs up, and the utilities mentioned above include the option to archive files. Instead of only retaining the latest version, archiving keeps a copy of each version of the file. In the event that you discover that one of your files has become corrupted, you can step back through the versions until you find one that is not.

Offsite backups can save you in the event of catastrophes like fires or floods. Cloud storage is becoming more affordable, but storage space is usually limited and backing up even a few gigabytes of photos to cloud storage can take hours, if not days. An effective way of doing offsite storage is to backup your files to a rotating set of drives that you put into a safe deposit box or send away to a remote location.

If you're rotating three drives, for example, you could retrieve the first drive as you send out the third. Backing up to anything other than another hard drive takes a lot of time and probably requires more effort than it is worth, especially now that you can get 1 TB portable drives for under $150.

Web Resources

Francis Bacon—http://www.artnet.com/artists/francis-bacon/
William Henry Fox Talbot—http://bit.ly/1h9kAJu
Jerry Uelsmann—uelsmann.net

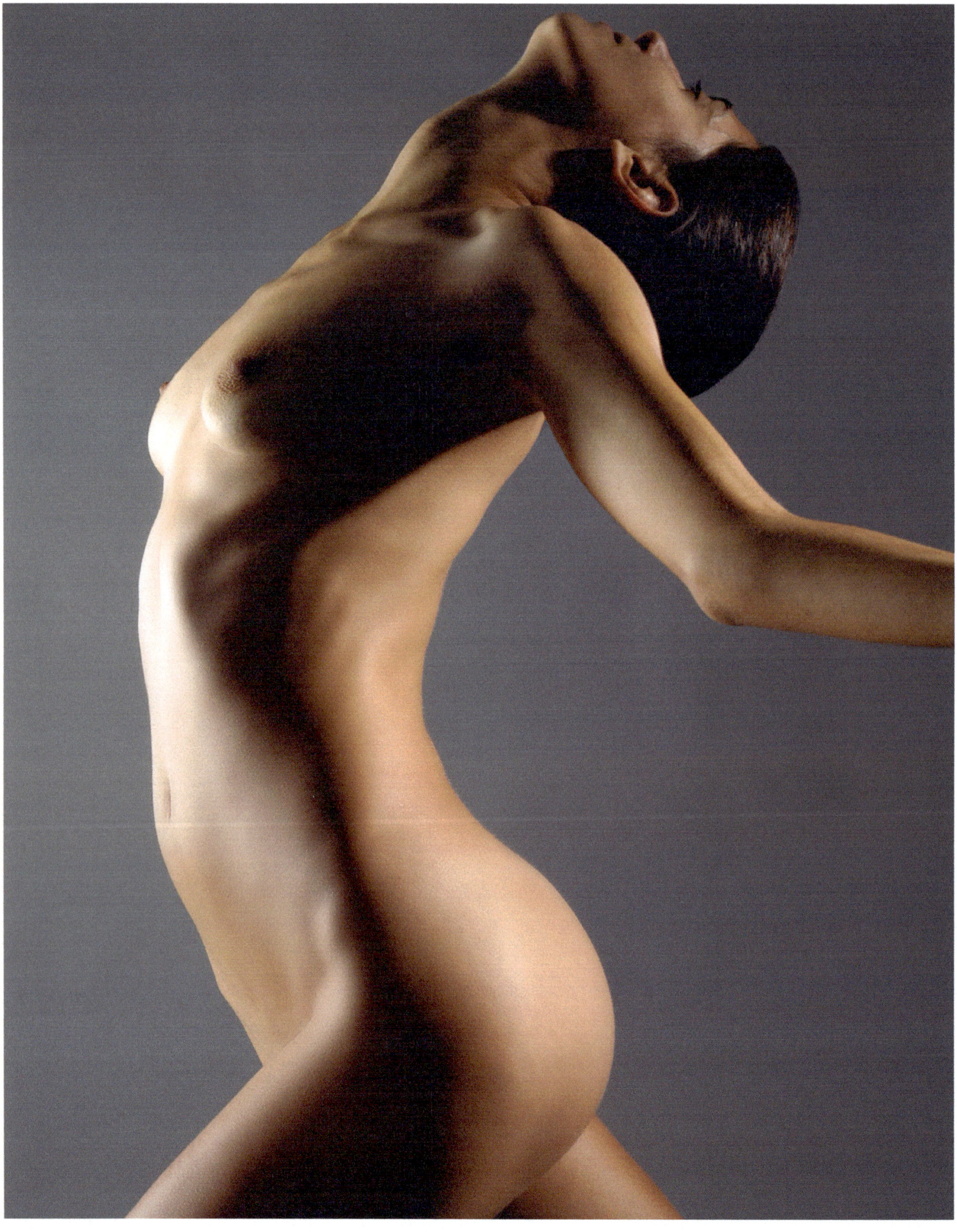

Chapter Eleven | Showing Your Stuff

"I'm in between an installation artist, video artist, and photographer. And when you work with nude bodies, you're immediately called a pornographer or a fashion photographer."
Spencer Tunick

ONE OF the fundamental truths about making art is that "showing up is half the battle." There is certainly satisfaction in the process of creating the work itself, but the circuit of communication—expressing yourself through your art—isn't completed until you put it out in front of people. You can create a personal website, a blog, or both. Galleries, photography clubs, and arts centers often post calls for entries to group shows and juried exhibitions. Answering the call and being selected can be your foot in the door to exhibiting in galleries. You can also approach galleries directly. Beyond conventional galleries, there are alternative spaces for exhibiting work. One more option is to submit work to magazines.

Once you have a site and a blog, you can cross-link them. You can promote both with social media, and use them to post announcements about gallery shows and publication in magazines. It is important to keep your online presence fresh—make it a point to update your blog frequently. Never consider any of your portfolios (online or print) a done deal, and make it a point to refresh them from time to time as well.

Grouping your work into distinct folios and carefully sequencing the presentation, rather than presenting a random assortment of "greatest hits," can

Facing: © Lou Benjamin. Model: Béu Tornaghi.

strengthen how audiences relate to it. The choice of titling your work, or leaving it "Untitled" can have a profound impact. Consider, for example, how often you've looked at a photograph and found yourself puzzled. You then read the title or caption, and it either became completely clear or got even murkier. The painter René Magritte understood this phenomenon and used it to create a powerful effect. His titles were designed to disorient the viewer and are an integral part of his work.

Once you begin to show your work, an interesting and sometimes frustrating thing happens—you lose control over how your work is interpreted, and your notion of what the work means becomes just one opinion among many. Participating in portfolio reviews, critiques offered by photography clubs, and even online can be helpful in finding out how others see your work. Some critiques have a ground rule that you can't say whether you like a photo or not, so as to focus on what works and doesn't work. This kind of feedback is worth seeking out.

Sharing Your Work on the Web

Putting your work on the Web makes it available to potential collectors and exhibitors. Aside from using the Web to present or sell work you have already done, you can use it to power your creative process by participating in communities of fellow photographers and collaborators, such as models, makeup artists, etc. Social networks specifically tailored to connecting photographers and models such as ModelMayhem and PurplePort were discussed in Chapter Nine. Many of the portfolio and site building tools discussed here make it easy to tie-in and repost to the major social networks, and even get comments and critiques on your work.

The blogging platforms Tumblr, 500px, and Instagram all have extremely active communities of photographers posting nude work (many have a presence on all three), and are particularly well-suited for easily sharing and promoting your work. Tumblr makes it extremely easy to "reblog" your posts, but a number of artists find their work reblogged with all references to themselves removed, and others are upset to find that their work has been reblogged to porn blogs (there are many on Tumblr). Many add notices such as "Reblogging OK with credits and links intact" and "No reblogging to porn blogs" to try to discourage this behavior.

Flickr and deviantART are designed to exhibit large archives of photographers' work. DeviantART galleries and Flickr photostreams function like a sketchbook, and seem better suited for networking with fellow photographers and drawing inspiration from others' work, than for self-promotion.

When you want to create separate, self-contained online portfolios, two options in Lightroom are to create and share collections as discussed in Chapter Ten or generate HTML galleries with the Web module. The generated galleries can be uploaded and linked to your site in a number of ways. Another route is to create a portfolio on 500px. The platform is designed for sharing and selling photos, and combines social networking, search, and e-commerce features. It has apps for iOS, Android, Windows 8, and Chrome OS. Photoshelter and Zenfolio allow you to create portfolio sites with a home page and galleries of images. Both offer responsive designs based on HTML5, which fluidly adapts to mobile screens. Portfolio.deviantart.com offers free and premium accounts.

Challenging subject matter is likely to meet resistance, and many online communities expect you to label work depicting nudity NSFW (Not Safe For Work), or possibly 18+. Pay attention to guidelines for posting and labeling and remember that they sometimes change. Not doing so can result in having your work deleted, your account terminated, or your IP address banned. Another potential issue is abuse by anonymous trolls. One photographer removed his substantial collection of work from deviantART because he kept getting anonymous messages that were demeaning and even threatening toward his models.

Creating your own website offers you the greatest control over content, style, and features. Your site can have a domain name such as YourNamePhoto.com and include all the portfolios, blogs, contact forms, password-protected pages, and other exhibits you need, in precisely the format you want. To set up a site, you will need to register your domain name, get a hosting service, and put your content up on the server provided by your web host. Domain, hosting, site building, and content management can be purchased à la carte or bundled together in different ways.

All-in-one service providers such as SquareSpace and WIX can handle hosting and domain registration for you. Both offer themes and tools to make site building and customization easy. If you register your domain separately, Weebly offers bundled hosting and site-building. WIX and Weebly both offer free plans, but you will likely want a premium plan, which removes branding, allows you to use your own domain (instead of username.wix.com/sitename, for example), and gives you more storage for photos and portfolios.

Another option is to handle domain registration and hosting separately and use WordPress to build and maintain your entire website—it's not just for blogs. You can register your domain with a company like Network Solutions or GoDaddy. Both companies also offer hosting as well, but Bluehost has specialty options, including one-button WordPress installation and servers optimized for WordPress. Once WordPress is installed, choose a theme from a vast selection designed for photographers and creatives, and build your site with features such as menus, pages, blog posts, galleries, etc.

Copyright

Whenever you post work online, you should assume that it will be taken and used by others without your permission. Even if the site blocks right-clicks and drag-and-drop downloading, there are ways around those features, and people can always grab screen shots. Some use appropriated work as stock for their own compositions, while others simply post it on their own blogs, too often stripping your credits in the process. Still others properly attribute the work to you, but feel they have every right to crop, convert your work to black and white or manipulate it in whatever way they see fit. These are all copyright violations.

Even though copyright is automatically granted to the photographer the moment the shutter falls, you can't recover damages in court unless you register your images (for a fee) with the Copyright Office before you sue. It's best to register within three months after the date of first publication/uploading to the Web, or before the infringement occurs. Of course, once you upload images to the Web, it can be just a matter of minutes before someone has grabbed them.

The easiest and most economical way to register is in bulk, before the images are published. Your pictures should always run with a copyright notice that reads © + year of first publication + your name. This format is recognized internationally. ASMP recommends adding a border to your photos and including a watermark with your copyright notice instead of degrading the image by placing the watermark across it. Regardless of where you place the watermark, they are easily removed, and are more valuable as branding than for preventing people from appropriating your work.

Be sure to use the legally recognized "circle c" copyright symbol ©. A C in parentheses (C) is not legally recognized. To type the copyright symbol on Mac, use Option + G. On Windows, press and hold Alt while typing 0169. You can find out much more at the Copyright Office website (copyright.gov) and the ASMP copyright tutorial pages: https://asmp.org/tutorials/copyright-tutorial.html.

Copyright enforcement is up to you, and lawyers do not pursue copyright violation cases *pro bono*. You can approach the violator on your own and ask them to attribute the work to you or ask that they take the photo(s) off their website. When approached about copyright violations, you may encounter any of these reactions:

- Some are genuinely unaware that they're violating copyright law. They tend to be embarrassed and apologetic and simply comply immediately.
- Some are aware of the law and hope to get away with something. They comply as soon as they realize they've been busted.
- People who post in volume are usually aware of the law and the cost of pursuing a copyright suit. They often have a "make me" attitude.

If you have registered your work early and the infringer is a corporation, you may be able to recover damages and come out ahead of your outlay for legal representation. Otherwise, you can consider the less expensive options of having your copyright lawyer send a cease and desist letter or filing a DMCA takedown notice on your own.

Magazine Submissions

A wide range of magazines, including art, fetish, tattoo, and even mainstream magazines publish artistic nudes. Magazines are now published online, in downloadable PDF format, printed on-demand, or printed traditionally. There is no money to be made in getting your work published in magazines, but it can help to get your work in front of a different audience. Some models will even negotiate a better rate for projects that generate tear sheets from publication.

A Google search for "nude photography magazine submissions" will turn up leads for online magazines. For print magazines, look for the appropriate editor on the masthead. Magazines have different philosophies, editorial approaches, and audiences. It's best to read a few issues of the publication to get a feel for how your work might fit before contacting them about submissions.

Submission criteria vary widely, and it's important to follow the guidelines precisely. Many require a link to your website—more incentive to get one set up. Some guidelines specifically prohibit showing genitalia (really crotches), while others draw a finer line. For example, Blur-Magazine.com has posted this policy statement: "there is a clear distinction between the artistic portrayal of the nude human body and graphical pornographic content, which is not tolerated. However, we do accept images that depict genitalia, as well as aesthetically thoughtful imagery of the sexual act, as long as it's done in a tasteful and artistic manner. Our editorial staff reserves the right to interpret such imagery independently and will not enter into any discussions over its decisions not to publish a certain photo."

Galleries and Other Spaces

If you are interested in exhibiting your work in galleries, the entire art object, and the context you create for it, is of interest to the curator and your audience. Your artist's statement and anything the curator writes about your work can be helpful in creating context. The size of your editions and the pricing of your work will be important considerations, because galleries often take commissions of 40 percent or more. Editions that are too small can be a problem, especially if the work is priced too cheaply and the edition sells out. On the other hand, editions that are too large decrease the value of the work because it lacks scarcity. Cultivating relationships with galleries can be a lengthy process that may begin with participating in calls for entry or portfolio reviews. Each gallery can be very different from the next, and a successful relationship requires a good fit between your work and the vision of the gallery.

Member-operated and "pay to play" galleries are alternatives to commercial galleries. Member galleries typically offer opportunities to participate in group shows and to present solo shows. Pay to play galleries are spaces that you can rent to mount a show and sell your work. Dues and fees for these alternative spaces vary greatly. If you are courting commercial galleries, you should also bear in mind that pay to play venues are not looked upon favorably—you might want to keep those shows off your artist resume.

Many bars, clubs, coffee shops, and other customer-facing establishments are regularly on the look-out for art to display. They also tend to censor or decline to show artwork representing nudity on the grounds of protecting minors from what might be considered indecent in some communities, or simply to avoid controversy. As with commercial galleries, and even magazines, there needs to be a good fit.

Interview with Jason Franz
Executive Director, Manifest (www.manifestgallery.org)

Manifest operates a non-profit gallery and drawing center in Cincinnati, Ohio. The gallery is not an art retailer, but sales are encouraged with proceeds benefiting the artists, the operation of the gallery, and the community. The nude is the central theme of their annual curated exhibition, which includes photography. A distinguishing trait of the gallery is its academic slant. Manifest's drawing center and artist residency programs set it apart from most galleries, and highlight some ways in which photographers can continue to expand and develop their work.

How does working with a gallery impact the way an artist works?

▶ This would depend on the type of gallery they're working with, and this is incredibly varied. I feel that too many artists allow the gallery paradigm to make them think about their work as products, akin to products they see in our modern industrial culture. They are not taught, or do not realize, that the value obtained through great art is not a direct A to B correlation to cash in the bank. But artists sensationalized in the art-media tend to suggest that one can make a breakthrough, gain a gallery's representation, and make a lot of money selling one's art. While artists certainly must think of themselves as businesses of a sort (and stop thinking of themselves as charitable causes), they generally must realize that the equation is more complicated than it may appear.

How is your approach different from that of a commercial gallery?

▶ People often assume that "all galleries are the same." As a 501(c)(3) the organization is not unlike most art museums or art centers in the U.S., many colleges and universities, and other charitable educational and cultural institutions.

So, the primary, but by no means only, differentiation between Manifest and commercial galleries is that Manifest removes the criteria of salability from all its curatorial decision-making when creating exhibitions. We set out to exhibit the best work being made in the world today, regardless of its ability to be converted into cash via a sale. With this, our goal is to create an experience of quality in visual art and to disentangle the public's value of "art" from its perception of monetary value of products.

You have featured the international competitive exhibit NUDE, which explores the uncovered human form in current art, since 2008. You invite artists to submit works in any media. Have many photographers submitted works or been selected?

▶ Yes. I could not easily tell you how many photographs were submitted because we do not capture this data outside our raw info. But in the past two years' exhibits about 25 percent of the works included were photographic in nature.

Do you have any thoughts for photographic artists who are working with the nude and interested in exhibiting their work?

▶ Sure!

1. Why photography? Don't make the media your content. The "why" of your work should be clear, and the media, whatever it is, should be appropriate to achieving it.
2. Why nude? The human nude in photography is ubiquitous. This makes it disappear. Or, it makes it all the more tempting to push boundaries of all sorts in order to differentiate it from the rest. This can be a good exercise, but it can also look desperate and silly. Make good photography, make good ART, regardless of what the subject is. I see so many submissions of nudes that look like so many others, it is embarrassing and redundant.
3. Tell a story. It's not just about an object/subject. Something can be happening, or about to happen, or have just happened.
4. Use mystery. It does not have to be "what you see is what you get." Too much photography is just this.
5. Craft the object! When it comes to exhibiting a physical object in a physical space, the crafting

of the "thing" that you ship and we hang on the wall makes all the difference in the world. It is with photography more than any other media that we see a great disparity between the apparent quality of the art (as seen in a jpeg file submitted for review) and the actual art (as delivered to our gallery). Frame, mat, printing, paper, or other presentation options truly do mean everything in support of the image itself. Without them the experience will often fail completely. Many artists, especially including photographers, neglect this part of the art-making process to their detriment. That said, when you have made the object what it should be, document this with detailed images or alternate views to show the gallery so we know what we're looking at—what we can expect to see when it arrives at the gallery. No surprises, or pleasant surprises, is a good thing.

6. One can look at an image and get a sense that it's a decent photograph. But then one can look at an image and get a sense that it is incredibly good art. Aim for the second. Learn the fundamentals, and use them as the tools they are!

Would you say that the proliferation of online image-sharing platforms has made photographers even less conscious of the importance of the object qualities of the work?

▶ Yes, however I think that the first reason photographers are so often guilty of neglecting the object is related to the process mentioned above—that of looking through the viewfinder and developing the assumption that the art is all inside, or through, that frame. I also find that presentation methods and theory are not taught effectively in college art programs. Frames or other presentation choices just become a sloppy afterthought, or an expensive burden. Ironically it is that final touch that, sure enough, will make or break a work's chances of being purchased. This is because it can severely impact the quality of the experience of the art itself. And that is what a patron is buying, or a gallery is looking to exhibit.

Are there any special issues that need to be dealt with in exhibiting nude work? Have you seen changes in attitudes to exhibits involving nudity, from collectors, the general public, or governmental bodies in the last five to ten years?

▶ We have had very little negative feedback related to our annual NUDE exhibitions. We are conscientious of the fact that two of our galleries face a public street and have lights on 24/7. So we are cautious to not place works that are potentially blatantly offensive or inappropriate for children in those spaces. But we have included the NUDE exhibit in them from time to time. The truth is we have rarely exhibited anything that would fall into those categories (offensive or inappropriate). The question comes down to understanding how different people see representations of the human body, and respecting this even while we may feel otherwise. We present our exhibits with tact and a sense of respect for everyone involved, and this is generally appreciated. The most vocal someone has ever been has come not as a direct complaint about the art in our gallery, but as a complaint that a local cultural paper reproduced a full frontal nude male (a highly realistic drawing) in an article about the exhibit. A man called to complain about the exhibit he had not himself seen, because the paper had shown the nudity, and his young daughter saw (or could have seen) the paper.

The vision statement for the Drawing Center program says that, "To learn to draw is to learn to see." That's very striking because many photographers are conscious of the importance of seeing—Dorothea Lange even said "the camera is an instrument that teaches people how to see without a camera." Is there a difference between photographic seeing and the seeing required for drawing? Do you think that photographers would do well to learn to draw?

▶ I believe photographers would benefit very much from a drawing discipline. And I also happen to believe that drawers (and other visual artists, especially those working from perception) would benefit from a photography discipline.

In good photography one is always composing, recognizing the four sides of the format as the "frame" and first compositional element to be dealt with. But once the photograph is made, those edges disappear and cease to be such a tangible element for the viewer—we look past them. In drawing one has to concentrate to do this, and see the "picture" instead of the subject, taking account of the edges of the paper or drawn format, and planning a composition as much by virtue of focus and selection as by omission and suggestion. The nature of the crafting of a drawing places the viewfinder in the mind's eye, whereas in photography the viewfinder is a separate tangible object. In drawing the "seen" is as often the drawing itself as the subject being drawn. In photography it is the subject that is the seen.

Interview with Pet Silvia
Artist and Curator

Pet Silvia has been both artist and curator, creating exhibitions that celebrate the human body and sexuality, for over 35 years. With his wife, Tammey Stubbs, Pet opened Art at Large gallery in January of 2002 in Hell's Kitchen in New York City. Operating under the tagline "Art that excites," the mission of the gallery was to promote and sell the work of artists that are a significant contribution to life and longing in the twenty-first century. Represented artists include H. R. Giger, Annie Sprinkle, Barbara Nitke, Carolyn Weltman, Frances Turner, Charles Gatewood, Spider Webb, Tom of Finland, and photographs from the Quentin Crisp Archives. After approximately six years of operation, they closed the gallery space and now only conduct sales by appointment.

What's the best advice or feedback you've ever received regarding your work?

▸ "Get your stuff out of here and don't come back," has been my favorite. Rejection makes you hard, and if you are ever to be successful in anything, you need to get over your fears and forge ahead.

The mainstream tends to conflate nudity, sexuality, and (im)morality. What are your thoughts about that?

▸ That's why it's called the "mainstream." Whatever the art form, or creative discipline, we have to search out our audience. If you work within the stifled parameters of mainstream, for whatever reason that is, then you will probably meet with success more easily. But as soon as you enter into the realms of sexuality, or religion, or politics, that is where you will be constantly met with strong opinions about what you do, and often a rather oblique opposition. The only thing you can do to keep from going insane is to come to grips with this fact early on, and stay true to your guns. But realize, that it is a double-edged sword, because few can ever attain the degree of recognition and success that they would hope for.

The phrase "Art That Excites" is at least a double-entendre. One reading of it is an allusion to arousal, which some would say is the primary function of pornography. Do you think it's necessary to distinguish erotic fine art from pornography, and why?

▸ I use that tag-line for Art At Large, for several reasons. First, because the word "erotic" is a misleading word for the general public. They immediately associate the word "pornography" with it. As a business person, I'm always trying to find new markets for these works of art, that I think deserve better attention. So, yes, from a business point of view, it's vital that the mind of the collector who is new to this genre be educated to the subtle nuances of the erotic. The only really distinguishable differences between erotic and pornographic are the venue, and the vehicle. Erotic is one or several pictures in an art gallery or art website. Porn is hundreds or thousands upon thousands of pictures in a magazine or website that you pay to look at. I've done both, and porn has a more immediate monetary reward. Erotic art, as with any controversial genre, takes time for acceptance.

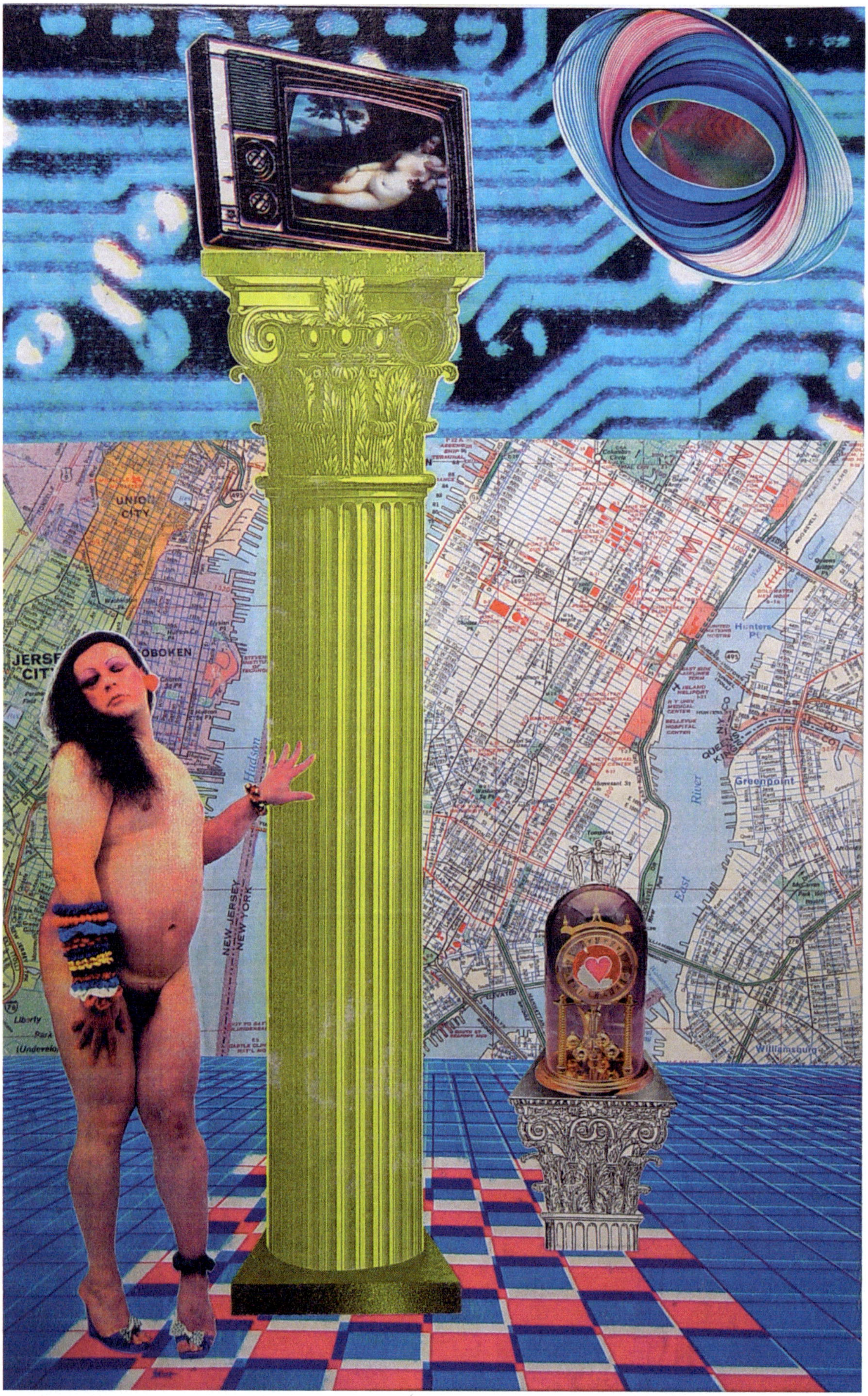

Hudson
NEW JERSEY
NEW YORK
River
East
Greenpoint
Williamsburg
Liberty
Park

How much of curating is about shaping tastes and how much is about responding to them?

- Curating is more about the former than the latter. You take a given amount of talent and make things go together visually in some kind of coherent fashion, or thematic assembly. The responses come from the audience viewing what you have amassed to present to them. They then form opinions, likes, dislikes, etc. based on the notion that they are paying attention to what you are telling them with your collection of works. Hopefully, they "get it," and that's my reward.

What is the most important aspect of your art, and what's the most important aspect of your curating?

- As an artist, I try to maintain an original and thought-provoking process. Art, after all, is mostly about process for the artist, and it certainly holds true for a curator. As a curator, I look for those same qualities in the works of others. I always tell new talent that I find to "show me something I've never seen before." It's still surprising that I always find that, either with what I've come up with as an artist, or in the works of others as curator.

Who or what has most influenced your visual style?

- I do think that Tom of Finland, perhaps more than any other artist, has been more of an inspiration to erotic artists than anybody else. From his notoriety, influence on gay culture, and recently being accepted into the permanent collection of MoMA in New York, is a pretty big deal. When I first found out about his work and the foundation, I couldn't believe they existed. A very crucial artist and organization for erotic artists of all orientations.

Pierre Molinier's work also looked at gender identity and longing in interesting ways. Are you familiar with his work, and do you see any connections with your own?

- I love his work! I discovered Molinier's work a good five years or so after I began my self-erotic portrayals. I saw several exhibitions of his photographs, but I found him to be much darker than me in his execution. Also, much freer in his works that are kaleidoscopic in nature. But people have told me I have sexier legs than he did.

Has making your work taught you anything about yourself? About others?

- Yes. It's a tough way to make a living. Any art that is not within the mainstream of the art world is truly a labor of love. All of the artists I've met over the years have the same thing in common. They all really love what they do, and I've tried to help them to understand that it is most important for them to keep doing it, despite all of the pitfalls they'll come across.

Web Resources

Ruth Bernhard—www.artnet.com/artists/ruth-bernhard/
Bill Brandt—www.houkgallery.com/artists/bill-brandt/
Quentin Crisp Archives—crisperanto.org
Charles Gatewood—charlesgatewood.com
H. R. Giger—hrgigermuseum.com
Dorothea Lange—http://bit.ly/1cRrGyB
Manifest, NUDE—www.manifestgallery.org/nude/
Pierre Molinier—artnet.com/artists/pierre-molinier/
Barbara Nitke—barbaranitke.com
Annie Sprinkle—anniesprinkle.org
Alfred Stieglitz—http://bit.ly/1CVad3K
Tom of Finland—http://bit.ly/1al9KlC
Frances Turner—http://bit.ly/1ykyrpq
Spider Webb—spiderwebbtattoo.com
Carolyn Weltman—artid.com/members/carolynweltman
Edward Weston—edward-weston.com

Facing: © Pet Silvia. While working as manager of a reprographics firm in Morristown, New Jersey, Silvia discovered and fell in love with the xerographic process as an alternative form of photography. Color and black and white images could be produced, reprocessed, and manipulated, to make art. He began posing himself in front of the camera out of necessity, rather than a quest for self-portraiture, or ego satisfaction. It started out as an experiment in duality and became about pansexuality. Silvia is still his own model.

Conclusion

"Art is life seen through man's inner craving for perfection and beauty—his escape from the sordid realities of life into a world of his imagining. Art accounts for at least a third of our civilization, and it is one of the artist's principal duties to do more than merely record life or nature. To the artist is given the privilege of pointing the way and inspiring towards a better life."
Paul Outerbridge

WE END as we began—with imagination. It shapes your art and your artistic process, so please remember to feed it. The clarity of your vision makes all the difference. Get closer to your passion, tune in to your influences, and use them as fuel. Leave the Web behind and go see some works of art in the physical world; it might even be better if it's not photography. Carry a notebook. When you notice that you like something, try to articulate what it is that you like about it. Wherever you find inspiration, steal some ideas.

Most of all, make more work. Get out there and shoot, but don't forget that the camera is a stubborn collaborator that does not see things as we do. Whether you're creating naked honesty or sublime nudity, make the effort to coax out the images that you imagine in spite of the technology. The camera encourages us to copy, so let your imagination take you beyond simply replicating your inspirations.

It has been a privilege to have you read this book. I hope that you have found value in it. Just as with the first edition, I learned a lot as I put it together. The insights and inspiration I have gained will fuel the next leg of my artistic journey. I wish you creativity and luck on yours.

Index

Page numbers in italic refer to figures.